£16.99

Language Development

7

Essential Readings in Developmental Psychology

Series Editors: Alan Slater and Darwin Muir

Queen's University, Kingston, Ontario and the University of Exeter

In this brand new series of nine books, Alan Slater and Darwin Muir, together with a team of expert editors, bring together selections of readings illustrating important methodological, empirical and theoretical issues in the area of developmental psychology. Volumes in the series and their editors are detailed below:

Infant Development	*Darwin Muir and Alan Slater*
Childhood Social Development	*Wendy Craig*
Childhood Cognitive Development	*Kang Lee*
Adolescent Development	*Gerald Adams*
The Psychology of Aging	*William Gekoski*
The Nature/Nurture Debate	*Steven Ceci and Wendy Williams*
Teaching and Learning	*Charles Desforges and Richard Fox*
Language Development	*Michael Tomasello and Elizabeth Bates*
Children and the Law	*Ray Bull*

Each of the books is introduced by the volume editor with a rationale behind the chosen papers. Each reading is then introduced and contextualised within the individual subject debate as well as within the wider context of developmental psychology. A selection of further reading is also assigned, making each volume an ideal teaching resource for both classroom and individual study settings.

Language Development
The Essential Readings

Edited by Michael Tomasello and
Elizabeth Bates

BLACKWELL
Publishers

Copyright © Blackwell Publishers Ltd 2001
Editorial matter and organization copyright © Michael Tomasello,
Elizabeth Bates, Alan Slater and Darwin Muir 2001

2 4 6 8 10 9 7 5 3 1

Blackwell Publishers Inc.
350 Main Street
Malden, Massachusetts 02148
USA

Blackwell Publishers Ltd
108 Cowley Road
Oxford OX4 1JF
UK

British Library Cataloguing in Publication Data

A CIP catalogue record for this book is available from the British Library.

Library of Congress Cataloging-in-Publication Data
Language development : essential readings / edited by Elizabeth Bates and Michael Tomasello.
    p.   cm. – (Essential readings in developmental psychology)
Includes bibliographical references and index.
ISBN 0-631-21744-4 (alk. paper) – ISBN 0-631-21745-2 (pbk.: alk. paper)
1. Language acquisition.   I. Bates, Elizabeth.   II. Tomasello, Michael.   III. Series.
P118 .L263 2001
401'.93 – dc21

2001025967

Typeset in 10 on 12½ pt Photina
by Best-set Typesetter Ltd., Hong Kong
Printed in Great Britain by MPG Books Ltd, Bodmin, Cornwall

This book is printed on acid-free paper

Contents

Acknowledgments

The editors and publishers gratefully acknowledge the following to reproduce copyright material:

Akhtar, Nameera, "Acquiring Basic Word Order: Evidence for Data-Driven Learning of Syntactic Structure." *Journal of Child Language* 26, 1999. (Cambridge University Press, Cambridge, 1999).

Bates, Elizabeth & Goodman, Judith C., "On the Inseparability of Grammar and the Lexicon: Evidence from Acquisition, Aphasia, and Real-time Processing." *Language and Cognitive Processing*, 1997.

Bloom, Lois, Rispoli, Matthew, Gartner, Barbara, & Hafitz, Jeremie, "Acquisition of Complementation." *Journal of Child Language* 16, 1989. (Cambridge University Press, Cambridge, 1999).

Budwig, Nancy, from "An Exploration into Children's Use of Passives." *Linguistics* vol. 28.6, 1990, reprinted by permission of Mouton de Gruyter, New York.

Caselli, Maria Cristina, et al. "Lexical Development in English and Italian." *Cognitive Development*, 1995.

Clancy, Barbara, & Finlay, Barbara, "Neural Correslates of Early Language Learning" excerpted from E. Bates, D. Thal, B.L. Finlay, & B. Clancy, "Early Language Development and Correlates" (in press). To appear in I. Rapin & S. Segalowitz (eds.), *Handbook of Neuropsychology, Volume 6, Child Neurology* (2nd edn.) (Elsevier, 2001).

Elman, Jeffrey L., "Connectionism and Language Acquisition."

Fernald, Anne, Pinto, John P., Swingley, Daniel, Weinberg, Amy, & McRoberts, Gerald W., "Rapid Gains in Speed of Verbal Processing by Infants in the 2nd Year." *Psycho-*

logical Science 9, 1998. Reprinted by permission of American Psychological Society and Blackwell Publishers, Oxford.

Gómez, R.L. & Gerken, L.A., "Infant Artificial Language Learning and Language Acquisition." *Trends in Cognitive Sciences* 4, 2000. Reprinted by permission of Elsevier Science.

Jusczyk, Peter W., "Finding and Remembering Words: Some Beginnings by English-Learning Infants." *Current Directions in Psychological Science* 6, 1997. Reprinted by permission of American Psychological Society and Blackwell Publishers, Oxford.

Karmiloff-Smith, Annette, "Development Itself Is the Key to Understanding Developmental Disorders". *Trends in Cognitive Sciences* 2, 1998. Reprinted by permission of Elsevier Science.

Köpcke, Klaus-Michael, "The Acquisition of Plural Marking in English and German Revisited: Schemata Versus Rules." *Journal of Child Language* 25, 1998. (Cambridge University Press, Cambridge, 1999).

Markson, Lori & Bloom, Paul, "Evidence Against a Dedicated System for Word Learning in Children." *Nature* 385: pp. 813–15 copyright © 1997 Macmillan Magazines Ltd.

Ramus, Franck, Hauser, Marc D., Miller, Cory, Morris, Dylan, & Mehler, Jacques, "Language Discrimination by Human Newborns and by Cotton-top Tamarin Monkeys." *Science* 288, 2000, reprinted by permission of American Association for the Advancement of Science.

Shwe, Helen I., & Markman, Ellen M., "Young Children's Appreciation of the Mental Impact of Their Communicative Signals." *Developmental Psychology* 33, 1997. Copyright © 1997 by the American Psychological Association. Reprinted with permission.

Slobin, Dan I., "Form/Function Relations: How Do Children Find Out What They Are?" (edited) from M. Bowerman & S. Levinson (eds.), *Language Acquisition and Conceptual Development* (Cambridge University Press, Cambridge, 2001).

Tomasello, Michael, "Perceiving Intentions and Learning Words in the Second Year of Life" from M. Bowerman & S. Levinson (eds.), *Language Acquisition and Conceptual Development* (Cambridge University Press, Cambridge, 2001).

Tomasello, Michael, "The Item-Based Nature of Children's Early Syntactic Development." *Trends in Cognitive Sciences* 4, 2000. Reprinted by permission of Elsevier Science.

Werker, Janet F. & Desjardins, Renée N., "Listening to Speech in the 1st Year of Life. Experiential Influences on Phoneme Perception." *Current Directions in Psychological Science* 4, 1995. Reprinted by permission of American Psychological Society and Blackwell Publishers, Oxford.

General Introduction

All animal species with complex social lives have complex systems of communication. Arguably the most complex and distinctive of these are the 6,000 human languages of the world, each of which comprises tens of thousands of meaningful elements that may be used in combination to create innumerably many communicative messages. The fact that there are so many different languages in the world, each with its own distinctive set of linguistic conventions, means that no particular linguistic elements are biologically given to the species – the way they are biologically given in honey bee dance communication, for example. Instead, each human child must learn the specific linguistic conventions used by the people around her. Children are biologically prepared for this prodigious task, of course, but it still takes many years of active and continuous learning to become a competent speaker of a natural language. This is a longer period of learning with more things to be learned – by many orders of magnitude – than is required of any other species on the planet.

At first glance, the way children learn a language seems straightforward. They observe what other persons are doing with language, and they "do the same thing." But anyone who has attempted to learn a foreign language knows that this general description obscures many difficulties. (One might just as well say that to become a champion tennis player one has simply to watch champion tennis players and do what they do.) Among the most important of these are three major types of problems that face a language learner.

- Problems of speech perception and production. Simply hearing clearly the different sounds speakers are producing, and then segmenting these into words and other meaningful units, is a very difficult task – and then reproducing those sounds competently is another difficult task on top of this.
- Problems of communication and meaning. Having segmented an identifiable unit of speech, it is still far from straightforward to comprehend precisely how a speaker of an unknown language uses that linguistic unit to direct the attention or behavior of other persons communicatively (i.e., what does the unit mean?).

- Problems of grammar and creativity. Mastering the use of many different sound units and their conventional meanings is still not enough, however, because much of the language a person hears and produces every day is novel, and so it must be interpreted or constructed creatively out of, or on analogy with, known units.

Attempting to discover how children solve these three acquisition problems has resulted in the wide variety of different theoretical approaches and research paradigms that currently constitute the field of study known as developmental psycholinguistics.

For this introductory volume of "essential" readings we have chosen to focus on what we consider to be the "most essential" psycholinguistic processes at work in child language acquisition, namely, those involved in solving our three basic acquisition problems. There are many important aspects of language development that we might have included as well but could not due to limitations of space. Among these are: bilingualism; child-directed speech; the acquisition of sign language; individual differences; babbling and phonological development; discourse, conversational, and narrative skills; literacy skills; and many others. Nevertheless, in our view, the papers in the current volume should provide the empirical and theoretical foundation that interested students will need in order to explore these other areas of research on their own.

In the remainder of this introduction we provide some general background for each of our three major problems, and also introduce some perspectives from allied fields. At the beginning of the appropriate sections in the volume, we provide further details on the particular theoretical and empirical issues involved in the collected papers.

Speech Perception and Production

Listening to a foreign language, especially one far removed from one's own native language, provides some perspective on the child's initial problem of segmenting speech into manageable units. When a monolingual English speaker listens to Italian or Chinese, for example, it is very difficult even to distinguish words in the continuous flow of speech. Human infants may be in a better position than adults in this regard, however, since they do not have a competing sound system (English in the case of our example) to get in the way. Indeed, it turns out that human infants begin to become familiar with the speech sounds they hear around them – in terms of the types of sounds of their language and the voices of particular speakers such as their mothers – while they are still in utero (DeCasper et al., 1994). By the time they are near their first birthdays, infants have already begun to zero in on the particular sounds they need to know to speak the language they are born into – in terms of both perception and production – to the extent that they are beginning to lose the ability to perceive and produce the sounds of other languages (Werker & Desjardins, this volume).

The human vocal-auditory apparatus biologically prepares human infants to acquire the specific sound and speech patterns of any human language. As researchers have attempted to discover precisely how this works, much attention has been focused on mechanisms that were originally thought to be specialized for language processing and unique to the human species. Thus, a variety of studies in the 1970s showed that very young human infants perceived phonemes categorically. That is, when they hear a series of closely related sounds, such as those that provide a continuous bridge between *ba* and *pa*, they make a sharp discrimination – classifying all the sounds up to a certain discrete point as *ba* and all those after this point as *pa*. It turns out, however, that other mammals do the same thing (Kuhl & Miller, 1975), and so this aspect of human speech perception is not specialized for language but rather represents the use of general mammalian vocal-auditory competencies for a new evolutionary function. More recently, it has been shown that very young infants – well before they show any signs of language comprehension or production – discriminate utterances in the particular language they hear around them from those in other languages. They do not do this when the utterances are played to them backward – showing that the temporal organization of the constituent sounds as present in normal human speech is crucial (Ramus et al., 1999). But tamarin monkeys who are exposed to a human language for a relatively brief period of time end up making the same kind of discrimination (including a lack of discrimination of the backward version; Ramus et al., this volume). And so the empirical discovery is that human languages are adapted to general mammalian perceptual capabilities more than the other way around.

Speech production is another story. Human speech has clearly evolved with the production of language as its primary adaptive context. Human beings can make sounds that no other primate can make, especially those that involve the blocking and rerouting of expelled air with the lips, tongue, and other parts of the mouth, that is to say, consonants. Unique features of the anatomy of the human vocal apparatus – for example, the lower positioning of the larynx in the throat – as well as adaptations for the voluntary control of various muscles in the oral cavity, ensure that human beings make their own species-unique sounds (although some bird species can make very similar sounds using different speech mechanisms). These of course conform with the general primate auditory system, or else they would be of no use. This specialization of the vocal tract began to take place, by most accounts, late in human evolution, perhaps after some less than fully linguistic forms of symbolic communication (both gestural and vocal) had already emerged (Lieberman, 1985). Human infants begin babbling a wide range of sounds from very early in ontogeny, and they begin gradually to restrict themselves to producing only the sounds they hear around them by the second half of the first year of life (Boysson-Bardies et al., 1984; but see Oller et al., 1999, for a cautionary note on just how early language-specific speech sounds are produced).

And so, to begin the process of language acquisition, human children must be equipped with a general primate auditory apparatus and a specialized human speech mechanism, and these of course must be "in tune" with one another. Precisely how these work in concert to enable the human infant to discriminate phonemes, to segment speech into words and other meaningful units, to perceive different intonational patterns, and to produce native-like speech is the story to be told by the papers in Part I of this volume. It is perhaps worth mentioning at this point that some children acquire a different king of natural language – one of the several hundred sign languages of the world – without the aid of a normal vocal-auditory apparatus (Volterra and Erting, 1990). This fact speaks volumes about the flexibility of human linguistic communication; it is a process that human beings may effect in various ways, even on the most basic perceptual and motor levels.

Word Learning

Most children in the industrialized world begin to comprehend and produce language sometime soon after their first birthdays. In a large norming sample for American children (based on the MacArthur Communicative Development Inventories, a widely used parent-report instrument for measuring young children's early language development – Fenson et al., 1994), 18-month-old infants were reported to produce between 50 and 100 words, on average. But about one-quarter of the children produced more than double that number, another one-quarter produced less than half that number, and it is not at all uncommon for an 18-month-old American child to produce no recognizable language at all (about 10%). In terms of rate (again using the MacArthur norms, supplemented by studies from older children; Bloom, 2000) American 1-year-olds learn about 1 new word per day, 2-year-olds learn about 2 new words per day, and 3- to 6-year-olds learn about 3 new words per day (by "words" we mean distinct lexical items like "dog" regardless of the specific grammatical form that these words take, e.g., "dog" or "dogs"). In other cultures, of course, a somewhat different developmental timetable may hold. Although we know from many ethnographic reports that in virtually all cultures 2-year-old children are beginning to produce substantial amounts of comprehensible language, there are almost no quantitative data on 1-year-olds or on overall rates of learning from cultures other than industrialized, mostly European, nations.

One interesting question is why children begin to use language at the age they do. Very young human infants are able to consistently associate particular sounds with particular perceptual experiences (Haith, 1994), but apparently that is not enough to acquire a linguistic symbol. Children must mot only be able to identify particular speech sounds, identify particular perceptual or conceptual experiences, and associate the two, but they must also be able to understand that language is used to communicate – to manipulate the attention and mental states of other people. This takes us beyond simply perceiving sounds and things in the world and into the realm of children reading other people's minds. But, the fact is that this is precisely what differentiates the learning of a linguistic convention or symbol from learning associations in general (e.g., the way a household pet might come to associate the sound "Dinner" with a specific object or event). Linguistic communication is about discerning what other people intend for you to pay attention to or think about when they use a linguistic convention, and then, in complementary fashion, using those same conventions yourself to manipulate the intentional and mental states of other persons. Cognitive development is crucial to the process as well, of course, as one cannot talk about something that one cannot in some way understand and conceptualize.

Although it is common to characterize word learning as something entirely separate from the acquisition of grammar, the fact is that children do not hear or use words in isolation; they experience and use them as parts of entire utterances, speech acts whose aim is interpersonal communication. Word learning is thus often characterized as a kind of mini-linguistics lesson in which adults point to and name objects for children, similar to the way some vocabulary lessons happen in the classroom. But this is not the actual situation. First, adults in many cultures do not stop what they are doing to name things for children at all, and even the most pedagogically conscious Western parents do not do this for words other than object labels (i.e., parents do not say to their child: "Look! Giving." or "Look! Of.") Instead, the way most of the world's children experience most words is in the ongoing flow of social interactions in which adults use language to regulate their behavior ("Sit down!"), anticipate their desires ("Do you want more?"), announce future events ("I'll put it here."), make proposals ("Let's roll the ball together."), describe past events ("You fell down."), narrate ongoing events ("You're blowing bubbles."), and perhaps sometimes name objects ("That's a tape recorder."). To learn a new word in these contexts, children must understand the adult's communicative intentions as they relate to the ongoing events around her.

Second, and moreover, a child very seldom hears an adult produce a single-word utterance, and even when they do that single-word utterance is associated with a particular speech act function with an associated intonation contour. For instance, if a mother tells her child to "Sit down!", the child must determine that the lexeme *sit down* is used to refer to a particular activity, and that the requestive part of the speech act comes from the imperative intonation with which it is said. When an adult asks the child: "Do you want a piece of cake?", to comprehend the adult's communicative intention in full detail the child must understand what role is being played by the interrogative intonation contour, what role is being played by the phrases "do you want" and " a piece of cake" (and perhaps each of the words in each of these phrases as well). And there are some relational words – for example, the prepositions "from," "for," and "of" – that only have a distinctive meaning inside some larger phrase containing the elements to be related. And so, not only must the word-learning child be able to discern the adult's communicative intention in the ongoing social situation, she must also be able to extract the phonetic substance of a new word from a larger utterance and then identify the functional role that word is playing in the communicative intention as a whole.

On the production side, children's first words sometimes occur within so-called holophrases, such as "Ball!" meaning "I want the ball" or "Ball?" meaning "Where is the ball?" – with the difference in meaning being indicated mostly by the different intonation contours involved (nonlinguistic context is important as well). And many of children's early holophrastic utterances actually correspond to adult utterances containing more than one word, such things as "I-wanna-do-it," "Lemme-see," and "My-turn," with no evidence that these are recognized as multiword at all (Pine and Lieven, 1993; Peters, 1983). In these cases, the child's first "words" must indeed be broken down for her to comprehend the internal grammar of the utterance. And, strangely enough, from the English point of view, in highly agglutinating languages such as Inuktitut (spoken by some Native Americans living mostly in Canada) this breaking-down process is the normal case. In these languages the normal case is that 2-year-old children regularly hear and produce word-sentences such as "Taartaulirtunga," meaning "Something is in my way" or "Tuqutaulangasivungaa!", meaning "I'm going to get killed!" (Allen, 1996) – which have to be broken down into morphemes before any of their elements can be used productively in other utterances. The overall point is simply that children do not learn words in some vocabulary acquisition game in which the word and referent are carefully isolated for them, and they do not produce words in isolation either. Children must acquire words by extracting their forms from complex utterances and their meanings from complex social-communicative situations; and to produce them they must integrate them into their larger communicative intentions.

And so word learning is actually only one part of a very complex set of processes by means of which children learn to associate linguistic forms with their intended meanings. Word learning may have some special properties, as words are, by all accounts, a special unit of language structure. But viewing the acquisition of words as a series of mini-linguistics lessons and the acquisition of grammar as a totally abstract and rule-governed process without connections to adult linguistic models is inaccurate and unproductive, and indeed one of the challenges in future research is to integrate our theoretical accounts of how children learn the many and diverse linguistic structures – including both words and grammatical constructions – that they hear around them. The papers selected for Part II of this volume make some first steps in this direction.

Grammatical Development

One could imagine that children learn holophrases, or perhaps even words disembodied from any particular speech act function, and then combine these in situations in which they both are relevant – with both words having roughly equivalent status. For example, a child might learn to name a ball and a table and then spy a ball on a table and say, "Ball table." There may be some initial linguistic productions that are like this for some children. But most of children's early multi-word speech shows a functional asymmetry between constituents; that is, there is one word (or morpheme or phrase) that seems to structure the utterance in the sense that it determines the speech act function of the utterance as a whole (often with help from an intonational contour), with the other linguistic item(s) simply filling in variable slot(s). This kind of organization is responsible for what has been called the "pivot look" of early child language, which is characteristic of most children learning most of the languages of the world (Braine, 1976; Brown, 1973). Early multi-word productions are thus things like: *Where's the X?, I wanna X, More X, It's a X, I'm X-ing it, X gone, Put X here, Let's X it, Throw X, I X-ed it, Sit on X, Open X, X here, There's a X, X broken,* and so forth (with this kind of analysis working with individual morphemes in the case of languages like Inuktitut). These early word combinations serve the same kinds of functions as early holophrases (indeed many begin their life as holophrases); they simply have a bit more grammatical structure in the sense that they have constant linguistic material that (1) has some internal complexity in some cases, and (2) has at least one open slot into which many different lexical items and phrases may be placed.

Across all the languages of the world, the kinds of things children talk about with these pivot-like expressions are similar as well (Brown, 1973; Braine, 1976). Among the most common are:

- the presence–absence–recurrence of people, objects, and events (*hi X, bye X, X gone, more X, X again, another X, stop X-ing, X away*)

- the exchange-possession of objects with other people (*give X, have X, share X, my X, X mine, Mommy's X*)
- the movement-location of people and objects (*X come, X go, X up, X down, in X, out X, on X, off X, put X, X here, X there, X outside, bring X, take X, Where X go?*)
- the states and changes of states of objects and people (*open X, close X, X falldown, X break, fix X, X wet, X pretty, little X, big X*)
- the physical and mental activities of people (*eat X, kick X, ride X, draw X, hug X, kiss X, throw X, roll X, want X, need X, look-at X, do X, make X, see X*)

Children's early linguistic expressions thus reflect the kinds of activities and states of affairs they engage in and find important throughout their daily lives, and these are, in a very general way, highly similar in all of the different cultures of the world.

The question then becomes how children move beyond these semi-concrete formulae to the more abstract grammatical constructions characteristic of adult linguistic competence. In the domain of morphology – the systematic and productive creation of new word forms – there is one group of theorists who believes that there is a stark dichotomy between regular and irregular forms (Clahsen, 1999; Pinker, 1999). For example, the regular past tense forms in English are formed by adding an *-ed* to the verb root, and this process is productive, as witnessed by the fact that mature speakers can easily turn the made-up verb *moop* into its past tense form *mooped*, even though they have never before heard this form. Irregular past tenses like *thought* (from *think*) must simply be learned on their own, without the benefit of a rule. To explain these phenomena, this group of theorists has proposed a Dual Process view of morphological development, in which language learning in children (and language use in adults) requires the application of two distinct "modules": one for words, and another for rules. Other theorists, however, have pointed out that there are mini-regularities among some irregular forms; for example, many adults would form the past tense of the made-up verb *pling* as *plang*, on analogy with *sing-sang, ring-rang*, etc. This phenomenon is much more acute in languages that have more complex morphology than English; for example, in German there are 9 different ways to form the plural of a noun, about half of which are quite productive (Köpcke, this volume). Moreover, researchers using connectionist computer models have found that a single generalization process working on different kinds of exemplars reproduces quite accurately children's linguistic behavior (Plunkett & Marchman, 1996). In this approach, then, both regulars and irregulars are generated by the same learning mechanism (the Single Process view); the difference we observe in the development of regulars and irregulars lies in the data that this mechanism is given.

In the domain of syntax, the question of how children create ever more abstract linguistic constructions is even more difficult because in this case we are talking about many parts of a construction all being abstract at once. Thus, for example, if a mature English speaker is told that *mooping* refers to the activity of sending someone a message via mental telepathy, they would very likely be able to generate the utterances "He is mooping her a message" and "The message is being mooped to her now." The reason they can do this is they have mastered whole abstract sentence patterns – in the first case, the ditransitive construction (as in *He gave her a penny*) and, in the second case, the passive (as in *The package is being sent to her today*) (see Goldberg, 1995). How best to characterize these abstract constructions, and how children go about acquiring them, depends on one's theoretical stance. On the one hand, followers of the linguist Noam Chomsky believe that all children of the world are born with the same innate universal grammar, and so even their earliest language is best described with an adult-like formal grammar. In this view, all the child must do to acquire adult-like linguistic competence is to link the particular language she is learning to this innate universal grammar – which then yields immediate competence with all kinds of linguistic abstractions (e.g., Pinker, 1994). On the other hand, more usage-based, constructivist theorists do not believe that human beings are born with an innate universal grammar (e.g., Bates & MacWhinney, 1989; Tomasello, 2000; Slobin, 1997; who follow linguistic theories such as those of Langacker 1987, 1991, and Goldberg, 1995). This means that children must do much more work to learn their language than they would have to do if Chomsky's account were true. In the constructivist view, children must actually construct the abstract categories and schemas of their language based on the patterns they can discern in the language they hear around them. These patterns have been created historically through patterns of grammaticalization – the way that the English of Chaucer and Shakespeare has been transformed into the English of today (Traugott & Heine, 1991) – and in the course of "finding" the structures in their language, children recapitulate at least a part of this original creative process (see especially Slobin, this volume).

The central issue in the study of grammatical development is thus the nature of children's linguistic representations – especially in terms of abstractness – and how those representations change over development. If a distributional analysis of children's spontaneous language is performed, the answer is clear: children use specific linguistic items and expressions only in very limited ways, failing to generalize them to many contexts that are normal for adults. Experimentally, if they are told about the mental telepathy verb *mooping*, they do not then produce, as adults do, a creative utterance like "He's mooping her a message." The inference is thus that children's early language is *not* based on highly abstract linguistic structures and constructions – which should allow very broad-based generalizations – but rather it consists entirely of an inventory of highly specific, item-based schemas that develop from pivot-like structures in piecemeal fashion over the early childhood years (see Tomasello, 2000, this volume). Generative grammarians counter that children's limited ability to generalize simply reflects "performance limitations"; the child possesses adult-like linguistic structures but simply has not linked them all up yet to the particular language she is learning. Unfortunately, very little research has been aimed at identifying and measuring potential performance factors that might prevent children from displaying their supposed adult-like linguistic competence.

For purposes of the current collection of basic readings, we have chosen to focus in Part III on the processes that young children use to learn the specific grammatical conventions of the specific language they are learning. From this more usage-based, constructivist side of the theoretical spectrum, some of the issues of most current importance are: (1) What is the relationship between the acquisition of words and the acquisition of grammar? (2) Do verbs and other relational words play an especially important role in early grammatical development? (3) What are the cues children use to discern the communicative function of grammatical elements in an utterance such as case markers or word order? (4) How do children make generalizations across different exemplars of abstract constructions (such as different exemplars of the English transitive construction)? (5) How do children piece together previously mastered constructions to create novel and more complex utterances? (6) How do children create "slots" in linguistic constructions, such as those in pivot constructions? (7) What is the role of frequency of exposure in the learning of grammatical constructions? (8) How are children's different concrete and abstract constructions related to one another? (9) Are there important cross-linguistic and/or individual differences in basic processes of grammatical development?

Other Perspectives

It is clear from all of the foregoing that children need to be able to do and experience a number of things if they are to acquire a natural language. Unfortunately for many children, a delay in any one of them can hold up the entire process. In cultures or homes in which speaking to prelinguistic infants is not the norm, perfectly healthy children may begin to acquire language later than in other cultures simply because they do not have as much early exposure to language (Hart, 1991). Delays are also observed in some children despite rich child-directed input. For example, some children seem to have special difficulties in either hearing or reproducing adult-like phonological sequences (or both), and they often turn out to be especially slow and error-prone as they start producing language (see Bishop, 1997, and Leonard, 1998, for reviews). Children with autism seem to have problems understanding that others have attentional or mental states that they may attempt to manipulate via language. Many investigators now believe that this social and cognitive limitation is responsible (at least in part) for the fact that many children with autism acquire no language at all, while others display very late and/or atypical language (Sigman & Capps, 1997, Happe & Frith, 1996). Children with Down Syndrome, who have trouble with conceptual development in general, acquire their language skills but only very slowly and with much difficulty (Chapman, 1995; Mervis & Robinson, 2000; Vicari et al., 2000). The lesson is simply that there are many skills involved in learning and using linguistic conventions, and so there are many ways to go wrong – and many reasons for individual differences.

We thus end the volume with some basic tutorials on theory and mechanism that integrate the ideas and phenomena reviewed in Parts I–III. These include a paper by Clancy and Finlay reviewing the latest evidence on human brain development before and during language acquisition (the neural substrates for the kinds of learning reviewed in Parts I–III). There is also a short chapter by Elman – written especially for this volume – on computational approaches to the language-learning problem, emphasizing artificial neural networks as tools for the simulation of language acquisition in real live children. Finally, we end with a chapter on developmental disorders by Karmiloff-Smith, which shows how small perturbations in the "starting state" of human psychology prior to language (due to defective genes) can lead to deviant cognitive, social, and linguistic outcomes.

Conclusion

Human children inherit things from their forebears both biologically and culturally. In the case of language development, children inherit the capacity to acquire a natural language and, of course, they also inherit the language itself – in the sense that they grow up in the midst of other human beings communicating with one another linguistically. Developmental psycholinguists study the processes by means of which human children use their dual inheritances over a several-year period to become competent speakers of one or another of the world's 6,000 natural languages. The process is a multifaceted one, requiring just about all of the child's perceptual, cognitive, social-communicative, and learning skills – applied over several years of nearly continuous interaction with mature language users.

The readings collected in this volume are intended to introduce students to some of the many dimensions of this rich and interesting phenomenon of the natural world, and to prepare its readers for 21st-century research on language learning and development.

References

Allen. S. (1996). *Aspects of argument structure acquisition in Inuktitut.* Amsterdam: John Benjamins.

Bates, E., & MacWhinney, B. (1989). Functionalism and the competition model. In B. MacWhinney, & E. Bates (Eds.), *The crosslinguistic study of sentence processing* (pp. 3–76). New York: Cambridge University Press.

Bishop, D.V.M. (1997). *Uncommon understanding: Development and disorders of comprehension in children.* Hove, UK: Psychology Press.

Bloom, L. (2000). *How children learn the meanings of words.* Cambridge, MA: MIT Press.

Boysson-Bardies, B., Sagart, L., & Durand, C. (1984). Discernible differences in the babbling of infants according to target language. *Journal of Child Language, 11,* 1–15.

Braine, M.D.S. (1976). Children's first word combinations. With commentary by Melissa Bowerman. *Monographs of the Society for Research in Child Development, 41*(Serial No. 164)

Brown, R. (1973). *A first language: The early stages.* Cambridge, MA: Harvard University Press.

Chapman, R. (1995). Language development in children and adolescents with Down Syndrome. In P. Fletcher, & B. MacWhinney (Eds.), *The handbook of child language* (pp. 641–663). Oxford: Basil Blackwell.

Clahsen, H. (1999). Lexical entries and rules of language: A multidisciplinary study of German inflection. *Behavioral and Brain Sciences, 22* (6), 991–1013, 1055–1060.

DeCasper, A.J., Lecanuet, J.P., Busnel, M.C., Granier-Deferre, C., & Maugeais, R. (1994). Fetal reaction to recurrent maternal speech. *Infant Behavior and Development, 17* (2), 159–164.

Fenson, L., Dale, P., Reznick, S., Bates, E., Thal, D., & Pethick, S. (1994). Variability in early communicative development. *Monographs of the Society for Research in Child Development, 59* (5, Serial No. 242).

Goldberg, A.E. (1995). *Constructions: A construction grammar approach to argument structure.* Chicago: University of Chicago Press.

Haith, M.M. (1994). Visual expectations as the first step toward the development of future-oriented processes. In M.M. Haith, J.B. Benson, R.J. Rogers, Jr., & B.F. Pennington (Eds.), *The development of future-oriented proceses* (pp. 11–38). Chicago: The University of Chicago Press.

Hart, B. (1991). Input frequency and children's first words. *First Language, 11,* 289–300.

Happé, F., & Frith, U. (1996). The neuropsychology of autism. *Brain, 119,* 1377–1400.

Kuhl, P.K., & Miller, J. (1975). Speech perception by the chinchilla: Voiced-voiceless distinction in alveolar plosive consonants. *Science, 190,* 69–72.

Leonard, L.B. (1998). *Children with specific language impairment.* Boston MA: MIT Press.

Langacker, R.W. (1987). *Foundations of cognitive grammar.* Stanford, CA: Stanford University Press.

Langacker, R. (1991). *Foundations of cognitive grammar, Volume 2.* Stanford University Press.

Lieberman, P. (1985). On the evolution of human syntactic ability. Its pre-adaptive bases. *Journal of Human Evolution, 14,* 657–668.

Mervis, C.B., & Robinson, B.F. (2000). Expressive vocabulary ability of toddlers with Williams syndrome or Down syndrome: A comparison. *Developmental Neuropsychology, 17* (1), 111–126.

Oller, D.K., Eilers, R.E., Neal, A.R., & Schwartz, H.K. (1999). Precursors to speech in infancy: The Prediction of speech and language disorders. *Journal of Communication Distorders, 32* (4), 223–245.

Peters, A. (1983). *The units of language acquisition.* Cambridge: Cambridge University Press.

Pine, J., & Lieven, E. (1993). Reanalyzing rote-learned phrases: Individual differences in the transition to multi-word speech. *Journal of Child Language, 20* (3), 551–571.

Pinker, S. (1994). *The language instinct: How the mind creates language.* New York: William Morrow.

Pinker, S. (1999). *Words and rules: The ingredients of language.* New York: Basic Books.

Plunkett, K., & Marchman, V. (1996). Learning from a connectionist model of the English past tense. *Cognition, 61* (3), 299–308.

Ramus, F., Nespor, M., & Mehler, J. (1999). Correlates of linguistic rhythm in the speech signal. *Cognition, 73* (3), 265–292.

Sigman, M., & Capps, L. (1997). *Children with autism: A developmental perspective.* Cambridge, MA: Harvard University Press.

Slobin, D. (Ed.). (1997). *The crosslinguistic study of language acquisition* (Vol. 4). Hillsdale, NJ: Erlbaum.

Slobin, D. (Ed.). (1997). *The crosslinguistic study of language acquisition* (Vol. 5). Hillsdale, NJ: Erlbaum.

Tomasello, M. (2000). Do young children have adult syntactic competence? *Cognition, 74,* 209–253.

Traugott, E.C., & Heine, B. (1991). *Approaches to grammaticalization.* Amsterdam; Philadelphia: J. Benjamins.

Vicari, S., Caselli, M.C., & Tonucci, F. (2000). Asynchrony of lexical and morphosyntactic development in children with Down Syndrome. *Neuropsicologia, 38* (5), 634–644.

Volterra, V., & Erting, C. (Eds.). (1990). *From gesture to language in hearing and deaf children.* New York: Springer-Verlag.

Part I

Introduction to Speech Perception

Introduction to Part I

Speech perception and its development in children is one of the richest and liveliest sub-fields in language research. Because speech is a physical as well as a psychological phenomenon, it has lent itself more easily to experimental study than some of the "higher" (and more controversial) levels of language and language processing. This solid grounding in reality has permitted a remarkable amount of progress – and yielded a lot of big surprises.

In the past few decades a series of technical breakthroughs have made it possible for scientists to visualize the acoustic signals that support speech, using sound spectrograms and other instruments. Figure 1 (below, from Aslin et al., 1983) illustrates a schematic ("cleaned up") version of the sound spectrogram for two syllables, \di\ (pronounced "dee") and \gu\ (pronounced "goo"). Time in milliseconds is plotted on the horizontal axis. The vertical axis represents a graded series of frequency bands, or "formants" (as in a car radio tuner). The black bands in this two-dimensional space represent changes over time in the distribution of energy within those frequency bands. The visible shifts in Figure 1.1 of energy from one formant to another are called "formant transitions," long believed to play a key role in signaling systematic contrasts between speech sounds (e.g., between "d" and "g"). With such instruments, scientists are able to modify the signal in many different ways, and then play it back to see how those modifications sound to real human beings. A major motivation for this research (then and now) has been to construct artificial systems that can understand speech, so we can talk to our computers directly, bypassing the keyboard. In principle, this kind of mechanism might also be very useful to people who are congenitally deaf.

Considering all the time and money that has gone into this enterprise, the first big surprise is that we still have so far to go. Today's computers can be trained to understand a finite set of words uttered by a single speaker ("his master's voice"), or a very small set of words uttered by a much larger array of speakers (like the numbers 0–9, or the words "calling card" and "collect" that we find ourselves yelling at telephone company computers). Much more flexible and sophisticated speech-understanding systems may be just around the corner. But we are still well below the level reached by healthy human infants across the first year of life. The problem of speech perception has proven to be especially difficult to solve, because the relationship between physics (the actual acoustic events, like those in Figure 1) and experience (the sounds we hear) is not at all transparent. Three examples of this problem include the following.

- Violations of linearity. If the mapping from sound to experience were straight-forward, then we should expect the first part of each pattern in Figure 1 to sound

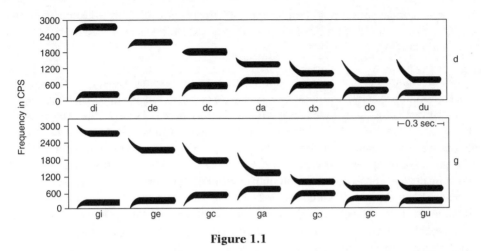

Figure 1.1

like a consonant ("d" or "g") while the second part would sound like a vowel ("eee" or "ooo"). For the vowel portion, the prediction works. However, when the formant transitions that signal different consonants are played back without their vowel contexts, they do not sound like speech at all! Instead, they sound like clicks or brief chirps that disappear when these bits of sound are placed back into a speech context.

- Violations of invariance. If the mapping from sound to experience were transparent, then we would also expect the formant transitions that signal "d" and "g" in Figure 1 to play more or less the same role in other vowel contexts. So if we spliced the first part of \di\ in front of the vowel \u\, then we would expect the resulting spectrogram to sound like \du\. But that is not what happens! These bits of sound do not behave like letters of the alphabet. For example, the "d" component of the syllable "du" looks like the "g" component of the syllable "ga." Furthermore, the shape of the visual pattern that corresponds to a constant sound can even vary with the pitch of the speaker's voice, so that the "da" produced by a small child results in a very different-looking pattern from the "da" produced by a mature adult male. The bottom line is that the physical components that make up speech sounds are not invariant over contexts; they are highly context dependent, changing their colors completely depending not only on the vowels they precede and follow, but on the voice of the person who is doing the talking (i.e., the "fundamental" or carrier frequency that characterizes the difference in sound quality between men and women, or adults and children). We perceive speech sounds as "same" or "different," but the basis for this difference in experience is not obvious from the physical signal itself.
- Categorical perception. Consonants like \p\ and \b\ differ along a dimension called voice onset time (VOT), a difference between the point in time at which the vocal chords begin to vibrate and the discontinuous point at which we open our lips to allow that continuous sound to emerge. It is possible to make up artificial tokens of \p\ and \b\ that differ continuously along this VOT dimension. However, native speakers do not hear this as a gradual change. Instead, they hear a sudden or "categorical" transition from \p\ to \b\. The physical basis for this

categorical shift is not at all obvious, a surprising result that led some investigators to conclude that the boundary is imposed by the listener's auditory processing system.

As peculiarities like these began to mount, it became obvious that speech-understanding systems would not be as easy to construct as we had originally hoped. Some investigators concluded that human beings process speech the way they do because we have a special-purpose speech perception device built into our brains, imposing psychological experiences upon an underdetermined physical event. Some of the pioneers of speech perception research also proposed that this innate, special-purpose device is based not on audition per se but on the human system for speech production. This theory (called the Motor Theory of Speech Perception) is based on a kind of "analysis by synthesis": that is, we perceive auditory input as speech by "coming up to meet it" with an internal model of what that person we are listening to was trying to produce with an articulatory system very much like our own. This theory led to several clear predictions: (1) speech perception should be unique to humans; (2) speech perception makes use of a neural substrate that is separate from the neural system used for other kinds of audition; (3) the system should be innate, up and running at birth.

Evidence in favor of this view (especially the third point) began to appear in 1975, with an influential paper by Peter Eimas showing that very young infants (2–4 months old) are not only able to hear the phoneme contrasts that characterize natural languages, but to hear them categorically (Eimas, 1975). Habituated on one set of sounds (e.g., \ba\), the infants showed signs of surprise (e.g., vigorous sucking on an electronically monitored pacifier) when the signal shifted to \pa\, with a sharp border roughly around the point at which adults also show a categorical boundary. Following this discovery, many more studies of infant speech perception, using a variety of methods, led to the clear conclusion that infants are born able to perceive most if not all of the speech contrasts used by natural languages. As Patricia Kuhl has put it, infants are born "citizens of the world," able to hear and learn any natural language without prejudice.

It is now quite clear that the ability to perceive speech contrasts is present very early, and is probably (within limits) an innate property of the human auditory system. This does not mean, however, that our innate perceptual abilities are unique to speech, or unique to humans. For example, subsequent studies have shown that categorical perception also occurs with sequences of pure tones (Cutting & Rosner, 1974) and with sequences of lights (the famous flicker-fusion phenomenon). Perhaps the most important and surprising finding in this regard lies in a growing literature showing that categorical perception of speech sounds occurs in non-human species, e.g., chinchillas (Kuhl & Miller, 1975) and quail (Lotto et al., 1997). The article by Ramus et al. (2000, and in this volume) pushes these observations one step further, showing that tamarin monkeys can discriminate the same speech contrasts perceived by human infants, and are (like human infants) unable to make those discriminations when these speech sequences are played backwards – suggesting that the pereception is not just of random sound sequences but rather of something concerning patterned human speech.

The overwhelming conclusion from studies like these is that human speech perception evolved to exploit pre-existing dimensions and categories that were already present in the mammalian auditory system. Crudely put, the mouth evolved to meet the ears, and not vice versa. Given such evidence, research on speech perception and its development has shifted from the initial state of the organism (What can humans perceive at birth? Virtually all speech contrasts – but this is not unique to humans) to a focus on the process by which children learn to tune in to the 40 or so phonemes used by their own native language (out of an array of up to 4,000 possibilities). Even more surprises have emerged out of this research effort. For example, we now know that human infants develop a bias toward certain sounds from their native language in utero (DeCasper et al., 1994; Ramus et al., 1999). This remarkable finding was viewed with considerable skepticism when it first appeared in the literature, but current evidence regarding brain development in humans (Clancy & Finlay, this volume) confirms that the human brain is "up and running" and capable of learning before the third trimester. A large and comprehensive body of research by Kuhl, Werker, Jusczyk, and others (see especially Jusczyk, this volume) testifies to the rich and intricate patterns of language-specific speech contrasts (i.e., phonotactics) that infants develop during the first year of life, zeroing in like homing pigeons first on the vowels favored by their language, and then on consonantal boundaries, rhythmic biases, and constraints on the kinds of sounds that can and cannot occur together.

The paper by Gerkin and Gomez reviews exciting new evidence suggesting that human infants (by at least 6–8 months of age) are so skilled at learning that they are able to pick up statistical patterns in their perceptual input with 2 minutes or less of exposure to a disembodied voice, played while the infants are playing on the floor and seemingly paying little attention. They go on to show that the same statistical learning process that operates on speech (locating possible word boundaries) are also capable of supporting the induction of artificial grammars with many of the properties that underlie the natural grammars that infants will acquire many months later. Gerkin and Gomez also cite studies by other investigators showing that infants can extract these same kinds of patterns from other kinds of perceptual inputs as well, for example, sequences of arbitrary tones or even lights (e.g., Saffran et al., 1999). This suggests the existence of a very general perceptual pattern extractor – not one specific to language – from relatively early in infancy. Moreover, in more recent work Ramus et al. (2000) have shown that tamarin monkeys can extract patterns from speech in exactly the same way as human infants – suggesting in this case that the pattern extractor is not even specfic to humans. We thus see, once again, that human language evolved to fit with pre-existing primate (or mammalian) perceptual processes, not the other way around.

In this fashion, the center of gravity in research on infant speech perception has shifted from what children are able to perceive (which seems to be just about everything we can throw at them) to what they are (eventually) unable to perceive. As adults, native speakers of Japanese find it extremely difficult to perceive the contrast between \ra\ and \la\ – a contrast that is very easy for listeners in a language like English, in which that contrast is used productively to distinguish between possible words. In the same vein, native speakers of English lose the ability to hear a Thai consonant contrast that falls somewhere between the English consonants \d\ and \t\ (see Werker & Desjardins, this volume). Interestingly, this loss starts around 10 months of age – right around the age at which children start to show systematic evidence of word comprehension. In order to tune into one's native language and find those packages of sound that really matter, human infants have to learn to "tune out" the array of sound contrasts that matter far less in their particular language. But there is an interesting twist: the infant's open mind about the languages she can learn is closed not by some mysterious maturational process depending on an invariant and inflexible "critical period," but by the very act of learning her own native language. Tuning in involves tuning out. The gradual (but very efficient) process of tuning in to possible and actual words in the speech stream is illustrated very clearly in the paper by Fernald et al., who use infants' looking behavior as an index of the strength, speed, and efficiency of word recognition across the second year of life.

References

Aslin, R.N., Pisoni, D.B., & Jusczyk, P.W. (1983). Auditory development and speech perception in infancy. In P.H. Mussen (Series Ed.) & M.M. Haith & J.J. Campos (Vol. Eds.), *Handbook of child psychology: Vol. II. Infancy and developmental psychobiology* (4th edn, pp. 573–687). New York: John Wiley & Sons.

Cutting, J.C., & Rosner, B.S. (1974). Categories and boundaries in speech and music. *Perception & Psychophysics, 16*, 564–570.

DeCasper, A.J., Lecanuet, J.P., Busnel, M.C., Granier-Deferre, C., & Maugeais, R. (1994). Fetal reaction to recurrent maternal speech. *Infant Behavior and Development, 17* (2), 159–164.

Eimas, P.D. (1975). Auditory and phonetic coding of the cues for speech: Discrimination of the (R-L) distinction by young infants. *Perception & Psychophysics, 18* (5), 341–347.

Kuhl, P.K., & Miller, J. (1975). Speech perception by the chinchilla: Voiced-voiceless distinction in alveolar plosive consonants. *Science, 190*, 69–72.

Lotto, A.J., Kluender, K.R., & Holt, L.L. (1997). Perceptual compensation for coarticulation by Japanese quail (Coturnix coturnix japonica). *Journal of the Acoustical Society of America, 102* (2), Pt. 1: 1134–1140.

Ramus, F., Nespor, M., & Mehler, J. (1999). Correlates of linguistic rhythm in the speech signal. *Cognition, 73* (3), 265–292.

Ramus, F., Hauser, M.D., Miller, C., & Morris, D. (2000). Language discrimination by human newborns and by cotton-top tamarin monkeys. *Science, 288* (5464), 349–351.

Saffran, E.M., Aslin, R.N., & Newport, E.L. (1996). Statistical learning by 8-month-old infants. *Science, 274*, 1926–1928.

Saffran, E.R., Johnson, E.K., Aslin, R.N., & Newport, E.L. (1999). Statistical learning of tone sequences by human infants and adults. *Cognition, 70*, 27–52.

ONE

Finding and Remembering Words:
Some Beginnings by English-Learning Infants

Peter W. Jusczyk

Learning to speak and understand a language involves acquiring a vocabulary. At a minimum, the learner must be able to recognize and identify a set of sound patterns and attach these to their appropriate meanings. If the sound patterns were presented one at a time, or with clear pauses between adjacent words, then the first step would be a matter of discriminating and remembering the different patterns. However, in everyday speech, talkers rarely pause between words. Instead, they are more apt to run one word into the next. Adults are rarely aware of this difficulty in their own language because they have learned to use cues to word boundaries that are available in the speech signal. The word segmentation problem typically becomes apparent when one listens to speech in an unfamiliar language. Then, it becomes difficult to know where one word ends and the next one begins. Because different languages cue word boundaries in different ways, learners must discover the cues that are most useful in segmenting words for their native language.

Although infant-directed speech is generally slower and has more exaggerated pitch contours than adult-directed speech (Fernald & Simon, 1984), the lack of clear boundaries between successive words is still present. Nevertheless, the word segmentation problem might not pose a serious difficulty for acquiring a vocabulary if new words were always presented to infants as isolated utterances. However, even when parents are explicitly instructed to teach their children new words, they present these words in isolation only about 20% of the time (Woodward & Aslin, 1990). Consequently, to make real headway in acquiring a vocabulary, learners need to solve the word segmentation problem.

Potential Cues to Word Boundaries

There are several different sources of information that could potentially inform listeners about likely word boundaries in fluent speech. One possibility is that listeners rely on their knowledge of predominant word stress patterns. This notion figures prominently in the Metrical Segmentation Strategy proposed by Cutler and her colleagues

(Cutler, 1994; Cutler & Carter, 1987; Cutler & Norris, 1988). Noting that a very high proportion of content words in English conversational speech are stressed on their initial syllables, Cutler and her colleagues have suggested that, as a first-pass strategy, listeners might identify the potential onsets of words with the occurrence of stressed syllables.

Phonotactic constraints (restrictions on the permissible sequences of phonetic segments in words) have also been suggested as a potential source of information about word boundaries (Brent & Cartwright, 1996; Myers et al., 1996). For example, knowledge that English does not allow certain sequences of consonants, such as "db" or "kt," at the beginnings of words could be used to infer a potential word boundary between such consonants.

In the linguistics literature, the fact that certain allophones (different pronunciations of the same speech sound) are restricted to particular contexts has been suggested as a possible cue to word boundaries in speech (Bolinger & Gerstman, 1957; Hockett, 1958). For example, as Church (1987) has noted, in English, "t's" are aspirated (i.e., produced with a large puff of air) when they occur in the initial position of stressed syllables, but unaspirated elsewhere. Thus, a listener sensitive to the occurrence of an aspirated "t" in speech might infer that it marks the beginning of a new word.

Finally, it has also been suggested that distributional evidence (i.e., information about the kinds of contexts that a particular sound pattern appears in on different occasions) can serve as a cue to a word boundary (Brent & Cartwright, 1996; Saffran et al., 1996; Suomi, 1993). For example, hearing the word "milk" in a variety of different contexts (e.g., "the milk," "an old milk bottle") may help that word to "pop out" as a unit in the speech stream. Subsequently, the learner might be able to use this knowledge to infer information about word boundaries of two unfamiliar words (i.e., "chocolate" and "carton") in the sequence "chocolate milk carton."

It should be noted that none of these potential cues is completely reliable by itself in predicting word boundaries in English. Rather, each of them points to probable locations of word boundaries, and it is likely that in segmenting words from speech, listeners rely on some appropriately weighted combination of these cues.

When Does Word Segmentation Begin?

Investigating the word segmentation abilities of infants requires the use of a test procedure that allows for the presentation of long strings of speech. Aslin and I adapted the head-turn preference procedure for this purpose (Jusczyk & Aslin, 1995). We familiarized English-learning infants with pairs of words like "feet" and "bike." There were 15 different versions of each word. On a given familiarization trial, one of the words began to play when the infant looked at a flashing red light on one of two side panels. Repetitions of the word continued playing until either the trial was completed (i.e., after all 15 versions were played) or the infant turned away from the light for two consecutive seconds. At the completion of a familiarization trial, a green center light began to flash to attract the infant's attention to the center. Then the next trial began with one of the two red side lights flashing. This familiarization procedure continued until the infant accumulated at least 30 s of listening time to each word. Then, the infants heard four different passages, each consisting of six sentences. Two of the passages contained one of the familiarized words in each sentence (e.g., a "feet" passage and a "bike" passage), and two similarly contained repetitions of two words not heard during familiarization. On a given trial, as during the familiarization period, the test passage began to play when the infant was looking at the flashing red light. The passage either continued to its conclusion or was stopped when the infant turned away from the light for two consecutive seconds. Estimates of listening times to each passage were based on how long the infants looked at the flashing light per trial.

When 7.5-month-olds were tested with this procedure, they listened significantly longer to the passages that contained the words that they had been familiarized with, suggesting that they detected the occurrence of the familiarized words in these passages. By comparison, 6-month-olds tested with the same materials displayed no significant preferences for the passages with the familiarized words. Hence, in English-learners, the ability to detect familiar words in fluent speech appears to develop between 6 and 7.5 months of age.

How Does Word Segmentation Begin in English-Learners?

Now that we know when word segmentation abilities develop, the next issue to resolve concerns the means by which infants accomplish this task. Previous work has shown that infants' sensitivity to predominant word stress patterns and to phonotactic constraints in the native language increases between 6 and 9 months of age (Echols et al., 1997; Friederici & Wessels, 1993; Jusczyk et al., 1993a; Jusczyk et al., 1993b; Morgan & Saffran, 1995). These findings suggest that such sources of information may be available to infants in segmenting words from speech.

My co-workers and I have recently focused our investigations on whether infants might rely on some form of the Metrical Segmentation Strategy (Cutler & Norris, 1988). Using the same procedure as Aslin and I did, we familiarized 7.5-month-olds with pairs of words that each had an accented first syllable followed by an unaccented second syllable (Houston et al., 1995; Newsome & Jusczyk, 1995). These *strong-weak* words included "doctor" and "candle" (or "kingdom" and "hamlet"). Following the familiarization phase, the infants were tested on passages either with or without the familiarized target words. The infants listened significantly longer to the passages containing the target words.

One interpretation of these results is that 7.5-month-old English-learners can segment words with strong-weak stress patterns from fluent speech. However, another possibility is that the infants were responding only to the strong syllables of these words (i.e., not to "candle," but to "can"). To explore this possibility, we ran another experiment in which infants were familiarized with just the isolated strong syllable of each word (i.e., "dock" and "can" or "king" and "ham") and then heard the passages containing the original strong-weak words. The infants did not listen longer to the passages with the strong-weak words (e.g., "hamlet" and "kingdom") that corresponded to the strong syllables from the familiarization period (e.g., "ham" and "king"). Nor did infants familiarized with isolated strong-weak words like "hamlet" or "kingdom" listen longer to fluent speech passages containing the words "ham" or "king."

Further experimentation indicated why infants recognized the whole word instead of just the embedded strong syllable. One consequence of using a strategy that identifies stressed syllables with the onsets of words in speech is that words beginning with unstressed syllables would be missegmented. To examine whether learners encounter such difficulties, we conducted comparable experiments using weak-strong words (i.e., an unaccented syllable followed by an accented one). Thus, infants were familiarized with "guitar" and "surprise" (or "beret" and "device"). In contrast to the earlier results, 7.5-month-olds familiarized with weak-strong words gave no evidence of subsequently recognizing these words in sentential contexts. However, infants familiarized with just the strong syllables of these words (i.e., "tar" and "prize") did listen significantly longer to the passages containing the whole weak-strong words (i.e., "guitar" and "surprise"). It was as if the infants perceived the "tar" from "guitar" as initiating a new word when it occurred in a fluent speech context.

Why do infants match familiarized strong syllables to words they hear in the test passages in the case of weak-strong words, but not in the case of strong-weak words? The distributional properties of the sentential contexts apparently are the key. Whenever a strong-weak word occurred in a sentence, its strong syllable was always followed by the same weak syllable (i.e., the one in the word). This was not true for the strong syllable of a weak-strong word. For example, the "tar" of "guitar" was followed by "is" on one occasion, by "has" on another, and by a sentence boundary on another. These differences across the various sentential contexts may help to signal a word boundary at the end of "guitar." Indeed, Saffran et al. (1996) found that 8-month-olds can use distributional cues to segment wordlike patterns from strings of nonsense syllables. In the present case, the strong-syllable segmentation strategy posits a word onset at the strong syllable "tar." This, plus the distributional evidence, makes "tar" pop out of the context as a word. To test this hypothesis, we rewrote our sentential materials to use a constant word following a particular target word. For example, "guitar" was always followed by "is," and "surprise" was always followed by "in." This time, when 7.5-month-olds were familiarized with the isolated syllables "tar" and "prize," they did not listen significantly longer to the passages with "guitar" and "surprise." One suggestion is that the context led them to segment the pseudowords "taris" and "prizin." This interpretation was verified when infants familiarized with "taris" and "prizin" did listen longer to passages that included the word sequences "guitar is" and "surprise in." Thus, when the distributional context is favorable, using stressed syllables to mark word onsets may cause infants to missegment speech as containing a possible strong-weak word.

Our results suggest that English-learning 7.5-month-olds begin to segment speech by using the occurrence of strong syllables to indicate onsets of new words. Although this strategy is helpful for words beginning with strong syllables, it is problematic for words that begin with, or consist solely of, weak syllables. Further experiments that we have conducted with 10.5-month-olds suggest that by this age, infants have resolved their problems with weak-strong words by supplementing their initial strategy, using additional cues to word boundaries. For example, although 9-month-olds gave no evidence of using context-sensitive allophones in segmenting words, 10.5-month-olds are able to use these kinds of cues (Jusczyk et al., 1998). Picking up these additional sources of information may be facilitated by the use of stress-based cues to break the input into smaller sized chunks, which may provide the learner with more opportunities to detect the correspondence between certain allophones (and also phonotactic patterns) and their relation to the onsets and offsets of possible words in the speech stream. Thus, the learner may progress by a "divide and conquer" strategy of segmenting utterances into smaller pieces and then tracking regularities within these.

Remembering Words

Segmenting words from speech will be of little help in building a vocabulary unless learners encode and remember the sound patterns of these words. There is evidence that even at 7.5 months of age, infants are storing information about sound patterns that they hear frequently. For example, in one study (Jusczyk & Hohne, 1997), 8-month-olds were visited 10 times during a 2-week period. On each occasion, they heard audio recordings of the same three children's stories (although by different talkers or in different orders on different days). Two weeks after the last home visit, the infants were brought into the laboratory, and lists of words were played. Half of the lists contained words that had occurred frequently in the stories (these words were new examples of the words, spoken in isolation and recorded separately from the stories). The other lists were made up of foils – words that had not appeared in the stories. The foil words occurred with the same typical frequency in child-directed speech as the story words and had phonetic properties similar to those of the story words. The infants who had heard the stories listened significantly longer to the story words than to the foils. By comparison, a control group of infants who had not heard the stories showed no preference for either type of word list. Thus, the results suggest that the infants who had heard the stories did segment and remember, over a 2-week period, some of the frequently occurring words in the stories.

Because recognition of the story words was indexed by an overall preference for lists of words from the stories, we cannot say whether the infants remembered all the words or just a few of the words that occurred on the lists. In an effort to obtain information about infants' memory for specific items, Houston, Tager, and I adapted the procedure and test materials Aslin and I had used to study when infants develop word segmentation abilities (Houston et al., 1997). In our first experiment, 7.5-month-olds were familiarized for 30s each to either "feet" and "bike" or "cup" and "dog." The next day, the infants were tested on four passages, each of which used one of these words in every sentence. Even after the 24-hr delay, the infants listened significantly longer to the passages that contained the familiarized words. Hence, infants do appear to remember these specific sound patterns for at least a day.

Results of additional studies suggest that at this age, long-term memory for words may be closely tied to characteristics of the talker's voice. When testing immediately followed familiarization, infants listened longer to passages containing the familiarized words even when the isolated words were produced by one talker and the passages were produced by a different talker of the same gender. But this generalization across talkers failed when a 24-hr delay intervened between familiarization and testing. Under these circumstances, the infants were just as likely to listen to the passages with the novel words as they were to listen to those with the familiarized words. These findings suggest that, at least initially, infants' representations of words may be stored exemplars of previously heard words rather than abstract prototypes.

Conclusions

The studies reviewed provide some indication that the lexicon begins to develop relatively early in the second half of the 1st year. English-learners display some capacity for segmenting words from fluent speech by about 7.5 months of age. These earliest attempts at word segmentation appear to draw on information about predominant word stress patterns and distributional cues. This first-pass strategy succeeds in correctly segmenting many words, but not others. Yet, the strategy may also facilitate the acquisition of information about other potential cues (e.g., context-sensitive allophones and phonotactic constraints) to word boundaries in the language. Even at this early stage of language development, there is evidence that infants retain information about words that occur frequently in the input. At the same time, there is some evidence that these early memory representations of words are relatively limited. Further experience may be required to generalize from words produced by one talker to those produced by a different talker.

Acknowledgments

The author is grateful to Cynthia Fisher and Karla Jusczyk for comments on a previous version of the present manuscript, and to his many collaborators on the research projects reported here.

References and Further Reading

Bolinger, D.L., & Gerstman, L.J. (1957). Disjuncture as a cue to constraints. *Word, 13,* 246–255.

Brent, M.R., & Cartwright, T.A. (1996). Distributional regularity and phonotactic constraints are useful for segmentation. *Cognition, 61,* 93–125.

Church, K.W. (1987). *Phonological parsing in speech recognition.* Dordrecht, The Netherlands: Kluwer Academic.

Cutler, A. (1994). Segmentation problems, rhythmic solutions. *Lingua, 92,* 81–104.

Cutler, A., & Carter, D.M. (1987). The predominance of strong initial syllables in the English vocabulary. *Computer Speech and Language, 2,* 133–142.

Cutler, A., & Norris, D.G. (1988). The role of strong syllables in segmentation for lexical access. *Journal of Experimental Psychology: Human Perception and Performance, 14,* 113–121.

Echols, C.H., Crowhurst, M.J., & Childers, J.B. (1997). Perception of rhythmic units in speech by infants and adults. *Journal of Memory and Language, 36,* 202–225.

Fernald, A., & Simon, T. (1984). Expanded intonation contours in mothers' speech to children. *Developmental Psychology, 20,* 104–113.

Friederici, A.D., & Wessels, J.M.I. (1993). Phonotactic knowledge and its use in infant speech perception. *Perception & Psychophysics, 54,* 287–295.

Hockett, C.F. (1958). *A course in modern linguistics.* New York: Macmillan.

Houston, D., Jusczyk, P.W., & Newsome, M. (1995, November). *Infants' strategies of speech segmentation: Clues from weak/strong words.* Paper presented at the 20th Annual Boston University Conference on Language Development, Boston.

Houston, D., Jusczyk, P.W., & Tager, J. (1997, November). *Talker-specificity and the persistence of infants' word representations.* Paper presented at the 22nd Annual Boston University Conference on Language Development, Boston.

Jusczyk, P.W. (1997). *The discovery of spoken language.* Cambridge, MA: MIT Press.

Jusczyk, P.W., & Aslin, R.N. (1995). Infants' detection of sound patterns of words in fluent speech. *Cognitive Psychology, 29,* 1–23.

Jusczyk, P.W., Cutler, A., & Redanz, N. (1993a). Preference for the predominant stress patterns of English words. *Child Development, 64,* 675–687.

Jusczyk, P.W., Friederici, A.D., Wessels, J., Svenkerud, V.Y., & Jusczyk, A.M. (1993b). Infants' sensitivity to the sound patterns of native language words. *Journal of Memory and Language, 32,* 402–420.

Jusczyk, P.W., & Hohne, E.A. (1997). Infants' memory for spoken words. *Science, 277,* 1984–1986.

Jusczyk, P.W., Hohne, E.A., & Bauman, A. (1998). Infants' sensitivity to allophonic cues for word segmentation. *Perception & Psychophysics, 61,* 1465–1476.

Morgan, J.L., & Saffran, J.R. (1995). Emerging integration of sequential and suprasegmental information in preverbal speech segmentation. *Child Development, 66,* 911–936.

Myers, J., Jusczyk, P.W., Kemler Nelson, D.G., Charles Luce, J., Woodward, A., & Hirsh-Pasek, K. (1996). Infants' sensitivity to word boundaries in fluent speech. *Journal of Child Language, 23,* 1–30.

Newsome, M., & Jusczyk, P.W. (1995). Do infants use stress as a cue for segmenting fluent speech? In D. MacLaughlin & S. McEwen (Eds.), *Proceedings of the 19th Annual Boston University Conference on Language Development* (Vol. 2, pp. 415–426). Somerville, MA: Cascadilla Press.

Saffran, J.R., Aslin, R.N., & Newport, E.L. (1996). Statistical learning by 8-month-old infants. *Science, 274,* 1926–1928.

Suomi, K. (1993). An outline of a developmental model of adult phonological organization and behavior. *Journal of Phonetics, 21,* 29–60.

Woodward, J.Z., & Aslin, R.N. (1990, April). *Segmentation cues in maternal speech to infants.* Paper presented at the biennial meeting of the International Conference on Infant Studies, Montreal, Quebec.

TWO

Listening to Speech in the 1st Year of Life: Experiential Influences on Phoneme Perception

Janet F. Werker and Renée N. Desjardins

The use of language to share thoughts, ideas, and feelings is a uniquely human characteristic. And to learn a language is one of the biggest challenges of infancy and early childhood. In order to be successful at this momentous task, the child must break down the speech stream, which consists of highly encoded and overlapping information, into smaller units such as clauses, phrases, and words. A yet smaller unit is the phoneme. Two words may differ by only one phoneme (e.g., *bat* vs. *pat*), yet this difference is enough to convey different meanings. Thus, a critical part of the language acquisition process is the ability to distinguish individual syllables on the basis of minimal differences in phonemes. In this review, we discuss the kinds of initial abilities infants bring to the task of phoneme perception, how these sensitivities are influenced by experience in a particular linguistic community, and whether events that occur during the prelinguistic period help prepare the child for the important task of language acquisition.

Mapping the Changes in Phoneme Perception

Sensitive experimental techniques that were developed in the early 1970s allowed testing very young infants' speech perception abilities. These techniques revealed that infants can not only discriminate minimally distinctive phonemes, but can also distinguish phonemes from all the world's languages – including phonemes not used in their language-learning environment. In contrast, research with adults, using different techniques, had led scientists to believe that adults cannot readily discriminate all phonemic distinctions that are not used in their native language. Because adults typically perform better than infants at virtually any task given to them, this counterintuitive pattern of results was most intriguing. Our work was designed to explore the age at which experience first begins to influence phonemic perception and the mechanisms that might be responsible for this change.[1]

To explore the counterintuitive suggestion that infants discriminate nonnative phonemes better than adults, we first compared the two groups directly. In order to do this, we needed a procedure that would be adaptable to both infants and adults. The procedure we chose is a category change procedure. In this task, the subject monitors a continuous background of syllables from one phonemic category (e.g., /ba/) and presses a button to signal when the stimuli change to a contrasting phonemic category (e.g., /da/). Correct button-presses are reinforced with the presentation of a flashing light (as feedback for older children and adults) or an electronically activated animal (as a reward for younger children). Incorrect button-presses are not reinforced, and misses are not signaled.

In the infant version of this procedure, called the conditioned head turn task, the infant sits on the parent's lap facing an experimental assistant who maintains the infant's interest by showing toys. The infant is conditioned to turn his or her head toward the sound source when he or she detects a change in the phonemic category. Correct head turns are reinforced with the illumination and activation of clapping and drumming toy animals inside a Plexiglas box. In addition, the experimental assistant claps and gives praise and encouragement. As is the case with children and adults, incorrect responses are not reinforced. In our laboratory, the criterion for successful discrimination is set at 9 out of 10 correct consecutive responses within a series of 25 trials, approximately half of which are control trials in which no change occurs.

In the first series of experiments, we compared infants and adults on their ability to discriminate two distinctions that are phonemic (i.e., can differentiate words) in Hindi but not in English and one that is phonemic in both Hindi and English. The Hindi-only contrasts were chosen to vary in their potential difficulty. The first contrast, /Ta/–/ta/, involves two phonemes that both sound like *t* to a native English speaker. The difference between them involves where the tongue is placed. For /Ta/, the tongue is curled back and the tip of the underside hits the roof of the mouth. This is called a retroflex consonant. For /ta/, the tip of the tongue is placed against the front teeth. This is called a dental consonant. An English speaker makes a /t/ by placing the tongue against the alveolar ridge directly behind the front teeth. This alveolar consonant is articulated at a place in between the dental and retroflex consonants.

The second contrast was a Hindi voicing contrast that also involves two phonemes that sound like *t* to an English speaker. In this case, the difference involves the timing and shape of the opening of the vocal cords. Hindi /t^h/ and /d^h/ involve a slightly different combination of timing and shape than is used in production of English phonemes. For linguistic and acoustic reasons, this voicing contrast is potentially easier to discriminate than the retroflex-dental contrast.

Subjects were also tested on the contrast between /ba/ and /da/, which is used in both Hindi and English. This contrast served as a control to ensure that the subjects understood (and, in the case of the infants, were willing to perform) the task.

In the first study done collaboratively with Richard Tees, John Gilbert, and Keith Humphrey, English-learning infants aged 6 to 8 months were compared with both English-speaking adults and Hindi-speaking adults. Virtually all subjects in all groups could discriminate the /ba/–/da/ contrast, and the English-learning infants and the Hindi-speaking adults could easily discriminate both Hindi contrasts. However, the English-speaking adults had difficulty discriminating the Hindi contrasts, and showed particular trouble with the difficult retroflex-dental distinction. A short training procedure (25 trials) was effective in raising the proportion of English-speaking adults who could discriminate the Hindi voicing contrast, but this amount of training did not improve adult performance on the retroflex-dental distinction.

This experiment confirmed what many researchers had expected. Testing using comparable procedures verified that infants discriminate nonnative phoneme contrasts better than adults. But we had no idea as to the age in development when the performance decrement occurs. An influential view at the time was Lenneberg's hypothesis that there is a "critical period" for language acquisition up to the onset of puberty. Extrapolating from this hypothesis led us to test children on the verge of adolescence, as well as two younger age groups. To our surprise, the results indicated that English-speaking children 12, 8, and even 4 years old perform as poorly as English-speaking adults on the Hindi contrasts not used in English. This effect was evident even though the 4-year-old children could easily discriminate the English contrast, and even though Hindi-learning children of age 4 discriminated both Hindi contrasts successfully when tested with the same procedure.

These results showing that language experience affects phoneme perception by age 4 led to additional tests of children between 6 months and 4 years old. A series of pilot tests led to a focus on the 1st year of life.

Infants between 6 and 12 months of age were tested on the difficult retroflex-dental contrast taken from Hindi, as well as on a new contrast taken from a Native Canadian language, Nthlakampx (one of the Interior Salish languages). The new contrast, glottalized velar /k'/ versus glottalized uvular /q'/, involves a difference in the position of the tongue in the back part of the vocal tract. English listeners hear these two sounds as "funny" *ks*. We found that although English-learning infants aged 6 to 8 months can discriminate both of these contrasts with ease, infants of 10 to 12 months, like English-speaking adults, fail to discriminate the difference in either non-English contrast. The same pattern of results was replicated in a study in which the same infants were tested at 6 to 8, 8 to 10, and 10 to 12 months of age. Thus, it appeared that the change occurs between 6 and 12 months of age.

In a final manipulation, we tested a small number of 11- to 12-month-old infants who were being exposed to either Hindi or Nthlakampx in the home. Infants in each language group discriminated the contrast from their native language with ease, confirming that the change between 6 and 12 months reflects language-specific experience and is not just an age-related decrement in performance on difficult contrasts.

In a subsequent study, we tested English-learning infants using synthetically produced stimuli that varied in equal steps along a continuum from bilabial /ba/ to dental /da/ to retroflex /Da/. We found that English-learning infants aged 6 to 8 months can group stimuli according to the English boundary between labial and dental stimuli, and according to the Hindi boundary between retroflex and dental, but not according to an arbitrary boundary location that does not correspond to any known phonemic category. English-learning infants aged 10 to 12 months can group only according to the bilabial-dental boundary. These results confirm that the sensitivities shown by young infants prior to language-specific tuning are not arbitrary, but rather conform to potential phonemic categories. Also, with these synthetic stimuli, we replicated our finding that language-general perception shifts to language-specific perception between 6 and 12 months of age.

More recently, Best and colleagues replicated this finding with both the Nthlakampx /k'/–/q'/ contrasts and three contrast from the Zulu language that are not used in English.[2] Best found that infants 6 to 8 months old could discriminate nonnative contrasts, whereas infants 10 to 12 months old could not. These findings are of particular interest as Best used a habituation-dishabituation looking procedure,[3] rather than the conditioned head turn procedure. Taken together, these replications with new phonemic contrasts and different testing procedures provide strong confirmation that listening experience brings about a change in nonnative consonant perception within the 1st year of life.

How to Explain This Pattern of Results?

One possible explanation to account for these results is that phoneme sensitivities that exist in the young infant will be maintained only if those phonemes are present in the language input (a maintenance/loss view). Without such experience, the infant will lose the ability to discriminate those phonemes permanently. Originally, we thought the loss was tied to events at the level of neuronal functioning. However, a series of experiments with adults convinced us that this explanation was not adequate. Specifically, we found that adult performance varied as a function of the testing conditions. Under conditions that match the demands required in natural language use, adults fail to discriminate the nonnative contrasts. However, when memory demands are minimized (via a shortened interstimulus interval), or uncertainty is dimished (via practice or training), adults show a continued sensitivity even to the most difficult nonnative phoneme distinctions. For this reason, we began to refer to the age-related change in cross-language perception as a reorganization rather than a loss. We assumed the reorganization resulted in a restructuring of initial sensitivities to map on to those required to contrast meaning in the native language.

Recently, Best has developed a model that predicts how listeners will perceive nonnative phoneme contrasts on the basis of how those contrasts map on to the sound system of the native language. According to her perceptual assimilation model (PAM), English-learning infants 10 to 12 months old fail to discriminate the retroflex-dental distinction because retroflex and dental *t* are assimilated to a single phonemic category in English. Nonnative phonemes that fall into two different English phonemic categories may be easier to discriminate. Finally, if the two nonnative phonemes are completely unlike any sounds used in the native language, there should be no pressure for reorganization, and high levels of discrimination should be maintained.[4]

To test this model, Best, McRoberts, and Sithole used a series of clicks from the Zulu language.[4] These clicks are not recognizable as speech to native English speakers. In one such contrast, [|] – [||], the first click sounds to an English speaker like a "tsk-tsk" of disapproval, and the second sounds something like the click used to make a horse move faster. Consistent with their predictions, Best and her colleagues found that English-learning infants of all ages and English-speaking adults discriminate this contrast easily. However, Best has shown that other Zulu contrasts that can be assimilated into English phonemic categories pattern like the consonants in our previous work: They are easily discriminated by young infants, but not by English-learning infants of 10 to 12 months or by English-speaking adults.

Recently completed research in our laboratory has shown that similarity to native language sounds is not the only factor influencing reorganization. Pegg tested infants on their ability to discriminate two variants of a single phonemic category (allophones) that occur systematically in the English language but are not used to distinguish meaning.[5] The allophones she tested can be illustrated by the phonetic difference between "the stalls" and "these dolls." Both the [t] in *stall* and the [d] in *doll* sound like the English phoneme /d/; however, there are subtle differences that are discriminable to adults and that may help listeners find word boundaries. Pegg found that many English-learning infants 6 to 8 months old are sensitive to these subtle differences and can distinguish the two allophones. Infants 10 to 12 months old, however, cannot. The performance of the older infants suggests that exposure to a systematic difference in speech sounds is not enough to maintain discriminability. Apparently, it is necessary that the distinction be used to contrast meaning in the native language.

New Directions

The work we have discussed so far focused exclusively on consonant perception. An area of current interest is whether experience affects vowel perception similarly. There are several reasons why vowel perception might pattern differently. Vowels carry paralinguistic information concerning the speaker's identity, emotional tone, and pragmatic context in addition to carrying specifically phonemic information. Thus, very young infants may listen to vowels for their prosodic as well as for their phonemic information. Also, the boundaries between vowel categories are less rigid than the boundaries between consonant categories: Both adults and infants can discriminate "within-category" differences better for vowels than for consonants. Finally, discrimination of nonnative vowel contrasts is typically easier than is discrimination of nonnative consonant contrasts.

In an early study of cross-language vowel perception in infancy, Trehub reported that English-learning infants aged 5 to 17 weeks discriminated a French vowel contrast that is not used in English, thus showing the same pattern of language-general sensitivity in vowel perception as has been shown for consonant perception.[6] In recent work, Kuhl and colleagues showed there are language-specific influences on the internal structure of vowel categories by 6 months of age in both Swedish- and English-learning infants.[7] This finding suggests that language-specific experience might affect vowel perception at a younger age than it affects consonant perception. However, because Kuhl's research involved testing infants' ability to generalize to other exemplars within a single vowel category rather than to discriminate across two phonemic vowel categories, it is not analogous to the studies of consonant perception.

To compare vowel and consonant perception directly, Polka and the first author tested English-learning infants and English-speaking adults on their ability to discriminate two German vowel contrasts.[8] Each pair contrasted a high, front, rounded with a high, back, rounded German vowel in a "d-VOWEL-t" context. For example, in one pair, the vowel in "boot" (high, back, rounded) was contrasted with a German vowel produced like the

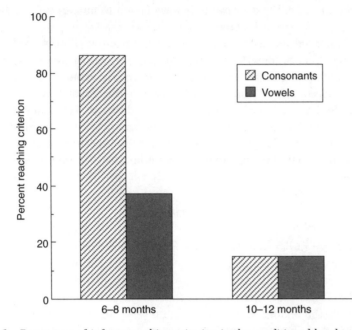

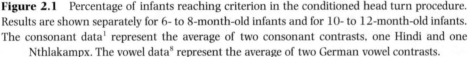

Figure 2.1 Percentage of infants reaching criterion in the conditioned head turn procedure. Results are shown separately for 6- to 8-month-old infants and for 10- to 12-month-old infants. The consonant data[1] represent the average of two consonant contrasts, one Hindi and one Nthlakampx. The vowel data[8] represent the average of two German vowel contrasts.

vowel in "beet" but with the lips rounded (high, front, rounded). Pretesting with adults showed that although these distinctions are not phonemic in English, they are relatively easy for English-speaking adults to discriminate. All subjects were also tested on an English contrast (/dit/ vs. /dat/) to make sure they could perform the task.

Using two different procedures to test English-learning infants from 4 to 12 months of age, we found that the effects of experience begin earlier for vowels than for consonants, but that experiential influences continue to be seen up to 10 to 12 months of age. Infants aged 4 months performed better than infants aged 6 months on the German contrasts when tested in a habituation-dishabituation looking procedure (a procedural change necessary for testing younger infants). When tested in the conditioned head turn procedure, infants aged 6 to 8 months performed significantly better than the 10- to 12-month-old infants, but not as well as 6- to 8-month-old infants typically perform on nonnative consonant contrasts (see figure 2.1).

This study suggests that vowel perception is like consonant perception, but that experience begins to influence initial language-general capabilities at an earlier age for vowels than for consonants. However, as this is the first cross-language study of this type that has been reported using vowels, additional research is required before we can be confident about the results. Indeed, there are some reports that vowel perception may initially be organized quite differently than consonant perception, and that the effects of experience may not always be as pronounced for vowel perception as they are for consonant perception.[9]

It is important to note that researchers have begun to investigate whether experience affects other aspects of language processing in addition to phoneme perception. Although it is beyond the scope of this article to review this burgeoning literature, it seems that infants become increasingly sensitive to many aspects of the native language, including stress pattern, rules for sequencing sounds, and cues to word boundaries.[10] Indeed, infants may show sensitivity to the global prosody of the native language within the first few days after birth.[11] Finally, there is evidence that babbling changes across the 1st year of life to reflect the characteristics and distribution of sounds used in the native language.[12] An exciting question is how all these capabilities come together to prepare the child to move on to the task of word learning.

Summary

During the 1st year of life, long before uttering his or her first words, an infant makes remarkable progress toward mastering the sound structure of the native language. The biases and proclivities that allow the neonate to detect regularities in the speech stream are, by 1 year of age, exquisitely tuned to the properties of the native language. Our work documents the infant's movement from universal to language-specific phoneme perception. What we have described, however, represents only a part of the infant's remarkable journey toward becoming a native listener. The challenge for future work is to determine what makes the movement from language-general to language-specific perception possible, and how sensitivity to the various properties of the native language is linked to the functional task of language acquisition.

Notes

1   For a review of the studies discussed in this introduction, see J.F. Werker, Becoming a native listener, *American Scientist*, *77*, 54–9 (1989).

2   C.T. Best, Learning to perceive the sound pattern of English, in *Advances in Infancy Research*, C. Rovee-Collier and L. Lipsitt, Eds. (LEA, Hillsdale, N), in press).

3   In this procedure, infants' looking time to a visual display is used as an index of their attention to the speech stimuli. During the habituation phase, the infants are familiarized to instances of a single phoneme. Across trials, looking time decreases. A novel phoneme is then presented. If infants are able to discriminate the difference between the novel and familiar phonemes, they show an increase in looking time.

4   C.T. Best, G.W. McRoberts, and N.N. Sit-hole, The phonological basis of perceptual loss for non-native contrasts: Maintenance of discrimination among Zulu clicks by English-speaking adults and infants, *Journal of Experimental Psychology: Human Perception and Performance*, *14*, 345–60 (1988).

5   J.E. Peggy and J.F. Werker, Infant perception of an English allophone [Abstract], *Infant Behavior & Development*, *17*, 862 (1994).

6   S.E. Trehub, The discrimination of foreign speech contrasts by infants and adults, *Child Development*, *47*, 466–72 (1976).

7   P.A. Kuhl, K.A. Willams, F. Lacerda, K.N. Stevens, and B. Lindblom, Linguistic experience alters phonetic perception in infants by 6 months of age, *Science*, *255*, 606–8 (1992).

8   L. Polka and J.F. Werker, Developmental changes in perception of nonnative vowel contrasts, *Journal of Experimental Psychology: Human Perception and Performance, 20,* 421–35 (1994).

9   L. Polka and O. Bohn, *A cross-language comparison of vowel perception in English-learning and German-learning infants,* poster presented at the International Conference on Infant Studies, Paris (June 1994).

10   See, e.g., P.W. Jusczyk, A. Cutler, and N.J. Redanz, Infant's preference for the predominant stress patterns of English words, *Child Development, 64,* 675–87 (1993); P.W. Jusczyk, A.D. Friederici, J.I. Wessels, V.Y. Svenkerud, and A.M. Jusczyk, Infants sensitivity to the sound patterns of native language words, *Journal of Memory and Language, 32,* 402–20 (1993).

11   J. Mehler, P.W. Jusczyk, G. Lambertz, N. Halstead, J. Bertoncini, and C. Amiel-Tison, A precursor of language acquisition in young infants, *Cognition, 29,* 143–78 (1988).

12   See, e.g., B. De Boysson-Bardies and M. Vihman, Adaptation to language: Evidence from babbling and early words in four languages, *Language, 61,* 297–319 (1991); D.H. Whalen, A.G. Levitt, and Q. Wang, Intonational differences between the reduplicative babbling of French- and English-learning infants, *Journal of Child Language, 18,* 501–16 (1991).

Recommended Reading

Jusczyk, P.W. (1994). Infant speech perception and the development of the mental lexicon. In J.C. Goodman & H.C. Nusbaum (Eds.), *The Transition From Speech Sounds to Spoken Words: The Development of Speech Perception.* Cambridge, MA: MIT Press.

Werker, J.F., Lloyd, V.L., Pegg, J.E., & Polka, L.B. (in press). Putting the baby in the bootstraps: Toward a more complete understanding of the role of the input in infant speech processing. In J. Morgan and K. Demuth, (Eds.), *Signal to Syntax: The Role of Bootstrapping in Language Acquisition.* Hillsdale, NJ: LEA.

Werker, J.F., and Tees, R.C. (1992). The organization and reorganization of human speech perception. *Annual Review of Neuroscience, 15,* 377–402.

THREE

Language Discrimination by Human Newborns and by Cotton-Top Tamarin Monkeys

Franck Ramus, Marc D. Hauser, Cory Miller,
Dylan Morris, and Jacques Mehler

A fundamental question in the study of language evolution and acquisition is the extent to which humans are innately endowed with specialized capacities to comprehend and produce speech. Theoretical arguments have been used to argue that language acquisition must be based on an innately specified language faculty,[1,2] but the precise nature and extent of this "language organ" is mainly an empirical matter, which notably requires studies of human newborns as well as nonhuman animals.[3-5] With respect to studies of humans, we already know that newborns as young as 4 days old have the capacity to discriminate phonemes categorically[6] and perceive well-formed syllables as units;[7-9] they are sensitive to the rhythm of speech, as shown in experiments in which newborns distinguish sentences from languages that have different rhythmic properties but not from languages that share the same rhythmic structure;[10,11] however, newborns do not discriminate languages when speech is played backward,[10] and neurophysiological studies suggest that both infants and adults process natural speech differently from backward speech.[12,13] All these studies indicate that humans are born with capacities that facilitate language acquisition and that seem well attuned to the properties of speech. Studies of nonhuman animals, however, show that some of these capacities may predate our hominid origins. For example, insects, birds, nonprimate mammals, and primates process their own, species-typical sounds in a categorical manner, and some of these species perceive speech categorically.[14-18]

Our aim here is to extend the comparative study of speech perception in three directions. First, using the same design and the same material, we have conducted joint experiments on human newborns and on monkeys. Second, whereas most studies of nonhuman animal speech perception involve extensive training before testing on a generalization task, our experimental approach – the habituation-dishabituation paradigm – involves no training and parallels the method used in studies of infant speech perception. Thus, conditions are met to appropriately compare the two populations. Third, most studies of speech processing in animals involve tests of phonemic perception. Here, we extend the analysis to sentence perception, thereby setting up a much broader range of perceptual problems.

Our experiments were run on human newborns and cotton-top tamarin monkeys (*Saguinus oedipus oedipus*). The stimuli consisted of 20 sentences in Japanese and 20 sentences in Dutch uttered by four female native speakers of each language. Conditions in which the two languages are pitted against one another were compared with conditions in which speakers of the same language are contrasted. In addition, sentences within a session were played either forward or backward. To more readily control for prosodic features of the signal, we reran all conditions with synthesized exemplars of the original sentences. Synthesized sentences were created with the MBROLA diphone synthesizer.[19] Phoneme duration and fundamental frequency were preserved, whereas the phonetic inventory was narrowed to only one phoneme per manner of articulation: all fricatives were synthesized as /s/, vowels as /a/, liquids as /l/, plosives as /t/, nasals as /n/, and glides as /j/. Thus, each synthesized sentence preserved only the prosodic characteristics of its natural counterpart while eliminating lexical and phonetic information.[20]

We tested newborns with the high-amplitude sucking procedure and a habituation/dishabituation design. Sentences were elicited by the newborns' sucking on a pacifier. In the language change condition, newborns were habituated to 10 sentences uttered by two speakers in one language and then switched to 10 sentences uttered by two different speakers in the other language. In the speaker change condition, newborns were habituated to 10 sentences uttered by two speakers from one language and then switched to two different speakers in the same language. A significant increase in sucking after the language change, compared with the speaker change, is taken as evidence that newborns perceive a significant difference between the two languages.[21]

We tested 32 newborns[22] on the natural language-forward experiment: 16 in the language change condition and 16 in the speaker change condition. Figure 3.1A shows that the two groups did not differ significantly and thus that newborns failed to discriminate the two languages ($F_{(1,29)} < 1$).[23] This result appears to conflict with previous experimental work showing that newborns discriminate English and Japanese. However, our experiment exposes newborns to great speaker variability (four voices),[24] and this factor has previously been shown to impair the discrimination abilities of infants.[25] If speaker variability is responsible for the absence of discrimination, then we would predict successful discrimination with fewer speakers. To test for this possibility, we ran a second experiment using synthesized speech, thereby reducing the number of voices to one, that of the speech synthesizer.[26]

We tested 32 additional newborns[27] on the forward language and speaker discrimination using the synthesized versions of the original sentences. Figure 3.1B shows that newborns in the language change condition increased their sucking significantly more during the 2 min after the switch than newborns in the speaker change condition ($F_{(1,29)} = 6.3$, $P = 0.018$). This indicates that, relying exclusively on prosodic cues, newborns discriminate sentences of Dutch from sentences of Japanese. Moreover, this result shows that the failure of newborns to discriminate in experiment 3.1A was probably due to speaker variability.

To determine the specificity of the newborns' capacity to discriminate languages, we tested 32 more newborns with the same synthesized sentences played backward.[28] Figure 3.1C shows that newborns fail to discriminate languages played backward

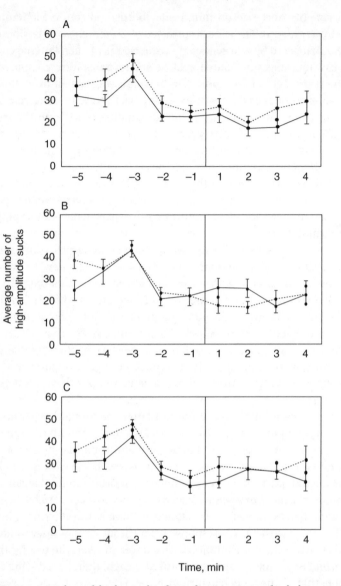

Figure 3.1   Average number of high amplitude sucks per minute for babies oin the control (speaker change, dotted lines) and experimental (speaker and language change, solid lines) groups. Minutes are numbered from the time of change. Error bars represent ±1 SEM. (A) Natural sentences played forward. (B) Same sentences synthesized. (C) Same sentences synthesized and played backward.

$(F_{(1.29)} < 1)$.[29] Moreover, the interaction between experiments 1B and 1C (forward vs. backwards) is marginally significant ($F_{(1,59)} = 3.6$, $P = 0.06$). The finding that newborns discriminate two nonnative languages played forward but not backward suggests that the newborns' language discrimination capacity may depend on specific properties of speech that are eliminated when the signal is played backward. However, before drawing such a conclusion, it is important to directly assess the speech specificity of this capacity by testing it on another species.

We tested cotton-top tamarins ($n = 13$) with the same stimulus set as the newborns. Instead of sucking rate, however, we used a head orientation response toward the loud-speaker. During the habituation phase, a tamarin was presented with sentences uttered by two speakers in one language and then tested with a sentence uttered by a different speaker, either in the same language (speaker change condition) or in the other language (language change condition). Recovery of orientation toward the loudspeaker was interpreted as an indication that the tamarin perceived a difference between the habituation and test stimuli.[30]

Experiment 2A involved natural sentences of Dutch and Japanese played either forward or backward.[31] Figure 3.2A shows that 10 of 13 tamarins ($P < 0.05$; binomial test) dishabituated in the language change condition, whereas only 5 of 13 dishabituated to the speaker change ($P = 0.87$). The difference between language and speaker change is significant ($P < 0.05$; χ^2 test). This result suggests that the tamarins discriminated Dutch from Japanese regardless of speaker variation. Surprisingly, such a pattern was not observed when the sentences were played backward: only 5 of 13 tamarins dishabituated to the backward language change ($P = 0.87$); this pattern is not significantly different from the speaker change condition ($P > 0.2$). These results parallel those obtained with newborns on the synthetic stimuli.

In experiment 2B, we tested the same tamarins on both the speaker and the language conditions but with synthesized sentences. Figure 3.2B shows that 10 of 13 tamarins dishabituated to the forward language change ($P < 0.05$). Although the number of subjects dishabituating to the speaker change failed to reach statistical significance ($P = 0.29$), the increased numbers in this condition led to a nonsignificant difference between language and speaker change for the synthesized sentences ($P > 0.3$). For backward sentences, subjects failed to show a statistically significant level of dishabituation to either the language or the speaker change ($P = 0.29$ and $P = 0.13$). Experiment 2B suggests that the ability of tamarins to discriminate Dutch and Japanese is diminished when only prosodic cues are available.

When the data from experiments 2A and 2B are pooled (figure 3.2C), the overall result is clear: when sentences are played forward, tamarins significantly dishabituate to the language change ($P = 0.005$) but not to the speaker change ($P = 0.58$), and the difference between language and speaker change is significant ($P < 0.05$). When sentences are played backward, no such effect is observed. This overall result parallels that obtained with human newborns: both species discriminate sentences of Dutch and Japanese played forward but not backward.

The pattern of our results suggests striking similarities as well as differences between the monkey and the human auditory systems. First, we have shown that tamarins, like human newborns, are able to process not just isolated syllables but also whole strings of continuous speech and to extract enough information to discriminate between Dutch and Japanese. Second, their ability to do so above and beyond speaker variability suggests that they are able to extract auditory equivalence classes – that is, to extract abstract linguistic invariants despite highly variable acoustic shapes.[17,32] Third, the fact that, like newborns, tamarins fail to discriminate when speech is played backward suggests that their language discrimination capacity relies not on trivial low-level cues

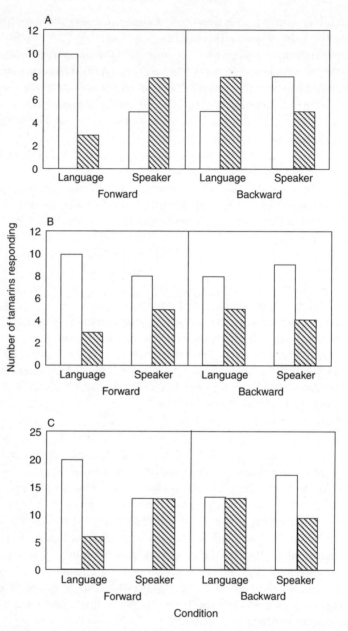

Figure 3.2 Number of tamarins responding positively (white bars) and negatively (hatched bars) to test sentence depending on condition: language or speaker change, sentences played forward or backward. (A) Natural sentences. (B) Synthesized sentences. (C) Data from experiments 2A and 2B pooled together, $^{*}p < 0.05$. $^{**}p < 0.01$.

but rather on quite specific properties of speech. Because tamarins have not evolved to process speech, we infer in turn that at least some aspects of human speech perception may have built upon preexisting sensitivities of the primate auditory system. Finally, unlike newborns, tamarins fail to discriminate the language change more than the speaker change when speech is resynthesized. This leaves open the possibility that human newborns and tamarins may not be responding to exactly the same cues in the sentences: tamarins might be more sensitive to phonetic than to prosodic contrasts.

References and Notes

1   N. Chomsky. *Language and Problems of Knowledge* (MIT Press, Cambridge, MA, 1988).
2   S. Pinker. *The Language Instinct.* (William, Morrow, and Co. New York, 1994).
3   A. Doupe and P. Kuhl, *Annu. Rev. Neurosci.* **22**, 567 (1999).
4   A. Chazanfar and M. D. Hauser, *Trends Cogn. Sci.* **3**, 377 (1999).
5   E. S. Spelke and E. L. Newport, in *Handbook of Child Psychology. Volume 1: Theoretical Models of Human Development.* R. M. Lerner. Ed. (Wiley, New York, 1998), pp. 275–340.
6   P. D. Eimas, E. R. Siqueland, P. W. Jusczyk, J. Vigorito, *Science* **171**, 303 (1971).
7   J. Bertoncini and J. Mehler, *Infant Behav. Dev.* **4**, 247 (1981).
8   J. Bertoncini, C. Floccia, T. Nazzi, J. Mehler, *Lang. Speech* **38**, 311 (1995).
9   R. Bijeljac-Babic, J. Bertoncini, J. Mehler, *Dev. Psychol.* **29**, 711 (1993).
10 J. Mehler et al., *Cognition* **29**, 143 (1988).
11 T. Nazzi, J. Bertoncini, J. Mehler, *J. Exp. Psychol. Hum. Percept. Perform.* **24**, 756 (1998).
12 H. J. Neville and D. L. Mills, *Mental. Retard. Dev. Disabil. Res. Rev.* **3**, 282 (1997).
13 D. Perani, et al., *Neuroreport* **7**, 2439 (1996).
14 G. Ehret and B. Haack, *Naturwissenshaften* **68**, 208 (1981).
15 R. A. Wyttenbach, M. L. May, R. R. Hoy, *Science* **273**, 1542 (1996).
16 P. K. Kuhl and J. D. Miller, *Science* **190**, 69 (1975).
17 P. Kuhl, in *Categorical Perception: The Groundwork of Cognition.* S. Hamad, Ed. (Cambridge University Press, Cambridge, 1987), pp. 355–386.
18 M. D. Hauser, *The Evolution of Communication* (Bradford Books/MIT Press, Cambridge, MA, 1996).
19 T. Dutoit, V. Pagel, N. Pierret, F. Bataille, O. van der Vrecken. *The MBROLA Project: Towards a Set of High-Quality Speech Synthesizers Free of Use for Non-commercial Purposes* (ICSLP'96, Philadelphia, 1996). This software is available free from tcts.fpms.ac.be/synthesis/mbrola.html.
20 Production of this kind of stimuli is described in detail in [F. Ramus and J. Mehler, *J. Acoust. Soc. Am.* **105**, 512 (1999)]. Supplementary material is available at www.sciencemag.org/feature/data/1047866.shl.
21 The experiment takes place in a sound-attenuated booth with only the baby and the experimenter inside. The experimenter is blind to the experimental condition and listens to masking noise during the test. Newborns are randomly assigned to the control or experimental group. Order of presentation of languages is counterbalanced across subjects. During a given phase, sentences corresponding to the condition are played in random order. The habituation phase lasts at least 5 min. The habituation criterion is a 25% decrease in sucking during two consecutive minutes compared with the maximum number of sucks previously produced in 1 min. Because increases in sucking rate can occur in the absence of stimulation (C. Floccia, thesis, l'Ecole des Hautes Etudes en Sciences Sociales, Paris, 1996), we compared sucking rate increase of the experimental and the control groups. This

is done with a covariance analysis, comparing the average number of sucks during the 2 min after the switch (dependent variable) between the two groups and taking account of the average number of sucks during the 2 min before the switch (covariate). This analysis is detailed in [A. Christophe, E. Dupoux, J. Bertoncini, J. Mehler, *J. Acoust. Soc. Am.* **95**, 1570 (1994)] and has been used since.

22   Subjects are full-term healthy newborns, between 2 and 5 days old, recruited at the Port-Royal maternity hospital in Paris. Forty-two additional babies were tested, and their results were discarded for the following reasons: rejection of the pacifier (1), sleeping or insufficient sucking before the switch (12), crying or agitation (9), failure to meet the habituation criterion (9), sleeping or insufficient sucking after the switch (6), loss of the pacifier after the switch (4), and computer failure (1).

23   The slight tendency for babies in the control group to suck more overall than those in the experimental group, although visible in Fig. 1A, is not significant ($F_{(1,31)} = 2.6$, $P = 0.12$).

24   In the English-Japanese discrimination experiments by Nazzi et al. (11), the variability due to the four voices was much reduced by low-pass filtering the stimuli. In other experiments (10), a single bilingual speaker was used.

25   P. W. Jusczyk, D. B. Pisoni, J. Mullenix, *Cognition* **43**, 253 (1992).

26   Although the resynthesis process reduces all voices to one, other (prosodic) characteristics of the different speakers are preserved. We did not test discrimination of the natural sentences played backward because of failure of the newborns to discriminate these sentences even when played forward.

27   Twenty additional babies were tested, and their results were discarded for the following reasons: sleeping or insufficient sucking before the switch (6), crying or agitation (4), failure to meet the habituation criterion (1), sleeping or insufficient sucking after the switch (3), and loss of the pacifier after the switch (6).

28   Seven additional babies were tested, and their results were discarded for the following reasons: crying or agitation (1), sleeping or insufficient sucking after the switch (4), and loss of the pacifier after the switch (2).

29   The tendency for babies in the control group to suck more than those in the experimental group during the habituation phase is not significant ($F_{(1,31)} = 2.7$, $P = 0.11$).

30   Before these experiments were run, all tamarins had participated in a habituation-dishabituation experiment involving their own species-typical vocalizations. Thus, all subjects were familiar with the general test set-up. Subjects sit in the test cage within the acoustic chamber and do so without stress. They also sit or hang on the front panel during testing thereby allowing relatively unambiguous observations of head-turning behavior. Experiments were run by transporting a tamarin from the home room to a test room, which was acoustically and visually isolated from all other tamarins. Two observers watched the session from a monitor outside the test room. Stimuli were played back from a concealed speaker only when the subject's head and body were oriented about 180° away from the speaker. A positive response was scored if the subject turned and oriented toward the speaker within the playback period. If the response was ambiguous, we ran the trial again but with a different exemplar from the habituation series. A subject was considered habituated if he or she failed to respond on two consecutive trails. After habituation, the test stimulus was played. The final trial of the session was a post-test playback, presenting the long call of a tamarin. Given the salience of the long call, we expected the tamarins to respond. If they failed to do so, we excluded the entire session, under the assumption that failure to respond to all stimuli represents general habituation to the test setup. The intertrial interval within a session was set at a minimum of 15 and a maximum of 60s. All trials were videotaped. After a session was run, trials were digitized onto a computer and then scored blind with

respect to test condition by stepping through the experiment frame-by-frame. Two observers scored each test trial: interobserver reliability was 0.92.

31 Each tamarin was tested in the four conditions, with the order of presentation of languages counterbalanced across subjects. The intersession interval was no less than 4 days, with a median of 7 days. When a session's data were excluded because of an ambiguous response to the test sentence or failure to respond to the post-test trial, the tamarin was tested again in the same condition after 1 to 3 weeks in order to complete all the conditions. The significance of the proportion of monkeys reacting to a given change was assessed with a binomial test, and the difference between two conditions was assessed with a 2×2 χ^2 test.

32 The fact that newborns fail under this very condition in experiment 1A is likely due to their immature auditory system, because susceptibility to speaker variability appears to resolve a few months after birth (25).

FOUR

Infant Artificial Language Learning and Language Acquisition

Rebecca L. Gómez and LouAnn Gerken

Language acquisition is one of the most complex learning tasks imaginable. The daunting nature of the undertaking arises from conflicting pressures to generalize beyond the stimuli encountered without generalizing too far. The logical and computational difficulties raised by this problem have traditionally caused researchers to conclude that language is unlearnable except by a specialized learning device.[1-3] Rather, humans must be born with some number of built-in constraints for deciding when and how to generalize from the stimuli they encounter. This view of a constrained language learner has dominated the field for the past 30 or so years. However, recent advances in cognitive science are causing us to reconsider the types and degree of constraint placed on the learner. Of particular interest, and the focus of this article, are recent studies on infants' ability to acquire information about miniature artificial languages.

The complexity of natural language often makes it difficult to isolate the exact factors responsible for language learning. Language researchers have thus turned to artificial languages to obtain better control over the input to which learners are exposed, both in terms of testing precise learning abilities and controlling for prior input. This new approach has led to exciting discoveries regarding the learning mechanisms available during infancy.[4-8]

Word Segmentation

A problem encountered by all language learners is the identification of words in running speech. This would be easy if words were consistently demarcated by physical cues as they are in written text, but they are not. The difficulty of this task is made all the more salient by recalling what it is like to listen to a completely unfamiliar language. For most of us, the words all seem to run together.

A reasonably consistent cue to when a series of syllables forms a word is that syllables within words usually have higher transitional probabilities than syllables spanning words (the conditional probability of Y given X is calculated by normalizing the co-occurrence frequency of X and Y by the frequency of X).[7] For example, in the learner's experience, the likelihood that *by* will follow *ba* in the phrase *pretty baby* is much higher than the likelihood that *ba* will follow *ty*. Why? Many words other than *baby* may follow *pretty* (*pretty doggie, pretty mommy, pretty girl, pretty flower, pretty dolly*).

Saffran, Aslin, and Newport[7] investigated whether infants could use these probabilities to segment word-like units in running speech. In their study, 8-month-old infants listened to two minutes of continuous speech consisting of four tri-syllabic nonsense words strung together in random order (e.g., bidakupadotigolabubidakutupiropadoti . . .). Infants were then tested to see whether they would discriminate two of the familiarized words (e.g., tupiro and golabu) from two non-words (dapiku and tilado). Infants' listening preferences for different stimuli were measured using the head-turn preference procedure.[9] (Stimuli in this procedure are presented auditorily from the infant's left or right side. The amount of time the infant orients toward the source of sound is taken as the dependent measure.) Words and non-words were drawn from the same syllable set, but differed in terms of the transitional probabilities between syllable-pairs (with words having mean transitional probabilities of 1.0 and non-words having mean transitional probabilities of zero). The only cue to whether or not a stimulus was a word was the difference in mean transitional probabilities, and so differences in looking times to words versus non-words would demonstrate sensitivity to such probabilities. Infants indeed discriminated, suggesting the presence of fairly sophisticated learning abilities. Later studies[8] demonstrated that infants were also sensitive to transitional probabilities over tone sequences, demonstrating that this ability was more general than one dedicated solely to processing linguistic stimuli. Whether infants will go on to treat constituents extracted from speech as lexical items is still open, but it is certainly a question that can be investigated empirically.

Words in Sequence

In addition to segmenting words in running speech, learners must also acquire the legal ordering of words in sentences. Gómez and Gerken[5] investigated this issue by exposing 12-month-olds to a subset of strings produced by one of two finite-state grammars. Although word order was constrained by these grammars, there was still considerable variability in terms of the orderings of words in individual sentences. For instance, in one grammar, PEL could occur in first position (PEL-TAM-RUD), second position (VOT-PEL-JIC-RUD-TAM), both second and third position (VOT-PEL-PEL-JIC), or not at all (e.g., VOT-JIC-RUD-TAM). Similarly, JIC could occur after VOT, PEL, or TAM, but its position varied as a function of whether the sentence began with PEL or VOT, whether PEL occurred after VOT or TAM, and whether PEL repeated in the string. After brief exposure to a subset of strings in their training grammar (less than 2 minutes), infants were tested to see if they would discriminate new strings from the two grammars. Both grammars began and ended with the same words and contained the same vocabulary. However, they differed in terms of the ordering of word pairs so, for example, the transition TAM-JIC found in one grammar never occurred in the other. Infants listened longer to new strings from their training grammar than to strings from the other grammar, regardless of which grammar they heard during training. Although the constraints placed on word ordering were the same during training and test, infants were never tested on strings encountered earlier, demonstrating that learning was not confined to memory for old strings, but instead was flexible enough to generalize to novel strings with familiar co-occurrence patterns.

Words in Abstract Patterns

Although sensitivity to word order is necessary for tracking sequential information in sentences, learners must ultimately abstract beyond the ordering of specific words. Gómez and Gerken investigated early abstraction abilities by training 12-month-old infants on strings in one vocabulary and testing them on strings in novel vocabulary.[5] For instance, infants heard strings like FIM-SOG-FIM-FIM-TUP during training but heard strings like VOT-PEL-PEL-JIC at test. Thus, although constraints on grammatical structure remained constant, vocabulary did not. Critically, because test strings were instantiated in new vocabulary, infants could not distinguish the two grammars based on transitional probabilities between remembered word pairs. This task was all the more difficult because *none of the underlying strings occurred in both training and test.* Infants discriminated grammatical from ungrammatical strings despite the change in vocabulary, demonstrating the ability to abstract beyond the specific transitions encountered during training.

In a complementary set of studies, Marcus and colleagues exposed 7-month-olds to 3-minute speech samples of strings with ABA (*wi-di-wi* and *de-li-de*) or ABB (*wi-di-di* and *de-li-li*) word patterns.[6] In these studies the underlying strings were the same for training and for test, but vocabulary was not. As in the Gómez and Gerken study, infants were able to discriminate strings with the training pattern from those with a different pattern (e.g., *ba-po-ba* vs. *ba-po-po*) despite the change in vocabulary.

Marcus et al. interpreted these findings as evidence that infants are capable of abstracting algebra-like rules (involving the substitution of arbitrary elements in abstract variables). However, although these findings are important for indicating the presence of early abstraction abilities, it is premature to claim that the abstraction demonstrated in these studies is the same as that implicated in the abstraction of variables found in natural language. Compare the pattern-based representation ABA to the category-based representation Noun Verb Noun. Although superficially similar, these examples differ along a critical dimension. Abstracting the pattern ABA from *ba-po-ba* involves noting that the first and third elements in sequence are physically identical. With category-based abstraction, however, learners must identify the first and third elements as members of the abstract category *noun*. That is, *Dogs eat pizza* and *John loves books* share the same category-based structure, despite the fact that the category members are physically dissimilar. These determinations cannot be based on a perceptual identity relation and thus (unlike the ABA case) are at least one step removed from the physical stimulus. Although identity relations play an important role in other linguistic phenomena (e.g., relations between pronouns and antecedents, and between moved elements and their traces), again, the abstraction required of such phenomena is a step removed from the way in which identity is used in the infant studies.

Category-based Abstraction

The ability to abstract over categories is fundamental to linguistic productivity. A learner who identifies a novel word as belonging to a particular category has immediate access to all of the rules involving that category.[10-11] Even very young learners are privy to such information. Preschool children seeing and hearing "*Here is a wug. Now there are two of them,*" and asked to complete the sentence "*There are two ___,*" respond with the answer "*wugs*".[11]

Category-based abstraction has been of particular interest to researchers investigating language acquisition with older learners, and has focused on the problem of how learners acquire relations between grammatical classes.[12-14] For example, English-speaking children need to learn that the determiners *the* and *a* precede nouns and not verbs, whereas auxiliaries like *was* and *is* precede verbs, but not nouns. This problem can be conceptualized in terms of filling in the cells of matrices (such as the ones shown below), where learners must acquire the knowledge that MN and PQ are legal sentences of a language, but MQ and PN are not.[14] In these studies, learners are exposed to most, but not all, grammatical pairings during training to see whether they will generalize to new grammatical pairs at test. If learners acquire the categories M, N, P, and Q, and learn the dependencies between them, then they should distinguish a new grammatical pair such as M_1N_3 from the ungrammatical M_1Q_3.

	N_1	N_2	N_3
M_1	x	x	?
M_2	?	x	x
M_3	x	?	x

	Q_1	Q_2	Q_3
P_1	x	?	x
P_2	x	x	?
P_3	?	x	x

As it happens, these kinds of distributional relations are practically impossible for learners to acquire.[12-14] Although adults learn readily that M- and P-words occur first and N- and Q-words occur second, they do not learn the dependencies between classes. This difficulty is ameliorated, however, when a subset of category members are marked with salient conceptual or perceptual cues.[12,13] Now that we have some understanding of the requirements for inducing category-based structure in adults, the next step will be to investigate how younger learners master such abstraction.

Summary

A prevailing assumption has been that linguistic input is too impoverished and learning mechanisms too rudimentary to otherwise explain how young children converge on language. Such mechanisms are either too weak to generalize appropriately or they result in rampant overgeneralization. However, if artificial language learning research demonstrates anything it is that infants are equipped with remarkable abilities for parsing linguistic input. Such abilities enable them to identify word-like constituents in fluent speech,[4,7] as well as constraints on grammatical word order.[5] There is also evidence of some ability to abstract.[5–6] Furthermore, abstraction does not result in rampant overgeneralization. As these studies show, distributionally-based category abstraction results only when there is sufficient evidence for learners to distinguish the categories in question. This should not be surprising given previous work demonstrating the importance of systematically related cues in language learning.[15–19] Thus this approach has been informative with respect to a number of tasks faced by language learners.

Additionally, all of the artificial language learning studies discussed above have examined learners' sensitivity to linguistic form in the absence of semantic content. In so far as these studies are tapping sensitivities used in real language acquisition, they challenge many accounts in which language development is driven by a mapping between meaning and form.[3,20–21] This is not to say that learners do not ultimately need to map the syntactic forms they encode during infancy onto meaning. Obviously they do. However, the fact that infants are able to acquire certain aspects of form prior to acquiring the meaning of these forms changes the nature of the language acquisition problem in a fundamental way.

A final implication of the research on infant artificial language learning concerns the specificity of the constraints on the learner. On many accounts, these constraints have been construed such that for every aspect of language to be acquired, the child is born with a specific constraint or parameter that guides him/her to the correct representation.[22–23] However, data showing that infants can use transitional probabilities to segment grammatical tone sequences suggests that they apply statistical learning to linguistic and non-linguistic stimuli alike.[8] This ability is admittedly far from the constraints discussed by linguistic nativists (involving such language-specific notions as whether or not declarative sentences in a particular language must have an overt subject).[24] Nevertheless, the hypothesis that language (although a specialized human cognitive domain) may be acquired via general purpose learning mechanisms is likely to be investigated with increasing vigor over the next decade.

Although the abilities demonstrated thus far are remarkable, there are a number of issues yet to address. With respect to considerations of learnability, it is important to demonstrate that learners adapt their strategies to the information of most relevance in the input. For example, memory-based computations (involving transitional probabilities) are useful for segmenting words, but not necessarily for identifying frequently occurring syntactic patterns (involving agreement between auxiliaries and verb inflections, determiners signaling noun phrases, etc.). In fact, the transitional probability of any open-class element given a preceding closed-class element decreases as the set of open-class elements grows in number. In contrast, a characteristic of frequently occurring patterns is that they tend to be invariant with respect to the elements occurring around them. The ability to capitalize on invariant structure, then, could be particularly useful. Learners must also be able to apply their strategies selectively. Thus, we are currently asking whether learners can switch between memory- and invariance-based strategies depending on the information of most relevance in the input. Adults show clear evidence of doing so, and thus ongoing research is investigating when in development infants will also.[25]

Another issue has to do with the ability to generalize from a reduced (or limited) set of input (like that characterizing caregiver speech). Although limited, a salient aspect of such input is that it involves multiple presentations of a reduced set of forms.[26] A sufficiently powerful abstraction mechanism, then, would enable learners to generalize as well after exposure to a small set of grammatical exemplars (presented repeatedly) as compared to a much larger set. Research with adults shows them capable of such abstraction,[27] motivating similar research with younger learners.

Other important issues have to do with explaining how learners generalize despite imperfections in the input and whether linguistic generalization involves the use of rules. Learning approaches will also need to begin addressing the acquisition of specific syntactic phenomena. Although there are more than likely to be specialized constraints on language learning, a major contribution of the research conducted thus far is in suggesting that a greater burden of the task may be handled by general devices than has been traditionally posited.

References

1   Chomsky, N. (1965). *Aspects of a theory of syntax*. MIT Press.
2   Gleitman, L.R., & Wanner, E. (1982). Language acquisition: The state of the art. In E. Wanner & L.R. Gleitman (Eds.), *Language acquisition: The state of the art*. Cambridge University Press.
3   Pinker, S. (1984). *Language learnability and language development*. MIT Press.
4   Aslin, R.N., Saffran, J.R., & Newport, E.L. (1998). Computation of conditional probability statistics by 8-month-olds infants. *Psychological Science, 9,* 321–324.
5   Gómez, R.L., & Gerken, L.A. (1999). Artificial grammar learning by one-year-olds leads to specific and abstract knowledge. *Cognition, 70,* 109–135.
6   Marcus, G. et al. (1999). Rule learning by seven-month-old infants. *Science, 283,* 77–80.
7   Saffran, J.R., Aslin, R.N., & Newport, E.L. (1996). Statistical learning by eight-month-old infants. *Science, 274,* 1926–1928.
8   Saffran, J.R. et al. (1999). Statistical learning of tonal structure by adults and infants. *Cognition, 70,* 27–52.
9   Kemler Nelson et al. (1995). The Head-turn Preference Procedure for testing auditory perception. *Infant Behavior and Development, 18,* 111–116.
10 Maratsos, M.P. (1982). The child's construction of grammatical categories. In H.E. Wanner & L. Gleitman (Eds.), *Language Acquisition: The state of the art*. The University Press.
11 Berko, J. (1958). The child's learning of English morphology. *Word, 14,* 150–177.
12 Braine, M.D.S. (1987). What is learned in acquiring word classes – A step toward an acquisition theory. In B. MacWhinney (Ed.), *Mechanisms of language acquisition*. Erlbaum.
13 Frigo, L., & McDonald, J.L. (1998). Properties of phonological markers that affect the acquisition of gender-like subclasses. *Journal of Memory and Language, 39,* 218–245.
14 Smith, K.H. (1969). Learning co-occurrence restrictions: Rule learning or rote learning? *Journal of Verbal Learning and Verbal Behavior, 8,* 319–321.
15 Billman, D. (1989). Systems of correlations in rule and category learning: Use of structured input in learning syntactic categories. *Language and Cognitive Processes, 4,* 127–155.
16 Jusczyk, P.W. (1997). *The discovery of spoken language*. MIT Press.
17 Kelly, M.H. (1992). Using sound to solve syntactic problems: The role of phonology in grammatical category assignments. *Psychological Review, 99,* 349–364.
18 Morgan, J.L., & Newport, E.L. (1981). The role of constituent structure in the induction of an artificial language. *Journal of verbal learning and verbal behavior, 20,* 67–85.

19   Morgan, J.L., Meier, R.P., & Newport, E.L. (1987). Structural packaging in the input to lan-
      guage learning: contributions of prosodic and morphological marking of phrases to the
      acquisition of language. *Cognitive Psychology, 19*, 498–550.
20   Bates, E. (1976). *Language and context: studies in the acquisition of pragmatics.* Academic Press.
21   Bowerman, M. (1973). *Early syntactic development: a cross-linguistic study with special refer-
      ence to Finnish.* Combridge University Press.
22   Chomsky, N. (1980). *Rules and representations.* Foris.
23   Wexler, K., & Manzini, R. (1987). Parameters and learnability in binding theory. In T. Roeper
      and E. Williams (Eds.), *Parameter setting.* Foris.
24   Hyams, N.M. (1986). *Language acquisition and the theory of parameters.* Reidel.
25   Gómez, R.L. (2000). Adaptive strategies for acquiring grammatical structure. Poster pre-
      sented at the Finding the Words Conference, Stanford, CA, April.
26   Snow, C. (1972). Mothers' speech to children learning language. *Child Development, 43*,
      549–565.
27   Gómez, R.L., & Gerken, L.A. (1999). Generalization from limited input. Poster presented at
      the 40th Annual Meeting of the Psychonomic Society, Los Angeles, November.

FIVE

Rapid Gains in Speed of Verbal Processing by Infants in the 2nd Year

Anne Fernald, John P. Pinto, Daniel Swingley, Amy Weinberg, and Gerald W. McRoberts

The language abilities of human infants improve dramatically during the 2nd year of life (e.g., Bates et al., 1988). Most 12-month-old infants are just beginning to speak, and acquire new words at a slow pace. At around 18 months of age, many infants show a "vocabulary burst," shifting to a much faster rate of acquisition (Bloom, 1973; Goldfield & Reznick, 1990), and by age 24 months, infants can typically produce 200 to 500 words (Fenson et al., 1994). Research on the early development of linguistic competence has focused much more on what infants can say than on what they can understand, in part because speech production is directly observable whereas comprehension is not. However, during this period of rapid expansion in productive vocabulary, infants also make impressive gains in their receptive language abilities. Here we provide the first fine-grained analysis of the time course of spoken-word understanding by infants ages 15 to 24 months. By monitoring the ongoing process of word recognition by infants in a behaviorally relevant context, we found that both the speed and the accuracy of speech processing increase steadily over the 2nd year.

Comprehension is a mental event that must be inferred from overt behavior and the context in which it occurs. One common method for assessing the early development of comprehension skills is to ask parents what words they think their child understands (Fenson et al., 1994). Other laboratory methods test comprehension by asking infants to choose a named object from among alternatives (e.g., Woodward et al., 1994). Such parental-report and object-choice measures allow inferences about which words an infant understands, but not about the actual process of word recognition. In adults, much more sophisticated methods are available for studying temporal aspects of spoken-language understanding. Research using various on-line measures of speech comprehension has shown that word recognition by adults is extremely fast and efficient, occurring as soon as there is sufficient acoustic information to disambiguate alternative word candidates (e.g., Altmann, 1990; Grosjean, 1980; Warren & Marslen-Wilson, 1987). However, it has not been possible to examine the speed and efficiency of speech comprehension in infants using such on-line behavioral techniques, because the task demands are too difficult and because infants cannot be instructed to respond quickly and accurately.

Studying the process of word recognition in infants requires a technique that has minimal task demands and that can be used in a naturalistic context. Because infants tend to look at a familiar object when it is named, longer looking at a named target object than at an unnamed distractor object has been used as a measure of word recognition (e.g., Golinkoff et al., 1987; Reznick, 1990). In previous research using a preferential looking procedure, we found that 19-month-old infants oriented more reliably to pictures of familiar named objects than did 12- or 15-month-old infants (Fernald et al., 1992). We also found an age-related increase in the flexibility of speech processing: Although 15-month-old infants could recognize a familiar word in sentence-final position ("Over there there's a *ball*"), they failed to recognize the same word in a perceptually more challenging context, when it was embedded in the middle of the sentence ("There's a *ball* over there"). However, 19-month-old infants performed well regardless of the position of the word in the sentence. Thus, during the period of rapid expansion in productive vocabulary in the 2nd year, infants also develop greater proficiency in extracting lexical information from continuous speech.

These findings motivated us to monitor in greater detail the actual time course of word recognition by infants during this period. A promising approach used with adults has been to observe their gaze patterns as they look at an array of objects while listening to speech related to the objects. By examining sequences of eye movements time-locked to particular words, it is possible to monitor the rapid mental processes involved in understanding spoken language (Tanenhaus et al., 1995). Fine-grained analyses of eye movements have also been used to measure infants' response to visual stimuli, although only in nonlinguistic contexts (cf. Haith et al., 1988; Hood & Atkinson, 1993; Johnson et al., 1994). By increasing the resolution of our coding system, we were able to track infants' eye movements as they looked at pictures while listening to speech naming one of the pictures. To examine the time course of word recognition, we identified the point at which infants initiated a shift in gaze toward the named picture, measuring their eye movements from the beginning of the spoken target word. Our goal was to assess developmental changes in the speed and accuracy of word recognition by infants from 15 to 24 months of age.

Method

Subjects

Subjects were 72 infants from monolingual English-speaking families in a predominantly middle-class population. We tested 24 infants in each of three age groups: 15 months (range: 14.5–15.5), 18 months (range: 17.5–18.5), and 24 months (range: 24.0–25.0). An additional 41 infants were tested but not included in the final sample for the following reasons: fussiness during testing (20), failure to look at pictures during one or more of the trials (6), eyes difficult to see during coding (6), parental interference during testing (4), and experimenter error or equipment failure (5). Parents were administered the MacArthur Communicative Development Inventory (see Fenson et al., 1994); only infants whose parents reported that they were familiar with all four target words were included in the analysis. Informed consent was obtained from the parents of all infants participating in this study.

Stimuli

The auditory stimuli consisted of sentences containing four target words, *doggie, baby, ball,* and *shoe,* typically among the first object names acquired by English-learning infants. The four target words were similar in duration (752–794 ms) and were always presented in the same two carrier frames ("Where's the___? See the___?"). These sentences were spoken in infant-directed speech style, in which words are typically longer in duration than in adult-directed speech (Fernald et al., 1989). The visual stimuli consisted of four colored pictures of familiar objects, one matching each of the target words. The pictures were presented in pairs (ball-shoe or dog-baby), with side of presentation of the objects in each pair varied across trials, and order of object presentation counterbalanced across subjects.

Procedure

Each subject was observed in a three-sided testing booth located in a darkened, sound-treated room (see Swingley et al., 1998, 1999, for details). The infant sat on his or her caregiver's lap 72 cm from two adjacent computer monitors, which were positioned at the infant's eye level. During each trial, one object picture was shown on each monitor. As a guard against bias, the caregiver's view of the pictures was blocked by an opaque curtain. After a 4-s silent familiarization period, the infant heard two sentences naming one of the objects. Each of the four objects served as the target on two trials and the distractor on two trials. Eight 6-s test trials were interspersed with three filler trials showing different pictures, to maintain the infant's interest. Visual and auditory presentations were controlled by a Macintosh computer located in an adjacent room.

Infants' patterns of looking to the two pictures were recorded with a video camera concealed between the monitors. A time code accurate to 0.1 s was superimposed on the video record. Eye movements were analyzed off-line frame by frame from the videotapes by highly trained coders who were unaware of the side of the target object on each trial. For every 100 ms, coders assessed whether the child was looking at the target, at the distractor, or at neither object. These measurements of the looking pattern on each trial were then analyzed in relation to the onset and offset of the first spoken target word, located by visual inspection of the acoustic waveform. A subset of the trials was coded independently by two or more coders, to determine interobserver reliability in measurement of eye movements. Kappas ranged from .85 to .99 ($M = .92$).

Results

A preliminary analysis verified that infants in each age group demonstrated recognition of the target words. Examining the overall proportions of looking time to the target and distractor objects for the 4-s period following the offset of the target word, we found that infants looked significantly more at the target objects than at the distractor objects

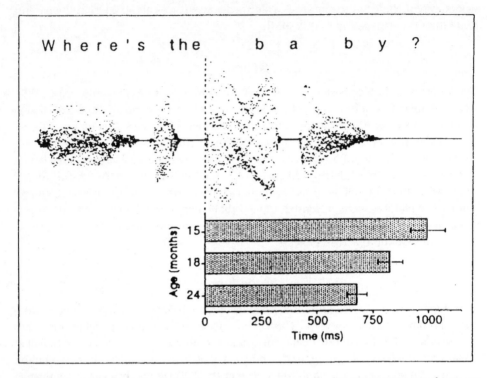

Figure 5.1   Mean latencies to initiate a shift in gaze from the distractor picture to the target picture, measured from the beginning of the spoken target word, for 15-, 18- and 24-month-old infants. This analysis included only those trials on which the infant was initially looking at the incorrect picture and then shifted to the correct picture when the target word was spoken. The graph is aligned with an amplitude waveform of one of the stimulus sentences.

in response to naming. Performance was well above chance (50%) at all ages: 15 months, 65.4%, $t(23) = 5.5, p < .0001$; 18 months, 72.3%, $t(23) = 8.7, p < .0001$; and 24 months, 77.2%, $t(23) = 13.4, p < .0001$.

In the next analysis, we focused on developmental changes in the speed of word recognition, calculating infants' reaction time to seek out the correct picture in response to the spoken target word. Because the infants could not anticipate the side on which the target object would be presented, they were equally likely to be looking at the distractor or the target object at the beginning of a trial. At the onset of the target word, infants were looking at the distractor picture on 39.8% of the trials, at the target picture on 38.4% of the trials, and at neither picture on 21.8% of the trials, averaged across the three age groups. Using only those trials on which the infant was initially fixating the distractor object, we calculated reaction time by measuring the infant's latency to initiate a shift in gaze from the distractor to the target object when the target word was spoken. Mean response latency decreased significantly with age: 995 ms for 15-month-olds, 827 ms for 18-month-olds, and 679 ms for 24-month-olds, as shown in figure 5.1. The overall age effect was reliable, $F(2, 63) = 6.83, p < .01$. Comparisons between age groups revealed that 18-month-olds were reliably faster than 15-month-olds, $t(41) = 1.75$, $p < .05$, and 24-month-olds were reliably faster than 18-month-olds, $t(43) = 2.04$, $p < .05$.

The final analysis compared correct shifts in gaze (distractor to target) and incorrect shifts in gaze (target to distractor) in response to the target word. This analysis included all trials in which the infant was on task, excluding those trials in which the infant was looking away from both pictures when the target word was spoken. In the graphs shown in figure 5.2, the lines show the proportion of trials on which the infants shifted fixation from the picture they were initially looking at to the other picture, calculated every 100 ms from the beginning of the target word. Solid lines represent the proportion of correct responses, when the infants started out looking at the distractor picture and then shifted to the target, and dashed lines represent the proportion of incorrect responses, when the infants started out looking at the target picture and then shifted to the distractor. As more of the word was heard, correct shifts outnumbered incorrect shifts at all three ages. However, the lines diverge earlier and to a greater extent at 24 months, indicating that older infants were not only faster, but also more accurate in matching familiar spoken words with their referents.

Discussion

These findings reveal that infants, like adults, respond spontaneously to a familiar spoken word by rapidly fixating the visual referent that matches the word they hear. Moreover, during their 2nd year, infants make dramatic gains in speed and efficiency in understanding familiar words in continuous speech. Although 15-month-old infants demonstrated recognition of the four target words by reliably looking at the correct picture in response to naming, they did not initiate a shift in gaze to the correct picture until after the target word had been spoken. In contrast, 24-month-olds were 300 ms faster, on average, shifting their gaze to the correct picture before the end of the spoken word. These results demonstrate that by 2 years of age, children are rapidly progressing toward the highly efficient performance of adults, making decisions about words based on incomplete acoustic information (e.g., Tanenhaus et al., 1995; Warren & Marslen-Wilson, 1987).

Infants' response latency to a spoken word in this task was influenced not only by the time required for linguistic processing, but also by the time required to program a shift in gaze to the correct picture. It is important to note that our reaction time measure was based on the time it took the infant to initiate an eye movement from one picture to the other and did not include the actual shift in gaze. An analysis of the duration of shifts in gaze from one picture to the other revealed no significant age differences in speed of executing eye movements. It might still be the case that the longer response latencies of the younger infants were due to the fact that they required more time to program an eye movement. This explanation seems unlikely, however, because eye movement control in infants is more adultlike than any other motor system (Haith et al., 1993). In infants as young as 3 months of age, the minimum latency to initiate a shift in gaze to a peripheral picture in a nonlinguistic task is about 150 ms, approaching adult reaction time in such situations (Canfield et al., 1997). Thus, the most plausible explanation for the age differences in infants' response latency to spoken words is

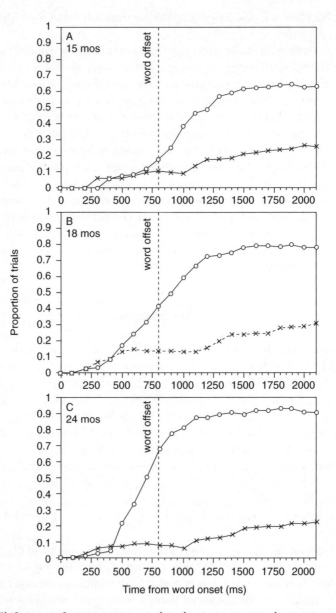

Figure 5.2 Shifts in gaze from one picture to the other in response to the target word, for infants ages (a) 15 months, (b) 18 months, and (c) 24 months. Solid lines represent correct responses, shown as the proportion of trials on which infants were initially fixating the distractor object at the onset of the distractor word and then shifted to the target picture (distractor-to-target shifts); dashed lines represent incorrect responses, shown as the proportion of trials on which infants were initially fixating the target object and then shifted to the distractor picture (target-to-distractor shifts).

that they reflect differences in speed of linguistic processing rather than maturation of the oculomotor system.

Our data show that during the period of rapid expansion in speaking vocabulary at the end of the 2nd year, infants also get much faster at understanding the words they hear. Neuropsychological research on infants' responses to spoken words during the same period reveals a major shift in cerebral organization that appears to be closely linked to language knowledge (Mills et al., 1993). Such developmental changes in neural responses to known words may underlie the increase in speed and efficiency revealed in our on-line behavioral measures of verbal processing. Our results also show that under experimental conditions that are both well controlled and naturalistic, eye movements can be used effectively to monitor the time course of word recognition by infants. This paradigm will enable investigation of a wide range of questions related to the early development of competence in understanding spoken language.

Acknowledgments

We thank Praveen Menon-Johansson, Andrea Heberlein, and the undergraduate research assistants at the Center for Infant Studies for their dedication and skill in testing infants and coding eye movements. We also thank the parents and infants who participated in this study.

References

Altmann, G.T.M. (Ed.). (1990). *Cognitive models of speech processing.* Cambridge, MA: MIT Press.

Bates, E., Bretherton, I., & Snyder, L. (1988). *From first words to grammar.* New York: Cambridge University Press.

Bloom, L. (1973). *One word at a time.* The Hague, Netherlands: Mouton.

Canfield, R.L., Smith, E.G., Brezsnyak, M.P., & Snow, K.L. (1997). Information processing through the first year of life: A longitudinal study using the visual expectation paradigm. *Monographs of the Society for Research in Child Development, 62* (2, Serial No. 250).

Fenson, L., Dale, P.S., Reznick, J.S., Bates, E., Thal, D.J., & Pethick, S.J. (1994). Variability in early communicative development. *Monographs of the Society for Research in Child Development, 59* (5, Serial No. 242).

Fernald, A., McRoberts, G.W., & Herrera, C. (1992, May). *Prosodic features and early word recognition.* Paper presented at the 8th International Conference on Infant Studies, Miami, FL.

Fernald, A., Taeschner, T., Dunn, J., Papousek, M., de Boysson-Bardies, B., & Fukui, I. (1989). A cross-language study of prosodic modifications in mothers' and fathers' speech to preverbal infants. *Journal of Child Language, 16,* 477–501.

Goldfield, B.A., & Reznick, J.S. (1990). Early lexical acquisition: Rate, content, and the vocabulary spurt. *Journal of Child Language, 17,* 171–183.

Golinkoff, R.M., Hirsh-Pasek, K., Cauley, K.M., & Gordon, L. (1987). The eyes have it: Lexical and syntactic comprehension in a new paradigm. *Journal of Child Language, 14,* 23–45.

Grosjean, F. (1980). Spoken word recognition and the gating paradigm. *Perception & Psychophysics, 28,* 267–283.

Haith, M.M., Hazan, C., & Goodman, G.S. (1988). Expectation and anticipation of dynamic visual events by 3.5-month-old babies. *Child Development, 59,* 467–479.

Haith, M.M., Wentworth, N., & Canfield, R.L. (1993). The formation of expectations in early infancy. In C. Rovee-Collier & L.P. Lipsitt (Eds.), *Advances in infancy research* (Vol. 8, pp. 251–297). Norwood, NJ: Ablex.

Hood, B.M., & Atkinson, J. (1993). Disengaging visual attention in the infant and adult. *Infant Behavior and Development, 16,* 405–422.

Johnson, M.H., Posner, M.I., & Rothbart, M.K. (1994). Facilitation of saccades toward a covertly attended location in early infancy. *Psychological Science, 5,* 90–93.

Mills, D.L., Coffey-Corina, S.A., & Neville, H.J. (1993). Language acquisition and cerebral specialization in 20-month-old infants. *Journal of Cognitive Neuroscience, 5,* 317–334.

Reznick, S.J. (1990). Visual preference as a test of infant word comprehension. *Applied Psycholinguistics, 11,* 145–166.

Swingley, D., Pinto, J.P., & Fernald, A. (1998). Assessing the speed and accuracy of word recognition in infants. In C. Rovee-Collier, L. Lipsitt, & H. Hayne (Eds.), *Advances in Infancy Research* (Vol. 12, pp. 257–277). Norwood, NJ: Ablex.

Swingley, D., Pinto, J.P., & Fernald, A. (1999). Continuous processing in word recognition at 24 months. *Cognition, 71,* 73–108.

Tanenhaus, M.K., Spivey-Knowlton, M.J., Eberhard, K.M., & Sedivy, J.C. (1995). Integration of visual and linguistic information in spoken language comprehension. *Science, 268,* 1632–1634.

Warren, P., & Marslen-Wilson, W. (1987). Continuous uptake of acoustic cues in spoken-word recognition. *Perception & Psychophysics, 41,* 262–275.

Woodward, A.L., Markman, E.M., & Fitzsimmons, C.M. (1994). Rapid word learning in 13- and 18-month-olds. *Developmental Psychology, 30,* 553–566.

Introduction to Word Learning

Introduction to Part II

Learning to perceive and produce the sounds of a language is, of course, only half the story of language acquisition – and indeed the poorer half if we recall that many children learn a natural language in the visual-manual modality (i.e., sign language). The essence of language acquisition is the comprehension and production of conventional symbols that may be used to direct the attentional and mental states of other persons. Just as human infants move gradually into the perception and production of the sounds of the language they are learning, they also move gradually into the ability to symbolize conventional meanings.

At around 9 months of age human infants begin to gesture (and sometimes to vocalize with cries or "grunts") in order to get adults either (1): to do something from them (e.g., get an object for them or perform some activity), or (2) to share attention with them to some object or ongoing event. This is the same age at which they first begin to respond appropriately to adult attempts to direct their attention to outside objects and events via pointing and other gestures as well. These acts of protoimperative gesturing (requesting a concrete action) and protodeclarative gesturing (requesting shared attention) provide the foundation for the communicative dimension of children's early language (Bates et al., 1975). Many studies have found that virtually all infants gesture with adults and that the use of gesture represents a very important transitional phase in children's acquisition of skills of linguistic communication (Iverson et al., 1994). Moreover, the function of children's gestures changes as they begin to acquire conventional linguistic skills – from the primary carriers of communicative intent to a more supplementary function. The importance and robustness of gesture as a communicative device is evidenced by the facts that (1) even young blind children gesture while communicating (Iverson & Goldin-Meadow, 1998), and (2) gesture remains an important aspect of human communication throughout childhood and even into adulthood (Goldin-Meadow, 1999). From this point of view, the existence of fully grammaticized sign languages and their ready acquisition by deaf children is not so surprising.

In the current set of readings, Shwe and Markman find that two-year-olds do a number of different things in an effort to communicate with adults, both gesturally and verbally. By reacting to those attempts in different ways, these investigators were able to determine that children do not just communicate in order to manipulate the behavior of adults, but rather to influence their interest and attention to entities in their shared environment. An important part of language acquisition is thus the reading of minds. Another important part of the process – not represented in the current readings – is young children's ability to conceptualize the world in terms of the "same" objects and events as adults. Thus, progress in word learning depends crucially on general cognitive developments in different domains. For example, Gopnik and Meltzoff (1986) review evidence showing that it is only when young children can understand nonverbally the invisible displacement of objects (Piagetian object permanence development) that they can learn words indicating such things as the disappearance and reappearance of objects (e.g., *gone, another*, etc.).

Caselli et al. report a number of quantitative findings with regard to the ages at which and the speed with which young children acquire their earliest words in both English and Italian. As is well known, comprehension precedes production and many children make especially rapid progress in the second half of the second year of life. These investigators also document young children's acquisition of different types of words, including grammatical function words (e.g., articles, prepositions, demonstrative, etc.). Perhaps of special interest, these investigators provide evidence relevant to the controversy of whether young children find it easier to learn nouns or verbs. Although Gentner (1982) surveyed reports from children learning many different languages and concluded that children learn nouns before they learn verbs, recent results with children learning some non-Western languages in which verbs are more salient in speech to young children have called this result into question (e.g., for Chinese, Tardif, 1996; for Korean, Gopnik & Choi, 1995; for Tzotzil, de Léon 2000; for Tzeltzal, Brown, 2000). Because Italian should be a very "verb-friendly" language, the finding of Caselli et al. that Italian children learn nouns before verbs generally supports Gentner's hypothesis and conflicts with these more recent findings. However, there are difficult methodological issues concerning sampling, as young children quite often use a few verbs very widely and frequently whereas they use each of their nouns less widely and frequently – which may give verbs an advantage in a relatively brief sampling of spontaneous speech. The Caselli et al. study uses the McArthur Communicative Development Inventory – a measure based on parent report that is not as sensitive as are spontaneous speech samples to issues of frequency and sampling. Overall, the issue of whether children learning all languages in all kinds of social contexts find it easier to learn nouns than verbs is still an open question.

The next two readings in this section concern not so much what children are learning, but how they are learning it, that is, the *process* of word learning. For more than a decade this problem has been framed in the context of the problem of referential indeterminacy, as first outlined by the philosopher Wittgenstein (1955). The point was crystalized by the philosopher Quine (1960) in his parable of a native who utters the expression "Gavagai!" to a foreigner as a rabbit runs past. The problem is that there is basically no way that the foreigner can know whether the native's novel expression is being used to refer to the rabbit, its color, its running action, a part of its body, or to any of an infinite number of aspects of the situation. In the modern study of word learning, a number of scholars believe that children have initial biases about what some novel word might be used to refer to in the outside world; for example, children might begin by assuming that a novel word refers to a class of objects for which they currently have no word (Markman, 1989). A variation on this theme is the recent work of Golinkoff and Hirsch-Pasek (1999) on "principles of word learning."

Other investigators do not believe that such constraints or principles are necessary in the early stages because there are many aspects of children's cognitive and social development that may serve to constrain the word-learning process without positing distinct entities called "word-learning constraints." Tomasello's paper in the current volume represents this view. He reviews a number of experimental studies showing how different cues in the ongoing social interaction may serve to orient children to the adult's referential intentions. One unique aspect of these studies is that these cues direct children in very similar situations to infer that the novel word they are hearing refers to either an object or to an activity (i.e., they use social cues to differentiate nouns and verbs). Very few experimental studies of word learning concern word types other than object labels, and so more work on verbs and other kinds of early words is sorely needed (but see Tomasello & Merriman, 1995).

The word-learning study reported by Markson and Bloom investigates more quantitative aspects of the word-learning process. Most importantly, it demonstrates that children may learn new words relatively quickly and remember them for a reasonably long length of time without further exposure. And they do this with learning skills that do not seem to differ in kind from those used to acquire other pieces of information about the world. One of the issues raised by this study is the issue of the precise number of exposures to a new word the child needs in order to learn it, and how long they recall a word if they do not hear it repeated. These simple but important quantitative questions have not received the research attention they deserve. Although not addressed by the Markson and Bloom study in particular, Bloom (2000) argues that young children do not go through any kind of "vocabulary spurt" at 18 months of age, as some researchers have proposed. The process of word learning is relatively continuous, with children becoming more skillful – and so learning new words at an ever-faster rate – across childhood and into early adulthood.

In the final reading of this section, Bates and Goodman provide a bridge from the study of word learning to the study of grammatical development. In a review of findings from language development, language breakdown, and real-time processing, they conclude that the distinction between the lexicon and grammar has been exaggerated. Many lexical items serve grammatical functions in larger syntactic constructions, and many syntactic constructions represent symbolic patterns that must be learned in the same basic way as words. Their studies show that there is a very strong correlation between vocabulary size and the emergence of grammatical speech in young children. In studies of language breakdown, they also find that lexicon and grammar are closely intertwined. Bates and Goodman conclude by offering the basics of a connectionist learning model that does not distinguish in any important way between lexicon and grammar.

In thinking about the process of word learning, it is thus important not to lose sight of the fact that children for the most part do not hear people speaking words in isolation. Children experience other people using utterances to achieve communicative goals, and words are simply one component of this communicative act. To acquire a new word, therefore, requires that the learner perform some kind of functional analysis of the utterance as a whole in order to determine precisely which aspects of the utterance the speaker is using to indicate precisely which aspects of the referential context. The future of research in word learning lies in studies that investigate word learning as it occurs in real-time linguistic communication, with words and grammatical constructions conceptualized as simply two interrelated aspects of the same ongoing comprehension process.

References

Bates, E., Camaioni, L., & Volterra, V. (1975). The acquisition of performatives prior to speech. *Merrill-Palmer Quarterly, 21,* 205–224.

Bloom, L. (2000). *How children learn the meanings of words.* Cambridge, MA: MIT Press.

Brown, P. (2000). The conversational context for language acquisition: A Tzeltal (Mayan) case study. To appear in M. Bowerman & S. Levinson (Eds.), *Language acquisition and conceptual development.* Cambridge: Cambridge University Press.

de León, L. (2000). The emergent participany: Interactive patterns in the socialization of Tzotzil (mayan) infants. *Journal of Linguistic Anthropology, 8,* 131–161.

Gentner, D. (1982). Why women are learned before verbs: Linguistic relativity versus natural partitioning. In S. Kuczaj (Ed.), *Language Development,* vol. 2. Hillsdale, NJ: Erlbaum.

Goldin-Meadow, S. (1999). The role of gesture in communication and thinking. *Trends in Cognitive Science, 3,* 419–429.

Golinkoff, R., & Hirsh-Pasek, K. (1999). Emerging cues for early word learning. In B. MacWhinney (Ed.), *The emergence of language.* Mahwah, NJ: Erlbaum.

Gopnik, A., & Choi, S. (1995). Names, relational words, and cognitive development in English- and Korean-speakers: Nouns are not always learned before verbs. In M. Tomasello & W. Merriman (Eds.), *Beyond names for things: Young children's acquisition of verbs* (34pp. 63–80). Hillsdale, NJ: Lawrence Erlbaum.

Gopnik, A., & Meltzoff, A. (1986). Relations between semantic and cognitive development in the one-word stage – the specificity hypothesis. *Child Development, 57,* 1040–1053.

Iverson, J.M., Capirci, O., & Caselli, M.C. (1994). From communication to language in two modalities. *Cognitive Development, 9* (1), 23–43.

Iverson, J.M., & Goldin-Meadow, S. (1998). Why people gesture when they speak. *Nature, 396* (6708), 228–228.

Markman, E.M. (1989). *Categorization and naming in children.* Cambridge, MA: Bradford Books.

Quine, W.V. (1960). *Word and object.* Cambridge, MA: Technology Press of the Massachusetts Institute of Technology.

Tardif, T. (1996). Nouns are not always learned before verbs: Evidence from Mandarin speakers' early vocabularies. *Developmental Psychology, 32* (3), 492–504.

Tomasello, M., & Merriman, W. (Eds.) (1995). *Beyond names for things: Young children's acquisition of verbs.* Hillsdale, NJ: Lawrence Erlbaum.

Wittgenstein, L. (1955). *Philosophical investigations.* New York: MacMillan.

SIX

Young Children's Appreciation of the Mental Impact of Their Communicative Signals

Helen I. Shwe and Ellen M. Markman

Adults understand that one important function of language is to the influence the thoughts, desires, intentions, and beliefs of others. They are aware that their communicative signals have an impact on their listener's mind. With respect to development, some authors argue that young children's communicative acts indicate that they too appreciate the mental impact of their signals, whereas others interpret these behaviors as only persistent efforts to achieve a material goal. Existing studies do not convincingly resolve this issue. The present work attempted to clarify whether young children (30-month-olds) recognize that their signals can affect the mental states of others.

Recent research by Baldwin (1991, 1993) and Tomasello (1995; Tomasello & Barton, 1994; Tomasello & Kruger, 1992) on infants' early communicative abilities suggests that infants understand that others' attentional cues provide necessary information about the intended referent of a novel word. For example, Baldwin presented young infants with a scenario in which they could potentially map a novel label to the wrong referent – this might occur when an adult utters a novel object label at a time when the infant is looking at something other than the correct object. She found that infants (16 months and up) had the ability to gather information about a speaker's focus of attention and thus avoided mapping errors. Moreover, by around 2 years of age, children can discriminate between intentional and unintentional actions that signal the speaker's communicative intent.

In summary, Baldwin and Tomasello (Baldwin, 1991, 1993; Tomasello & Barton, 1994; Tomasello & Kruger, 1992) have shown that infants seem to be aware of the mental lives of others and can use the attentional focus of others to interpret the meaning of a novel word. It is still not clear, however, whether young children use their own communicative signals to influence the mental life of others. One line of early research that begins to address this question is the work on intentional signals. Researchers have used the term *intention signal* to describe a range of behaviors that infants begin producing at about 1 year of age (e.g., Bates et al., 1979; Bretherton & Beeghly, 1982; Bretherton, 1984; Golinkoff, 1986, 1993). For example, infants request help from others in obtaining objects, give and show objects to others, and reject objects that others offer them. According to these researchers, such behaviors indicate that infants are aware of other people's mental lives and are trying to influence others' mental experience.

These claims, however, go well beyond the data. Shatz (1983) argued that infants may be engaging in *magical thinking* when they produce intentional signals. She proposed that children may create the "illusion" of trying to influence the mental life of others by persisting in their attempts to achieve certain goals. That is, Shatz claimed that infants' intentional signals are used to manipulate their listener's behavior and not to influence the mental processes underlying those behaviors.

In opposition to Shatz, Golinkoff (1986, p. 456) argued that certain behaviors that infants produce in events she called the "negotiation of failed messages" suggest that infants are intentionally communicating. She claimed that prelinguistic children are communicating to get their point across and not just to gain material ends. To support this claim, Golinkoff drew upon findings from a longitudinal study of communicative episodes between preverbal infants (12- and 18-month-olds) and their mothers. By analyzing the distribution of various types of behaviors that infants produced in negotiation episodes (i.e., at least one comprehension failure by mother). Golinkoff provided three types of evidence that she interpreted as indicating that infants appreciate the mental impact of their signals: (a) infants initiate negotiation episodes, (b) infants reject incorrect interpretations of signals, and (c) infants creatively repair their failed signals. These findings do not, however, provide compelling evidence for the claim that infants appreciate the mental impact of their signals because they can all be explained by alternative behavioral explanations. For example, infants may reject incorrect interpretations of their signals because they want to change another person's behavior (e.g., removing an undesired object), not because they want their listener to understand their initial signal.

In response to Golinkoff's (1986) claim that infants appreciate the mental processes that underlie certain behavioral responses. Shatz and O'Reilly (1990) conducted an observational study that examined miscommunication episodes between children (age 2 years 6 months) and their parents in free play sessions. Shatz and O'Reilly concluded from the results of their study that Golinkoff seriously overestimated infants' and young children's ability to understand the mental aspect of communicative signals. Shatz and O'Reilly classified child utterances eliciting parental requests for clarification into one of two categories: (a) request for action or information or (b) assertion. They hypothesized that children would persist more in achieving mutual understanding with their parent when their original utterance was a request rather than an assertion because this would indicate that children use communicative signals mainly to achieve behavioral goals. Shatz and O'Reilly found that children responded to requests for clarification made of their own requests significantly more frequently than they responded to clarification requests made of their own assertions (means of 94% and 84%, respectively). They interpreted these results to support their claim that young children use communicative signals mainly to get things.

Golinkoff (1993) responded to Shatz and O'Reilly's (1990) criticisms by arguing that the high rate (84%) at which children clarified their assertions supports her claim that children communicate for the sake of being understood. Furthermore, Golinkoff pointed out that even adults will provide more repairs when they are trying to obtain an overt goal and not just providing some information to others.

In summary, although Golinkoff (1993) argued that infants' early gestural behaviors demonstrate their appreciation of the mental component of communicative interactions, there are alternative explanations for these findings. A weaker claim that is supported by these findings is that infants and young children have goals and persist in their attempts to achieve them. In line with Golinkoff's work, a handful of observational studies in the theory of mind literature suggest that 2-year-olds are aware of the mental lives of others (Garvey, 1984; Keenan & Schieffelin, 1976). These studies have documented the active attempts of children to ensure that they and their communicative partners are attuned to the same topic. Garvey investigated young children's attempts to inform another person about an object or event by recording their conversations with adults and peers at home and school. These observations showed that 2- and 3-year-olds persisted in establishing a common label for an object for the purposes of talking about that object or helping a communicative partner recall something to talk about a previous event. In addition, Keenan and Schieffelin observed 3 children (during the period from 16 to 35 months of age) and recorded their attempts to initiate and sustain topics of conversation. These children used a number of verbal (e.g., verbs such as *see* and *look*, deictic particles such as *there*) and nonverbal (e.g., pointing, eye contact) devices to focus the attention of their listeners on present objects or events. These observations of young children's persistence in establishing a common label for an object or event suggest that they monitor the attentive focus of their listener.

These observational studies, however, do not provide clear evidence to answer whether young children use communicative signals to influence the cognitive state of their listener or simply to manipulate the listener's behavior. This question must be addressed by using a method that can separate the factors of gaining overt goals from influencing the cognition of others. The present study was designed to address this issue by creating a situation in which children's persistence could be interpreted only as trying to obtain listener understanding.

In a set of recent studies with 2-year-olds, O'Neill (1996) introduced experimental manipulations to investigate whether toddlers take into account their mothers' knowledge states when communicating with them. Children had to ask their mothers for help in retrieving an object in two different conditions. In one condition, mothers had witnessed the object's placement; in the other condition, the mother had not witnessed the object's placement (e.g., she was out of the room or covered her eyes). As predicted, O'Neill found that 2-year-olds named the object, named its location, and gestured to its location significantly more often when their mother had not witnessed the object's placement than when they had witnessed its placement. Thus, young children altered their verbal and nonverbal communication according to the knowledge state of their communicative partner.

Thus, under some circumstances, 2-year-olds monitor their listener's knowledge state and can tailor their signals appropriately. Yet we still do not know whether young children care that their goal oriented requests are understood or whether they only care that they achieve their goal. When young children are faced with a situation in which they desire an object, the motivation to achieve their goal might swamp any incipient ability they have to monitor their listener's comprehension.

To address whether children are able to monitor their listener's comprehension when a salient goal is at stake, we must distinguish between efforts to be understood per se and efforts to achieve a goal. Refusal of a child's request is one situation in which the components of listener comprehension and obtaining some goal are distinguishable. For example, a child requests a ball and the listener responds by saying "You want the ball? You may not have the ball now." In this scenario, the listener conveys to the child that she understood the child's request but at the same time does not satisfy the request for the object. So in this case, the elements of listener understanding and obtaining a material goal are not confounded.

In the present study, we investigated young children's understanding of the mental aspect of their communicative signals by presenting children with situations in which their listener conveys either misunderstanding or comprehension of their request for an object. In one set of conditions, children were presented with two situations in which they did not get what they wanted. In one of those conditions, the experimenter expressed understanding; in the other, she conveyed misunderstanding of the request for an object. In another set of conditions, children obtained what they wanted: one in which the experimenter conveyed understanding of their request and one in which she did not. If children persist in their attempts to get their point across to their listener even after their goal has been achieved, then the hypothesis that children appreciate the mental component of their signals would have even stronger support. In summary, if young children care whether their signals are being understood per se, then they should persist in clarifying their signals more when the listener misunderstands compared to when the listener understands their request, regardless of whether they achieve their overt goal.

Method

Participants

Twenty-two healthy children (M age = 30 months 17 days, range = 30 months 2 days to 31 months 7 days, 11 boys and 11 girls) participated in this study. They were recruited through ads in local parent newspapers and magazines and received either a small object or $5 for their participation. Eight additional children participated in the study but were not part of the final data set because of failure to choose objects consistently or failure to complete the procedure.

Materials

Stimuli

Each child saw 10 objects that were presented in pairs. Every child in the study was presented with a duck, a car, a train, a ball, a turtle, a plane, a boat, and a pig paired with either a shirt or a sock in the eight experimental trials. The duck toy was a mother with her baby attached to her stomach. When the baby duck was pulled away from the mother, the mother flapped its wings and walked across the table. The car was a battery-powered car that made noise and drove in circles on the table when a button was pushed. The train and turtle moved across the table when pushed. The ball was soft, somewhat bouncy, and bright pink. The plane had Big Bird sitting in it and was a children's flashlight that made noise and lit up when you pushed it. The pig talked when its stomach was pushed. In the filler trial (first trial), children were presented with an additional set of familiar objects.

On each trial, the child was presented with one action object and one boring object (shirt or sock). Pilot studies indicated that children found the action objects (duck, car, train, ball, turtle, plane, boat, and pig) very attractive. The shirt and sock were both blue with no interesting features. Pilot work indicated that children typically did not request these objects and were noticeably dissatisfied when handed a shirt or sock instead of an interesting object. An action toy was paired with a less interesting object in the hope that children would consistently choose the same object in the experimental conditions and would care which object the experimenter gave them. We expected children to request the action toy and be somewhat dissatisfied when the experimenter handed them the sock or shirt.

Equipment
A video camera equipped with a stopwatch function was used to tape each session.

Design

There were two experimental conditions in which children did not get the object they requested but that differed in terms of whether the experimenter indicated she understood their request or not. These two conditions were Understanding/Wrong Object and No Understanding/Wrong Object. In addition, there were two experimental conditions in which children obtained the requested object. These two conditions were Understanding/Correct Object and No Understanding/Correct Object.

Each child participated in all four conditions with two trials of each. The order of each set of test trials was random so that children got one trial of each condition in the first block of four trials and the same for the second block of trials. Children were presented with a different pair of objects on each of the eight experimental trials. The test trials were preceded by one filler trial in which the experimenter simply gave the requested object to the child (i.e., no verbal response from experimenter). This filler trial was used to familiarize the baby with the game that involved requesting only one object instead of both. To make the game more interesting for the children, the experimenter often used a puppet to retrieve the objects from the child.

Procedure

In all of the conditions, children were shown two objects and were prompted to request one of the objects from an experimenter. After the child clearly requested one of the objects by pointing, reaching, or labeling, the experimenter placed one of the objects in a bucket on the far corner of the table leaving only one object in front of the child. For example, in the two conditions in which children obtained the requested object, the other (undesired) object was taken away and placed in the bucket. The object was placed in a bucket on the table instead of removing it from the table so that children's responses (i.e., persistence in requesting an object) would be clear for coding purposes. That is, if children persisted in requesting an object, they would have a specific referent at which to direct their verbal requests. The opaque bucket was used to make the procedure less frustrating for the children – having the desired object in their direct line of sight would have been upsetting. After the experimenter gave a verbal response to the child's request, she handed the object on the table to the child.

Gestural forms of requests by the child were coded as requests in this study. We did not require a verbal request from young children because in pilot work we had to eliminate too many children on the basis of their low frequency of verbal requests. However, simply by placing the two objects on the table in front of the children but out of reach we were able to reliably elicit gestures. That is, children clearly indicated the desired object by pointing or reaching. These gestures were often accompanied by eye gaze and verbalizations such as "that" or "want that one," which made coding gestural requests clear and straightforward in most cases. The test trials of 12 participants were coded independently by two coders, and they agreed 100% of the time on which object the child requested. Although gestural requests indicated which object the child desired, verbalizations were coded as the dependent measure after children's initial request for an object. Thus, children's original requests could be gestural, but their rerequests were only coded if they were verbal.

Listener comprehension was conveyed by having the experimenter correctly repeat the label of the object that the child requested. In contrast, misunderstanding was conveyed by having the experimenter incorrectly repeat the label of the unrequested object. In all four conditions, the same carrier phrases and intonation were used when the experimenter expressed understanding or misunderstanding of the child's request and refused or complied with the child's request (e.g., "You asked for the *object label 1*. I think you want the *object label 1*. I'm going to give you the *object label 2*. Here's the *object label 2*."). For example, in the Understanding/Wrong Object condition, if the child requested the duck, the experimenter said, "You asked for the *duck*. I think you want the *duck*. I'm going to give you the *shirt*. Here's the *shirt*." These carrier phrases were used so that the experimenter would convey her understanding or misunderstanding of the child's request and nothing more.

Children were seated at a table, with their parent seated next to them and the experimenter seated across the table. The experimenter presented the child with two objects by placing them approximately 60 cm apart on the table in front of the child but out of reaching distance. The experimenter then prompted the child to request one of the objects (if necessary) by saying, "Which object do you want to see? Would you like to see the___ or the___?" After the child clearly requested one of the objects, the experimenter placed one of the objects in a bucket on the far corner of the table, gave the appropriate verbal response, and then handed the object left on the table to the child. The following examples of each condition pertain to a trial where the experimenter presents a car and sock, and the child requests the car.

For the two conditions in which children did not get the requested object, the experimenter placed the requested object (car) in the bucket on the corner of the table. Thus, the boring object was in front of the child just out of reach, and the requested object was put away out of sight. At this point the experimenter then gave the relevant verbal response:

1 Understanding/Wrong Object: "You asked for the *car*. I think you want the *car*. I'm going to give you the *sock*. Here's the *sock*."
2 No Understanding/Wrong Object: "You asked for the *sock*. I think you want the *sock*. I'm going to give you the *sock*. Here's the *sock*."

After the experimenter gave a verbal response to the child's request, she handed the child the other object (sock). Then the experimenter waited approximately 10 s until she retrieved the object and began the next trial.

For the two conditions in which children obtained the requested object, the experimenter placed the other object (sock) in the bucket on the corner of the table. Thus the desired object was in front of the child just out of reach, and the boring object was put away out of sight. At this point the experimenter gave the appropriate verbal response for the condition:

1 Understanding/Correct Object: "You asked for the *car*. I think you want the *car*. I'm going to give you the *car*. Here's the *car*."
2 No Understanding/Correct Object: "You asked for the *sock*. I think you want the *sock*. I'm going to give you the *car*. Here's the *car*."

After the experimenter gave a verbal response to the child's request, she handed the child the requested object (car). Then the experimenter waited approximately 10 s until she retrieved the object and began the next trial.

Results

If young children appreciate the mental component of their signals, then they should persist in clarifying their signal more when their listener misunderstands them than when their listener understands their request. This comparison can be made between two sets of conditions when children did not receive what they requested (Understanding/Wrong Object vs. No Understanding/Wrong Object) and when they did obtain the requested object (Understanding/Correct Object vs. No Understanding/Correct Object). Children's verbalizations were coded to determine whether they followed the predicted pattern. We predicted that children would repeat the label of the requested object and verbally reject the undesired object more when the experimenter conveyed misunderstanding than when she conveyed understanding of their request.

Coding

Children's reactions were compared in the four conditions by coding two types of verbalizations – repetitions of the requested object label and rejections of the undesired object. Children's nonverbal responses (e.g., looking, touching, reaching for objects) were not coded in this study because pilot work indicated that these data were difficult to interpret, and only a few trends in the predicted direction were observed.

The number of repetitions was calculated for children's request of the desired object and their rejection of the undesired object. The verbalizations of children's request for the desired object included phrases such as "Want duck," "Give me the duck," and "Please duck," in addition to repetitions of the other object label in isolation. Children rejected the unrequested object by using a number of different verbalizations: "I don't want that," "No sock," and "I don't like it."

Each trial started when the experimenter placed one of the objects in a bucket on the far corner of the table. At this point one of the objects had been removed, leaving only one object visible to make it clear which object the experimenter is about to hand over to the child. Thus, the verbal data is not open to a behavioral explanation because the coding started at the point when children should know which object they were going to get. That is, in pilot versions of the study, children did not know which toy the experimenter was going to hand them until after she provided a verbal response to their request. Children may have persisted more when they heard the label of the undesired toy because they recognized that as a sign that they were not going to get what they wanted. In the present study, the experimenter provided a verbal response to the children's requests only after the children knew which toy they were going to get. The trial ended when the experimenter retrieved the object from the child.

The test trials of all 22 participants were coded independently by two coders. Reliability was calculated with Cohen's (1960) kappa. The two coders showed relatively strong agreement (94%, $\kappa = .89$) in their judgments of the number of times each participant requested the desired object but somewhat weaker agreement (82%, $\kappa = .72$) in their judgments of the number of times each participant rejected the unrequested object. Each discrepancy was carefully reexamined by both coders at which time they came to an agreement about what the child had said or done. All of the disagreements resulted from one of the coders' failing to record a behavior that the child exhibited. That is, each coder had failed to notice some verbalization on a small number of trials. The final coding used in the data analyses was the agreed upon responses from both coders.

All conditions

A first set of analyses was conducted to compare all four conditions: Understanding/Wrong Object, No Understanding/Wrong Object, Understanding/Correct Object, and No Understanding/Correct Object. Children's verbalizations were analyzed in a 2 (object: correct, incorrect) × 2 (response: understanding, misunderstanding) × 2 (trial: trial 1, trial 2) × 2 (gender: male, female) analysis of variance (ANOVA). Two such analyses were conducted: one analysis with the requested object (requesting the object in the bucket) verbalization measure and the second with the no (rejecting the object given by the experimenter) response measure. As predicted, these analyses revealed a significant main effect of response for the number of repetitions of the requested object,

Table 6.1   Repetitions of requested object

Condition	Wrong object	Correct object
Understanding		
M	.16	0.00
SD	.43	0.00
No understanding		
M	.48	.77
SD	.88	.86

$F(1, 20) = 27.69, p < .001$. That is, children repeated the label of the requested object more when the experimenter expressed misunderstanding ($M = .63$ repetitions) than when she conveyed understanding ($M = .08$ repetitions). Furthermore, these omnibus ANOVAs revealed a significant main effect of response for verbally rejecting the object given by the experimenter. $F(1, 20) = 6.96, p < .01$. Children verbally rejected the given object more when the experimenter misunderstood their signal ($M = .49$ repetitions) than when she understood ($M = .09$) their request. In addition to the predicted main effects of response, these analyses revealed a significant Object × Response interaction for the number of repetitions of the requested object and a significant main effect of object for verbally rejecting the given object. To better understand these findings, we will first consider the responses of children when they did not obtain the requested object and then examine their responses in the conditions in which they obtained the requested toy.

Understanding/Wrong Object versus No Understanding/Wrong Object

We compared children's verbalizations in the conditions in which children did not get the requested object but were understood in one condition and misunderstood in the other. The two categories of verbalizations analyzed were requested object (requesting the object in the bucket) and no (rejecting the object given by the experimenter). Children's verbalizations were analyzed in a series of 2 (condition) × 2 (gender) × 2 (trial) ANOVAs. As predicted, children who did not get the desired object tended to repeat the requested object label more when the experimenter expressed misunderstanding ($M = .48$ repetitions) than when she conveyed understanding ($M = .16$ repetitions) of the children's request, $F(1, 20) = 5.03, p < .05$ (see Table 6.1 for summary of results). Eight of the children repeated the label of the requested object more when their listener conveyed misunderstanding than when she expressed understanding, whereas 3 children showed the opposite pattern. This difference, however, did not reach significance (binomial test, $p = .11$). Children verbally rejected the given (undesired) object more when the experimenter expressed misunderstanding ($M = .70$ repetitions) than when she conveyed understanding ($M = .18$ repetitions) of their request, $F(1, 20) = 8.94, p < .01$ (see Table 6.2 for summary of results). Thirteen of the children verbally rejected the undesired object more when their listener expressed misunderstanding than when she

Table 6.2   Rejections of undesired object

Condition	Wrong object	Correct object
Understanding		
M	.18	0.00
SD	.54	0.00
No understanding		
M	.70	.27
SD	1.11	.58

conveyed understanding, but none of the children showed the opposite response pattern (binomial test, $p < .001$).[1]

Understanding/Correct Object versus No Understanding/Correct Object

In addition to comparing the two conditions in which children did not get the object they requested, we compared children's verbalizations in the two conditions in which children obtained the requested object. Children who obtained the requested object repeated the label of the desired object more when the experimenter expressed misunderstanding than when she conveyed understanding of their request. Children repeated the label of the requested object a mean of .77 times when she conveyed misunderstanding, whereas they never uttered the label of the requested object when the experimenter expressed understanding of their request, $F(1, 20) = 28.47, p < .001$. Seventeen (of the 22) children who obtained the requested object repeated the label of the desired object more when the experimenter conveyed misunderstanding than when she expressed understanding of their request, whereas none of the children showed the opposite pattern (binomial test, $p < .001$). Furthermore, children who obtained the desired object verbally rejected the unrequested object more when the experimenter expressed misunderstanding of their request. Children verbally rejected the undesired object a mean of .27 times when the experimenter conveyed misunderstanding, whereas they never verbally rejected the undesired object when she expressed understanding of their request, $F(1, 20) = 6.15, p < .05$. Seven children verbally rejected the undesired object more when their listener conveyed misunderstanding than when she expressed understanding of their request, but none showed the opposite response pattern (binomial test, $p < .01$).

In summary, when children did not get the requested object, they tended to repeat the label of the other object and verbally rejected the given object more when the exper-

---

[1]   We replicated these findings in a previous study with 24 children who were 30 months old. Children repeated the other object label significantly more in the No Understanding/Wrong Object than the Understanding/Wrong Object trials. Furthermore, the boys also verbally rejected the given toy more in the No Understanding/Wrong Object than in the Understanding/Wrong Object trials. The girls showed no difference between the two conditions.

imenter expressed misunderstanding than when she conveyed understanding of their request. Furthermore, even when children obtained the requested object, they showed an analogous pattern of responses. That is, they repeated the label of the requested object and verbally rejected the undesired object significantly more when the experimenter conveyed misunderstanding than when she expressed understanding of their request for an object.

Receiving the desired object versus rejected object

Turning back to the findings from the omnibus ANOVAs, a significant interaction between response and object was found for the number of repetitions of the requested object. As expected, children never repeated the label of the requested object when the experimenter conveyed understanding of their signal and they obtained the requested toy. Also as expected, children persisted to clarify their signal at a relatively low rate (M = .16 repetitions) when the experimenter expressed understanding but they did not get what they wanted. The puzzling findings, however, is the comparison between the two cases in which the experimenter expressed misunderstanding; in one case the children obtained the requested toy, and in the other they did not. That is, children persisted to clarify their signal more when they got what they wanted but the experimenter misunderstood (M = 0.77 repetitions) than when they got the wrong object and the adult misunderstood (M = 0.48 repetitions). Although this finding is somewhat counterintuitive, one possible explanation is that when children are faced with a situation in which they are misunderstood and, on top of that, do not get what they want, they may be too frustrated or upset to clarify their signal. In the case in which they at least get what they want (but are still misunderstood), children can devote some of their resources to clarifying their signal.

The omnibus ANOVAs also revealed a significant main effect for object for children's verbal rejection of the toy given by the experimenter. That is, children verbally rejected (e.g., "No"; "Don't want it") the undesired toy more than the requested toy (Ms = 0.44 and 0.14 repetitions, respectively). Part of this main effect can be attributed to the obvious expectation that when children were understood, they verbally rejected the wrong object more than the requested object (Ms = 0.18 and 0.00, respectively). More interestingly, even when children were misunderstood, they verbally rejected the wrong object more (M = 0.70 repetitions) than the correct object (M = 0.27 repetitions). Although this main effect for object was not one of the main predictions, it makes sense given the different responses children could give to clarify their signal. On the one hand, when children did not obtain the requested toy, they could either repeat the label of the requested toy or verbally reject the undesired toy to clarify their signal. On the other hand, when children obtained the requested toy, it made more sense for them to repeat the label of the requested toy to clarify their signal when the experimenter misunderstood them. That is, it did not make much sense for children to clarify their signal by saying "No" or "I don't want it" when they obtained the requested toy but the experimenter misunderstood them. Thus, these young children were showing some signs of modulating their corrections to be appropriate for the kind of misunderstanding the experimenter expressed (i.e., whether children obtained the requested or rejected toy).

Discussion

The results of this study suggest that young children are aware that their communicative signals have an impact on the mental state of their listeners. Children persisted in clarifying their signals more when their listener expressed misunderstanding than when she conveyed understanding in situations in which children did not fulfill their goal of obtaining an attractive object. Furthermore, the predicted pattern of differences in children's verbalizations was found even when children obtained the object they requested.

These findings provide evidence that young children appreciate the mental component of their signals and treat their listeners as more than just manipulable objects. In reference to the debate between Golinkoff (1986) and Shatz and O'Reilly (1990), our results are consistent with Golinkoff's claim that young children are communicating to get their point across and not just to get things they want. Our findings do not support Shatz and O'Reilly's interpretation of the results from their study on miscommunication episodes with 2-year-olds. Our findings indicate that young children care whether their signals are being understood, regardless of whether their request is successful. This work helps to resolve the debate between Golinkoff and Shatz and O'Reilly by providing a controlled experiment that distinguishes between intentions and overt goals. It remains to be seen, however, whether babies as young as 18–24-month-olds appreciate the mental impact of their signals.

Our results also help clarify the issue of exactly how to characterize 2-year-olds' understanding of the mental world. These findings support the conclusions of Garvey (1984) and Keenan and Schieffelin (1976) regarding young children's ability to ensure that they are their communicative partners are focused on the same topic of conversation. More specifically, in a request scenario, it is vital for children to ensure that their listener is attuned to the same topic. Our results indicate that young children use verbal devices to focus the attention of their listener on the correct (requested) object.

Furthermore, our results corroborate O'Neill's (1996) finding that 2-year-olds take into account their communicative partner's knowledge state and can adjust their level of informativeness accordingly. Although O'Neill's procedure differs markedly from ours in many respects, the two procedures tap some of the same basic communicative abilities in young children. For example, in O'Neill's procedure, children had to monitor their mothers' knowledge state (inferred from what the mother witnesses) and then adjust their level of informativeness accordingly to obtain a desired object. Similarly, in our procedure, children had to monitor their listener's knowledge state (inferred from what label she used) to determine whether a higher level of persistence was required to obtain listener comprehension. Discussions of attention in infancy have focused on infants' abilities to take into account the direction of the gaze of another person (Baldwin, 1991, 1993; Baldwin & Moses, 1993). O'Neill suggested that children in her task were not simply monitoring the direction of their mothers' eye gaze but rather assessing which events their mothers were jointly attending to with them. She suggested that although the ability to determine an adult's gaze is useful for infants in many situations, as children grow older their understanding of joint attention must incorporate other factors as well.

A similar conclusion can be made in relation to our findings – children could not simply monitor the eye gaze or other attentional cues of their listener to determine whether she understood them or not. That is, in all of the experimental conditions, the listener looked at the child (and not at one of the objects) when giving the verbal response to the children's request. Children in our task were clearly using their receptive language comprehension to determine whether the experimenter understood their request or not. Thus, 2-year-olds' understanding of attention goes beyond monitoring specific attentional cues such as eye gaze and pointing in communicative interactions. Our findings support the conclusion that 2-year-olds are not limited to these sorts of information about an adult's attention focus but, rather, have a number of resources at their disposal to monitor the focus of attention and knowledge state of their listener. Furthermore, these findings suggest that when they are misunderstood, young children tailor their clarification responses to accommodate the context of the misunderstanding (i.e., whether they received the desired object). Our results, in combination with O'Neill's (1996) findings, suggest that 2-year-olds are broadening their understanding of attention, which, in turn, will help them monitor the knowledge state of their listener across an increasingly wide range of situations.

In conclusion, young children's persistence in clarifying their communicative signals regardless of whether they achieve their goal is striking, given their strong desire for an interesting object. Children were presented with attractive toys and encouraged to request them from an experimenter in the present procedure. Young children's strong desire for a toy easily could have masked their communicative competence, resulting in no difference between the conditions. In fact, when children were misunderstood, they tended to clarify their signal more when they obtained the requested toy. Yet when children did not get what they wanted, their disappointment did not completely overshadow their ability to clarify their communicative intent to their listener. Thus, young children monitor their communicative partner's knowledge state and care about their listener's comprehension over and above getting what they requested.

Acknowledgements

Portions of these findings were presented at the March 1995 biennial meeting of the Society for Research in Child Development in Indianapolis, Indiana. We would like to express our appreciation to the parents and infants who generously participated in this research. We thank Judith Wasow for administrative help and Nancy Lin, Amy Jones, and Cindy Lupin for their diligence in coding videotapes.

References

Baldwin, D.A. (1991). Infants' contribution to the achievement of joint reference. *Child development, 62*, 875–890.

Baldwin, D.A. (1993). Infants' ability to consult the speaker for clues to word reference. *Journal of Child Language, 20*, 309–418.

Baldwin, D.A., & Moses, L.J. (1993). In C. Lewis, & P. Mitchell (Eds.), *Origins of an understanding of mind*. Hillsdale, NJ: Erlbaum.

Bates, E., Benigni, L., Bretherton, I., Camaioni, L., & Volterra, V. (1979). *The emergence of symbols: Cognition and communication in infancy.* New York: Academic Press.

Bretherton, I. (1984). Social referencing and the interfacing of minds: A commentary on the views of Feinman and Campos. *Merrill-Palmer Quarterly, 30*, 419–427.

Bretherton, I., & Beeghly, M. (1982). Talking about internal states: The acquisition of an explicit theory of mind. *Developmental Psychology, 18*, 906–921.

Cohen, J. (1960). A coefficient of agreement for nominal scales. *Educational and Psychological Measurement, 20*, 37–46.

Garvey, C. (1984). *Children's talk.* Cambridge, MA: Harvard University Press.

Golinkoff, R.M. (1983). The preverbal negotiation of failed messages: Insights into the transition period. In R.M. Golinkoff (Ed.), *The transition from prelinguistic to linguistic communication.* Hillsdale, NJ: Erlbaum.

Golinkoff, R.M. (1986). "I beg your pardon?": The preverbal negotiation of failed messages. *Journal of Child Language, 13*, 455–476.

Golinkoff, R.M. (1993). When is communication a "meeting of minds"? *Journal of Child Language, 20*, 199–207.

Keenan, E.O., & Schieffelin, B.B. (1976). Topic as a discourse notion: A study of topic in the conversations of children and adults. In C.N. Li (Ed.), *Subject and topic* (pp. 335–384). New York: Academic Press.

O'Neill, D.K. (1996). Two-year-old children's sensitivity to a parent's knowledge state when making requests. *Child Development, 67*, 659–677.

Shatz, M. (1983). Communication. In P.H. Mussen (Series Ed.), J. Flavell, & E. Markman (Vol. Eds.), *Handbook of child psychology: Vol. 3. Cognitive development* (4th edn. pp. 841–889). New York: Wiley.

Shatz, M., & O'Reilly, A. (1990). Conversation or communicative skill? A reassessment of two-year-olds' behavior in miscommunication episodes. *Journal of Child Language, 17*, 131–146.

Tomasello, M. (1995). Joint attention as social cognition. In C. Moore, & P. Dunham (Eds.), *Joint attention: Its origins and role in development* (pp. 103–130). Hillsdale, NJ: Erlbaum.

Tomasello, M., & Barton, M. (1994). Learning words in nonostensive contexts. *Developmental Psychology, 30*, 639–650.

Tomasello, M., & Kruger, A. (1992). Joint attention on actions: Acquiring verbs in ostensive and non-ostensive contexts. *Journal of Child Language, 19*, 311–333.

SEVEN

Lexical Development in English and Italian[1]

M.C. Caselli, P. Casadio, and E. Bates

In the last 25 years, there has been a marked increase in cross-linguistic research on language development, at every level from speech perception in infancy (Goodman & Nusbaum, 1994; Kuhl, 1991; Werker, 1994), through the acquisition of grammar (Slobin, 1985–1997; see also MacWhinney & Bates, 1989), to the finer details of narrative discourse from preschool through the elementary school years (Berman & Slobin, 1994). At all levels (phonetic, lexical and/or grammatical), cross-linguistic variation in content and order of acquisition has been observed, but this variation is complemented by evidence for constraints on learning, perception, and production that operate in every language. In this paper, we will investigate the interplay between universal and language-specific factors in lexical development from 8 to 30 months, a crucial period in which children make the passage from first words to grammar. We will compare profiles of development in English and Italian, with special emphasis on the onset and growth of nouns, verbs, and function words as a function of total vocabulary size. As we shall see, these two languages provide strong evidence for universal constraints on the development and composition of vocabulary, although subtle cross-language variations in content are observed as well.

Some language-specific variations are inevitable in early lexical development, reflecting cultural factors (e.g., the relative frequency of "spaghetti") as well as language-specific variations in phonetic difficulty (e.g., the Italian word "macchina" may be harder to say than the English word "car," even though they are equivalent in frequency, conceptual difficulty, and attractiveness to children). Nevertheless, universal stages of lexical growth have been proposed, hypothesized to reflect universal cognitive and social constraints that override language- and culture-specific variations in content. Perhaps the best-known proposal of this kind comes from Gentner (1982),

---

[1] *A redaction of:*

   Caselli, M.C., Bates, C., Casadio, P., Fenson, L., Fenson, J., Sanderl, L., & Weir, J. (1995). A cross-linguistic study of early lexical development. *Cognitive Development, 10,* 159–199.

   Caselli, M.C., Casadio, P., & Bates, E. (1999). A comparison of the transition from first words to grammar in English and Italian. *Journal of Child Language, 26,* 69–111.

who has argued that verbs must develop later than nouns in all human languages (more on this below). Based on our own findings for English (Bates et al., 1988; Bates et al., 1994) and Italian (Bates et al., 1979; Caselli & Casadio, 1995), we have expanded Gentner's noun-verb proposal into a four-stage model of lexical development that includes hypotheses about lexical content before and after the noun-verb transition, as follows.

1 **Routines and word games.** In the very first phase of lexical development, when expressive vocabularies range from 0–10 words, children tend to produce words that are difficult if not impossible to classify into adult part-of-speech categories, including sound effects for animals and vehicles, social routines like "bye," "hi" and "uh-oh," and names for favorite people. These verbal routines are best viewed as *speech acts* or *performatives*, vocal conventions that children use in familiar and well-structured situations to achieve some social function (see also Dromi, 1987; Lieven & Pine, 1990; Nelson & Luciarello, 1985; Ninio, 1993). In fact, categories like "noun" and "verb" may not be operating at all in this early phase of development (Tomasello, 1992).

2 **Reference.** When expressive vocabulary grows to between 50 and 200 words, the overwhelming majority of words are nominals (broadly defined). Even when we restrict the definition of nominals to common nouns (i.e., names for classes of concrete objects), it is difficult to escape the conclusion that nouns predominate and grow sharply, in absolute numbers and as a proportion of all word types. There are large individual differences along this dimension. For example, Nelson (1973) observed that some children have extraordinarily high proportions of nouns (a propensity called "referential style"), while other children have far fewer nouns and continue to produce routines and word games that defy classification in adult terms (a propensity called "expressive style"). Nevertheless, for most children this period of development revolves primarily around words that establish reference.

3 **Predication.** Verbs and adjectives are very rare in the first two periods of lexical development, comprising between 0 and 5% of all words for most English-speaking children. These categories undergo a notable increase after the first 100 words, in absolute numbers and as a proportion of all word types. It has been argued that this change in vocabulary composition reflects the emergence of predication, i.e., the ability to encode relational meanings. Indeed, it is probably no coincidence that word combinations do not appear before the 50-word point (Nelson, 1973), and are not produced consistently until children achieve vocabularies between 100 and 200 words (Fenson et al., 1994).

4 **Grammar.** Grammatical function words are also extremely rare in the first stages of lexical development. Bates et al. (1994) report that these terms constitute less than 5% of all words in the first and second year of life, and do not display proportional growth until children achieve a total expressive vocabulary between 300 and 500 words. The occurrence of function words prior to the 400-word point appears to be uncorrelated or even negatively correlated with measures of grammatical development after that point, suggesting that the first function words are learned as memorized routines that may bear little relation-

ship to the emergence of productive grammar. By contrast, the proportional growth of function words after the 400-word point coincides and correlates with various indices of grammatical productivity, including mean length of utterance in morphemes and alternative measures of inflectional productivity.

These changes in the composition of vocabulary are hypothesized to reflect universal developments in the logical and conceptual substrates of meaning (O'Grady, 1987). A compelling rationale for at least one part of this story appears in Gentner (1982), who argued that concrete nouns *must* precede verbs in early language development because nouns are easy to grasp (based on concrete objects that "hold still" long enough to support word learning), while verbs reflect relational meanings that are harder to perceive and (more important) defined by a network of meanings that are subject to language-specific and situation-specific variations (e.g., the difference between "give" and "put," which depends on the animate or inanimate nature of the dative object). However, this proposed universal has been challenged recently in cross-linguistic studies of Korean (Gopnik & Choi, 1990, 1995; Choi & Gopnik, 1995) and Chinese (Cheng, 1994; Tardif, 1996; Tardif et al., 1996), with implications for the whole chain of events leading up to grammar that we have just described. In particular, it has been proposed that children who are learning Korean or Chinese do not display the same early bias toward nouns that has been observed in children learning English (e.g., Gopnik & Choi, 1995; Tardif, 1996). These investigators argue that the proposed universal transition from nouns to verbs may be an accidental by-product of English and Anglo-American culture. They also note that most studies reporting an early noun advantage have been based on parental report and/or on data collection in cultural contexts that emphasize object naming. By contrast, data for children learning Korean or Chinese suggest that verbs may be far more common in these languages, even within the very first stages of lexical learning. Indeed, Tardif claims that verbs may actually predominate statistically over nouns in many Chinese children, a direct challenge to the hypothesized universal-stage model described above.

To explain their findings for Korean, Gopnik and Choi point out differences between this language and the others studied to date that could reduce or eliminate the oft-reported noun advantage. For example, Korean is an SOV (subject–object–verb) language, which means that verbs are usually in a salient position. Korean also makes extensive use of both subject and object omission, which means that verbs are often the only content word in sentences spoken to young children. In addition to these differences in linguistic structure, the authors point out some potentially relevant cultural differences between English-speaking and Korean-speaking mothers, revolving around the relative emphasis on object play (with object naming) and other forms of social interaction. Arguments in the same spirit are offered by Tardif for Chinese. Unlike Korean and like English, Chinese is predominantly an SVO language. However, Chinese permits far more word order variation than English, and (like Korean) Chinese also permits extensive omission of both the subject and the object. In addition, Chinese has no grammatical inflections of any kind that might be used to distinguish between nouns and verbs, a fact which may make it easier for children to cross the boundary between adult form classes at an early age.

We believe that Italian provides a good test case for the early onset of verbs. Fo. example, although Italian is an SVO language, it permits extensive word order variation. It is also a pro-drop language in which subjects are omitted around 70% of the time in informal conversation (Bates, 1976). Because of these characteristics, verbs are often located in sentence-initial or sentence-final positions that are easy for children to perceive, a situation analogous to the one described for Korean and Chinese. Unlike these two languages, however, Italian has an extremely rich system of verb morphology, and verb agreement plays a crucial role in conveying basic sentence relations. Indeed, current evidence suggests that Italian children are sensitive to verb agreement from a very early age, in both comprehension and production (Devescovi et al., 1998; Pizzuto & Caselli, 1992, 1993). Taken together, these features of Italian would appear to provide a solid basis for cross-language variation in verb onset and verb growth.

A second goal of the present study is to provide a cross-linguistic test of the relationship between vocabulary size and growth of grammatical function words (Bates & Goodman, 1997; Bates & Goodman, this volume; Bates et al., 1994; Fenson et al., 1994; Marchman & Bates, 1994). Prior studies of English have noted a proportional increase in number of function words described above for children with vocabularies over 400 words, together with a tight nonlinear correlation between vocabulary size and sentence complexity. Bates and Goodman argue that the strong interdependence of grammar and the lexicon during this period of development provides evidence in favor of lexicalist theories in which the development of vocabulary and grammar are based on common mechanisms, and against theories in which grammar is an autonomous module that is structurally and developmentally separate from the lexicon. If this argument is correct, then such interdependence ought to be observed across all natural languages.

Thanks in large measure to pioneering research by Dan Slobin and his international network of collaborators (Slobin (ed.), 1985–1997; Slobin, this volume), there is now an ample cross-linguistic literature on early grammatical development, including variations and universals in the acquisition of function words. For example, several projects have uncovered universal patterns in the acquisition of locatives (including locative markers on nouns, and locative prepositions, e.g., Johnston, 1985). These universals appear to reflect universal cognitive constraints (e.g., locatives that express complex spatial relations like "in front of" and "behind" emerge later than locatives that encode simpler relations like "in" and "on"). However, more recent studies of locatives in English and Korean (Choi & Bowerman, 1991; McDonough et al., 1997) have shown that linguistic input can influence the order in which some locative prepositions are acquired, and affect the way that space is carved up for linguistic expression. Similar cross-linguistic findings have been reported for linguistic terms that mark the relations between space and time (Weist et al., 1997) and the distinction between count and mass nouns (Gathercole & Min, 1997; Imai & Gentner, 1997). In this chapter, we will investigate the emergence of grammatical function words in relation to overall lexical size, and we will look at similarities and differences between English and Italian in the order of emergence of specific function words.

All of the results presented below are based on English and Italian versions of a parental report instrument called the MacArthur Communicative Development Inventory, or CDI. The CDI contains two separate scales: the Words and Gestures Scale, designed to measure word comprehension, word production, and gesture between 8 and 16 months, and the Words and Phrases Scale, used to assess word production and various aspects of grammar between 16 and 30 months. The 8–30-month data for Italian come from norms collected by Caselli & Casadio (1995); the corresponding American data are taken from the CDI norming study by Fenson et al. (1993; see also Fenson et al., 1994). These large data sets offer a unique opportunity to compare aspects of vocabulary composition in unusually large samples of English- and Italian-speaking children, controlling for age and for changes in vocabulary size. Of course there are clear limitations on our ability to investigate the details of grammar using a parental report technique. Such procedures will never replace traditional free speech and/or experimental measures in advancing our knowledge of lexical and grammatical development. Nevertheless, we can learn something about the relative onset and growth of adult word classes (nouns, verbs, adjectives, function words), providing some working hypotheses for more focused observational and experimental studies.

One might also argue that comparisons based on the CDI provide an unfair test of cross-linguistic differences. In particular, because the CDI was originally developed for English, adaptations of that instrument to other languages may be strongly biased toward English. There are two reasons why we believe that this criticism does not apply here. First, all non-English adaptations of the CDI are true adaptations, not translations of the English scales. Items are drawn from the existing literature on early development in that language, selected to reflect the lexical and grammatical forms that are known to appear in the relevant windows of development (Bottari et al., 1993; Cipriani et al., 1993; see also Jackson-Maldonado et al., 1993). They are also pre-tested with parents who are native speakers of the language, seeking their advice about items that should be added or dropped. Second, there is a unique historical relationship between the English and Italian versions of the CDI. Starting with a joint study in the 1970s of English and Italian infants between 9 and 13 months (Bates et al., 1979), the respective English and Italian instruments have been developed in parallel, in a series of joint and independent projects across a 20-year period. Hence the English version did not precede the Italian one in any relevant sense.

We will summarize results from two separate cross-linguistic studies of lexical development: the infant study from 8–16 months, using the Words and Gestures Scale (from Caselli et al., 1995), and the toddler study from 18–30 months, using the Words and Phrases Scale (from Caselli et al., 1999). For the sake of economy, the reader is referred to those two papers for methodological and statistical details.

Method

Participants

The two English samples included 659 infants between 8 and 16 months of age, and, 1,001 children between 18 and 30 months (for the Words & Phrases Scale), all participants in the three-city norming study for the American version of the MacArthur CDI (Fenson et al., 1994). The two Italian samples included 195 infants between 8 and 16 months, and 386 children between 18 and 30 months, taken from the norming samples for the Italian version of the CDI (Caselli & Casadio, 1995). There were approximately equal numbers of males and females within each age level. In both language communities, these samples represent families across the socioeconomic spectrum, but are disproportionately weighted toward the top. Based on a parental questionnaire about family and medical history, we excluded children with serious medical problems, neurological deficits, and/or mental retardation, as well as children with significant exposure to languages other than English or Italian.

Materials

In both languages, the CDI: Words & Gestures Scale (which we will refer to here as the Infant Scale) is composed of two sections. Part I is a checklist of 396 words. Next to each word, the parent is asked to indicate if the child (a) understands that word, and (b) understands and produces that word. Part II is a checklist of 63 communicative and/or symbolic gestures that also develop in this age range; these results will not be considered here. The Words & Phrases Scale (hence for the Toddler Scale) contains 680 words in the English version, 670 words in the Italian version (the number of content words is the same on both scales; the 10-word difference comes entirely from the list of grammatical function words, due primarily to language-specific differences in the prepositions, articles, and quantifiers that are acquired early in each language). Part II of the Toddler Scale assesses various aspects of grammatical development, and will not be considered here. The checklists at both age levels are organized into semantic categories: sound effects (e.g., "moo," "vroom"), animal names, vehicle names, toys, food items, articles of clothing, body parts, furniture, household objects, outside things and place to go, people (including proper nouns), rountines and games (e.g., "peekaboo"), verbs (called "action words" on the CDI form), words for time, adjectives (called "descriptive words" on the CDI form), pronouns, question words, prepositions, auxiliaries, modals, articles, and quantifiers. All forms are presented in their "citation form" (e.g., verbs are listed as stems).

Data reduction

In order to test the four-stage model described above, proportion scores were calculated for the following groups of words (following Bates et al., 1994): (1) Nominals, broadly defined to include common nouns, proper nouns, places to go, and sound effects that are often used by young children to refer to animals and objects; (2) Common nouns, more stringently defined to include only words from the adult language that stand for concrete objects (animal names, vehicles, toys, food and drink, clothing, body parts, furniture and rooms, small household objects); this count excludes names for people, sound effects, and "places to go"; (3) Proper nouns and terms for people; (4) Sound effects (e.g., "vroom," "meow"); (5) Routines (a heterogeneous category that includes social words like "hi" and "bye," daily routines or events like "breakfast" or "nap"), and familiar commands like "don't"; (6) Verbs; (7) Adjectives; (8) Grammatical function words.

All of these classifications were carried out from the point of view of adult part-of-speech categories. We do not and should not assume that these categories are somewhere in the mind of the child. Rather, we treat adult categories like noun and verb as independent variables, a short-hand way of referring to semantic, grammatical, and/or phonological differences in the input to which small children are exposed. To the extent that children treat nouns differently from verbs in the first stages of lexical development, we may infer that they have been influenced by these differences in their linguistic input. That is, there is something "in the child" that responds differently to nouns and verbs, reflecting characteristics that distinguish nouns from verbs (and from adjectives and function words) in the adult language.

Results

Results are based on between-subject analyses of variance, grouping children by language, age, and/or vocabulary level. Main effects and interactions are reported as significant if they fall below an alpha level of $p < .05$. For the sake of economy, full statistical details have been eliminated here; the reader can find them in Caselli et al. (1995) for the Infant Scale, and Caselli et al. (1999) for the Toddler Scale.

Age-related changes in vocabulary size

In word comprehension from 8–16 months, there were no significant differences between the English and Italian samples. In word production, the Italian group lagged slightly but significantly behind the larger American sample at both age levels (8–16 months; 18–30 months). Because of these differences, all of the word type analyses presented below (for both production and comprehension) are based on vocabulary size rather than age. Hence children in the two languages are "vocabulary matched." Before we consider the word type analyses, let us look briefly at the age-based data for overall vocabulary development within each language.

Figure 7.1 compares average growth within each language on the Infant Scale, for word comprehension and production, respectively. Collapsed over languages, the comprehension means started around 36 words at 8 months and reached a mean of 191 words at 16 months. The production means were (not surprisingly) far behind the means for comprehension, hovering near zero for both languages at 8 months, reaching an average of around 40 words by 16 months. Individual differences around these means were huge, in both languages and in both modalities. For example, the average number of words comprehended (collapsed over age) was 105 words (105 for English, 107 for Italian), with a range from 0 (no words at all) to 396 (all of the words on the list!).

Figure 7.2 compares rates of growth for English and Italian children on the Toddler Scale, for expressive vocabulary only. Although English children were (again) slightly ahead of their Italian counterparts, individual differences were very large in both languages. For example, the average 24-month-old was reported to produce around 300 words in both languages. However, the range in number of words produced at 24 months varied from under 50 to over 600, again in both languages.

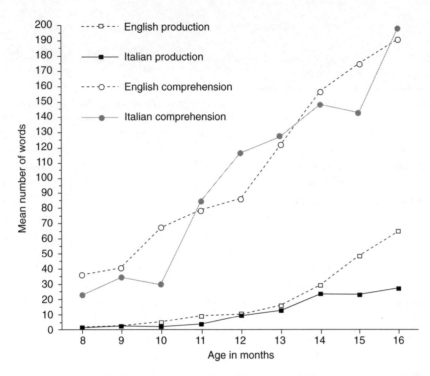

Figure 7.1   Growth of comprehension & production vocabulary from 8–16 months.

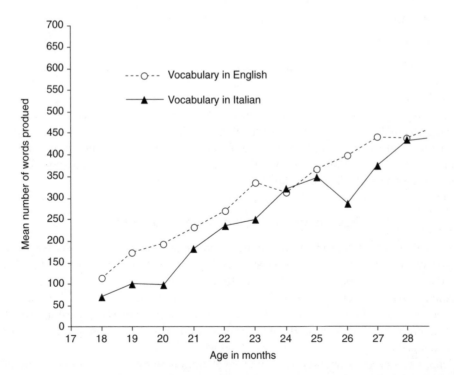

Figure 7.2   Vocabulary size as a function of age from 18–30 months in English & Italian children.

Table 7.1   Composition of production vocabulary from 18–30 months as a function of language and vocabulary size

Variable	Language	Number of words in production vocabulary					
		1–5	6–10	11–20	21–50	>50	Total
% Nominals	English	80.4	75.4	70.7	72.8	73.6	75.5
	Italian	91.0	84.5	74.7	70.4	72.6	82.0
% Common nouns	English	16.4	22.9	32.9	44.5	54.1	30.2
	Italian	20.6	28.1	31.4	36.5	46.2	28.8
% People	English	32.3	24.8	16.5	10.7	6.5	21.1
	Italian	35.1	35.4	19.6	16.9	11.1	27.6
% Sound effects	English	30.7	27.1	20.4	15.5	7.7	22.7
	Italian	35.3	21.0	23.6	16.5	11.8	25.3
% Routines	English	14.2	19.5	18.7	15.0	9.1	15.5
	Italian	7.8	13.3	20.7	20.1	16.4	13.8
% Verbs	English	0.5	1.1	2.1	2.7	6.8	2.1
	Italian	1.3	0.7	2.8	4.1	4.5	2.3
% Adjectives	English	1.7	0.5	2.7	4.3	4.8	2.5
	Italian	0.0	0.4	0.5	1.0	2.1	0.5
% Predicates	English	2.2	1.5	4.8	7.0	11.6	4.6
(Verb + Adj)	Italian	1.3	1.0	3.3	6.0	6.6	2.8
% Function words	English	3.2	3.6	5.8	5.2	5.4	4.4
	Italian	0.0	1.1	1.3	3.5	4.0	1.4

For the remainder of this chapter, we turn away from analyses over age to analyses in which children are grouped by vocabulary size, in search of possible cross-linguistic differences in the onset and growth of different word types as a function of language level. We start with findings on the Infant Scale (both production and comprehension) and end with results for the Toddler Scale (vocabulary production only).

Expressive vocabulary from 8–16 months

For analyses of word production, children were divided into six groups based on their total vocabulary size: (1) zero words, (2) 1–5 words, (3) 6–10 words, (4) 11–20 words, (5) 21–50 words, and (6) more than 50 words (see Caselli et al., 1995, for details). Table 7.1 reports mean proportion scores in production for each vocabulary level, for each language. These data will give us our answer regarding possible cross-linguistic differences in the relative onset and growth of nouns, verbs and other word types.

For expressive vocabulary, the category Nominals (broadly defined) accounted for 75.5% of total production vocabulary in the English sample, compared with 82% in Italian. So, contrary to predictions based on verb salience, there was actually a slight

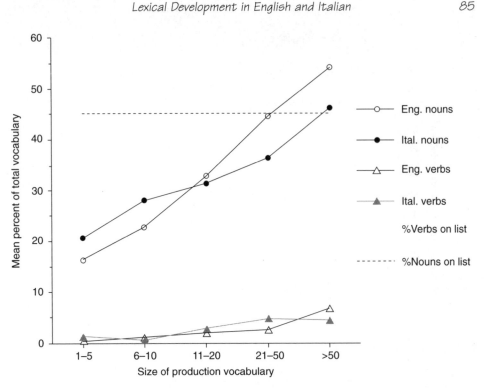

Figure 7.3   Percent nouns vs. verbs in production vocabulary for Italian vs. English children from 8–16 months.

advantage for nominals in the Italian group, reflected in a significant main effect of language. Further analyses showed that growth patterns for nominals were the same in English and Italian.

When analyses were carried out over the more restricted category of Common Nouns, we found a large main effect of vocabulary level, but no effect of language and no interaction. Hence the small nominal advantage for Italians disappeared with a stricter definition of "noun." In both languages, common nouns occupied a much smaller proportion of total expressive vocabulary than nominals more broadly defined: an average of 30.2% for English (compared with 75.5% for all nominals), and 28.8% for Italian (compared with 82% for all nominals). However, common nouns also grow proportionally as the lexicon expands, from 17.4% in children with only 1–5 words, to 52.7% in children with more than 50 words. In this respect, our results for Italian exactly mirror previous reports for English on the disproportionate representation and growth of object names in the first phases of lexical development (Bates et al., 1994). Figure 7.3 illustrates these developmental changes in the common-noun category, for each language. The flat dotted line around 45% is included to illustrate the proportion of the entire checklist composed of common nouns. As discussed by Bates et al. (1994), this line indicates the "checklist baseline." If acquisition of nouns were a constant or random process across this period of development, with no change in noun bias, then common-noun proportion scores should hover around 45% at every level of develop-

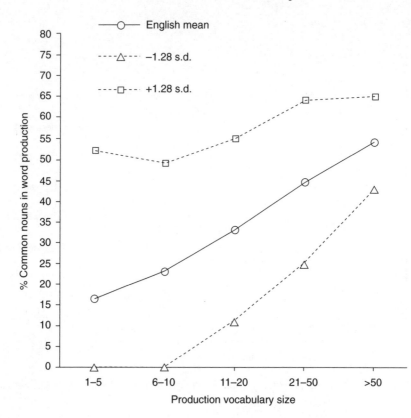

Figure 7.4a   Referential style (percent common nouns) in word production for English children 8–16 months.

ment, for both languages. Obviously this was not the case. In both groups, common nouns were underrepresented in the early stages but increased in importance with vocabulary growth.

We also looked at individual variation around the mean for common-noun scores, to see whether Italian children display the same dimension of variation in "nouniness" (also called "referential style") that has been described previously for English (Bates et al., 1988; Bates et al., 1994; Nelson, 1973). Figure 7.4a presents the mean percent common-noun scores at each vocabulary level for English, together with scores for children who are 1.28 standard deviations above and below the mean (parametric values that approximate the top and bottom 10th percentiles – Bates et al., 1994); figure 7.4b presents the corresponding values for Italian. It is clear from these figures that the same developmental and stylistic factors are at work in both languages. That is, nouns increase in importance across this developmental range for both groups, but there is also considerable variation in "nouniness" within each group.

We turn now to the critical comparison between nouns and verbs. As Table 7.1 shows, verbs occupied a very small proportion of total expressive vocabulary in both languages: 2.06% for English and 2.27% for Italian. In the analysis of variance for this category, there was no significant main effect of language, and no significant

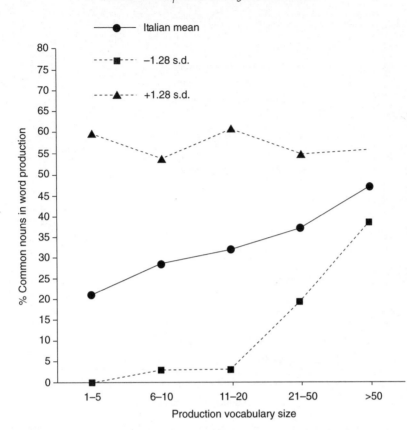

Figure 7.4b Referential style (percent common nouns) in Italian children from 8–16 months.

interaction. *In other words, we do not find the predicted "verb advantage" for Italians.* But there was a large main effect of vocabulary size, reflecting a gradual increase in the contribution of verbs to total vocabulary, from less than 1% in children with 1–5 words to 6.4% in children with more than 50 words. This developmental change is illustrated in figure 7.3 for both languages, to facilitate comparison between verbs and common nouns.

Before we accept the conclusion that nouns develop before verbs in both English and Italian, we need to consider a possible confound: The list as a whole contains far fewer verbs (14% of all items) than common nouns (45% of all items). To determine whether this difference in the absolute number of nouns and verbs was responsible for our findings, wee also carried out an analysis of the percentage of all noun and verb *opportunities* that were checked by parents of children at each vocabulary level. That is, we calculated a "noun opportunity score" (dividing the common nouns reported for each child by 182, the total number of common nouns provided on the list) and a "verb opportunity score" (dividing the verbs reported for each child by 55, the total number of verbs provided on the list). These scores were analyzed in a multivariate analysis of variance comparing noun vs. verb opportunity scores (hereafter Word Type) as a function of language and vocabulary level. Results of this analysis are illustrated in

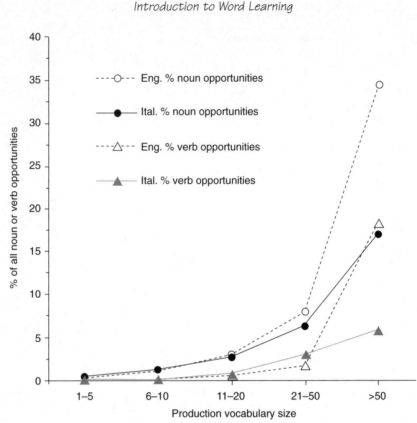

Figure 7.5 Percent of noun vs. verb opportunities acquired in expressive vocabulary from 8–16 months in English & Italian children.

figure 7.5. For our purposes here, the critical finding is this: the common-noun category "fills up" significantly faster than verb category in both language groups, even though this analysis has equated the two word types for the number of items available on the checklist.

As nouns and verbs go up, what comes down? Table 7.1 includes all language-by-vocabulary-level scores for proper nouns and names for people. Analysis of variance revealed a significant *decrease* in proper-noun proportion scores as a function of vocabulary level, from an average of 33% in children with 1–5 words, to 7% in children with more than 50 words. However, this category also differed significantly over languages, reflecting more production of names for people in the Italian sample. This means that the slight "nominal advantage" for Italian children was coming not from common nouns, but from a proportionally higher user of proper nouns – a finding that may reflect cultural differences in the number and proximity of grandparents and other family members (more on this below).

Sound effects are another category that decreases proportionally as total vocabulary grows. There was no language difference in the analysis of sound effects, nor was there a significant interaction, but there was a significant main effect of vocabulary level. For children with 1–5 words, the sound effect category constitutes a full 32% of total vocabulary, compared with 8.5% in children with more than 50 words. This confirms the oft-reported finding that sound effects are (like proper names) among the first nominals produced by one-year-old children. However, these items decrease in importance as "true" common nouns take off – a finding that holds for both language groups.

Routines like "bye" and "pattycake" also decrease in relative size as vocabulary expands. Indeed, just as proper nouns and sound effects constitute the "starter set" within the nominal category, these routines can be viewed as a "starter set" in the category of non-nominals. Analysis of variance revealed a significant main effect of vocabulary level, no main effect of language, but a reliable albeit small interaction between language and vocabulary size. In both language groups, the development of routines is characterized by an inverted U-shaped function, with an initial increase in routines followed by a decline. However, this decline in the contribution of social routines to total vocabulary is more protracted for Italian. This result may also reflect cultural differences in adult–child interaction, i.e., a tendency to "show off" to the relatively large number of aunts, uncles, and cousins that fill the lives of small Italian children.

We end these analyses of word production with the heterogeneous category of grammatical function words, known to be relatively rare in the first stages of language learning. As Table 7.1 shows, grammatical function words constitute 4.4% of total vocabulary for 8–16-month-old children acquiring English, compared with 1.37% for children acquiring Italian. Since function words constitute approximately 9% of the items on each checklist, this means that function words are indeed underrepresented in the vocabularies of 8–16-month-old English and Italian children. In other words, this result cannot be viewed as an artifact of the list itself. Analyses reveal no proportional growth in the function word category across this period of development. On average, score increase slightly from 2.4% in children with only 1–5 words, up to 5.2% in children with more than 50 words. As Bates, Marchman et al. (1994) have pointed out for English, the early use of function words bears no predictive relationship to the subsequent emergence of grammar. These first function words are restricted almost entirely to words that can be used alone in single-word commands and routines (e.g., "Mine!"). The small cross-linguistic difference favoring English comes from a handful of "stand-alone" items like these.

To summarize so far, there are far more similarities than differences in the composition of early productive vocabulary in English- and Italian-speaking children. Above all, there is no evidence whatsoever for an Italian advantage in verbs (narrowly defined) or non-nominals (broadly defined). Instead, both groups provide evidence for a developmental sequence from reference to predication, reflected in the early onset and growth of nouns and the paucity of verbs and other predicates. The few differences that we do see have more to do with culture than the structure of each language (i.e., more names for people and social routines in Italian).

Receptive vocabulary from 8–16 months

Previous studies comparing the early stages of comprehension and production have concluded that verbs play a much larger role in early receptive language (Bates et al.,

Table 7.2 Composition of receptive vocabulary from 8–16 months as a function of language and vocabulary size

Variable	Language	Number of words in receptive vocabulary						
		1–20	21–50	51–100	101–150	151–200	>200	Total
% Nominals	English	60.4	62.6	61.2	63.2	61.4	61.8	61.8
	Italian	66.8	67.0	63.7	64.2	60.4	60.7	63.8
% Common	English	22.0	37.2	44.2	48.6	47.5	48.4	41.5
nouns	Italian	31.7	44.5	47.0	49.2	47.8	48.2	45.2
% People	English	31.5	14.0	8.2	5.4	4.7	4.1	11.1
	Italian	29.4	14.8	8.6	6.4	4.8	4.0	10.9
% Sound effects	English	6.2	8.8	5.2	4.8	4.3	3.7	5.6
	Italian	5.1	7.0	5.4	4.5	3.7	3.5	4.9
% Routines	English	27.3	18.6	13.1	9.8	8.6	6.6	14.1
	Italian	25.2	18.7	12.5	9.9	8.4	6.4	13.3
% Verbs	English	6.8	10.0	14.6	15.0	16.6	16.0	13.2
	Italian	6.9	10.8	17.6	17.7	20.0	17.5	15.3
% Adjectives	English	2.8	5.2	6.7	6.9	7.2	7.8	6.1
	Italian	0.5	1.6	3.0	4.4	5.5	6.5	3.6
% Predicates	English	9.7	15.2	21.3	21.9	23.9	23.8	19.3
(Verb + Adj)	Italian	7.4	12.4	20.6	22.1	25.5	24.1	19.0
% Function	English	2.5	3.6	4.1	4.9	5.8	7.1	4.5
words	Italian	0.6	1.9	3.2	3.5	5.4	8.0	3.7

1979; Benedict, 1979; Goldin-Meadow et al., 1976). Hence, if there is a verb advantage in reports of word comprehension, we may be in a position to see cross-linguistic differences that did not emerge in our data on word production.

For analyses of word comprehension, children were divided into six groups based on vocabulary size, as follows: (1) 0–20 words, (2) 21–50 words, (3) 51–100 words, (4) 101–150 words, (5) 151–200 words, and (6) more than 200 words. Table 7.2 presents the nine proportion scores for word comprehension, for each of the language- and vocabulary-level groups in this 2 by 6 design. For the sake of economy, we will restrict our discussion to the critical comparison between common nouns and verbs.

For common nouns, proportion scores were actually larger for comprehension than they were for production, averaging 41.5% for English (compared with 30.2% in production) and 45.2% for Italian (compared with 28.2% in production). Analysis of variance on the common-noun scores in comprehension revealed a significant main effect of language, reflecting slightly larger common-noun proportion scores for Italians (again, the opposite of predictions based on verb salience). There was also a significant main effect of vocabulary size, and a small but reliable interaction. Figure 7.6 shows that common nouns make up an increasing proportion of total receptive vocabulary

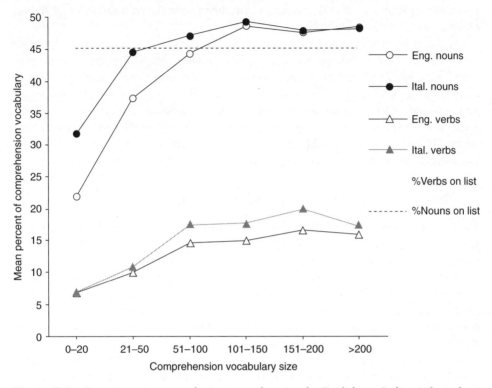

Figure 7.6 Percent nouns vs. verbs in comprehension for English vs. Italian infants from 8–16 months.

across this period of development, from 24.2% in children with fewer than 20 words to 48.3% in children with between 100 and 150 words (common-noun proportion scores hold steady after this point). The initial rise in common nouns starts somewhat earlier for children acquiring Italian, but the basic pattern is the same. Note also that the proportion of common nouns in comprehension actually "overshoots" the checklist ceiling (i.e., the dotted line indicated the 45% contribution of common nouns to the checklist as a whole). In other words, common nouns are overrepresented in children who understand between 50 and 200 words, similar to our findings for word production.

The developmental data for verbs in comprehension are also illustrated in figure 7.6 (plotted separately for each language), for comparison with comprehension of common nouns. Statistical analyses showed that verbs do increase markedly across this range of development. In fact (in contrast with our findings for production), verb proportion scores rise above the checklist baseline for children with more than 50 words in their receptive vocabulary. It is also clear from figure 7.6 that Italians are ahead by 1–2 percentage points in verb comprehension across this period of development, a small but significant effect. Hence we do find a minuscule version of the predicted Italian advantage on verbs in our data for comprehension, a difference that could be explained by two or three salient words (see item analyses below). However, the most important result here is that it is clear that nouns outnumber verbs for both English and Italian children, even in comprehension.

We conclude that the data for comprehension and production both provide evidence for a universal sequence from nouns to verbs and adjectives. This pattern holds up in both languages, and it holds up across modalities (even though verbs and adjectives do emerge earlier and grow faster in comprehension than production). The few cross-linguistic differences that we do find in vocabulary composition always involve differences of 1–3 percentage points – a difference that could be contributed by a few salient items. This brings us to a qualitative analysis of the first words acquired within each language, in production and in comprehension, from 8–16 months.

Item analyses for the Infant Scale

Table 7.3 presents the first 50 words in the expressive vocabularies of American and Italian children, where "first acquired" is defined in terms of the percentage of children in the sample who were reported to produce that word. Words are listed in order of acquisition within each language group. Within each list, words that would qualify as non-nominals according to the broad criteria used by Gopnik and Choi are marked with an asterisk (regardless of how those words were classified on the CDI). Those non-nominals that qualify as lexical verbs in the adult language are also marked with an asterisk, and presented in capital letters.

This table shows that lexical verbs do not appear at all among the first ten words produced by English or Italian children. And if we adopt the very broad criteria proposed by Gopnik and Choi, treating all non-nominals as verbs, then we actually find a small *disadvantage* in the non-nominal category for Italians – although this difference probably has more to do with the salience of words for people in the Italian culture (i.e., the first 10 words for Italian include "mommy," "daddy," "grandma" and "grandpa," while the first 10 words for English are restricted to "mommy" and "daddy"). However, this does not mean that children begin their lexical careers by naming objects. Instead, most of the items in the Top Ten for English and/or Italian are routines, sound effects, and names for people instead of common nouns. Moving further down the list, we find absolutely no lexical verbs among the first 50 words for English children. In Italian, the corresponding list contains exactly one lexical verb "*DARE" ("to give"). This word was used by only 5.1% of the sample (10 children out of 195). Hence we may conclude that lexical verbs are sorely lacking in the first stages of language development, in both languages.

In the same spirit, Table 7.4 presents the first 50 words reported for comprehension, in English and Italian. Although we do find some lexical verbs in this list, results complement and confirm what we have already learned from earlier analyses: nouns predominate over verbs in the first 50 words for each language, although verb proportions are somewhat higher in comprehension than they were in production.

To summarize so far, this cross-linguistic comparison of first words supports the following conclusions.

1   The first 5–10 words in each language contain sound effects, routines, and names for people, with a few common nouns scattered in. These are the very

Table 7.3 First 50 words in production for English vs. Italian infants

Rank	English		Italian		
	Word	% sample	Word	Translation	% sample
1.	daddy	54.9	mamma	mommy	49.7
2.	mommy	52.9	papa	daddy	46.7
3.	*bye	43.1	bau-bau	(dog sound)	41.5
4.	*hi	39.3	*pappa	(food/mealtime)	36.9
5.	*uh-oh	35.5	nonna	grandma	32.8
6.	baa-baa	31.9	brum-brum	(vehicle sound)	28.7
7.	ball	30.9	acqua	water	27.2
8.	dog	30.6	nonno	grandpa	23.1
9.	*no	28.5	*nanna	(sleep/bedtime)	21.5
10.	bottle	25.2	*no	no	21.5
11.	woof	24.9	miao	(cat sound)	21.0
12.	baby	24.6	*grazie	thanks	20.5
13.	*yum-yum	24.1	*ciao	hi/bye	17.9
14.	grr	23.5	*cuccu-settete	(hiding game)	16.9
15.	kitty	21.8	palla	ball	16.4
16.	vroom	20.2	muuh	(cow sound)	15.9
17.	book	19.9	*non c'è più	(is no more)	14.9
18.	bird	19.6	scarpe	shoes	14.4
19.	duck	18.8	coccode	(rooster sound)	13.8
20.	balloon	18.4	beh-beh	(sheep sound)	12.8
21.	cat	18.2	(child's own name)	–	12.8
22.	*night-night	17.1	ih-oh	(donkey sound)	12.8
23.	quack	17.0	bimbo	child	12.3
24.	shoe	17.0	*pronto	(hello on phone)	11.8
25.	meow	16.6	*bum	boom	11.3
26.	banana	16.3	grr	(lion sound)	10.8
27.	*hot	16.0	qua-qua	(duck sound)	10.8
28.	juice	15.4	(babysitter's name)	–	10.3
29.	eye	14.8	cip-cip	(bird sound)	10.3
30.	grandma	14.3	*si	yes	10.3
31.	moo	14.2	tuttu	(train sound)	10.3
32.	*thank-you	14.0	*zitto	hush/quiet	10.3
33.	*up	14.0	*(fare) popo/pipi	(make) pee/poo	9.7
34.	cookie	13.5	clop-clop	(horse sound)	9.2
35.	nose	13.5	*bua	hurt/owie	8.7
36.	*ouch	13.4	*(dare) toto	(give) spanking	8.2
37.	cracker	12.3	*mio	my/mine	8.2
38.	grandpa	12.3	pane	bread	8.2
39.	*shh	12.0	biscotto	cookie	7.7
40.	bath	11.8	cane	dog	7.2
41.	keys	11.8	ciuccio	pacifier	7.2
42.	bubbles	11.4	zio	uncle	7.2
43.	*down	11.4	latte	milk	6.7
44.	car	11.2	orologio	watch/clock	6.7
45.	*yes	11.0	zia	aunt	6.2
46.	cheese	10.9	banana	banana	5.6
47.	bear	10.7	*basta	enough/stop	5.6
48.	*hello	10.6	bambola	doll	5.1
49.	fish	10.4	***DARE**	to give	5.1
50.	*allgone	10.3	gatto	cat	5.1
51.	hat	10.3	mela	apple	5.1

* non-nominal according to Gopnik & Choi; bold = verb

Table 7.4 First 50 words in comprehension from 8–16 months for English vs. Italian infants

Rank	English		Italian		
	Word	% sample	Word	Translation	% sample
1.	mommy	95.0	mamma	mommy	91.3
2.	daddy	93.5	papa	daddy	88.2
3.	*bye	88.6	(child's own name)	–	82.6
4.	*no	86.3	*ciao	hi/bye	82.6
5.	*peekaboo	84.3	*pappa	(food/mealtime)	81.1
6.	bath	76.2	*cuccu-settete	(hiding game)	81.0
7.	ball	75.0	acqua	water	79.0
8.	bottle	75.0	*no	no	77.9
9.	*hi	74.0	palla	ball	75.9
10.	*allgone	71.9	bau-bau	(dog sound) ·	75.4
11.	dog	70.8	nonna	grandma	75.4
12.	book	68.7	cane	dog	74.9
13.	*night-night	68.5	biberon	bottle	71.8
14.	diaper	67.4	telefono	telephone	70.3
15.	*KISS	66.2	*bravo	good	67.7
16.	*uh-oh	65.1	nonno	grandpa	66.7
17.	*pattycake	62.6	scarpe	shoes	66.2
18.	juice	61.9	biscotto	cookie	65.6
19.	shoe	61.9	*BERE	to drink	65.1
20.	baby	61.6	miao	(cat sound)	64.6
21.	grandma	61.3	latte	milk	64.1
22.	outside	61.0	*nanna	(sleep/bedtime)	63.6
23.	car	60.1	mano	hand	63.1
24.	*EAT	59.7	*basta	(enough/stop)	62.6
25.	kitty	58.8	*pane	bread	62.6
26.	*DRINK	58.1	*(fare) bagno	(have/do) bath	62.1
27.	keys	56.3	*gatto	cat	62.1
28.	*DON'T	55.8	bimbo	child	60.5
29.	comb	55.4	*DARE	to give	59.5
30.	nose	55.4	*MANGIARE	to eat	59.5
31.	*HUG	54.9	piede	foot	59.0
32.	banana	54.4	*BACIARE	to kiss	59.0
33.	cookie	54.2	*BALLARE	to dance	59.0
34.	bathtub	53.2	automobile	car	57.9
35.	balloon	52.9	*non c'è più	(is no more)	56.9
36.	milk	52.9	panolino	diaper	56.9
37.	cat	52.7	*si	yes	56.9
38.	cracker	52.7	bavaglino	bib	56.4
39.	telephone	52.6	capelli	hair	56.4
40.	*yes	52.6	bocca	mouth	55.9
41.	cheerios	51.4	bicchiere	glass	54.9
42.	bird	50.4	uccellino	bird	54.4
43.	*yum-yum	50.4	passegino	stroller	53.8
44.	grandpa	50.1	*pronto	(hello on phone)	53.3
45.	woof	49.5	ciuccio	pacifier	51.3
46.	*DANCE	49.3	letto	bed	51.3
47.	baa-baa	49.0	naso	nose	50.3
48.	meow	48.3	televisione	television	49.7
49.	*LOOK	48.2	*ANDARE	to go	49.2
50.	mouth	48.2	cucchiaio	spoon	49.2
51.			*PETTINARE	to comb	49.2
52.			*SALUTARE	to greet	49.2

items that are hardest to classify in adult part-of-speech categories. In other words, the very first words produced by English and Italian children are *neither* nouns *nor* verbs.

2 When we expand our developmental window to include the first 50 words, the overwhelming majority are nominals (broadly defined); even when we restrict the definition of nominals to common nouns (i.e., names for classes of concrete objects), we cannot escape the conclusion that nouns predominate and grow sharply (in proportion to other items) across the first stages of lexical development, for both English and Italian, in both comprehension and production.

3 Verbs emerge earlier and grow faster in comprehension than they do in production, but they are still outnumbered by common nouns at every point across this period, in both English and Italian.

4 Grammatical function words are also very rare among the first 50–100 words acquired by English and Italian children, in both comprehension and production.

For reasons discussed in the introduction, verbs ought to be far more salient for Italian children. Had we seen any differences between English and Italian children in the emergence and growth of major lexical categories, we would be justified in concluding that children are influenced by differences in the relative salience of these categories in their respective input languages. Instead, we find a common sequence in both languages, in both modalities: from social words, to nouns, to verbs, to function words. The robustness of this sequence despite striking cross-linguistic differences in the input lead us to propose that this sequence may be a developmental universal. However, we should also note that the children studied here are considerably younger than the children studied by Gopnik and Choi in Korean, and by Tardif in Chinese. Hence a fairer test of cross-language differences in vocabulary composition might require a investigation of the next few stages of development, from 18–30 months. Data for older infants from Caselli et al. (1999) provides such a test for English and Italian.

Expressive vocabulary growth in toddlers (from Caselli et al., 1999)

For analyses of vocabulary composition, the 18–30-month-old children were divided into eight groups based on their total vocabulary size (following Bates et al., 1994): (1) 1–50 words, (2) 51–100 words, (3) 101–200 words, (4) 201–300 words, (5) 301–400 words, (6) 401–500 words, (7) 501–600 words, and (8) more than 600 words. Figure 6.7a illustrates changes as a function of vocabulary level in English, for percent common nouns, percent predicates, percent closed-class words, and percent social terms. Figure 7.7b illustrates the corresponding data for children acquiring Italian. The flat dotted lines in both figures (and those that follow) indicate the checklist ceiling for each category, i.e., absolute proportion of words from that category on the checklist as a whole. If development proceeded evenly across all word classes, with words added in accordance with their representation on the checklist as a whole, then the developmental functions would be flat (hovering around 40% for common nouns, 24% for verbs and adjectives, and so forth). It is obvious from visual inspection of figures 7.7a–b that this is not the case.

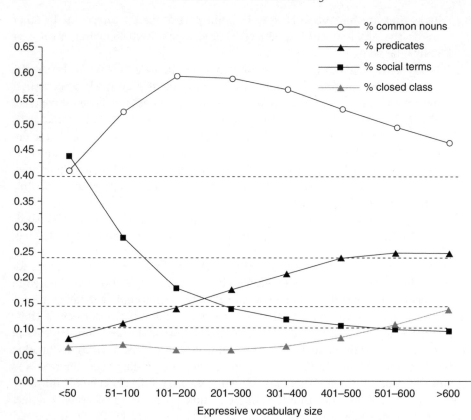

Figure 7.7a Vocabulary composition for English children from 18–30 months.

A quick comparison of figures 7.7a and 7.7b indicates that the four variables show similar overall patterns of growth across vocabulary levels in English and Italian. The most noteworthy similarities are the preponderance of common nouns, the slow growth of predicates (which do not outnumber nouns at any point), the rarity of closed-class words in early vocabularies, and the sharp nonlinear drop in social-word proportion scores after the earliest level. Despite these global similarities, figures 7.7a–b suggest that there may be subtle differences in the shape of these functions. To explore these differences, five separate 2 (Language) by 8 (Vocabulary Level) analyses of variance were conducted, on proportion scores for common nouns, predicates (verbs and adjectives combined), closed-class words, and social words, respectively. We also conducted a separate analysis on verbs alone, to provide the clearest possible test of the prediction that verbs will develop earlier in Italian. When significant language by level interactions appear, simple-effects analyses (one-way analyses of variance by language) were carried out at each vocabulary level, to uncover the locus of the interaction. (For further statistical details, see Caselli et al., 1999.)

The common-noun analysis yielded significant main effects of vocabulary level and language, and a significant language by vocabulary level interaction. This interaction is illustrated in figure 7.8, which shows that proportional growth in the common-noun

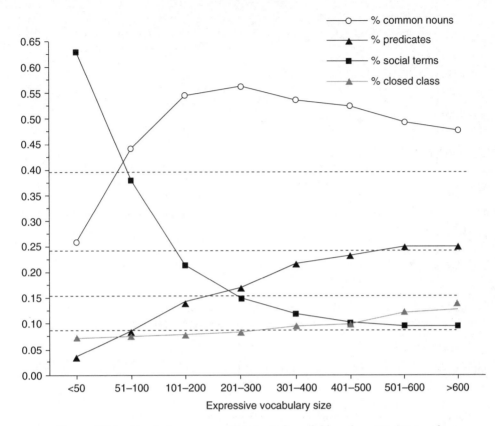

Figure 7.7b Vocabulary composition for Italian children from 18–30 months.

category has a similar shape in English and Italian; however, the function is somewhat higher for Americans, especially among children with fewer than 200 words. Simple-effects analyses showed that the two groups differed at all points except the two levels between 400 and 600 words. The advantage went to the American sample in every case except for the final level (over 600 words), where there was a very small but reliable difference favoring the Italians.

The analysis of variance over predicates also yielded significant main effects of vocabulary level and language, plus a significant interaction plotted in figure 7.9. Simple-effects analyses show that predicate scores were significantly larger for the American group at the first two vocabulary levels, contrary to predictions of a "verb advantage" in Italian, but similar to findings for younger children (above). There were no significant language differences after that point.

To clarify whether this does indeed mean that there is no verb advantage in Italian, we repeated the analysis of variance for verb proportion scores only. This analysis also yielded significant main effects of vocabulary level and language, plus a small but reliable interaction, illustrated in figure 7.10. This figure shows that the verb advantage does favor English-learning children, contrary to predictions, although the difference is only reliable at the first two vocabulary levels.

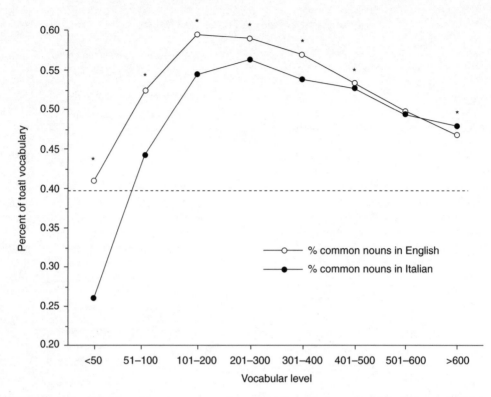

Figure 7.8 Common nouns as a proportion of total vocabulary size (dotted line = checklist ceiling).

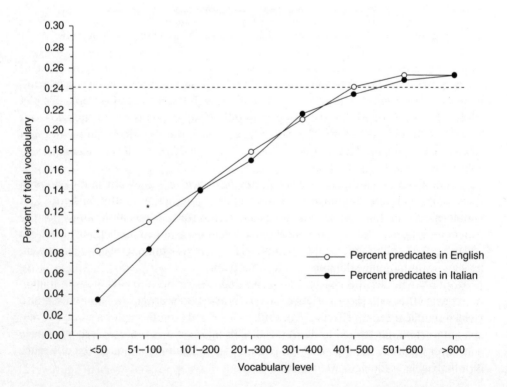

Figure 7.9 Predicates as a function of total vocabulary size (dotted line = checklist ceiling).

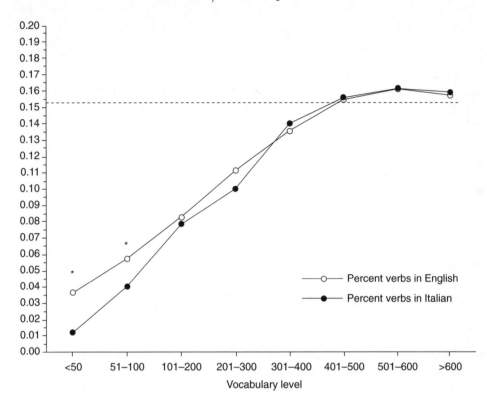

Figure 7.10 Verbs as a function of total vocabulary size (dotted line = checklist ceiling).

So far, it looks as though the English-speaking children are ahead on all the major categories. Because these are proportion scores, we know that the Italians must be making up the difference somewhere else. An analysis of variance on the social-word category yielded significant main effects for vocabulary level and language, as well as a language by level interaction. The interaction is plotted in figure 7.11, which shows that the Italians have a clear advantage in the social-word category in the early phases of lexical development. The contribution of social words to total vocabulary undergoes a sharp nonlinear drop for both languages, as we have already noted. However, post hoc analyses showed that the Italians maintained their advantage in this category at seven of the eight vocabulary levels. This is similar to results in Study 1, where we suggested that the greater representation of social words in Italian reflects cultural differences. Specifically, Italian children and their extended family tend to live in the same cities, a fact that gives Italian children more relatives to be named and more relatives to elicit routines, sound effects, and other language games on their frequent visits. Because our analyses are all based on proportion scores, the relatively greater number of social words in the Italian sample occurs at the cost of relatively smaller scores for content words in this language.

Finally, the analysis of variance for closed-class proportion scores yielded significant main effects of vocabulary level and language. The interaction was also reliable, although it was relatively small. The shape of this interaction can be seen in figure 7.12,

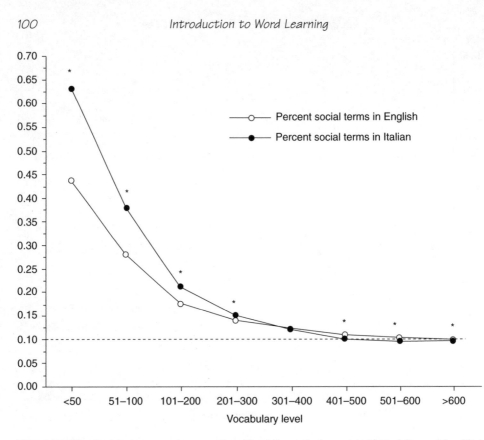

Figure 7.11 Social terms as a proportion of total vocabulary size (dotted line = checklist ceiling).

which shows that Italian children were slightly ahead of their American counterparts at every level, except for the final level when vocabularies exceed 600 words. Post hoc tests show that this difference is not reliable for children with vocabularies under 100 words, but it is reliable at all later levels.

In addition to these differences in the magnitude of closed-class proportion scores, figure 6.12 shows that the overall shape of the growth function for closed-class words is also somewhat different in these two languages. As Bates et al. (1994) have already shown, the English closed-class function is nonlinear; there is no detectable relationship between these proportion scores and total vocabulary size until the point at which total vocabulary exceeds 400 words (see Bates et al., 1994 for a detailed discussion of this point). By contrast, the Italian function approaches linearity, with gradual increases across the entire period in the proportional contribution of closed-class items to total vocabulary. Further analyses confirm that the shape of development for closed-class words is different in English and Italian, even though this category is still very small in both languages (see Caselli et al., 1999, for further details).

To summarize results for vocabulary composition, we again find no evidence for a verb advantage in Italian, replicating and extending results for younger children. The overall shape of development for both nouns and verbs is quite similar in these two lan-

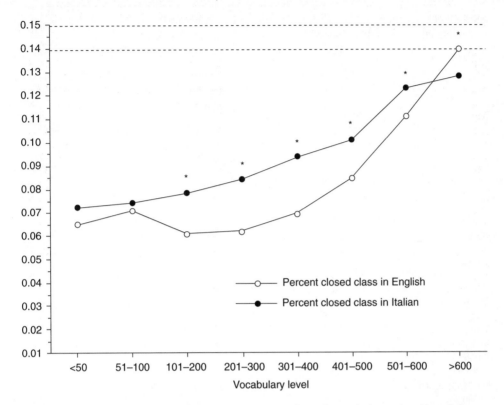

Figure 7.12 Closed-class words as a proportion of total vocabulary size (dotted line = checklist ceiling for English (15%) and Italian (13.7%)).

guages. There are small differences favoring the Americans in both these categories, but these can be attributed to the fact that Italian children have a correspondingly larger repertoire of social words. We do find a small but consistent advantage for Italian children in the proportional development of closed-class words, complemented by small but reliable differences in the shape of change within this category. To help us understand the different growth patterns for function words in English and Italian, we turn finally to a qualitative analysis of the order in which specific function words are acquired in each language.

Item analyses: growth of function words

Table 7.5 presents a full listing of the grammatical function words contained on each of the word checklists, organized by language (English on the left, Italian on the right) and type (pronouns and pronominal determiners, question words, prepositions, quantifiers and articles, connecting words and auxiliary verbs). Within each category, words are listed in their order of acquisition. Following Fenson et al. (1994), Caselli et al. (1995), and Caselli & Casadio (1995), age of acquisition is defined as the percentage of all children within each language who are reported to produce that item. As Fenson et

Table 7.5 Percent children reported to produce specific function words in English and Italian

PRONOUNS (including pronominal determiners)		PRONOMI	
Mine	78.7	Mio	82.38
Me	67.1	Io	66.58
That	55.2	Tuo/a	56.74
You	54.0	Quello/a	53.63
I	53.9	Questo/a	52.85
My	50.1	Tu	48.96
This	47.9	Me/Mi	38.34
It	42.7	Si	35.75
He	29.8	Te/Ti	27.20
These	26.5	Suo/a	26.68
She	24.8	Lo/a	24.09
Your	23.5	Che	22.80
Her	22.1	Lui	22.54
We	21.0	Lei	18.91
Him	20.6	Noi	18.65
Myself	20.0	Li/e	18.13
Those	18.5	Nostro/a	13.73
His	18.1	Ci	12.95
Them	16.9	Gli	9.59
They	15.7	Loro	8.29
Hers	15.5	Voi	5.70
Our	14.1	Vi	4.92
Us	11.2	Vostro/a	2.85
Their	11.0		
Yourself	8.3		
QUESTION WORDS		INTERROGATIVI	
What	54.8	Che/Che cosa?	37.82
Where	44.3	Chi	35.75
Why	35.7	Dove?	35.49
Who	30.6	Perché?	31.61
How	21.9	Come?	17.62
When	14.2	Quando?	15.03
Which	8.5	Quale?	13.73
PREPOSITIONS AND LOCATIONS		PREPOSIZIONI	
Down	79.4	Ecco	59.33
Up	76.2	Qui/Qua	59.07
Off	70.4	Giù	57.77
Out	69.4	Lì/Là	56.48
On	68.8	Fuori	46.11
Inside/In	58.5	Sotto	45.34
Here	50.7	Su	43.52
There	45.2	A	43.26
Back	42.5	Di	42.23
Away	37.9	Dentro	40.16
Under	36.4	Sopra	39.64
Over	35.2	Da	33.68
To	34.9	Con	28.76
With	31.1	Lontano	26.94
At	29.8	Vicino	24.87
For	27.9	In	23.83
On top of	25.8	Dietro	23.32
By	24.7	Per	22.28
Around	23.2	Davanti	21.24
Behind	22.6	Fra/Tra	5.96

Table 7.5 *Continued*

Next to	16.0			
Of	13.7			
Into	12.6			
Above	9.6			
About	9.6			
Beside	6.9			

QUANTIFIERS AND ARTICLES		ARTICLIE QUANTIFICATORI	
More	75.3	Ancora	58.81
Too	45.8	Tanto	48.96
Some	44.2	Tutto	47.41
All	41.4	Poco	46.89
A	34.5	La	40.67
The	32.5	Altro/Un altro	39.90
Not	29.9	Un/Uno//Una	37.31
Other	29.7	Niente	34.20
Another	29.6	II	31.87
Any	23.9	Un po'	31.61
A lot	23.6	Anche/Pure	28.24
None	19.4	I	27.20
Same	17.9	Nessuno	23.83
Much	16.9	Molto	22.28
Every	12.7	Lo	21.50
An	8.7	Le	21.24
Each	7.2	Di più	18.91
		Troppo	16.84
		Del/Della	15.28
		Dei/Delle	10.36
		Gli	9.84

CONNECTING WORDS		CONGIUNZIONI	
And	34.6	Perché	41.71
Because	20.9	E	30.57
So	15.6	Così	27.20
But	12.0	Ma	20.21
Then	11.0	Quindi/Allora	19.43
If	8.1	Se	10.62

HELPING VERBS		AUSILIARI	
Do	54.3	Voglio	45.08
Wanna	49.1	È	39.12
Don't	45.4	Ho	31.35
Lemme	41.2	Sono	31.09
Gonna	33.2	Sei	26.17
Can	32.2	Posso	24.87
Did	29.9	Vuoi	24.87
Is	28.8	Ha	23.83
Need to	28.8	Vuole	21.24
Try to	26.0	Hai	20.73
Am	25.0	Devo	16.58
Have to	23.8	Puoi	10.62
Are	20.4	Devi	10.62
Be	19.4	Può	10.36
Gotta	18.5	Deve	9.07
Will	18.2		
Does	17.0		
Was	15.4		
Could	11.6		
Were	9.0		
Would	8.6		

al. have shown, this simple statistic correlates highly with more complicated month-by-month estimates (e.g., the age at which 50% of the sample is reported to produce a given word, with adjustments for those words that are still not mastered by 50% of the sample by the end of the study at 2;6).

The most important finding in Table 7.5 is the high degree of similarity in order of acquisition of function words in English and Italian, even though the content of the two lists is not identical (and comparisons are simply not possible in some cases, e.g., the fact that Italian has multiple reflexive and clitic pronouns that have no counterpart in English). For example, singulars tend to come in earlier than plurals in every relevant class (e.g., pronouns, including pronominal determiners; auxiliaries). The pronominal determiner "Mine!" (Italian "mio") is the first item in the pronoun class in both languages, and "more" (Italian "ancora") is the first quantifier, facts that may reflect universal social and material concerns of one-year-olds. Within the pronoun class, person marking follows the same sequence in both languages, with first person < second person < third person (though Italians show a marked delay in informal second person plural forms like "voi," "vi," and "vostro"), and subject forms generally appear before their object counterparts (e.g., "we," "he," and "she" precede "us," "her," and "him," respectively). Question words appear in roughly the same order in both languages (what < where < why < how < when < which), although "where" seems to be earlier in English while "chi" ("who") is earlier in Italian. Connecting words follow the same sequence (["and," "because"] < "so" < "but" < "then" < "if"), although "and" precedes "because" in English while the opposite order occurs in Italian. Prepositions and locatives show a number of parallels here that have also been reported in free speech and experimental studies (Johnston, 1985): words that express direction or location of a single element emerge first (e.g., "down," "up," "off," "out," "here," and "there"), followed by locatives that mark a simple relationship of one entity to its base ("on," "inside," under," "over"), while the locatives that appear last are those that express a relationship between two entities and/or a relationship that requires assumptions about the orientation of the array relative to the speaker and listener (e.g., "next to," "beside," "behind"). Comparisons are harder to make within the categories of quantifiers and articles, and modals and auxiliaries, but there are similarities here as well. For example, the order "want" < "can" < ["have to," "gotta"] in English corresponds to the acquisition of the first conjugated form of each modal in Italian ("voglio" or "I want" < "posso" or "I can" < "devo" or "I must").

The few differences that remain can be explained by structural, statistical, and/or pragmatic differences between the two languages, superimposed on universals of cognitive development and infant social life. For example, the English subject pronoun "I" is the fifth pronominal form acquired, reported for 50.1% of the sample. The corresponding Italian subject pronoun "io" is the second pronominal form acquired, reported for 66.58% of the sample. Note that the pronoun "I" is far more frequent than the Italian "io," due to the prevalence of subject omission in Italian. Because subject pronouns can be omitted in Italian, "io" is only used for contrastive purposes; hence, when it is used, it is generally high in pragmatic and acoustic salience. Although this modest cross-linguistic difference will require a more careful test under comparable laboratory conditions, it suggests that salience is sometimes more important than sheer frequency during the first stages of grammatical development.

We would also like to underscore another similarity in Table 7.5 that transcends specific function word categories: Acquisition appears to be a gradual process that extends across the period from 1;6–2;6, with individual items acquired at different points in time depending on their frequency, regularity, salience, and utility to the child. There is no evidence here for a single "moment" when articles, pronouns, prepositions, or auxiliary verbs come in together as a block. In this respect, and in the order in which specific items emerge within each category, our results are largely (though not perfectly) compatible with previous free speech studies of grammatical development in English (e.g., Brown, 1973) and Italian (e.g., Devescovi & Pizzuto, 1995; Pizzuto & Caselli, 1992).

The picture that has emerged so far across all these analyses suggests that universal constraints dominate lexical development from 8–30 months of age. However, these analyses obscure some fundamental differences between early language in English and Italian. Specifically, Italian children have to learn to produce far more grammatical morphology than their English counterparts, including gender marking and gender agreement on nouns and all their modifiers, plus a far richer array of verb inflections. For this reason, we think it would be appropriate to contrast the similarities in grammatical development illustrated in Table 7.5 with just a few examples of the kinds of sentences that Italian and American parents report for children at comparable levels of vocabulary development. As we shall see, this kind of close, qualitative comparison reveals differences that are not captured by the measures that we have used so far.

To conduct these comparisons, we randomly selected 20 cases from the Italian data base, 5 boys and 5 girls at 24 months and 5 boys and 5 girls at 30 months. For each of those cases, we attempted to find a match in age and vocabulary size from the American sample, in order to compare the three longest utterances reported by parents within each language when vocabulary size is held constant. Some illustrative contrasts are offered in Table 7.6 (for further examples, see Caselli et al., 1999). It was extremely clear from these comparisons that Italian children are producing far more complex morphology than their English counterparts, even when carefully matched for vocabulary size as well as age. In other words, even though grammatical development appears to be paced by vocabulary growth in both languages, the amount of grammar displayed by Italian children appears to be greater when vocabulary size is controlled.

Summary and Conclusion

We set out to ask whether there are cross-linguistic differences in the development and composition of vocabulary, with special reference to (1) hypothesized differences in the onset and growth of nouns and verbs, and (2) universal vs. language-specific patterns in the development of function words.

On the noun-verb question, we found little or no evidence in favor of the idea that verbs or other predicative terms get off the ground earlier in Italian, even though there are many differences in the input to small children that ought to favor verbs in that language. In fact, we actually found evidence for a small English advantage in the proportional representation of both common nouns and predicates, compared with Italian

Table 7.6 Utterances reported for English vs. Italian children matched for vocabulary

Italian	English
Female, 24 months, 231 words Chicca e mamma mangiamo la stessa cosa *Chicca and mamma eat(1st. pl) the(fs) same (fs) thing(fs)*	*Female, 24 months, 235 words* Daddy work boat
Dal dottore no Chicca *To the(ms) doctor(ms) no Chicca*	Baby go night-night
Nonna Silvia cade, bua ginocco, naso, denti *Grandma Silvia falls(3rd. s), booboo knee, (ms) nose(ms), teeth(mpl)*	Mommy in there?
Male, 24 months, 364 words Il papa porta il gelato a Davide *The(ms) daddy (ms) brings(3rd. s) the(ms) icecream(ms) to Davide*	*Male, 24 months, 352 words* Daddy go work
Mamma andiamo dalla nonna in campagna con la macchina *Mommy, go(1st. pl) to the(fs) grandma(fs) in country with the(fs) car(fs)*	Happy day to you
Mamma fa il bagno a Davide *Mommy makes(3rd. s) the(ms) bath(ms) to Davide*	Wanna talk to Grandma phone
Male, 24 months, 479 words Prendiamo l'autobus e andiamo dalla zia *Take(1st. pl.) the(ell) bus(ms) and go(1st. pl.) to the(fs) aunt(fs)*	*Male, 24 months, 494 words* Mamma, Megan touched TV
Non c'è il sole oggi, mamma? *Not there-is(3rd. s) the(ms) sun(ms) today, Mommy?*	Go bye-bye see grandma, grandpa
La ruspa fa un buco grande grande, e poi se ne va a casa *The(fs) bulldozer(fs) makes(3rd. s) a(ms) hole (ms) big(uns) big(uns),* *and then (ref) (part) go(3rd. s) to home*	I want milk please
Male, 30 months, 590 words Metti l'acqua in questo bicchiere, l'altro e sporco *Put(2nd. s. imp.) the(ell) water(fs) in this(ms) glass(ms), the(ell) other(ms) is (3rd. s) dirty(ms)*	*Male, 30 months, 595 words* Daddy see lights on the ground, out the window
Prendo il mio orso e gli do la pappa *Take(1st. s) the(ms) my(ms) bear(ms)* *and it(dat) give(1st. s) the(fs) food(fs).*	Alan wants pizza from the pizza store
Voglio lavarmi i denti con lo spazzolino nuovo *Want(1st. s) to-wash-myself(1st. s ref) the(mpl) teeth(mpl) with the(ms) toothbrush(ms) new(ms)*	I got curly hair too

s = singular; p = plural; m = masc.; f = fem.; ell = ellided; un = gender unmarked; 1st–3rd = person; imp = imperative; dat = dative; ref = reflexive; part = partitive children matched for vocabulary level. However, these small differences appear to be the statistical reflex of a rather different phenomenon, namely, the fact that Italian children have a somewhat larger repertoire of social words (sound effects, names for people, social routines), particularly within the early stages when vocabularies do not exceed 200 words. Although other factors cannot be ruled out, we suspect that this particular cross-linguistic difference is the by-product of cultural differences between America and Italy, including the tendency for Italian families to live in the same city with an extended network of relatives and old family friends.

These findings for English and Italian differ from those of Gopnik and Choi for Korean, and Tardif for Chinese. However, these authors also used a different methodology (i.e., free speech samples complemented by a parental interview on small set of specific nouns and verbs). What would happen if our checklist methodology were applied to large samples of Korean or Chinese children in the same age range? Relevant findings come from an unpublished dissertation by Pae (1993), who adapted the MacArthur Infant Scale for Korean, and administered it to the mothers of 90 Korean infants between 12 and 23 years of age, all residents in middle-class apartment complexes in Seoul, Korea. Pae's results for both comprehension and production were remarkably similar to ours, suggesting that there are few differences among Korean, Italian, and English children in the onset and growth of nouns vs. verbs when comparable parental report methods are employed. She concludes that "Contrary to the verb bias argument, the Korean-speaking children in this sample did not show any sign of relative ease in learning verbs" (Pae, 1993, p. ii). The contrast between Gopnik and Choi's findings based on free speech and those of Pae using parental report lead to the suggestion that cross-linguistic differences in the emergence of non-nominal expressions (especially verbs) may reflect differences in the forms that children *prefer to use*, and not to differences in the words they are *able to use* (see also Bates et al., 1988). If this is the case, then we might expect to find differences between English and Italian children in early verb use in a free play situation – a possibility that we are currently pursuing.

On the function word issue, we found marked similarities in three aspects of development. First, closed-class words were rare in both languages in the early stages of lexical development (when vocabularies are under 200 words). Second, subsequent growth in the function word category was tightly correlated with overall vocabulary size in both languages. Third, an examination of the order in which specific function words are acquired yielded far more similarities than differences between languages. However, we also found interesting language-specific effects when the data are examined in another way. These include a significant difference in shape of the growth function for function words, which display a slow linear rise as a function of vocabulary size in Italian, compared with a sharp non-linear increase around 400 words in English. Finally, despite all the similarities in lexical growth, there were dramatic differences in morphological complexity for the longest sentences reported for Italian and English children who were carefully matched for vocabulary size as well as age.

We conclude lexical development reflects the operation of powerful universal social, cognitive, and perceptual constraints. Nevertheless, there are striking cross-linguistic variations in the amount and kind of grammar that children must acquire. These statistical and structural differences are even more evident when we control for overall vocabulary size as well as age – a procedure that we recommend for future cross-linguistic studies in this age range.

References

Bates, E. (1976). *Language and context: The acquisition of pragmatics.* New York: Academic Press.

Bates, E., Benigni, L., Bretherton, I., Camaioni, L., & Volterra, V. (1979). *The emergence of symbols: Cognition and communication in infancy.* New York: Academic Press.

Bates, E., Bretherton, I., & Snyder, L. (1988). *From first words to grammar: Individual differences and dissociable mechanisms.* New York: Cambridge University Press.

Bates, E., & Goodman, J.C. (1997). On the inseparability of grammar and the lexicon: Evidence from acquisition, aphasia and real-time processing. In G. Altmann (Ed.), Special issue on the lexicon, *Language and Cognitive Processes, 12*(5/6), 507–586.

Bates, E., Marchman, V., Thal, D., Fenson, L., Dale, P., Reznick, S., Reilly, J., & Hartung, J. (1994). Developmental and stylistic variation in the composition of early vocabulary. *Journal of Child Language, 21*(1), 85–124.

Benedict, H. (1979). Early lexical development: Comprehension and production. *Journal of Child Language, 6*, 183–200.

Berman, R.A., & Slobin, D.I. (1994). *Relating events in narrative: A Cross-linguistic developmental study* [in illaboration with Ayhan Aksu-Koc et al.]. Hillsdale, NJ: Erlbaum.

Bottari, P., Cipriani, P., Pfanner, L., & Chilosi, A.M. (1993). Inferenze strutturali nell'acquisizione della morfologia libera italiana [Structural inferences in the acquisition of free Italian morphosyntax]. In E. Cresti, & M. Moneglia (Eds.), *Ricerche sull'acquisizione dell'italiano* [Research on the acquisition of Italian]. Rome: Bulzoni.

Brown, R. (1973). *A first language: The early stages.* Cambridge, MA: Harvard University Press.

Caselli, M.C., Bates, C., Casadio, P., Fenson, L., Fenson, J., Sanderl, L., & Weir, J. (1995). A cross-linguistic study of early lexical development. *Cognitive Development, 10*, 159–199.

Caselli, M.C., & Casadio, P. (1995). *Il primo vocabolario del bambino: Guida all'uso del questionario MacArthur per la valutazione della comunicazione e del linguaggio nei primi anni di vita* [The child's first vocabulary: User's guide to the MacArthur questionnaire for the evaluation of language and communication in the first years of life]. Milan: FrancoAngeli.

Caselli, M.C., Casadio, P., & Bates, E. (1999). A comparison of the transition from first words to grammar in English and Italian. *Journal of Child Language, 26*, 69–111.

Cheng, S.-W. (1994). *Beginning words of three children acquiring Mandarin Chinese.* Manuscript, National Chung Cheng University, Taiwan.

Choi, S., & Bowerman, M. (1991). Learning to express motion events in English and Korean: The influence of language-specific lexicalization patterns. *Cognition, 41*(1–3), 83–121.

Choi, S., & Gopnik, A. (1995). Early acquisition of verbs in Korean: A cross-linguistic study. *Journal of Child Language, 22*(3), 497–529.

Cipriani, P., Chilosi, A.M., Bottari, P., & Pfanner, L. (1993). *L'acquisizione della morfosintassi in italiano: Fasi e processi* [The acquisition of morphosyntax in Italian: Stages and processes]. Padua: Unipress.

Devescovi, A., D'Amico, S., Smith, S., Mimica, I., & Bates, E. (1998). The development of sentence comprehension in Italian and Serbo-Croatian: local versus distributed cues. In D. Hillert (Ed.), *Sentence processing: a cross-linguistic perspective.* San Diego, CA: Academic Press.

Devescovi, A., & Pizzuto, E. (1995). Lo sviluppo grammaticale [The development of grammar]. In G. Sabbadini (Ed.), *Manuale di neuropsicologia dell' etá evolutiva* [Handbook of developmental neuropsychology] (pp. 260–285). Bologna: Zanichelli.

Dromi, E. (1987). *Early lexical development.* New York: Cambridge University Press.

Fenson, L., Dale, P., Reznick, J., Bates, E., Thal, D., & Pethick, S. (1994). Variability in early communicative development. *Monographs of the Society for Research in Child Development, Serial No. 242, vol. 59, No. 5.*

Fenson, L., Dale, P., Reznick, J., Thal, D., Bates, E., Hartung, J., Pethick, S., & Reilly, J. (1993). *The MacArthur Communicative Development Inventories: User's guide and technical manual.* San Diego, CA: Singular Publishing Group.

Gathercole, V., & Min, H. (1997). Word meaning biases or language-specific effects? Evidence from English, Spanish and Korean. *First Language, 17,* 31–56.

Gentner, D. (1982). Why are nouns learned before verbs: Linguistic relativity versus natural partitioning. In S. Kuczaj II (Ed.), *Language development, Vol. 2: Language, thought and culture.* Hillsdale, NJ: Erlbaum.

Goldin-Meadow, S., Seligman, M.E.P., & Gelman, R. (1976). Language in the two-year-old. *Cognition, 4,* 189–202.

Goodman, J.C., & Nusbaum, H.C. (Eds.) (1994). *The development of speech perception: Transitions from speech sounds to spoken words.* Cambridge, MA: MIT Press.

Gopnik, A., & Choi, S. (1990). Do linguistic differences lead to cognitive differences? A cross-linguistic study of semantic and cognitive development. *First Language, 10,* 199–215.

Gopnik, A., & Choi, S. (1995). Names, relational words, and cognitive development in English and Korean speakers: Nouns are not always learned before verbs. In M. Tomasello, & W. Merriman (Eds.), *Beyond names for things: Young children's acquisition of verbs.* Hillsdale, NJ: Erlbaum.

Imai, M., & Gentner, D. (1997). A cross-linguistic study of early word meaning: universal ontology and linguistic influence. *Cognition, 62,* 169–200.

Jackson-Maldonado, D., Thal, D., Marchman, V., Bates, E., & Gutierrez-Clellen, V. (1993). Early lexical development in Spanish-speaking infants and toddlers. *Journal of Child Language, 20*(3), 523–549.

Johnston, J.R. (1985). Cognitive prerequisites: the evidence from children learning English. In D. Slobin (Ed.), *The crosslinguistic study of language acquisition* (Vol. 2). Hillsdale, NJ: Erlbaum, 961–1004.

Kuhl, P.K. (1991). Perception, cognition, and the ontogenetic and phylogenetic emergence of human speech. In S. Brauth, W. Hall, & R. Dooling (Eds.), *Plasticity of development.* Cambridge, MA: MIT/Bradford Books.

Lieven, E., & Pine, J. (1990). [Review of the book *From first words to grammar: Individual differences and dissociable mechanisms.*] *Journal of Child Language, 17,* 495–501.

MacWhinney, B., & Bates, E. (Eds.) (1989). *The crosslinguistic study of sentence processing.* New York: Cambridge University Press.

Marchman, V., & Bates, E. (1994). Continuity in lexical and morphological development: A test of the critical mass hypothesis. *Journal of Child Language, 21,* 339–366.

McDonough, L., Choi, S., Bowerman, M., & Mandler, J. (1997). The use of preferential looking as a measure of semantic development. In E.L. Bavin, & D. Burnham (Eds.), *Advances in infancy research.* Norwood, NJ: Ablex.

Nelson, K. (1973). Structure and strategy in learning to talk. *Monographs of the Society for Research in Child Development, 38 (1 & 2, Serial No. 149).*

Nelson, K., & Lucariello, J. (1985). The development of meaning in first words. In M.D. Barrett (Ed.), *Children's single-word speech.* New York: Wiley.

Ninio, A. (1993). On the fringes of the system: Children's acquisition of syntactically isolated forms at the onset of speech. *First Language, 13,* 291–313.

O'Grady, W. (1987). *Principles of grammar learning.* Chicago: University of Chicago Press.

Pae, S. (1993). *Early vocabulary in Korean: Are nouns easier to learn than verbs?* Unpublished doctoral dissertation, University of Kansas, Lawrence, Kansas.

Pizzuto, E., & Caselli, M.C. (1992). The acquisition of Italian morphology: Implications for models of language development. *Journal of Child Language, 19*, 491–557.

Pizzuto, E., & Caselli, M.C. (1993). The acquisition of Italian morphology – A reply to Hyams. *Journal of Child Language, 20*(3), 707–712.

Slobin, D. (Ed.) (1985–1997). *The crosslinguistic study of language acquisition* (Vols. 1–5). Hillsdale, NJ: Erlbaum.

Tardif, T. (1996). Nouns are not always learned before verbs: Evidence from Mandarin speakers' early vocabularies. *Developmental Psychology, 32*(3), 492–504.

Tardif, T., Shatz, M., & Naigles, L. (1996). The influence of caregiver speech on children's use of nouns versus verbs: A comparison of English, Italian and Mandarin. *Abstracts of the VIIth International Congress for the Study of Child Language*, Istanbul.

Tomasello, M. (1992). *First verbs: A case study of early grammatical development.* Cambridge: Cambridge University Press.

Weist, R., Lyytinen, P., Wysocka, J., & Atanassova, M. (1997). The interaction of language and thought in children's language acquisition: a crosslinguistic study. *Journal of Child Language, 24*, 81–121.

Werker, J.F. (1994). Cross-language speech perception: Developmental change does not involve loss. In J.C. Goodman, & H.C. Nusbaum (Eds.), *The development of speech perception: The transition from speech sounds to spoken words* (pp. 93–120). Cambridge, MA: The MIT Press.

EIGHT

Perceiving Intentions and Learning Words in the Second Year of Life*

Michael Tomasello

In the modern study of language acquisition there are two main approaches to the problem of word learning: the constraints approach and the social-pragmatic approach. In the constraints approach a learner attempts to acquire a new word by: (1) creating a list of possible hypotheses about how the new word "maps" onto the real world, and (2) eliminating incorrect hypotheses in a semi-scientific manner (e.g., Markman, 1989, 1992; Gleitman, 1990). In all cases the learner's goal is to perform the task correctly and so to acquire accurately the mapping between word and world. The problem, as philosophers such as Quine (1960) have pointed out, is that there are too many possible hypotheses to be tested in a given case. Therefore, the child must be given a head start on the process. This head start takes the form of word learning "constraints" that eliminate certain hypotheses before they are seriously entertained.

One kind of constraint deals with the possible referents of novel words. For example, Markman proposes that young children are predisposed to assume that novel words refer to whole objects rather than to their parts, properties, or activities (whole object assumption). In Markman's account, children also know prior to language acquisition that two different words do not map onto the same real world object (mutual exclusivity); therefore, if an adult uses a new word in the presence of an object whose name they already know children assume that something other than the name of that whole object is the word's referent. Another kind of constraint deals with children's use of their a priori knowledge of syntax in determining the meaning of novel words (syntactic bootstrapping; Gleitman, 1990). In this account, the syntactic structures surrounding words, verbs in particular, provide additional constraints on their possible mappings to the world of events and states of affairs.

By all accounts – including those of Markman and Gleitman – these word-learning constraints cannot solve the word-learning problem by themselves. They only work if used in conjunction with social-pragmatic information about another person's specific referential intentions in specific contexts. That is, even if the child knows that an adult

* Modified version of chapter appearing in: M. Bowerman & S. Levinson (Eds.), *Language Acquisition and Conceptual Development*. Cambridge University Press.

is using a new piece of language to refer to a whole object or to a certain type of event, there is still the problem that in most word-learning situations there are multiple referents in the immediate context that fit within these specifications – especially for young children when their vocabularies are small. One way to supplement the constraints account is thus to add a few very specific pragmatic cues that, in combination with the various word-learning constraints, would be sufficient to enable the child to determine the referential significance of novel words. One obvious candidate is something like eye gaze direction. For example, in this account a child might know a priori that an adult is referring to a whole object, but would use eye gaze direction to specify which one of several possible candidates is intended (Baldwin, 1991, 1993a). The problem with this supplemental account is simply that gaze direction is itself insufficient in many cases of word learning, as adults quite often talk to children about referents that are not visually accessible. And children do learn words in these contexts as several empirical studies have demonstrated (Tomasello, 1992a; Tomasello & Kruger, 1992; and all of the studies to be reported here).

The social-pragmatic approach to the problem of referential indeterminacy takes a very different perspective on language and its acquisition. It begins by rejecting truth conditional semantics in the form of the mapping metaphor (the child maps word onto world), adopting instead an experientialist and conceptualist view of language in which linguistic symbols are used by human beings to invite others to experience situations in particular ways. Thus, attempting to map word to world will not help in situations in which the very same piece of real estate may be called: "the shore" (by a sailor), "the coast" (by a hiker), "the ground" (by a skydiver), and "the beach" (by a sunbather) (Fillmore, 1982; Lakoff, 1987). In the social-pragmatic view, each of the world's natural languages has its own set of communicative conventions, in the form of linguistic symbols created over thousands of years of human history, by means of which its speakers attempt to influence the interest and attention of other members of their speech communities (Talmy, 1996). This is not to deny that there are also universals in the way symbols are created, learned, and used across languages, reflecting universals both in the way human beings experience the world and in the ways they interact and communicate with one another socially. The main point is simply that there is nothing in human languages other than these symbols – which include grammatical symbols, categories of symbols, and syntactic constructions – and the experiences they symbolize (Langacker, 1987, 1991).

In the social-pragmatic approach to word learning in particular the focus is on two aspects of the process: (1) the structured social world into which the child is born – full of scripts, routines, social games, and other patterned cultural interactions; and (2) the child's capacities for tuning into and participating in that structured social world (Tomasello, 1992b). A word is one means by which adults attempt to induce children to attend to certain aspects of a shared social situation. In attempting to comply with linguistic exhortations – that is, in attempting to comprehend adult use of linguistic symbols and so to have the requested experiences – children use all kinds of interpretive strategies based on the pragmatic assumption that adult linguistic symbols are somehow *relevant* to the ongoing social interaction (Sperber & Wilson, 1986; Bruner, 1983; Bloom, 1993). In the social-pragmatic view, young children are not engaged in a reflective cognitive task in which they are attempting to make correct mappings of word to world based on adult input, but rather they are engaged in social interactions in which they are attempting to understand and interpret adult communicative intentions – so as to make sense of the current situation (Nelson, 1985). Having complied with adult instructions to experience a situation in a particular way in a given instance, children may then learn to produce the appropriate symbols for themselves when they wish for others to experience a situation in that same way – thus entering into the world of bi-directionally (intersubjectively) understood linguistic symbols (Tomasello, 1995).

In the social-pragmatic view, then, children acquire linguistic symbols as a kind of by-product of social interaction with adults, in much the same way they learn many other cultural conventions (Tomasello et al., 1993). The acquisition of linguistic symbols does not need external linguistic constraints in this theory because children are always participating in and experiencing particular social contexts, and it is these social contexts that serve to "constrain" the interpretive possibilities. The child who knows that his mother wishes him to eat his peas (she is holding them up to his mouth and gesturing), assumes that her utterance is relevant to that intention, and this is what guides his interpretations of any novel language in the situation. All of the philosophically possible hypotheses that Quine and others may create are simply not a part of the child's experience in this particular social context – assuming of course that by the time language acquisition begins young children do indeed have a reasonably adult-like understanding of at least some aspects of the social activities in which they participate.

Some early studies in the social-pragmatic perspective focused on the role of the adult in the acquisition process. Thus, it was found that when adults name new objects for young children by following into their already established focus of attention, as opposed to using the new language to direct their attention to something new, word learning is made easier (Tomasello & Farrar, 1986; Dunham et al., 1993). But this does not mean that the child is a passive participant in the word-learning process. Subsequent studies have shown that when there is a discrepancy between the adult and child's focus of attention – when young children hear a novel word in situations in which their focus of attention differs from that of an adult – they nevertheless are able to do the extra work to determine the adult's referential intentions, almost never assuming that the new word is being used for whatever is their current focus of attention irrespective of what the adult is attempting to do (Baldwin, 1991, 1993a). In all cases of word learning children make active attempts to understand adult referential intentions; it is just that some situations make it easier or harder for them to do so.

It is then clear that children do not learn words by employing mechanical mapping procedures or testing hypotheses, but rather that they learn them in the same basic way they learn other cultural skills and conventions: in the flow of naturally occurring social interaction in which both they and their interlocutors have various pragmatic goals toward the world and toward one another. Adults may do things that facilitate the learning process, but the child must always do some social cognitive work to determine the adult's referential intentions. Children learn words as an integral part of their social interactions with other persons as they attempt to understand what adults are trying to get them to do and as they attempt to get adults to do things for them (Bruner, 1983; Nelson, 1985; Tomasello, 1992b).

Learning Words "In the Flow" of Social Interaction

One of the main reasons that researchers have been drawn to the constraints view is that the prototypical case of word learning is assumed to be the learning of an object label in an ostensive context: an adult intends that a child learn a word and so "shows" her its referent (e.g., by holding up or pointing) in temporal contiguity with the utterance. In this case, the pragmatic understanding involved – that the adult intends to indicate the object held up or pointed to – is so basic and seemingly simple that it is often overlooked completely. However, in other word learning situations the situation is much more complex. In the studies that follow I attempt to demonstrate experimentally that this is indeed the case for children in their second year of life, that is, for children who have just caught on to the process of word learning and have begun to build their initial vocabularies. Moreover, by establishing something of the wide variety of situations in which nascent language learners can acquire new words, I attempt to undermine any attempt to characterize the process as wedded to any specific pragmatic cues such as gaze direction. Instead, I argue that learning new words is dependent on young children's ability to perceive and comprehend adult intentions, and they do this using a wide array of social-pragmatic cues.

The experimental studies my collaborators and I have recently performed share a number of features. The basic idea in all cases is to set up situations in which adults talk to children as they engage in various games, with novel words being introduced as naturally as possible into the ongoing flow of the game. In all cases there are multiple potential referents available; that is, there are multiple novel referents for which the child has no existing means of linguistic expression (this is checked before each study begins), and the novel word is introduced in a single type of linguistic context. Various pragmatic cues to the adult's intended referent are provided in different studies to see if children are indeed sensitive to them. The studies are designed so that none of the well-known word-learning constraints that various investigators have proposed (e.g., whole object, mutual exclusivity, syntactic bootstrapping) will be helpful to the child in distinguishing among possible referents. The studies are also designed so that eye gaze direction is never diagnostic of the adult's referential intentions.

Determining which object the adult intends to find

In our first study of this type, Tomasello and Barton (1994, Study 4) had a female experimenter say to 24-month-old children "Let's go find the toma" while looking directly into the child's eyes. The two of them then approached a row of five buckets. Each bucket contained a novel object, none of whose names the child knew beforehand, with the target object designated randomly across children. There were two experimental conditions. In the Without Search condition the adult went immediately to a bucket and excitedly found the target object and handed it to the child. In the With Search condition the adult went to the buckets, first extracted and rejected (by scowling at and replacing) two objects, and only then excitedly found and handed the child the target object (see figure 8.1). In both conditions the finding event was followed by the excited extraction of each of the other objects as the adult said "Let's see what's in this one."

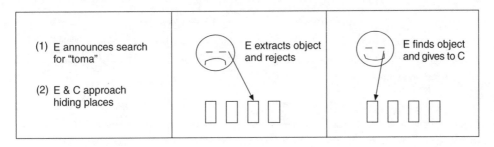

Figure 8.1   The With Search condition in Tomasello & Bates (1994, Study 4).

After several rounds of this procedure, comprehension and elicited production testing were conducted. The comprehension test consisted of the adult motioning in the general direction of all five objects (laid out in random order by a research assistant) and asking the child to bring her the toma. The elicited production task consisted of the adult holding up the target object and asking the child for its name (spontaneous productions at other times during the experiment were also recorded).

The outcome was that children learned the new word equally well in the two experimental conditions, both in comprehension and in production. Our interpretation of this result was as follows. Children could not have used a word-learning cue such as "the object at which the adult is looking while saying the new word" because the adult was always looking into the child's eyes at this time. Nor could they have used some simple extension of this cue such as "the first object the adult looks at after uttering the new word" (or first object the child sees), because then they would have performed better in the Without Search condition in which the target object was the first one extracted from the buckets; moreover, if they had used this cue in the With Search condition, they would have thought that the first object extracted and rejected was the toma (since the same object was always the first rejected object in all models for a given child) – which they did not, as they did not in a similar study by Baldwin (1993b). Because children performed equally well in the two conditions, our assumption was that: (1) the children understood from the beginning that the adult's intention was to find a particular object called a toma; and (2) they tracked the adult's behavior and emotional expression until she seemed to fulfill that intention by expressing excitement and terminating the search (i.e., with the first object extracted in the Without Search condition and the third object extracted in the With Search condition). We do not know precisely which aspect of the adult's behavior was critical for the children – her excited demeanor or the termination of the search, for example – but in either case the adult's behavior was a meaningful cue precisely because it was an indication that she had fulfilled her intention to find the toma.

Akhtar and Tomasello (1996, Study 1) had 24-month-old children participate in a variation of this game. There were two main differences. The first was that one of the buckets in the row of five was actually a very distinctive toy barn (again there was a novel, nameless object hidden in each container). The second was that there were some initial rounds of a finding game (in which the adult used no new words), so that the child would come to know which object was in the toy barn (randomized across

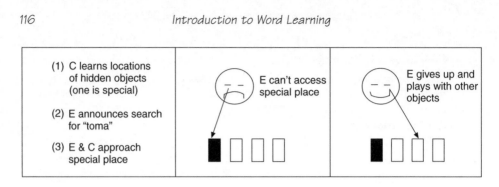

Figure 8.2   The Absent Referent condition in Akhtar & Tomasello (1996, Study 1).

children). The procedure was thus as follows. The adult and child went through the buckets and barn several times extracting the objects, with the adult saying things like "Let's see what's in here." After these initial extractions, the language models began, with the locations of all objects remaining constant for a given child and the object in the barn always serving as the target object. In the language-modeling rounds, the experimenter announced her intention to find a specific object: "Now let's find the toma!". There were two experimental conditions. In the Referent condition, the experimenter proceeded directly to the barn and extracted the target object (then followed by extraction of the other objects). In the Absent Referent condition, she proceeded to the barn and attempted to open it, but after being unsuccessful (and looking disappointed) had to inform the child "It's locked. I can't open it." (followed by extraction of the other objects; see figure 8.2). Thus, children in the Absent Referent condition **never** saw the target object after hearing the novel word. Language modelling was followed in both conditions by comprehension testing and elicited production.

Once again the outcome was that children learned the new word equally well in the two experimental conditions. (As an additional control to make sure that children were actually learning the word, additional subjects also participated in versions of the experimental conditions without the target language – the adult simply said of each container "Let's see what's in here" – and children performed at chance in the comprehension test.) As in the Tomasello and Barton study, this pattern of results indicated to us that (1) the children understood that the adult's intention was to find the toma, and (2) they then tracked her behavior and emotional expression in an attempt to determine when she had succeeded in doing so. In the Absent Referent condition, however, the adult did not succeed and thus never showed excitement in finding the target object – indeed she expressed her disappointment explicitly. Therefore, not only could children not have been using adult gaze direction, or "next object the adult sees," in this condition, they also could not have been using the adult's excitement as a cue; when the barn was locked the adult showed nothing but disappointment. Indeed, if they had used adult excitement as a cue, children would have inferred that the toma was the object extracted excitedly from the adjacent hiding place right after the failure, and almost no children did this. In this study children understood the adult's finding intention and used as a word-learning cue her disappointment at her failure, remembering or imagining in the process what it was she had intended to find.

Taken together these two studies demonstrate that children have multiple ways of understanding adult intentions in finding games. Children come to the experiment knowing about finding as an intentional activity. They soon come to understand that the adult intends to find this thing called a toma. They then monitor the adult's behavior to see when she has fulfilled her intention. Across the two studies they must do this in different ways: in one study understanding that the object the adult is excited about is the toma, while in the other study understanding that the object never seen – the one the adult is disappointed in not finding – is the toma. The implication is thus that in both of these studies children are employing a very flexible social understanding of adults' actional and communicative intentions and how they play themselves out in different circumstances. Recently Tomasello, Strosberg, and Akhtar (1995) have extended these two findings to children 18 months of age, demonstrating that these intentional understandings are not some late-developing word-learning strategy, but rather are an integral aspect of children's word-learning skills from very early in language development.

Determining which action the adult intends to perform

From the beginning of our thinking about the role of intentional understanding in word learning, the acquisition of verbs was seen as especially important. This is because many verbs (especially change of state verbs such as *give, put, make,* etc.) are only heard by young children as the adult requests an action of the child, anticipates the child's or her own impending action, or comments on a completed action – basically never using them in ostensive naming contexts (Tomasello & Kruger, 1992). Verbs are thus the prototype of words that are experienced by children in the ongoing flow of social interaction with others.

In our first experimental study along these lines, Tomasello and Barton (1994, Study 3) exposed 24-month-old children to two novel verbs, one in each of two experimental conditions, both involving an impending action on an apparatus affording two actions. In the Target First condition an adult experimenter used a novel verb to announce her intention to perform a novel action on the apparatus, saying, for example, "I'm going to plunk Big Bird!". She then performed the target action intentionally, saying "There!", followed immediately by another action on that same apparatus performed "accidentally," in an awkward fashion saying "Woops!". In the Target Last condition, the accidental action was performed first and the intentional action was performed second (see figure 8.3). (Because there were two apparatuses, each with two possible actions, which actions were intentional and which were accidental, as well as the order of intentional and accidental actions, was totally counterbalanced across children.) After several models of this type, the child was given a new character and asked "Can you go plunk Mickey Mouse?", with both apparatuses present. There were also attempts to get the children to produce the new word as the adult performed the action.

Results demonstrated that the children quite readily associated the new action word with the adult's intentional action, regardless of whether it occurred immediately after the novel word or later, after an intervening accidental action. As in the previous studies, the exact cues the children might have been using to distinguish intentional and accidental actions were not identified precisely; the adult both acted differently and

Figure 8.3   The Target Last condition in Tomasello & Barton (1994, Study 3).

used a different vocal marker for the two types of action. But again, as in the previous studies, whatever cues they might have used the children in this study apparently understood that the adult intended to plunk Big Bird, and they then tracked her behavior and emotional expressions to discover precisely what this plunking action might be.

Related to this finding is a study in which Akhtar and Tomasello (1996, Study 2) had an experimenter expose 24-month-old children to four novel actions using no new words. Each of these actions was uniquely associated with one and only one toy character and one and only one prop (e.g., catapulting was associated only with Ernie and only with a device for catapulting). Then came several language-modeling rounds using a novel verb (the target) associated with one of the four actions (counterbalanced across children). There were two experimental conditions. For subjects in the Referent condition, the experimenter set out the target action prop and announced her intention to perform an action, for example, "Let's pud Ernie!". She then proceeded to perform the target action (then followed by the other actions with their appropriate props and characters). For subjects in the Absent Referent condition, the experimenter also set out the target action prop and announced the same intention but, after searching, told the child she was unable to find Ernie and so she could not pud him (so she then went on to bring out the other props and characters and perform their respective actions; see figure 8.4). Children in this condition thus never saw the referent action after hearing the novel verb. Language modeling was followed in both conditions by comprehension testing and elicited production.

As in the very similar study with objects (see above), the outcome was that children learned the new word equally well in the two experimental conditions. (As an additional control to make sure that children were actually learning the word, additional subjects also participated in versions of the experimental conditions without the target language – the adult simply continued to say "Let's do this" – and they performed at chance in the comprehension test.) As in the similar study with objects, this pattern of results indicated to us that (1) the children understood that the adult's intention was to pub Ernie, and (2) they then tracked her behavior in an attempt to determine when she had done so. In the key condition, however, the adult never actually performed the action. Indeed, in the Absent Referent condition the next action the adult performed (after the disappointment of not being able to perform the target action) was one of the non-target actions. Thus, as in the similar study with objects, children in this study

Figure 8.4   The Absent Referent condition in Akhtar & Tomasello (1996, Study 2).

were able to understand in this highly scripted situation what the adult intended to do from her disappointment, without ever seeing the referent action paired with the novel verb.

These two studies with novel verbs thus demonstrate rather directly the role of children's understanding of intentional action in early word learning. Children know that adults use words to announce their intended actions, not their accidental actions (which would, of course, make no sense), and they have some ability in highly scripted situations to anticipate the adult's intended action even when it never actually happens and the adult shows disappointment – again evidencing a very flexible social understanding. We have not attempted these studies with younger children. However, two recent studies in which 16- and 18-month-old infants were asked to imitate novel actions on objects suggest that even at this younger age the ability to understand intentional action is present. In perfect parallel to the two verb-learning studies just reported: (1) Carpenter et al. (1998) found that 16-month-old infants were much more likely to imitate an adult's intentional than her accidental actions (cued mainly with the words "Woops!" and "There!" said with their appropriate intonations); and (2) Meltzoff (1995) found that 18-month-old infants were able to "imitate" actions that the adult only initiated but did not complete (and thus the intention was never actually fulfilled). It is thus possible that children this young could learn novel verbs in our two experimental paradigms as well.

Determining what is new for the adult

In each of four of the studies just reported there was some set of pragmatic cues indicating which object or action the adult intended to indicate with her novel word. In a fifth study attempting to demonstrate the role of children's intentional understanding in the word-learning process, Akhtar et al. (1996) set up a situation in which no special cues were associated with any one referent. In this study, 24-month-old children first played with three novel, nameless objects with two experimenters and a parent. The adults drew attention to each of the objects, handing them to the child and to one another excitedly, commenting on their characteristics, and in general playing with the objects enthusiastically. No language models were given during this initial play period. One experimenter and the parent then left the room while the child and the other experimenter played with a fourth object (the target) for an amount of time equal to

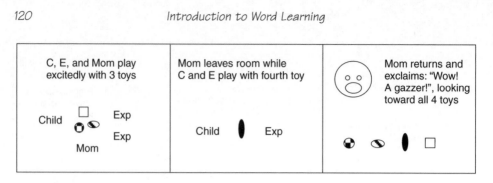

Figure 8.5   The Language condition in Akhtar, Carpente, & Tomasello (1996).

that for which they had played with the other objects. The experimenter then set all four of the objects in a row, in random order. The other adults then returned. What they then did constituted the two experimental conditions. In the Language condition the adults looked at the group of objects (none singled out by gaze) and said: "Look, I see a gazzer! A gazzer!" (see figure 8.5). In the No Language condition the adults behaved the same but said: "Look, I see a toy! A toy!" (There was also another control study in which the novel object was not the last one the child played with.) In both conditions, the language model was later followed by a comprehension test in which the experimenter who had left the room asked the child to bring her the gazzer, and there was an elicited production question as well.

The main result of this study was that children learned the word for the target object in the Language condition, but they behaved randomly in the No Language condition. This result means that the children: (1) knew which object was novel for the adults who had left the room; and (2) knew that adults only get excited about, and thus only use new language to talk about, things that are new to the discourse context. (Another way of expressing this second point is to say that the children knew that the adult had played with the other toys repeatedly previously and so it did not make sense for her to be excited about seeing them now, thus eliminating them as possible referents – analogous to the process of elimination in so-called fast mapping studies.) The important point is that the children in this study were able to single out the target object not on the basis of its being treated differently by the adults giving the language model; the pragmatic "cue" in this case was something much more distributed in terms of the child's understanding of the adults' experience during the entire experimental situation.

The power of this kind of understanding is underscored by another of our recent studies. Tomasello and Akhtar (1995, Study 1) were interested in whether children in this same general age range (24–26 months) could use their understanding of novelty from the adult point of view to help them determine to which ontological category a novel word might belong. The basic idea was that the language model would be given identically for all children, that is, using exactly the same language in exactly the same referential situation. What would differ across experimental conditions would be the experiences children had leading into that language model. There were two experimental conditions. In both conditions, children heard a novel word modeled as a one-word utterance ("Modi!") just as a nameless target object was engaging in a nameless target action. What preceded this model defined the experimental conditions.

Figure 8.6   Both experimental conditions in Tomasello & Akhtar (1995, Study 1).

In the Action Novel condition, children initially performed several actions on the target object, so that when the language model was presented the target action was the novel element in the discourse context. (The "feel" was supposed to be something like: first we do this with it, then we do that with it, **now** we "modi"). In the Object-Novel condition, children performed the target action on several objects so that when the language model was presented the target object was the novel element in the discourse context. (The "feel" was supposed to be something like: first we do it with this, then we do it with that, **now** we do it with "modi"). Figure 8.6 depicts both experimental situations.

There was an elicited production question and a comprehension test. The comprehension test was preceded by a pre-test (which actually took place at the very beginning of the experiment) in which children were given a cup, a spoon, and a ball. They were then asked to "Show me ball," "Show me bounce," and so forth, as a way of letting them know that with this one-sentence frame ("Show me ___") we might be asking for either an object or an action. Most children showed clearly from the beginning a tendency to hold up or give objects when they were requested, and to perform actions when they were requested. (Any children who did not were trained to do so, or, in a few cases, dropped from the study.) The target comprehension test was thus "Show me modi" addressed to the child in the presence of multiple objects (all of which had been played with equally) and multiple possible actions (all of which had been performed equally). Results indicated that the children associated the word *modi* with the element that was new to the discourse context at the time of the model: children in the Action Novel condition associated *modi* with the target action, whereas children in the Object Novel condition associated *modi* with the target object. This finding is especially significant because it indicates for the first time that the child's intentional understanding can even take them across ontological categories. That is, in all of the previous studies reported children have understood from the outset that the adult was referring to either an object or an action and their task was to determine **which one**; in this study the child's task was to determine **what kind** of entity the adult intended to indicate with her novel language.

These two studies thus show that young children can use something like novelty to the discourse situation to determine adult referential intentions. In the first study children had to determine which one of a number of objects was new, and they had to do this totally from the adult's point of view. In the second study novelty was equal for

	Action biasing: E prepares apparatus for C, alternates gaze between apparatus and C	Action biasing: E says: "Your turn, Jason. Wigit!"
E and C play with target object engaged in target action (no language)		
	Object biasing: E ignores apparatus, alternates gaze between object and C	Object biasing: E says: "Wigit, Jason! Your turn."

Figure 8.7   Both experimental conditions in Tomasello & Akhtar (1995, Study 1).

both the child and adult, but children had to use this novelty to determine what kind of entity, object or action, the adult intended to indicate. The ability to determine what is new in a situation for a potential communicative partner is of course not only an important skill in early word learning, it is also a crucially important skill in all aspects of language development as children learn to comprehend and produce utterances that are pragmatically appropriate to specific communicative contexts (e.g., for all kinds of topic-maintenance operations in discourse).

Determining what the adult intends for me to do

The final study in this series is Tomasello and Akhtar (1995, Study 2). The basic design is similar to that of the study just described: children saw a novel word modeled in a situation in which the adult might potentially be referring to either an object or an action. In this case, however, the adult behaved in a number of ways that differed between the two experimental conditions. To begin, all children saw an adult perform a novel and nameless action (target action) with a novel and nameless object (target object) on a special apparatus, and then they had the opportunity to perform the action with the object themselves – with no new words used at this time. Children in the Action Highlighted condition then watched as the adult prepared the apparatus so that the child could perform it again (by orienting the apparatus correctly for him). She then held out the object to the child and said "Your turn, Jason. Wigit!", while alternating her gaze between the child and the apparatus – as if requesting that the child perform the action. The experimenter behaved differently for children in the Object Highlighted condition. In this condition the experimenter did not prepare the apparatus for the child, and simply held out the object to the child and said "Wigit, Jason! Your turn," while alternating her gaze between the child and the object (never looking at the apparatus at all). Figure 8.7 depicts both of these conditions.

Elicited production and comprehension tests were then given, with the "Show me wigit" test, prepared by a pre-test, used to test comprehension as reported above (i.e., as in Tomasello and Akhtar, 1995, Study 1). The outcome was that children in the Action Highlighted condition learned the new word for the target action, whereas children in the Object Highlighted condition learned the new word for the target object. Once again a key aspect of this study was the fact that children did not know ahead of time whether we would be talking about a novel object or a novel action; it was only during the modeling itself that they learned the experimenter's referential intentions with respect to ontological category. The experimenter in this study did several things that differed in the two conditions: either prepared or did not prepare the apparatus, alternated gaze between the child and either the apparatus or the object, and said either "Your turn, Jason. Wigit!" or "Wigit, Jason! Your turn." Again in this case, therefore, we do not know the precise cue or cues used by children to determine the adult's referential intentions, but we do know that they used some aspects of the presented cue complex to distinguish situations in which the adult intended for them to perform an action from situations in which the adult intended to name an object for them.

It would also be interesting to perform this study, or something like it, with younger children. We have no experimental evidence that they could learn new words in this situation, but in Tomasello (1992a) I reported by daughter's acquisition of several verbs that seemingly were used by adults only in requestive situations (she sometimes complied and sometimes did not). A reasonable hypothesis is thus that even younger children could also learn novel verbs from utterances in which adults request behaviors of them (at least in comprehension) even if the actions are never actually performed – so long as the appropriate intention cues are present.

Summary

The fact that children can learn words in all of these different interactive situations – none of which consists of the adult stopping what she is doing to name something for the child – is a very important fact for theories of word learning. There are at least two possible explanations for this fact. On the one hand, it is possible that young children learn to deal with each of these learning situations separately, that is, they learn in each situation separately how the adult's new word "maps" onto one of the potential referents available: for example, through some kind of hypothesis testing procedure with general a priori constraints, individual cue learning, and subsequent feedback. On the other hand, it is also possible that word learning is not a hypothesis testing procedure needing to be constrained at all, but rather it is a process of skill learning that builds upon a deep and pervasive understanding of other persons and their intentional actions (i.e., social cognition in general) that is available to children by the time language acquisition begins.

Learning The First Word

All of the studies just reported concern children in the 18- to 24-month age range. This is the period during which many children have a "vocabulary spurt" and thus would seem to be the period during which they have become skillful at learning new words – to the tune of several new words per day for many children. It is thus possible that what these studies represent is a set of acquired strategies for word learning that only become operative after a certain developmental period. In this scenario children's acquisition of their first words in the first half of the second year of life might not depend on an understanding of the intentional actions of others in the same way as does their word learning later in the second year. The other possibility is that, perhaps with some minor twists, the basic process of word learning is the same throughout early development. Indeed, in this view the creation of linguistic conventions/symbols in the first place can only occur in organisms who understand their communicative partners as intentional agents. Children's learning of their first words is thus of a piece with their other social cognitive and cultural learning skills at this same developmental period early in the second year. This does not mean that word learning does not involve some additional complexities, only that it is not a completely modularized process in early development.

The story goes something like this. Human infants are social creatures from birth and so they clearly understand many things about other persons early in development. But they do not seem to understand other persons in terms of their intentional relations to the world. Five-month-old infants, for instance, do not do such things as follow the gaze of others to outside entities or imitate their behavior on outside objects, preferring instead to focus on their face-to-face interactions with others. All of this changes, however, at around the first birthday. Infants at this age begin for the first time to do such things as look toward objects at which adults are looking (gaze following), monitor adult emotional reactions to novel objects (social referencing), and act on objects in the way adults act on them (imitative learning). All of these skills emerge in rough developmental synchrony because all of them reflect the infant's emerging ability to understand other persons as intentional agents whose attention, emotion, and behavior to outside objects may be actively followed into and shared (Tomasello, 1995b). Experimental support for this view has recently been provided by the studies of Gergeley, Nádasdy, Csibra, and Biró (1995).

This social-cognitive revolution at the infant's first birthday sets the stage for the second year of life in which they begin to imitatively learn the use of all kinds of tools and artifacts, with linguistic symbols being one special case. In all of these cases the imitative learning involved is not just a mimicking of adult body movements, and not just a reproducing of interesting environmental effects by whatever means imaginable, but rather it is an actual reproduction of the adult's intentional relations to the world. In these interactions the infant perceives the adult's overt actions as composed of both a goal and a means for attaining that goal, and then actively chooses the adult's means of goal attainment in contrast to others it might have chosen. For example, in a study by Meltzoff (1988) 14-month-old children observed an adult bend at the waist and touch her head to panel thus turning on a light. Most of them imitatively learned this somewhat awkward behavior, even though it would have been easier and more natural for them simply to push the panel with their hands. The supposition is that that the infants understood that (1) the adult had the goal of illuminating the light, (2) chose one means for doing so, from among other possible means, and (3) if they had the same goal they could choose the same means. Imitative learning of this type thus relies fundamentally on infants' tendency to identify with adults, and on their ability to distinguish in the actions of others the underlying goal or intention and the different means that might be used to achieve it. This interpretation is supported by the recent finding of Meltzoff (1995) that 18-month-old infants also imitatively learn actions on objects that adults intend to perform, even if the adult is unsuccessful in actually performing them. It is likewise supported by Carpenter et al. (1998) who document that 16-month-old infants imitate adults' intentional actions on objects (indicated by "There!") and ignore their accidental actions (indicated by "Woops!") – in perfect parallel to the study of Tomasello and Barton (1994, Study 3 – as reported above).

The acquisition of linguistic symbols begins during this same developmental period quite simply because comprehending and producing language relies on the same basic understanding of persons as intentional agents as all of the other social cognitive and cultural learning skills that emerge at this same age. Nevertheless, linguistic symbols do have a special property. Unlike actions on objects, words are communicative actions directed to other persons; that is, words are social conventions and so involve a special application of social cognitive and cultural learning skills. This can be made clear by comparing the process by which infants imitatively learn an action on an object and the process by which they imitatively learn a linguistic convention.

Let us suppose that an infant observes an adult performing an intentional action on an object, and then imitatively learns that action herself. The process may be depicted as in figure 8.8a. Now suppose that an adult addresses a novel expression to a child, perhaps while pointing to an interesting event, for example, "A doggie!". The key is that the adult's intentional action in this case is not directed to the object, but rather to the child or, more specifically, to the child's intentions or attention. The child's comprehension of the adult's communicative act, therefore, requires an understanding that the adult is making this unfamiliar noise with the goal of getting *me* to do something intentional (i.e., focus my attention on some aspect of the ongoing event; see Gibson & Rader, 1979, for the argument that attention is intentional perception). Once the child understands this communicative intention, a linguistic convention is created when she then acquires appropriate use of that communicative act herself. This process is similar to other acts of cultural learning in that the child understands and reproduces the adult's intentional act. It is different, however, in that the imitative learning of communicative acts involves a role reversal. If the child understands the adult's act as "She is making that sound in order to get me to attend to the doggie," then imitatively learning this act means that the child must reverse the roles: if *I* wish *others* to focus on the doggie *I* must use the sound "doggie" toward *them* (see Figure 8.8b). As the child identifies with the adult and adopts her linguistic expression, of course, she retains the understanding that the adult also comprehends and uses it. The child's use of the expression thus creates a communicative convention, or symbol, whose essence is its bi-directionality or intersubjectivity (Saussure, 1916), which constitutes the quality of being socially "shared" (Akhtar & Tomasello, 1999).

It is important to note that not all communicative behaviors are bi-directional and shared in this same way. Thus, prelinguistic infants use a number of communicative gestures that are ritualized from noncommunicative behaviors; for example the "hands-up" gesture as a request to be picked up may be a ritualization of the infant trying to pull its way up to the parent's arms. There is no evidence that prelinguistic infants learn this gesture by imitative learning, or even that they comprehend these early gestures when they are produced by another person; if they do not, they cannot be viewed as bi-directional communicative conventions. The same may even be true of some of children's earliest "words," which may be learned through ritualization as well. That is, children may have some early "words" that they have acquired by simply mimicking an adult sound and then the adult responds in some predictable and interesting way. These so-called pre-symbolic forms are often characterized as being simply a part

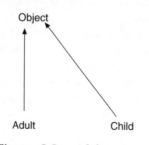

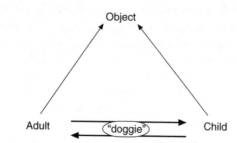

Figure 8.8a Adult acts on object and child imitatively learns that action.

Figure 8.8b Adult uses word to express intention (thick line) toward child's attention (thin line to object), and child imitatively learns that word with role reversal, thus creating a bi-directional linguistic convention/symbol.

of an activity, not a symbol standing for anything else in the activity (Bates, 1979). If they are of this nature, and they are not truly conventional (the child does not understand the adult's understanding of them), they are best called vocal signals.

Conclusion

To summarize, in the first half of the second year of life young children begin to learn language. The major social cognitive skill that underlies their ability to do this is their understanding of the intentional actions of others, especially their understanding that other persons have intentions toward their intentional states. Children's ability to reproduce these intentional communicative actions via some form of cultural or imitative learning involves a role reversal – the child has intentions toward that person's intentional states – which leads to the creation of linguistic conventions. Linguistic conventions are most clearly distinguished from other forms of communication precisely by virtue of their bi-directional or "shared" nature. Then, in the second half of the second year of life, young children go on to become more and more skilled at determining precisely what are the referential intentions of others in particular situations. They learn to do this in all kinds of ongoing social interactions, whose complexity and diversity preclude the possibility that this learning is of a straightforward mechanical variety in which word is mapped to world – either with or without a priori constraints.

Children's amazing skills at determining the referential intentions of other persons in a wide variety of communicative circumstances are only now being fully appreciated. Indeed, in addition to the many and varied word-learning contexts represented by the experimental studies summarized in this paper, there is also observational evidence that children in some, perhaps many, of the world's cultures even turn into the flow of social interaction between third parties and learn some linguistic conventions from **their** linguistic interactions (Brown and de Léon, this volume). Acquisition in this circumstance also depends on children's ability to perceive and understand the communicative intentions of others, but the specific social information used may be different. And we should not neglect in all of this concern with understanding nonlinguistic intentions that as children learn more language that language itself provides additional information for understanding the intentions of others.

References

Akhtar, N., Carpenter, M., & Tomasello, M. (1996). The role of discourse novelty in children's early word learning. *Child Development, 67,* 635–645.

Akhtar, N., & Tomasello, M. (1996). Twenty-four month old children learn words for absent objects and actions. *British Journal of Developmental Psychology, 14,* 79–93.

Akhtar, N., & Tomasello, M. (1999). Intersubjectivity in early language learning and use. In S. Braaten (Ed.), *Intersubjective Communication and Emotion in Ontogeny.* Cambridge University Press.

Baldwin, D.A. (1991). Infants' contribution to the achievement of joint reference. *Child Development, 62,* 875–890.

Baldwin, D. (1993a). Infants' ability to consult the speaker for clues to word reference. *Journal of Child Language, 2,* 395–418.

Baldwin, D. (1993b). Early referential understanding: Young children's ability to recognize referential acts for what they are. *Developmental Psychology, 29,* 1–12.

Bates, E. (1979). *The emergence of symbols: Cognition and communication in infancy.* New York: Academic Press.

Bloom, L. (1993). *The transition from infancy to language: Acquiring the power of expression.* Cambridge University Press.

Bruner, J.S. (1983). *Child's talk: Learning to use language.* NY: Norton.

Carpenter, M., Akhtar, N., & Tomasello, M. (1998). Fourteen-through 18-month-old infants differentially imitate intentional and accidental actions. *Infant Behavior and Development, 21,* 315–330.

Dunham, P.J., Dunham, F.S., & Curwin, A. (1993). Joint attentional states and lexical acquisition at 18 months. *Developmental Psychology, 29,* 827–831.

Fillmore, C. (1982). Frame semantics. In Linguistic Society of Korea (Ed.), *Linguistics in the morning calm.* Seoul: Hanshin.

Gergely, G., Nádasdy, Z., Csibra, G., & Biró, S. (1995). Taking the intentional stance at 12 months of age. *Cognition, 56,* 165–193.

Gibson, E., & Rader, N. (1979). Attention: The perceiver as performer. In G. Hale & M. Lewis (Eds.), *Attention and cognitive development.* Plenum Press.

Gleitman, L. (1990). The structural sources of verb meaning. *Language Acquisition, 1,* 3–55.

Lakoff, G. (1987). *Women, fire, and dangerous things: What categories reveal about the mind.* Chicago: University of Chicago Press.

Langacker, R. (1987). *Foundations of cognitive grammar, Volume I.* Stanford University Press.

Langacker, R. (1991). *Foundations of cognitive grammar, Volume II.* Stanford University Press.

Markman, E. (1989). *Categorization and naming in children.* Cambridge: MIT Press.

Markman, E. (1992). Constraints on word learning: Speculations about their nature, origins, and word specificity. In M. Gunnar & M. Maratsos (Eds.), *Modularity and constraints in language and cognition.* Hillsdale, N.J.: Lawrence Erlbaum.

Meltzoff, A. (1988). Infant imitation after a one week delay: Long term memory for novel acts and multiple stimuli. *Developmental Psychology, 24,* 470–476.

Meltzoff, A. (1995). Understanding the intentions of others: Re-enactment of intended acts by 18-month-old children. *Developmental Psychology, 31,* 838–850.

Nelson, K. (1985). *Making sense: The acquisition of shared meaning*. New York: Academic Press.

Quine, W. (1960). *Word and object*. Cambridge, MA: Harvard University Press.

Saussure, F. de (1916). *Course in general linguistics*. New York: Philosophical Library.

Sperber, D. & Wilson, D. (1986). *Relevance: Communication and cognition*. Harvard University Press.

Talmy, L. (1996). The windowing of attention in language. In M. Shibatani and S. Thompson (Eds.), *Grammatical constructions: Their form and meaning*. Oxford: Oxford University Press.

Tomasello, M. (1992a). *First Verbs: A Case Study of Early Grammatical Development*. Cambridge University Press.

Tomasello, M. (1992b). The social bases of language acquisition. *Social Development*, 1(1), 67–87.

Tomasello, M. (1995). Joint attention as social cognition. In C. Moore & P. Dunham (Eds.), *Joint Attention: Its Origins and Role in Development*. Lawrence Erlbaum.

Tomasello, M., & Akhtar, N. (1995). Two-year-olds use pragmatic cues to differentiate reference to objects and actions. *Cognitive Development*, 10, 201–224.

Tomasello, M., & Barton, M. (1994). Learning words in non-ostensive contexts. *Developmental Psychology*, 30, 639–650.

Tomasello, M., & Farrar, J. (1986). Joint attention and early language. *Child Development*, 57, 1454–1463.

Tomasello, M., & Kruger, A. (1992). Joint attention on actions: Acquiring verbs in ostensive and non-ostensive contexts. *Journal of Child Language*, 19, 311–334.

Tomasello, M., Kruger, A., & Ratner, H. (1993). Cultural learning. *Behavioral and Brain Sciences*, 16, 495–511.

Tomasello, M., Strosberg, R., & Akhtar, N. (1995). Eighteen-month-old children learn words in non-ostensive contexts. *Journal of Child Language*, 22, 1–20.

NINE

Evidence Against a Dedicated System for Word Learning in Children

Lori Markson and Paul Bloom

In two experiments (study 1 and study 2), 48 three-year-old children (mean age, 3 yr 7 months), 47 four-year-old children (mean age, 4 yr 5 months) and 48 undergraduate students first participated in a training phase that lasted for about twenty minutes. This phase involved the manipulation of ten kinds of objects, four of them familiar (for example, pennies) and six of them novel (see Methods). Subjects were asked to use some of the objects to measure other objects: for instance, they were asked to use pennies to measure the circumference of a plastic disk. Children were told it was a game, and adults were told it was a game designed to teach young children how to measure.

In the course of the training phase, subjects in both study 1 and study 2 were exposed to a new world – "koba" – used to refer to one of the six unfamiliar kinds of objects. Subjects in study 1 were also taught a new fact about one or more objects belonging to another kind. They were told that the object or objects were given to the experimenter by her uncle. Subjects in study 2 were given information about an unfamiliar object, presented visually. They watched as a sticker was placed on one of the unfamiliar objects, and were told that was where the sticker should go (see Methods).

In each of the studies, one-third of the subjects from each age group were tested for comprehension immediately after the training phase, one-third were tested after a 1-week delay (6–8 days), and one-third after a 1-month delay (28–30 days). Subjects were presented with the original array of ten items and asked to recall which object was the koba. Subjects in study 1 were also asked to recall which object was given to the experimenter by her uncle. Subjects in study 2 were handed a small sticker and instructed to put it where it should go (see Methods).

Children and adults successfully learned the novel object to which the label "koba" referred, and were able to remember the correct word–object mapping after all tested delays (figure 9.1). Adults were significantly better than the three- and four-year-olds when tested immediately, but there were no age differences at the longer intervals, and no significant decline in performance over time by any of the age groups.

Interestingly, however, subjects were equally good at remembering which novel object was "given to the experimenter by her uncle," suggesting that fast mapping[1-8] is not special to word learning. In fact, when tested immediately, children did significantly

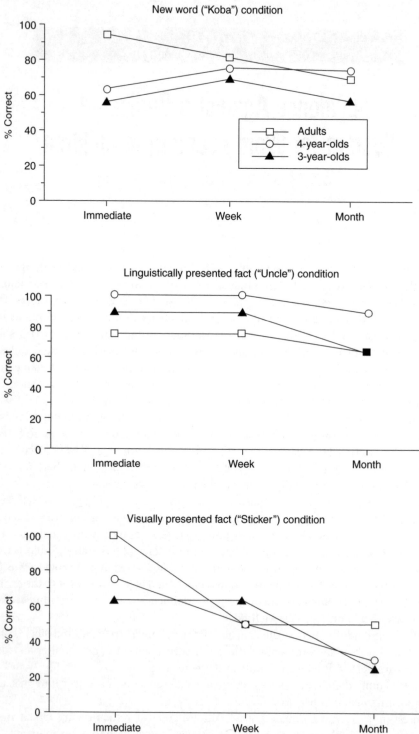

better in this condition than in the word-learning condition. In contrast to the "koba" and "uncle" conditions, both children and adults were considerably worse at learning and remembering which object had a sticker affixed to it. All age groups performed significantly better when tested immediately than when tested after a delay. The children performed significantly worse in the "sticker" condition than in the other two conditions, and only the adults in this condition performed significantly better than chance after a one-month delay; the children's performance after one month was indistinguishable from guessing.

One objection to the conclusion that fast mapping is not special to words is that the "koba" condition requires subjects to learn and store a novel phonological representation, whereas the "uncle" condition does not. It is possible that if both tasks involved a novel phonological form, subjects would do significantly worse at the non-word learning task. To test this, 15 three-year-olds (mean age, 3 yr 7 months), 15 four-year-olds (mean age, 4 yr 3 months) and 15 undergraduate students participated in a training phase in which they were taught an arbitrary fact that included an unfamiliar word. Specifically, subjects were taught that one of the unfamiliar kinds of objects "came from a place called Koba." They were tested on their memory of the new fact after a one-month delay by being asked to recall which object "came from a place called Koba."

Children and adults performed significantly above chance in this condition, and there were no significant age differences (3-year-olds: 87%; 4-year-olds: 67%; adults: 60%). In fact, after this one-month delay, there were no significant differences between subjects' ability to recall which object "came from a place called Koba" and their

◀──

Figure 9.1   Percentage of subjects who recalled the object to which the novel word referred, the object that had the property of being given to the experimenter by her uncle, and the object that had a sticker affixed to it. "Koba condition": Adults were significantly better than both the three- and four-year-olds when tested immediately (adults versus three-year-old, $X^2(1) = 6.0$; adults versus four-year-olds, $X^2(1) = 4.6$, both P values of <0.05). Unlike the two conditions below, in which chance performance was calculated as 1/10 (there were ten objects), chance performance was calculated as 1/6, because four of the ten objects were familiar, and children and adults assume that novel words are more likely to correspond to novel objects than to familiar ones.[15] As a result, even if subjects forgot which object the new word referred to, they might restrict their guess to the six novel objects. Based on these criteria, all ages performed significantly better than chance in all delay conditions. Also, the three-year-olds performed significantly better when the new word was presented in the singular rather than in the plural form ($P < 0.01$); this was the only effect of the singular/plural distinction. "Uncle" condition: All age groups again performed significantly better than chance in all delay conditions. When the three- and four-year-olds were combined into a single group, they did significantly better in the "Uncle" condition than in the "Koba" condition when tested immediately ($X^2(1) = 6.1$, $P < 0.05$). "Sticker" condition: Adults did significantly better when tested immediately than when tested after a week and when tested after a month (Fisher's exact tests, $P = 0.04$). The three- and four-year-olds' performance was significantly worse after a one-week delay than it was in the "Uncle" condition, and significantly worse after a one-month delay than it was in both the "Koba" and the "Uncle" conditions. Only the adults performed significantly better than chance after a one-month delay; the three- and four-year-olds declined over time, doing significantly worse after a month than when tested immediately (all P values < 0.05).

performance in the "koba" and "uncle" conditions. The fact that fast mapping still occurred when subjects had to learn a fact that contained a novel word alleviates the concern about task complexity.

In summary, children and adults were as good at learning and remembering an arbitrary linguistically presented fact about an entity as they were at remembering its name, even if the arbitrary fact contained a novel word. Nevertheless, fast mapping does not apply to any arbitrary memorization task, as illustrated by the children who, after a one-month delay, were unable to recall the location of a sticker. This raises the question of the scope of this process. One possibility is that it applies only to information conveyed through language. Another is that salience is a factor, and that the children and adults simply found the source of the object to be a more interesting fact than the placement of the sticker, and hence easier to remember. A third possibility is that fast mapping only applies in circumstances in which object identity or object category is considered relevant, as opposed to a property such as location. Nevertheless, although the precise scope of fast mapping remains a topic for further investigation, it is not limited to word learning.

In addition, we found no critical period for fast mapping; there was no advantage for children, at least for the time intervals studied here. In contrast, children are much better at learning phonology, morphology and syntax than adults,[9] consistent with the notion of a biological specialization for these aspects of language.[10,11] In this regard, then, word learning is different from other aspects of language development. This difference also surfaces in developmental disorders in which word learning is intact but other aspects of language are severely impaired,[12] as well as in event-related brain potential studies which find that lexical information is processed differently from grammatical information in both children and adults.[13] The finding that fast mapping is not restricted to word learning is therefore consistent with evidence from different sources which suggests that word learning is mediated by processes of human learning and memory that are not special to the domain of language.[14]

Methods

The novel objects were roughly equal in size and were selected according to the criterion that subjects would be unable to name them. They included a white plastic rectangle consisting of ten plastic bars connected by two longer bars, a gray plastic grid, a wooden stick with a black sponge tip, a trumpet-shaped piece of pasta, a blue plastic tube with a ridged surface, and a brown rubber disk that was smooth on one side and indented with various circles on the other. The familiar objects included pennies, a pencil, a ruler, and some string.

For half of the subjects in each study, the new word "koba" was used in the singular to describe a single object; for the rest, it was used to describe multiple identical objects of that kind. Subjects were told either "Let's measure the koba. We can count these to see how long the koba is. We can put the koba away now." or "Let's use the kobas to measure which is longer. Line up the kobas so we can count them. We can put the kobas away now."

Subjects who were taught a singular label learned a fact about multiple objects of the same kind, whereas subjects who were taught a plural label for multiple objects of the same kind were taught a fact about a single object. In study 1, subjects were told: "We can use the thing(s) my uncle gave to me to measure which is longer. My uncle gave these to me. We can put the thing(s) my uncle gave to me away now." Subjects is study 2 watched as a sticker was placed on one of the unfamiliar objects, and were told: "Watch where this goes. This goes here [placing the sticker onto one of the objects]. That's where this goes." The specific objects presented in the different conditions were counterbalanced across subjects.

Acknowledgements

We thank K. Wynn for helpful comments on a previous draft of this paper and E. Mallin for assistance with data collection.

References

1   Carey, S., & Bartlett, E. (1978). *Child Lang. Dev.*, *15*, 17–29.
2   Carey, S. (1978). In M. Halle, I. Bresnan, & G.A. Miller (Eds.), *Linguistic Theory and Psychological Reality*, 264–293. Cambridge, AMA: MIT Press.
3   Markman, E.M. (1989). *Categorization and Naming in Children: Problems of Induction*, 1–250. Cambridge, MA: MIT Press.
4   Baldwin, D.A. (1991). *Child Dev.*, *62*, 875–890.
5   Dickinson, D.K. (1984). *Appl. Psycholing.*, *5*, 359–373.
6   Dollaghan, C.A. (1987). *Speech Hear. Disord.*, *52*, 218–222.
7   Heibeck, T.H., & Markman, E.M. (1987). *Child. Dev.*, *58*, 1021–1034.
8   Rice, M.L., Buhr, J.C., & Nemeth, M. (1990). *J. Speech Hear. Disord.*, *55*, 33–42.
9   Newport, E. (1990). *Cogn. Sci.*, *14*, 11–28.
10 Chomsky, N. (1980). *Rules and Representations*, 1–299. Oxford: Blackwell.
11 Pinker, S. (1994). *The Language Instinct*, 1–494. New York: Morrow.
12 Curtiss, S. (1989). In M. Bornstein, & I. Bruner (Eds.), *Interaction in Human Development*, 105–137. Hillsdale, NJ: LEA.
13 Neville, H.J. (1991). In K.R. Gibson, & A.C. Peterson (Eds.), *Brain Maturation and Cognitive Development*, 355–380. Hawthorne, New York: Aldine de Gruyter.
14 Bloom, P., & Kelemen, D. (1995). *Cognition*, *56*, 1–30.
15 Markman, E.M., & Wachtel, G.F. (1988). *Cogn. Psychol.*, *20*, 121–157.

TEN

On the Inseparability of Grammar and the Lexicon: Evidence from Acquisition*

Elizabeth Bates and Judith C. Goodman

Linguistics is a field that is known for controversy. However, one general trend has characterized recent proposals in otherwise very diverse theoretical frameworks: more and more of the explanatory work that was previously handled by the grammar has been moved into the lexicon. In some frameworks (e.g., Chomsky, 1981, 1995), the grammatical component that remains is an austere, "stripped down" system characterized by a single rule for movement and a set of constraints on the application of that rule. In this theory, the richness and diversity of linguistic forms within any particular language are now captured almost entirely by the lexicon – although this is now a very complex lexicon that includes propositional structures and productive rules that govern the way elements are combined. The trend toward lexicalism is even more apparent in alternative frameworks like Lexical Functional Grammar (Bresnan, 2001) and Head-Driven Phrase Structure Grammar (Pollard & Sag, 1994). It reaches its logical conclusion in a framework called Construction Grammar (Fillmore et al., 1988; Goldberg, 1995), in which the distinction between grammar and the lexicon has disappeared altogether (see also Langacker, 1987). Instead, all elements of linguistic form are represented within a heterogeneous lexicon that contains bound morphemes, free-standing content and function words, and complex phrase structures without terminal elements (e.g., the passive). This lexicon can be likened to a large municipal zoo, with many different kinds of animals. To be sure, the animals vary greatly in size, shape, food preference, lifestyle, and the kind of handling they require. But they live together in one compound, under common management. The new lexicalist perspective is quite different from the modular proposals that characterized the first two decades or so of modern generative linguistics, which postulated separate but roughly equal components for semantics (including lexical description), grammar, and phonology (e.g., Chomsky, 1965).

The field of language acquisition has (with some exceptions) not kept up with this lexicalist movement in linguistic theory. Many investigators within the field are still firmly rooted in the modular perspective that characterized linguistic theory thirty

---

* Redacted from *Language and Cognitive Processes*, 1997, 12 (5/6), 507–584.

years ago, seeking a discrete and discontinuous boundary between grammar and the lexicon, and/or between those lexical items that do grammatical work and those that do not (e.g., the distinction between closed- and open-class words – Garrett, 1992; the contrast between regular and irregular morphology – Pinker, 1991). In this paper, we will review evidence on the relationship between lexical development and the emergence of grammar that supports a unified lexicalist view.

We will begin with evidence on the period between 8 and 30 months, when children make the passage from first words to grammar, showing that the emergence and elaboration of grammar are highly dependent upon vocabulary size. Then we will compare these results for normal children with studies of early language development in several atypical populations, including early talkers, children with focal brain injury, Williams Syndrome, and Down Syndrome. Results will show that (a) grammar and vocabulary do not dissociate in early talkers or in children with focal brain injury, at least not within this phase of development, (b) grammatical development never outstrips lexical growth, even in the Williams population (a form of retardation in which linguistic abilities are surprisingly spared in the adult steady state), and (c) grammatical development can fall behind vocabulary in some subgroups (e.g., Down Syndrome), but this apparent dissociation can be explained by limits on auditory processing. We conclude that the case for a modular distinction between grammar and the lexicon in language development has been overstated (see also MacDonald et al., 1994), and that developmental evidence is more compatible with a radically lexicalist theory of grammar (Goldberg, 1995; MacWhinney, 1993).

This does not mean that grammatical structures don't exist (they do), or that the representations that underlie grammatical phenomena are identical to those that underlie single-content words (they are not). Rather, we are suggesting that the heterogeneous set of linguistic forms that occur in any natural language (i.e., words, morphemes, phrase structure types) may be acquired and processed by a unified processing system, one that obeys a common set of activation and learning principles. There is no need for discontinuous boundaries.

I. Grammar and the Lexicon in Normally Developing Children

Af first glance, the course of early language development seems to provide a *prima facie* case for linguistic modularity. Children begin their linguistic careers with babble, starting with vowels (somewhere around 3–4 months, on average) and ending with combinations of vowels and consonants of increasing complexity (usually between 6 and 12 months). Meaningful speech emerges some time between 10 and 12 months, on average, although word comprehension may begin a few weeks earlier. After this, most children spend many weeks or months producing single-word utterances. At first their rate of vocabulary growth is very slow, but one typically sees a "burst" or acceleration in the rate of vocabulary growth somewhere between 16 and 20 months. First word combinations usually appear between 18 and 20 months, although they tend to be rather spare and telegraphic (at least in English). Somewhere between 24 and 30 months, most children show a kind of "second burst," a flowering of morphosyntax that Roger Brown (1973) has characterized as "the ivy coming in between the bricks."

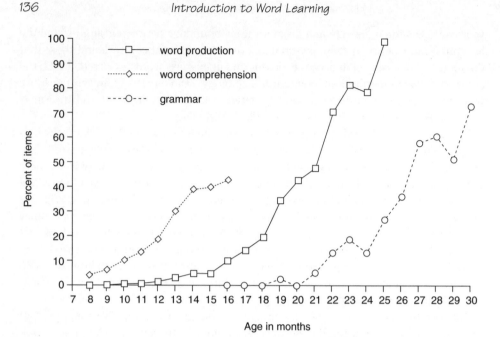

Figure 10.1   Median growth scores for word comprehension, production and grammar expressed as a percent of available items.

By 3–3.5 years of age, most normal children have mastered the basic morphological and syntactic structures of their language (defined by various criteria for productivity, including rule-like extension of grammatical structures to novel words).

   This picture of language development in English has been documented extensively. Of course this textbook story is not exactly the same in every language (Slobin, this volume), and perfectly healthy children can vary markedly in rate and style of development through these milestones (for reviews, see Bates et al., 1995a; Shore, 1995). At a global level, however, the passage from sounds to words to grammar appears to be a universal of child language development. A quick look at the relative timing and shape of growth in word comprehension, word production, and grammar can be seen in figure 10.1, taken from our own longitudinal study of language development from 8–30 months (Goodman, 1995). The word comprehension and production estimates are based on the same word checklist, and the grammar estimate is based on a 37-item scale for sentence complexity (note that these comprehension data were only collected from 8–16 months, and measurement of grammar did not begin until 16 months – see below for additional methodological details). Assuming for a moment that we have a right to compare the proportional growth of apples and oranges, this figure shows that all three domains follow a dramatic, nonlinear pattern of growth across this age range – although these "zones of acceleration" are separated by weeks or months.

   As Fodor (1983) has argued, one of the nine criteria that define a "mental module" is the observance of a "characteristic maturational course" (for discussion, see Elman et al., 1996). Indeed, it does look as though the basic modules of 1960s generative lin-

guistics emerge on a fixed and orderly schedule: phonology, followed by lexical semantics, with the grammatical component making its first appearance around two years of
age. Bickerton (1984) has taken this succession quite seriously. Following Chomsky,[1]
he argues that the period of babbling and single-word production prior to two years of
age is essentially "pre-linguistic." True language only begins when sentences begin,
around 2 years of age.

This kind of structural discontinuity in the passage from first words to grammar is
reminiscent of Jakobson's proposal for a discontinuity between babble and meaningful
speech (1968). Jakobson went so far as to suggest that children fall silent for a brief
period between these two stages. Furthermore, he suggested that the phonological
content of babble (i.e., the consonants and vowels that children prefer) is quite distinct
from the phonological content of first words. These were interesting ideas, but after 30
years of research on child phonology, we now know that Jakobson was wrong on both
these points (Goodman & Nusbaum, 1994). There is no silent period, and the specific
sounds that individual children prefer in their prelexical babble tend to predominate in
the same child's first attempts at meaningful speech. This continuous flow of preferred
and avoided phonemes suggests that phonological and lexical development are inter-
woven. What appeared at first glance to be an orderly and modular progression from
one linguistic component to another turns out, after a closer look, to involve bi-
directional causality and temporal overlap.

What about the passage from single words to grammar? We have known for some
time that, within individual children, the content, style, and patterning of first word
combinations is strongly influenced by the content, style, and patterning of single-word
speech (Bates et al., 1988; Bloom, 1991). But of course no one has ever proposed that
grammar can begin in the absence of words. Any rule-based device is going to have to
have a certain amount of lexical material to work on. The real question is: Just how
tight are the correlations between lexical and grammatical development in the second
and third year of life? Are these components dissociable, and if so, to what extent? How
much lexical material is needed to build a grammatical system? Can grammar get off
the ground and go its separate way once a minimum number of words is reached (e.g.,
50–100 words, the modal vocabulary size when first word combinations appear – Bates
et al., 1988; Nelson, 1973)? Or will we observe a constant and lawful interchange
between lexical and grammatical development, of the sort that one would expect if the
lexicalist approach to grammar is correct, and grammar does not dissociate from the
lexicon at any point? Our reading of the evidence suggests that the latter view is correct.
As we shall see, the function that governs the relation between lexical and grammatical growth in this age range is so lawful that it approaches Fechner's law in elegance
and power. The successive "bursts" that characterize vocabulary growth and the emergence of morphosyntax can be viewed as different phases of an immense nonlinear
wave that starts in the single-word stage and crashes on the shores of grammar a year
or so later.

Our first insights into this tight relationship came in a longitudinal study of 27 children who were observed at 10, 13, 20, and 28 months of age, using a combination of
structured observations (at home and in the laboratory) and parental report (Bates et
al., 1988). Among other things, we examined the concurrent and predictive relation
between vocabulary size and grammatical status at 20 and 28 months of age. Vocabu-

Table 10.1 Relations between grammatical development and vocabulary size from 20 to 28 months (From Bates et al., 1988)

	20-month vocabulary	20-month MLU[1]	28-month vocabulary	28-month MLU[1]
20-month vocabulary	–			
20-month MLU[1]	+.54**	–		
28-month vocabulary	+.64**	+.47*	–	
28-month MLU[1]	+.83**	+.48*	+.73**	–

* p < .05
** p < .01
[1] Mean length of utterance in morphemes.

lary size was assessed with a combination of video observations and parental report. Grammatical development was assessed in a standard fashion, calculating mean length of utterance in morphemes (MLU) from speech transcriptions, following the rules outlined by Brown (1973).[2] Table 10.1 summarizes the cross-lag correlations that we found between lexical and grammatical development within and across these two age levels. Results were very clear: The single best estimate of grammatical status at 28 months (right in the heart of the "grammar burst") is total vocabulary size at 20 months (measured right in the middle of the "vocabulary burst"). In fact, the correlation coefficient in this and related analyses with other grammatical variables hovered consistently between +.70 and +.84. Because we know that no measure can correlate with another variable higher than it correlates with itself (i.e., Spearman's Law of Reliability), it is interesting to note that separate samples of MLU at 28 months of age also tend to intercorrelate in the +.75–+.80 range. What this means, in essence, is that 20-month vocabulary and 28-month MLU scores are statistically identical; one could be used as a stand-in for the other in predicting a child's rank within his/her group. Of course this kind of correlational finding does not force us to conclude that grammar and vocabulary growth are mediated by the same developmental mechanism. Correlation is not cause. At the very least, however, this powerful correlation suggests that the two have something important in common.

In a more recent series of studies, we have developed a new parental report instrument called the MacArthur Communicative Development Inventory (CDI) to study the relationship between lexical and grammatical development in a much larger sample of 1,800 normally developing children, primarily middle class, all growing up in English-speaking households (Fenson et al., 1994). The CDI relies primarily on a checklist format to assess word comprehension (from 8–16 months), word production (from

8–30 months), and the emergence of grammar (from 16–30 months). Details concerning these two instruments (in English and Italian) are provided in Caselli et al. (this volume). For our purposes here, the most important aspects of this instrument are the vocabulary checklist (containing 680 words on the Words and Phrases Scale, intended for 16–30-month-olds), and the grammatical complexity checklist. The complexity checklist contains 37 sentence pairs, each reflecting a single linguistic contrast that is known to come in during this age range (e.g., "KITTY SLEEPING" paired with "KITTY IS SLEEPING"). Parents were asked to indicate (even if their child had not said this particular sentence) which sentence in each pair "sounds more like the way that your child is talking right now." Additional information about grammar comes from a second in which parents write out the three longest sentences that they can remember their child saying in the last couple of weeks (on the grounds that these would be sufficiently recent and striking events to have some validity even in recall mode). Finally, we provided a list of irregular nouns and verbs in their correct inflected forms (e.g., teeth; made), as well as a list of regularization errors that are common in young English-speaking children (e.g., tooths; maked). Parents were asked to check whether they had heard their child produce any of these forms. These three different modes of assessing early grammar were all highly correlated in the Fenson et al. study. More importantly still, the three measures correlate very highly with traditional laboratory measures of grammatical complexity (Dale, 1991; Dale et al., 1989), including correlations with MLU up to the statistical ceiling (i.e., as high as MLU correlates with itself in reliability studies). It is thus fair to conclude that these measures constitute a valid and reliable estimate of individual differences in grammatical development across the period from 16–30 months of age. In most of the results that follow, we will concentrate on the relation between vocabulary size and grammar using the 37-item grammatical complexity scale as our primary outcome variable. It is clear from the validation studies, however, that any of these parent report and/or laboratory estimates of gross progress in grammar would yield the same result.

As reported by Fenson et al. (1994), the relationship between grammatical complexity and vocabulary size in their large cross-sectional sample replicates and extends the powerful grammar/vocabulary relationship that had emerged in Bates et al. (1988). Figure 10.2 (from Fenson et al.) illustrates the relation between performance on the 37-item sentence complexity scale and productive vocabulary size (collapsed over age, with children divided into groups reflecting fewer than 50 words, 50–100 words, 101–200 words, 201–300 words, 301–400 words, 401–500 words, 501–600 words and >600 words). The linear correlation between these two measures is +.84 (p < .0001), but it is clear from Figure 10.2 that the function governing this relationship is nonlinear.

Of course there is some individual variation around this function. This is illustrated by the standard error of the mean in Figure 10.2, and by the separate lines in figure 10.3a, which indicate scores for children at the 90th, 75th, 50th, 25th, and 10th percentiles for grammar within each vocabulary group. These variance statistics make two points: (1) individual differences around the grammar-on-vocabulary function are relatively small, and (2) the variance is consistent in magnitude at every point along the horizontal axis beyond 50–100 words. Both these points are clarified further if we compare the tight correlation between grammar and vocabulary with the clear disso-

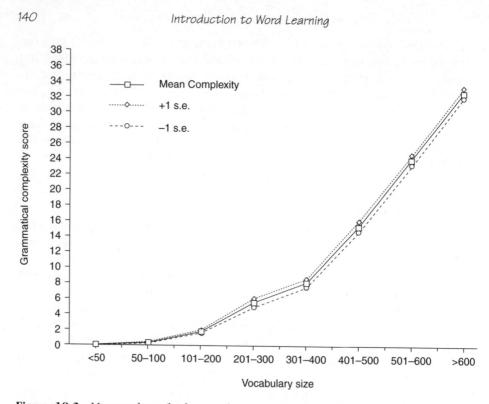

Figure 10.2 Mean and standard errors for grammatical complexity in children at different
vocabulary levels.

ciation between word comprehension and word production observed at an earlier
point in language development. Figure 10.3b displays the relation between expressive
vocabulary (on the vertical axis) and receptive vocabulary (on the horizontal axis),
collapsed over age in children between 8 and 16 months (redrawn from the MacArthur
norming study, Fenson et al., 1994). Analogous to figure 10.3a, figure 10.3b illustrates
the relation between domains by plotting scores at the 90th, 75th, 50th, 25th, and
10th percentile for word production within each comprehension group. What we see
in figure 10.3b is a classic fan-shaped pattern of variation, including children who are
still producing virtually no meaningful speech at all despite receptive vocabularies of
more than 200 words. Hence this figure captures a phenomenon that is well attested
in the child language literature: Comprehension and production can dissociate to a
remarkable degree. A certain level of word comprehension is prerequisite for expressive language to get off the ground, but comprehension (though necessary) is apparently not sufficient. If the same thing were true for the relationship between vocabulary
and grammar, we would expect the same kind of fan-shaped variance in figure 10.3a.
That is, we might expect vocabulary size to place a ceiling on grammatical development
up to somewhere between 50 and 200 words (when most children make the passage
into multiword speech). After that point, the variance should spread outward as the
two domains decouple and grammar takes off on its own course. Instead, we find that
grammar and vocabulary are tightly coupled across the 16–30-month age range.

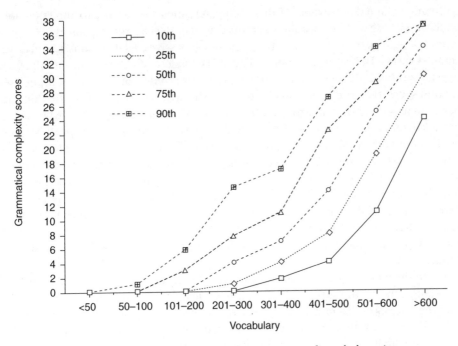

Figure 10.3a Relationship between grammar and vocabulary size.

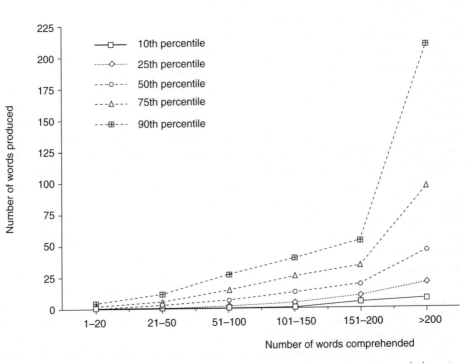

Figure 10.3b Variability in word production as a function of comprehension vocabulary size.

To understand the relevance of this finding, it is important to keep in mind that normally developing children are able to produce most of the basic grammatical structures of their language by 3–3.5 years of age, including passives, relative clauses, and other complex forms. Hence the function in figure 10.2 follows children right into the very heart of grammatical development, when productive control over crucial morphological and syntactic structures is well under way (Brown, 1973). We also note that this powerful function is not an artifact of age, because it remains very strong when age is partialed out of the correlation (Fenson et al., 1994). Indeed, age is a surprisingly poor predictor of both vocabulary and grammar within this 16–30-month window, for this large sample of healthy English-speaking children. Taken together, age and vocabulary size account for 71.4% of the variance in grammatical complexity. When age is entered into the equation after vocabulary size is controlled, it adds a statistically reliable but exceedingly small 0.8% to the total variance accounted for. However, when vocabulary size is entered into the equation after age is controlled, it adds a whopping 32.3% to the variance in grammar scores. (For similar results in Italian, see Caselli et al., this volume.)

Given the power of this relationship, we might suspect that another kind of artifact is lurking beneath the surface. After all, the vocabulary checklist includes grammatical function words like prepositions, articles, auxiliary verbs, pronouns, and conjunctions. Perhaps all that we really have in figure 10.2 is a tautological relation of grammar with itself! To control for this possibility, we recalculated total vocabulary size for the full MacArthur sample, subtracting out grammatical function words for each individual child. Figure 10.4 illustrates the relation between grammar and vocabulary that is observed when vocabulary counts are based entirely on the remaining content words. The nonlinear function that remains is, if anything, even more powerful than the original function where all words are included in the vocabulary total.

Another possible objection to these findings revolves around the cross-sectional nature of the normative sample. Because the functions in figures 10.1–10.4 are collapsed across different children at different age levels, we cannot assume that they represent patterns of growth for any individual child. In a more recent study (Goodman, 1995; Jahn-Samilo, 1995; Thal et al., 1997), we have used the MacArthur CDI to follow 28 individual children longitudinally, with parents filling out the forms on a monthly basis from 8 to 30 months of age. From 12–30 months, we also saw the children monthly in the laboratory, videotaping free speech and free play and administering structured measures of word comprehension, word production, and comprehension of grammar. There were striking similarities between this longitudinal sample and the large cross-sectional sample from the MacArthur norming study in both the mean and the range of variation observed across age levels in word comprehension, word production, and the development of grammar. Figure 10.5 compares the nonlinear function linking sentence complexity and vocabulary size in the respective cross-sectional and longitudinal samples. The two functions are remarkably similar, separated only by a very small lag (i.e., slightly lower complexity rates per vocabulary group in the longitudinal sample), well within the range of variation that we observe for the cross-sectional sample (figures 10.2, 10.3a).

Although this comparison does suggest that a common growth function is observed in both cross-sectional and longitudinal designs, we are still looking at group data in

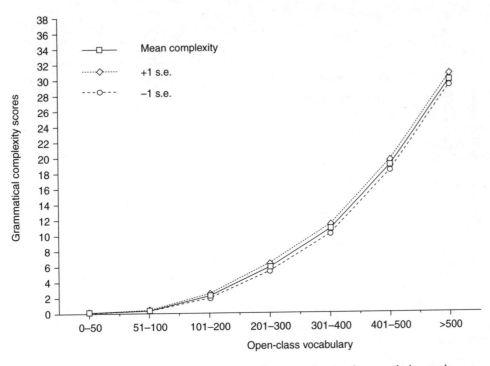

Figure 10.4 Grammatical complexity as a function of open-class vocabulary only.

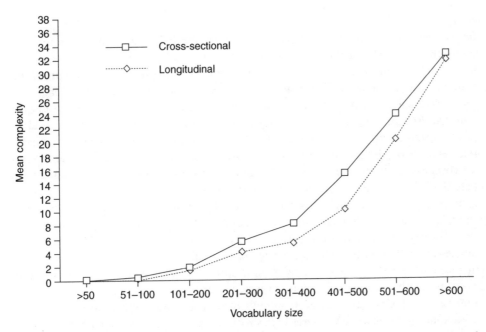

Figure 10.5 Grammatical complexity as a function of vocabulary size for the cross-sectional vs. longitudinal samples.

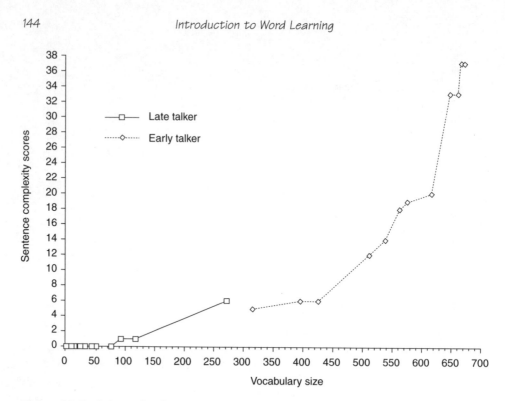

Figure 10.6   Relationship between grammatical complexity & vocabulary size for one late talker and one early talker.

both cases (i.e., results collapsed over many different children at each data point). We might therefore ask whether the growth curves in the longitudinal study look similar for individual children, or whether the commonalities in figure 10.5 represent group trends that mask sharp dissociations in at least some individual cases. To address this issue, we graphed the individual grammar-on-vocabulary functions for each of the 27 children. Results suggest a remarkable degree of similarity between these individual growth curves and the range of curves (from the 10th to the 90th percentile) summarized at the group level in figure 10.3a. To illustrate this point, we present the grammar-on-vocabulary functions for two individual children in figure 10.6, for each session between 16 and 30 months. These children were selected to represent extremes in rate of vocabulary growth, including one very late talker and one very early talker. Even though the two children overlap perfectly in age, there was absolutely no overlap in their vocabulary size across this period: the late talker produced only 272 words by the last session at 30 months, while the early talker already had a vocabulary of 315 words at 17 months, when administration of the grammar scales began. It is clear from figure 10.6 that both children are making progress in grammar that is directly commensurate to their lexical abilities, even though they reach their respective grammar-on-vocabulary levels at widely different ages within this period of development.

We have also had an opportunity to compare the grammar-on-vocabulary functions for two languages, English and Italian (Caselli et al., 1999). In both languages, the

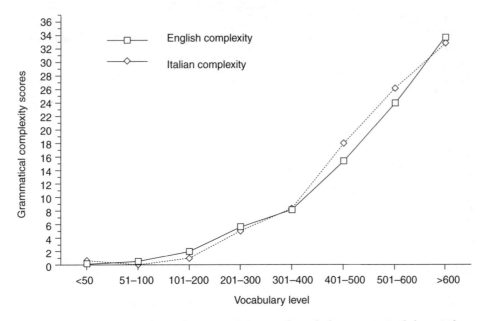

Figure 10.7 Grammatical complexity as a function of vocabulary size in English vs. Italian.

grammar scale of the CDI contained 37 pairs of sentences designed to pick up contrasts that are known to develop in that language between 17 and 30 months. However, the content of the respective grammar scales is entirely different (i.e., they are not translations). Despite these differences, figure 10.7 shows that the same lawful and powerful function is observed in two languages that differ markedly in their grammatical structure.

We are convinced by these data that there is a powerful link between grammar and lexical growth in this age range, a nonlinear growth function that holds for both cross-sectional and longitudinal designs, at both the individual and the group level. These results (even for individual children) are collapsed across a range of different grammatical structures. What does the relationship look like when we look at specific aspects of the grammar? Presumably, because we know that different grammatical structures come in at different points within this developmental window, we ought to expect individual forms to display different degrees and (perhaps) different types of "lexical dependence." For example, individual grammatical structures might require a different "critical mass" across the whole vocabulary, or they might require a critical number of lexical items within a specific class.

Some insights into this issue come from Marchman and Bates (1994), who used the MacArthur norming data to investigate the relationship between the number of verbs that children use and their progress on the verb morphology subscales on the CDI (i.e., the checklists of irregular, regular and overregularizes forms noted above). This study was motivated by the ongoing controversy between the connectionist "single mechanism" approach to grammatical development (Elman, this volume; Elman et al., 1996; MacWhinney, 1993; Plunkett & Marchman, 1993) and the symbolic "rote vs. rule"

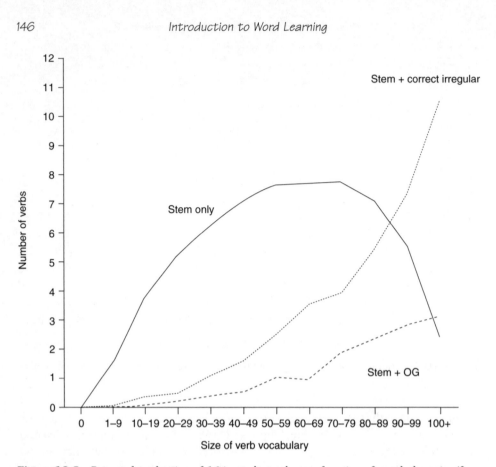

Figure 10.8   Reported production of 16 irregular verbs as a function of vocabulary size (from Marchman & Bates, 1994).

approach (Brown, 1973; Marcus et al., 1992; Pinker, 1991). Connectionist simulations of the acquisition of past-tense morphology have shown that a single mechanism can display many of the same behaviors that characterize grammatical learning in children. These include an initial stage in which the system produces high-frequency irregular past-tense forms correctly (e.g., CAME, WENT), a lengthy intermediate phase in which these correct forms coexist with occasional overregularizations (e.g., COMED, GOED), followed by an asymptotic convergence on the use of correct regulars and irregulars. However, as critics of the single-mechanism account have noted (e.g., Marcus et al., 1992), these changes are linked to the size and composition of verb vocabulary (e.g., high-frequency irregulars tend to dominate in the early stages; the appearance of overregularizations correlates with an increase in the proportion of regulars to irregulars in the network's "vocabulary"). This raises an important question: is past-tense learning in real children also tied to changes in vocabulary size?

Figure 10.8 from Marchman and Bates illustrates the relation between number of verbs in the child's vocabulary (based on the subset of verbs that are used in the vocabulary checklist and in the past-tense scale) and three forms of past-tense marking: zero stem (the child is reported to use the verb in the citation form only), correct irregulars, and incorrect overgeneralizations. This figure reveals a strong nonlinear relationship between verb vocabulary size and successive phases in the development of past-tense morphemes, similar to the relationship observed in connectionist simulations of this learning process.

This demonstration of a link between verb vocabulary and past-tense morphology is the only example we have right now of a link between specific grammatical structures and their requisite "critical mass" of lexical items. A great deal more work could be done in this area, to determine the lexical prerequisites (if any) for specific grammatical forms, which may vary substantially within and across languages. For now, we turn to a different set of questions. Is the powerful grammar–vocabulary relationship universal for anyone acquiring English, or can we find atypical populations in which dissociations between lexical and grammatical development are observed?

II. Grammatical Development and the Lexicon in Atypical Populations

Although grammatical development invariably follows a stage in which single words are acquired, the findings reviewed so far suggest that, aside from this temporal lag, there is no dissociation between grammar and lexical development in normal children. In view of the claims that have been made about the dissociability of these domains in adults, it seemed important to us to determine whether there are any individual children or any specific pediatric populations who deviate from the function displayed in figures 10.2–10.6.

In fact, the literature on older children with language disorders gives us reason to expect selective impairments in early grammar. Specific Language Impairment or SLI is defined as a delay in expressive language abilities that is at least 1 standard deviation below the mean for the child's chronological age, in the absence of mental retardation, frank neurological impairment, social-emotional disorders (e.g., autism), or any other serious biomedical risk factors that could account for the delay. Although the definition of SLI presupposes that language can be dissociated from the rest of cognition, the specificity of Specific Language Impairment is still controversial (Bishop, 1997; Gopnik, 1990; Leonard, 1998). For example, many investigators report that children with SLI score significantly below age-matched controls on at least some nonlinguistic measures, including mental imagery, symbolic play, shifting attention, and the ability to detect rapid temporal changes in auditory stimuli (see Bishop and Leonard for reviews). There is considerably more agreement about the nature of the language impairment in SLI. Within every linguistic domain that has been studied to date, the expressive and/or receptive abilities of children with SLI are qualitatively similar to those of younger normal children, but delays seem to be greater for grammar.

The vulnerability of grammar in SLI has led to some radical proposals. For example, Gopnik (1990) and Pinker (1991) described a family with what appeared to be a congenital version of SLI, manifested in a specific dissociation between regular and irregular grammatical morphology, with relative sparing of irregular forms. They suggested that such a dissociation is possible because irregulars are processed in the lexicon, while regulars are handled by a separate grammatical processor. However, a more comprehensive study of the same family by Vargha-Khadem et al. (1995) has shown that the

affected members of this family are equally impaired on both regular and irregular morphemes, as well as on a host of other language and nonlanguage measures. Marchman
et al. (1995) have investigated the proposed regular/irregular past-tense dissociation
in a large sample of children with SLI. They report significant impairments in past-tense
morphology for SLI children compared with age-matched controls. However, they find
no evidence whatsoever for a dissociation between regular and irregular forms. The
errors produced by children with SLI are quite similar to those of younger normal
children – there are just more of them (especially omissions).

Regardless of one's position on this question, we shall see later on that the selective
vulnerability of grammatical morphology is not specific to SLI. It has been observed in
a number of other child and adult populations, including children with Down Syndrome (Chapman, 1995; Contardi & Vicari, 1994). For present purposes, the point is
that a certain degree of dissociability has already been observed between grammatical
morphology and other aspects of language in older children and adults with language
impairments. What we want to determine next is whether analogous patterns of dissociation are observed in the period when grammar first develops.

Late and early talkers

Within a larger program looking for patterns of association and dissociation within and
across linguistic and cognitive domains, Thal and her colleagues have examined patterns of lexical and grammatical development in infants and preschool children at the
extreme ends of the normal distribution (Thal, 1991; Thal et al., 1996). This includes
"late talkers," defined as children in the bottom 10th percentile for expressive vocabulary between 18 and 24 months of age, in the absence of the same exclusionary factors
that are used to diagnose SLI in older children. It also includes "early talkers," defined
as children in the top 10th percentile for expressive vocabulary between 12 and 24
months of age. For our purposes here, we are interested in the relationship between
grammar and vocabulary in these extreme groups. If late talkers constitute an early
variant of SLI, then we might expect to find that grammar lags behind vocabulary level,
compared with children who reach the same vocabulary size closer to the normative
age. Alternatively, we might find some late talkers who have managed to develop grammatical abilities well in advance of their lexical levels. The same two extremes may also
be observed among the early talkers: children whose grammatical abilities are still tied
to chronological age, despite their lexical precocity, and children who are "grammar
geniuses," attaining levels of sentence complexity that are even greater than their
abilities in the lexical domain.

These were reasonable hypotheses, but they have not been supported by the data. In
study after study, grammatical development appears to be tied to lexical level even in
children at the far ends of the continuum, in patterns similar to those displayed by the
two extreme longitudinal cases in figure 10.6. Some further insights into this issue
come from case studies of children with extremely precocious language development
(Thal et al., 1996). In one of the children in this study, grammar did appear to lag
behind vocabulary level, suggesting some degree of dissociation. However, a detailed
comparison of the free-speech data and parent report data revealed an unexpectedly
strong association between vocabulary development and inflectional morphology for

both these children, even though one of them has barely moved out of the single-word stage!

This conclusion is illustrated in Table 10.2 (from Thal et al., 1996), which provides examples of the utterances produced by MW (17 months old with an expressive vocabulary of 596 words in the CDI) and SW (21 months old with an expressive vocabulary of 627 words on the CDI). With an MLU of 2.13, MW is right where we would expect her to be in grammar, given her vocabulary size (equivalent to performance by an average 28–30-month-old child in both domains). By contrast, SW has just begun to combine words (MLU 1.12) despite her huge vocabulary. In fact, her grammatical abilities are quite average for a 21-month-old child. At first glance it appears that SW represents a striking dissociation between grammar and vocabulary. However, the examples in Table 10.2 reveal a very curious phenomenon: production of words with contrasting inflections (e.g., 'falling . . . fell") in single-word utterances. This is a very odd phenomenon for children acquiring English, although it has been observed in children acquiring a highly inflected language such as Turkish (Slobin, 1985). Applying the criteria for morphological productivity developed by Brown (1973), Thal et al. discovered that both children have about as much control over English morphology as we would expect to find in a 2.5-year-old child. In fact, SW was actually more advanced than MW in grammatical morphology (i.e., productive control over more morphemes according to Brown's rules), although both children are well within the range that we would expect for children with more than 500 words (Marchman & Bates, 1994).

If the difference between MW and SW does not represent a clear dissociation between grammar and vocabulary, how can we explain their striking differences in utterance length? Thal et al. note that SW produced carefully articulated single words. By contrast, MW was observed to use longer utterances that often appeared formulaic in nature. Her parents indicated that MW could remember and produce a number of songs and idiomatic expressions (e.g., "No way, Jose," or "You little monkey!"). In fact, to the surprise and amusement of her mother and the experimenter, MW produced a novel juxtaposition of two established formulae during one of the experimental sessions: "No way, you monkey!" Thal et al. tentatively conclude that these two children differ primarily in the size of the unit that they are able to store in auditory memory, and/or the size of the unit that they are able to retrieve and reformulate in speech production (see also Peters, 1983). As we shall see shortly, this kind of processing account will prove useful in explaining the apparent dissociations observed in some clinical populations.

Early focal lesions

A different perspective on the relationship between early grammar and the lexicon comes from studies of infants and children with early focal brain lesions to the left or right hemisphere, usually due to pre- or perinatal stroke (Bates et al., 1997; Reilly et al., 1998). When cases with intractable seizures or other medical complications are excluded, most studies of this population report language abilities that are well within the normal range, regardless of lesion side, size, or site (Bates et al., 1999; Eisele & Aram, 1995; Feldman et al., 1992; Vargha-Khadem et al., 1994). As a group, children

Table 10.2 Examples of language production by two very early talkers (from Thal, Bates, Zappia, & Oroz, 1996)

MW:		SW:	
Age:	17 months old	Age:	21 months old
Vocabulary	596 words	Vocabulary:	627 words
Vocabulary age:	30 months	Vocabulary age:	>30 months
MLU:	2.13	MLU	1.19
MLU age:	28 months	MLU age:	20 months

MW	SW
Where cup went?	Pretty.
Where chair went?	Cute.
Teddy bear went?	Big.
Baby doing?	Round.
	Dry.
Wanna walk e baby.	Hungry.
Wanna put it on.	Wet.
Wanna go ride it.	Different.
Want mom get off.	Enough.
	Else.
Daddy take her. (referring to self)	More.
Help with the apple.	Minute.
Can't get the teddy bear.	Brushing.
Teddybear the bath.	Hiding.
	Baby crying.
Too much carrots on the dish.	
	Hold.
Move it around.	Hold it.
Clean e bottom.	Dropped it.
	Bring it.
Put ne sofa.	
Put in eye.	Falling.
	Fell.
Mommy wear hat.	
Mommy smell it.	Talk.
Mommy read the book.	Talking.
Mommy sit down.	
	Wash'em.
Find Becky.	Shirt on.
See Becky in the morning.	Teddy up.
Becky is nice.	Mommy shoe.
Saw Becky and goats.	

with unilateral brain damage tend to perform below normal controls, but do not qualify for a diagnosis of aphasia. This conclusion holds even for children whose injuries involve the classical language zones, and for some children who have had the entire left hemisphere removed. In fact, when children with early lesion onset are studied after 5–7 years of age, current evidence suggests that there are no significant differences at all between children with left- vs. right-hemisphere injury.

In view of all this evidence for plasticity, what can children with focal brain injury tell us about the relationship between grammar and the lexicon? The stereotypical view of aphasia in adults might lead one to expect that these children would provide evidence for a dissociation between grammar and the lexicon – at least in the early stages, when they are trying to get grammar off the ground. Instead, children with early brain injuries show a tight relationship between deficits observed in grammar and the lexicon across the years in which these skills develop (Bates et al., 1997; Vicari et al., 2000). Before 5–7 years of age, brain damage does exact a very heavy cost: regardless of side or site of injury, infants with early unilateral injuries are often 10–20 months behind the norm for their age. Furthermore, we can find specific effects of lesion side and site during the years in which language is first acquired – but surprisingly, these effects bear little resemblance to the lesion-symptom correlations observed in adults with aphasia. For example, initial delays in "cracking the code" (word comprehension and gesture from 10–20 months) are actually greater in infants with damage to the right hemisphere, exactly the opposite of what is typically seen in brain-injured adults. Children with damage involving the frontal lobes are often especially delayed in word and grammar production – but it doesn't seem to matter whether the frontal lobe injury occurs on the left or right side! So far, there is only one clue to the left-hemisphere specialization for language that usually emerges in uninjured adults: between 1 and 5 years of age (which is a fairly long time), delays in word production are greatest in children whose lesions include the temporal lobe (a sensory area) in the left hemisphere. It may seem strange that a sensory area is associated with production delays, but Bates et al. (1999) point out a possible reason for this correlation: When children are learning to talk for the first time, they have to carry out a much more detailed perceptual analysis of the speech signal ("hearing for production") than they need to figure out what those words mean in the first place ("hearing for understanding"). By 5–7 years of age (including longitudinal samples), all of these effects seem to disappear. Although brain-injured children are still slightly behind normal controls, there are no left–right differences (at least not in most well-controlled studies), and the children have almost all moved into the normal range.

One final conclusion is most important for present purposes: If children with early focal brain damage are delayed in vocabulary, they are delayed in grammar – and vice versa. There seems to be no evidence in this population for a specific lesion that selectively affects grammar (leaving vocabulary intact) or selectively affects vocabulary (leaving grammar intact). To illustrate this last point, figure 10.9 shows the relationship between grammar and vocabulary for 19 individual children in the Bates et al. (1997) study, compared with the means for normal controls at different vocabulary levels between 19 and 31 months of age from the MacArthur CDI norming study (Fenson et al., 1994). We have plotted grammatical complexity against vocabulary size in this figure in a form that facilitates comparison between the focal lesion data and the

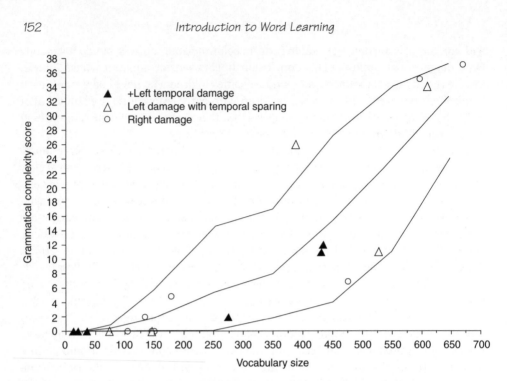

Figure 10.9   Grammar as a function of vocabulary size in children with focal brain injury (lines = 10th, 50th & 90th percentile for normals).

other populations considered so far. Separate symbols are provided to distinguish cases with left-hemisphere injuries involving the temporal lobe, left-hemisphere injuries that spare the temporal lobe, and right-hemisphere damage. The three lines in figure 10.9 represent the 10th, 50th, and 90th percentiles for grammar as a function of vocabulary size in the Fenson et al. normative sample. It should be clear from this figure that children with focal brain injury display the normal nonlinear relationship between grammar and vocabulary, even though some of them are markedly delayed on both (clustered in overlapping symbols in the bottom left quadrant). Of course there is some variance around this function, but the variance is no greater than we observe with normal children. Eighteen out of 19 focal-lesion cases fall within the 10-90 window for normal children, and one falls outside; we would expect between 1 and 4 cases to fall outside that window if we were drawing children randomly from the normal population. In short, there is no evidence for a dissociation between vocabulary and grammar in this phase of development, even in children who have suffered pre- or perinatal injuries to the classical language zones within the left hemisphere.

Williams Syndrome and Down Syndrome

Williams Syndrome (WMS) and Down Syndrome (DNS) are genetically based forms of mental retardation (Bellugi et al., 1994; Contardi & Vicari, 1994; Giannotti & Vicari, 1994; Mervis et al., 1999; Miller, 1992). In both groups, mean IQs generally hover between 40 and 60, although a broader range of IQ scores can be observed at every stage from infancy through adulthood. People with WMS and DNS tend to end up in the same special classrooms and residential centers; some adults are able to hold down simple jobs, but they are rarely able to live independently. Despite these similarities in global IQ and life experience, recent studies have revealed sharp contrasts between the two groups. For our purposes here, we are particularly interested in the claim that WMS and DNS represent a double dissociation between language and nonlinguistic cognition, and between lexical and grammatical aspects of language processing.

Children with DNS are markedly delayed in the acquisition of language. More importantly, their language abilities at virtually every stage (including the adult steady state) fall *below* the levels that we would expect based upon their mental age (Chapman, 1995; Miller, 1992). Furthermore, children and adults with DNS appear to be especially impaired in the production of bound and free grammatical morphemes, constituting a form of congenital agrammatism that is even more severe than the selective delays in grammatical morphology reported for children with Specific Language Impairment. The function word omissions and structural simplifications produced by older children with DNS are especially salient in a richly inflected language like Italian (Contardi & Vicari, 1994), resulting in profiles that are qualitatively similar to much younger normal children, although rates of omission are actually higher in DNS than controls when mean length of utterance is controlled (Fabbretti et al., 1997).

By contrast, older children and adults with WMS display levels of linguistic knowledge and language use that are surprisingly good when they are compared with the low levels of performance shown by children with DNS at the same mental age (Bellugi et al., 1994; Karmiloff-Smith et al., 1995; Mervis et al., 1999). This does not mean that individuals with WMS are "language savants." Those studies that have used normal controls have shown that the linguistic performance in WMS falls invariably below *chronological age* – which is, of course, not surprising for subjects with an IQ score around 50. When children with WMS are compared with younger normals matched for *mental age*, the picture is mixed. On most measures, performance is closely tied to mental age (Capirci et al., 1996; Giannotti & Vicari, 1994; Volterra et al., 1996). Performance above mental age is observed in children with WMS in two kinds of tasks: language tasks that draw heavily on auditory short-term memory (Wang & Bellugi, 1994), and/or language tasks that elicit affectively charged and colorful speech (Reilly et al., 1991).

The peculiar patterns of sparing and impairment that are observed within the language domain in WMS are complemented by equally interesting patterns of sparing and impairment outside of language. For example, people with WMS and DNS differ markedly in basic measures of information processing. WMS tend to be extremely sensitive to sound (i.e., hyperacusis), and they perform significantly better than IQ-matched individuals with DNS on tests of auditory short-term memory (Contardi & Vicari, 1994; Vicari et al., 1996; Wang & Bellugi, 1994). DNS is often associated with mild to moderate deficits in hearing, but DNS children show significantly better performance than age-matched WMS on gestural tasks, and DNS adults perform significantly better than WMS adults on measures of visual short-term memory. These differences in processing modality may be relevant to the contrasting grammatical profiles observed in WMS and DNS (see below).

Based on findings like these, the initial view of WMS as language savants has given way to an interest in this syndrome for the insight that this syndrome offers into language development under different conditions of information processing (especially auditory processing), affect and cognition (see Karmiloff-Smith, this volume). One of the most interesting questions revolves around the relationship between grammar and the lexicon in people with WMS. Earlier papers describing language in WMS suggested that grammar may be "spared" while semantics and pragmatics are deviant or "odd" (Bellugi et al., 1994; Reilly et al., 1991). Pinker (1991) has made the further suggestion that WMS may be particularly adept in the use of regular morphemes, resulting in overgeneralization errors on irregular forms (e.g., "goed" instead of "went"). However, more recent evidence suggests that grammar and lexical semantics are both abnormal in the WMS population. Rubba and Klima (1991) have shown that English-speaking WMS produce peculiar substitutions of prepositional forms. Karmiloff-Smith and colleagues have provided evidence suggesting that French-speaking WMS find it difficult to generalize regular gender morphology to novel words – even though they are very good at repeating the same novel items. Comparative studies of WMS and DNS in Italian suggest that both groups are markedly impaired in the production of grammatical morphemes, including both regular and irregular forms. However, the two groups differ markedly in the *kinds* of errors they produce. As noted above, Italian speakers with DNS tend to err by omission and simplification, yielding profiles similar to those that are observed in Italian Broca's aphasics, Italians with SLI, and very young Italian-speaking normals. By contrast, Italian speakers with WMS have been shown to produce a range of morphological substitutions that are rarely observed in normals at any age, bearing a distant resemblance to the substitution errors observed in Italian Wernicke's aphasics (Bates et al., 1991).

In view of the many contrasts observed in older children and adolescents with WMS syndrome vs. Down Syndrome, it is interesting to ask just how early the two groups separate in their profiles of language development. Is the language advantage in WMS (or the language disadvantage in DNS) present from the very beginning, or does it emerge only after some critical cognitive or linguistic milestone is reached? This question was addressed by Singer Harris et al. (1997), who used the MacArthur CDI to obtain early language data from a large sample of children with WMS or DNS between one and six years of age. In the period of development covered by the infant scale (equivalent to normal children between 8 and 16 months), WMS and DNS were equally and severely delayed in both word comprehension and word production. The predicted separation between WMS and DNS did not emerge until the period of development covered by the toddler scale (equivalent to normal children between 16 and 30 months). Both groups were still delayed by approximately two years at this point, with no significant difference in overall vocabulary size. However, Singer et al. found striking differences in the emergence of grammar. Interestingly, this difference reflects a *DNS disadvantage* rather than a *WMS advantage*.

To facilitate comparison across groups, we have plotted the data for individual WMS and DNS from Singer Harris et al. in figure 10.10, in the same format adopted throughout this chapter. Within WMS, grammatical development appears to be paced by vocabulary size, in the normal fashion. In fact, when these children are compared with lexically matched normal controls from the CDI sample, the relationship between

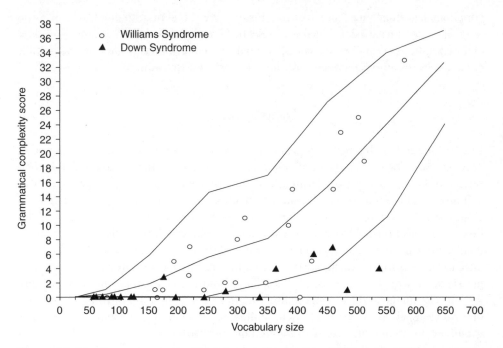

Figure 10.10 Grammar as a function of vocabulary size in children with Williams vs. Down Syndrome (lines = 10th, 50th & 90th percentile for normals).

grammar and vocabulary size is identical, following the same nonlinear accelerating function described above for normals and for children with focal brain injury. In short, there is no evidence for a dissociation between grammatical and lexical development in WMS – at least not in this early phase of grammatical development.

By contrast, the DNS sample provides our best evidence to date for a significant dissociation between grammar and the lexicon. In particular, DNS children scored significantly *below* the grammatical levels displayed by normal children and by WMS matched or vocabulary size (Figure 10.10). However, the term "dissociation" must be used with caution here. Correlational analyses show that grammar and vocabulary are tightly related in both children with WMS and children with DNS (correlating around +.70). There is a real difference between these groups, but it lies in the amount of vocabulary that children in each group seem to need in order to get grammar off the ground: *WMS need the same amount required by normal children of the same mental age, while DNS require more than the normal amount of vocabulary in order for grammar to emerge.*

As we noted earlier, there is a double dissociation in these two groups between auditory short-term memory (significantly better in WMS) and visual short-term memory (significantly better in DNS). It appears that DNS suffer from a selective impairment in one or more aspects of auditory processing, a deficit that is superimposed upon their more general cognitive delay. Under these circumstances, it is perhaps not surprising the DNS are selectively impaired in the ability to detect, store, and/or retrieve those aspects of their linguistic input that are lowest in what Leonard (1998) refers to as "phonological substance," or salience. This argument is similar to one that Tallal and her colleagues have used to explain the selective grammatical deficits displayed by older children with SLI (Tallal et al., 1985). We will return to this issue later on, with reference to selective impairments of grammar in brain-injured adults.

Explaining the Link

Why is the relationship between grammar and the lexicon so strong in this period of development? The same basic nonlinear relationship appears in longitudinal and cross-sectional data, in at least two dramatically different languages (see Caselli et al., this volume), in different domains of grammar, in children who are developing on a normal schedule and in children who are developing at an aberrant rate. We do find a violation of this relationship in children with Down Syndrome, but the deviation seems to involve not a dissociation between grammar and the lexicon, but a pathological difference in the amount of vocabulary required in order to learn grammar. There is no a priori reason why this had to be the case. For example, many adults who try to acquire a second language in the classroom find themselves in a situation in which their stock of grammatical rules outstrips their limited vocabulary. The dependence of early grammar on vocabulary size is so strong and the nonlinear shape of this function is so regular that it approaches the status of a psychological law, akin to the reliable psychophysical functions that have been observed in perception (e.g., Weber's Law, Fechner's Law). But explanation by legislation is not very satisfactory, and it is particularly unsatisfactory if better explanations are available. We can offer at least five reasons why grammar and vocabulary track each other so closely in this stage of language development. None of them are mutually exclusive.

1   **Perceptual bootstrapping.** Nusbaum and Henly (1992) have proposed that efficient word perception requires a certain amount of top-down processing, permitting the listener to weed out inappropriate candidates from a large pool of items that overlap (at least partially) with the blurred word tokens that so often occur in fluent speech. To the extent that this is true, it is probably even more true for the perception of grammatical function words and bound inflections. For a variety of reasons, these units are particularly hard to perceive (Herron & Bates, 1997; Hurlburt & Goodman, 1992; Leonard, 1998). They tend to be short and low in stress even in speech that is produced slowly and deliberately. In informal and rapid speech, speakers have a tendency to exploit the frequency and predictability of function words and bound morphemes by giving them short shrift, deforming their phonetic structure and blurring the boundaries between these morphemes and the words that surround them. In fact, when grammatical function words are clipped out of connected speech and presented in isolation, adult native speakers can recognize them no more than 40–50% of the time (Herron & Bates, 1997). This is true of speech directed to children as well as speech directed to adults (Goodman & Nusbaum, 1994). Under these circumstances, we should not be surprised that young children are unable to acquire grammatical

forms until they have a critical mass of content words, providing enough top-down structure to permit perception and learning of those "little sounds" that occur to the right or left of "real words."

2   **Logical bootstrapping.** Studies in several different languages have shown that verbs and adjectives are acquired later than nouns (see Caselli et al., this volume). Except for a few terms like "up" and "no" that can stand alone, function words tend to appear later still, well after the first verbs and adjectives appear. Furthermore, many relatively early prepositions (e.g., "up") may not be used in the same way by children as by adults. Adults use them to specify a relation between objects or a location. Children on the other hand use them to refer to events (Tomasello & Merriman, 1995) instead of using them as "grammatical glue." It has been suggested that this progression from names to predication to grammar is logically necessary, based on a simple assumption: Children cannot understand relational terms until they understand the things that these words relate. One can argue about the extent to which this assumption holds for individual structures, but it may provide a partial explanation for the dependence of grammar on lexical growth.

3   **Syntactic bootstrapping.** The perceptual and logical bootstrapping accounts both presuppose that the causal link runs from lexical growth to grammar. However, studies from several different laboratories have shown that children between 1 and 3 years of age are able to exploit sentential information to learn about the meaning of a novel word (Goodman et al., 1998; Naigles et al., 1993; Tomasello, 1992). Naigles et al. (1993) refer to this process as "syntactic bootstrapping," although it has been shown that children can use many different aspects of a sentence frame for this purpose, including sentence-level semantics, morphological cues, word order, and prosody. It is therefore possible that the accelerating function in Figures 10.2–10.10 is due in part to the effect of the child's emerging grammar on lexical growth.

4   **Nonlinear dynamics of learning in a neural network.** The above three accounts all support a link between lexical and grammatical development, but it is not obvious from these accounts why the function ought to take the nonlinear form that appears so reliably across populations and age levels. We noted earlier that the nonlinear functions governing the relation between verb vocabulary and the emergence of regular and irregular past-tense marking appear in a similar form in English-speaking children and in neural network simulations of past-tense learning (Elman, this volume; Marchman & Bates 1994; Plunkett & Marchman, 1993). This is only one example of a more general point: Multi-layered neural networks produce an array of nonlinear growth functions, reflecting the nonlinear dynamics of learning and change in these systems. The kinds of critical-mass effects that we have proposed to underlie the relation between lexical and grammatical growth may be a special case of this more general approach to the nonlinear dynamics of learning (Thelen & Smith, 1994).

5   **Lexically based grammar.** Finally, as we noted at the outset of this paper, the historical trend in modern linguistics has been to place in the lexicon more and

more of the work that was previously carried out in a separate grammatical component. The powerful relation between grammatical and lexical development
that we have observed here is precisely what we would expect if grammar is an
inherent part of the lexicon.

Points 1–4 all pertain to learning. Point 5 is a stronger claim, extending to the
relationship between grammar and the lexicon in the adult steady state. The data
that we have reviewed so far may be relevant only to the early stages of language
development, the period in which the fundamental properties of language-specific
morphosyntax are laid down. It is entirely possible that a modular distinction between
grammar and the lexicon may emerge at a latter point in development, in accordance
with the processes of "modularization" described by Karmiloff-Smith (1992); see also
Bates et al., 1988). This question is best addressed by looking at the literature on
language disorders in older children and adults, where strong claims about the
modularity of grammar and the lexicon have been made. Our review of this literature
suggests that the lexicalist approach stands up to the evidence for older children
and adults as well. For every clinical group for whom grammatical deficits have
been reported, lexical deficits have also been demonstrated. In fact, a deficit in word
finding (called "anomia") is the one symptom that is present in every form of adult
aphasia (Goodglass, 1993). Conversely, in every clinical group for whom lexical
deficits are reported, some kind of grammatical problem is observed as well. A particularly interesting observation about these links is the fact that grammar and the
lexicon tend to break down in the same way within individual patients. Non-fluent
Broca's aphasics tend to err by omission; they leave out grammatical inflections
and function words, but they also tend to leave out content words (especially verbs).
This omission profile is also seen (usually in a milder form) in children with Down
Syndrome and children with Specific Language Impairment. Fluent Wernicke's
aphasics tend to err by substitution, putting in the wrong content word (or a blend
of words). In richly inflected languages, the same tendency (called paragrammatism)
is observed for inflections and function words. This "substitution profile" is also
observed in children with Williams Syndrome, if they are acquiring a language
with enough morphology for such substitutions to surface (Volterra et al., 1996).
Finally, patients with Alzheimer's disease and patients with milder forms of aphasia
rarely make frank grammatical errors of any kind (omission or substitution).
However, they tend to avoid production of complex syntactic structures (e.g., the
passive, Bates et al., 1995b), a grammatical symptom that mirrors their problems
in lexical production (i.e., an overreliance on pronouns and other "light forms"). A
mild version of this "avoidance profile" is also seen in normal aging. In short, grammar
and the lexicon continue to travel together in adulthood, and they break down in
similar ways.

Grammar and the lexicon develop together in infancy, and they break down together
in brain-injured adults. In our view, the most parsimonious explanation for these facts
would be a mental/neural architecture in which grammar and the lexicon are represented together, and handled by the same mechanisms for learning and processing – in
short, a lexicalist view of the sort that has gained considerable acceptance in modern
linguistics.

Notes

1 "Observation of early stages of language acquisition may be quite misleading in this regard. It is possible that at an early stage there is use of languagelike expressions, but outside the framework imposed, at a later stage of intellectual maturation, by the faculty of language – much as a dog can be trained to respond to certain commands, though we would not conclude, from this, that it is using language." (Noam Chomsky, *Reflections on language* (p. 53). New York, Pantheon Books, 1975).

2 We also looked at many other metrics of grammatical development, including propositional complexity and morphological productivity. After all that work we were surprised to find that, at least in this period of development, MLU is so highly correlated with other, more sophisticated measures, that there was no point in using any other estimate of grammar in correlational analyses with other variables; for a discussion of this point, see Bates et al., 1988.

References

Bates, E., Bretherton, I., & Snyder, L. (1988). *From first words to grammar: Individual differences and dissociable mechanisms.* New York: Cambridge University Press.

Bates, E., Dale, P., & Thal, D. (1995a). Individual differences and their implications for theories of language development. In P. Fletcher & B. MacWhinney (Eds.), *Handbook of child language* (pp. 96–151). Oxford: Basil Blackwell.

Bates, E., Marchman, V., Harris, C., Wulfeck, B., & Kritchevsky, M. (1995b). Production of complex syntax in normal ageing and Alzheimer's Disease. *Language and Cognitive Processes, 11* (5), 487–539.

Bates, E., Thal, D., Trauner, D., Fenson, J., Aram, D., Eisele, J., & Nass, R. (1997). From first words to grammar in children with focal brain injury. In D. Thal & J. Reilly (Eds.), Special issue on Origins of Communication Disorders, *Developmental Neuropsychology, 13* (3), 275–343.

Bates, E., Vicari, S., & Trauner, D. (1999). Neural mediation of language development: Perspectives from lesion studies of infants and children. In H. Tager-Flusberg (Ed.), *Neurodevelopmental disorders* (pp. 533–581). Cambridge, MA: MIT Press.

Bates, E., Wulfeck, B., & MacWhinney, B. (1991). Crosslinguistic research in aphasia: An overview. *Brain and Language, 41,* 123–148.

Bellugi, U., Wang, P.P., & Jernigan, T.L. (1994). Williams Syndrome: An unusual neuropsychological profile. In S. Broman & J. Grafman (Eds.), *Atypical cognitive deficits in developmental disorders: Implications for brain function.* Hillsdale, NJ: Erlbaum.

Bickerton, D. (1984). The language bioprogram hypothesis. *The Behavioral and Brain Sciences, 7,* 173–187.

Bishop, D.V.M. (1997). *Uncommon understanding: Development and disorders of comprehension in children.* Hove, UK: Psychology Press.

Bloom, L. (1991). *Language development from two to three.* New York: Cambridge University Press.

Bresnan, J. (2001). *Lexical functional syntax.* Malden, MA: Blackwell.

Brown, R. (1973). *A first language: The early stages.* Cambridge, MA: Harvard University Press.

Capirci, O., Sabbadini, L., & Volterra, V. (1996). Language development in Williams syndrome: A case study. *Cognitive Neuropsychology, 13* (7), 1017–1039.

Caselli, M.C., Casadio, P., & Bates, E. (1999). A comparison of the transition from first words to grammar in English and Italian. *Journal of Child Language, 26,* 69–111.

Chapman, R.S. (1995). Language development in children and adolescents with Down Syndrome. In Paul Fletcher & Brian MacWhinney (Eds.), *The handbook of child language* (pp. 664–689). Oxford: Basil Blackwell.

Chomsky, N. (1965). *Aspects of the theory of syntax.* Cambridge, MA: MIT Press.

Chomsky, N. (1975. *Reflections on language.* New York, Pantheon Books, 1975).

Chomsky, N. (1981). *Lectures on government and binding.* New York: Foris.

Chomsky, N. (1995). *The minimalist program.* Cambridge, MA: MIT Press.

Contardi, A., & Vicari, S. (Eds.). (1994). *Le persone Down: Aspetti neuropsicologici, educativi e sociali.* Milano: FrancoAngeli.

Dale, P.S. (1991). The validity of a parent report measure of vocabulary and syntax at 24 months. *Journal of Speech and Hearing Sciences, 34,* 565–571.

Dale, P.S., Bates, E., Reznick, S., & Morisset, C. (1989). The validity of a parent report instrument of child language at 20 months. *Journal of Child Language, 16,* 239–249.

Eisele, J., & Aram, D. (1995). Lexical and grammatical development in children with early hemisphere damage: A cross-sectional view from birth to adolescence. In P. Fletcher & B. MacWhinney (Eds.), *The handbook of child language* (pp. 664–689). Oxford: Basil Blackwell.

Elman, J., Bates, E., Johnson, M., Karmiloff-Smith, A., Parisi, D., & Plunkett, K. (1996). *Rethinking innateness: A connectionist perspective on development.* Cambridge, MA: MIT Press/Bradford Books.

Fabbretti, D., Pizzuto, E., Vicari, S., & Volterra, V. (1997). A story description task in children with Down syndrome: lexical and morphosyntactic abilities. *Journal of Intellectual Disability Research, 41* (2), 165–179.

Feldman, H., Holland, A., Kemp, S., & Janosky, J. (1992). Language development after unilateral brain injury. *Brain and Language, 42,* 89–102.

Fenson, L., Dale, P., Reznick, J., Bates, E., Thal, D., & Pethick, S. (1994). Variability in early communicative development. *Monographs of the Society for Research in Child Development, Serial No. 242, Vol. 59, No. 5.*

Fillmore, C.J., Kay, P., & O'Connor, C. (1988). Regularity and idiomaticity in grammatical constructions: The case of Let Alone. *Language, 64,* 501–538.

Fodor, J.A. (1983). *The modularity of mind: An essay on faculty psychology.* Cambridge, MA: MIT Press.

Garrett, M. (1992). Disorders of lexical selection. *Cognition, 42,* 143–180.

Giannotti, A., & Vicari, S. (Eds.). (1994). *Il bambino con sindrome di Williams.* Milan: FrancoAngeli.

Goldberg, A.E. (1995). *Constructions: A construction grammar approach to argument structure.* Chicago: University of Chicago Press.

Goodglass, H. (1993). *Understanding aphasia.* San Diego: Academic Press.

Goodman, J.C. (1995). The shape of change: Longitudinal evidence about language development. *Society for Research in Child Development Abstracts, 10,* 111.

Goodman, J.C., McDonough, L., & Brown, N.B. (1998). The role of semantic context and memory in the acquisition of novel nouns. *Child Development, 69* (5), 1330–1344.

Goodman, J.C., & Nusbaum, H.C. (Eds.). (1994). *The development of speech perception: Transitions from speech sounds to spoken words.* Cambridge, MA: MIT Press.

Gopnik, M. (1990). Feature-blind grammar and dysphasia. *Nature, 344* (6268), 715.

Herron, D., & Bates, E. (1997). Sentential and acoustic factors in the recognition of open- and closed-class words. *Journal of Memory and Language, 37* (2), 217–239.

Hurlburt, M.S., & Goodman, J.C. (1992). The development of lexical effects on children's phoneme identifications. In J.J. Ohala, T.M. Nearey, B.L. Derwing, M.M. Hodge, & G.E. Wiebe (Eds.), *ICSLP 92 Proceedings: 1992 International Conference on Spoken Language Processing* (pp. 337–340). Banff, Alberta, Canada: University of Alberta.

Jahn-Samilo, J. (1995). Language comprehension and production in children from 8 to 30 months of age: A comparison of parent report and laboratory measures from a longitudinal study. *Society for Research in Child Development Abstracts, 10,* 112.

Jakobson, R. (1968). *Child language aphasia and phonological universals.* Paris: Mouton.

Karmiloff-Smith, A. (1992). *Beyond modularity: A developmental perspective on cognitive science.* Cambridge, MA: MIT Press.

Karmiloff-Smith, A., Klima, E.S., Bellugi, U., Grant, J., & Baron-Cohen, S. (1995). Is there a social module? Language, face processing, and theory of mind in subjects with Williams Syndrome. *Journal of Cognitive Neuroscience, 7* (2), 196–208.

Langacker, R. (1987). *Foundations of cognitive grammar.* Stanford: Stanford University Press.

Leonard, L.B. (1998). *Children with specific language impairment.* Boston MA: MIT Press.

MacDonald, M.C., Pearlmutter, N.J., & Seidenberg, M.S. (1994). Lexical nature of syntactic ambiguity resolution. *Psychological Review, 101* (4), 676–703.

MacWhinney, B. (1993). Connections and symbols: Closing the gap. *Cognition, 49* (3), 291–296.

MacWhinney, B., & Bates, E. (Eds.). (1989). *The crosslinguistic study of sentence processing.* New York: Cambridge University Press.

Marchman, V., & Bates, E. (1994). Continuity in lexical and morphological development: A test of the critical mass hypothesis. *Journal of Child Language, 21* (2), 339–366.

Marchman, V., Wulfeck, B., & Weismer, S.E. (1995). *Productive use of English past-tense morphology in children with SLI and normal language* (Tech. Rep. No. CND-9514). La Jolla: University of California, San Diego, Center for Research in Language, Project in Cognitive and Neural Development.

Marcus, G., Pinker, S., Ullman, M., Hollander, M., Rosen, T.J., & Xu, F. (1992). Overregularization in language acquisition. *Monographs of the Society for Research in Child Development, 57.*

Mervis, C., Morris, C., Bertrand, J., & Robinson, B. (1999). Williams syndrome: findings from an integrated program of research. In H. Tager-Flusberg (Ed.), *Neurodevelopmental disorders* (pp. 65–110). Cambridge, MA: MIT Press.

Miller, J. (1992). The development of speech and language in children with Down Syndrome. In E. McCoy and I. Lott (Eds.), Clinical care for persons with Down Syndrome (pp. 121–138). New York: Academic Press.

Naigles, L., Gleitman, H., & Gleitman, L.R. (1993). Children acquire word meaning components from syntactic evidence. In E. Dromi (Ed.), *Language and cognition: A developmental perspective* (pp. 104–140). Norwood, NJ: Ablex.

Nelson, K. (1973). Structure and strategy in learning to talk. *Monographs of the Society for Research in Child Development, 38 (1 & 2, Serial #149).*

Nusbaum, H.C., & Henly, A.S. (1992). Listening to speech through an adaptive window of analysis. In B. Schouten (Ed.), *The processing of speech: From the auditory periphery to word recognition.* Berlin: Mouton-De Gruyter.

Peters, A. (1983). *The units of language acquisition.* Cambridge: Cambridge University Press.

Pinker, S. (1991). Rules of language. *Science, 253,* 530–535.

Plunkett, K., & Marchman, V. (1993). From rote learning to system building: Acquiring verb morphology in children and connectionist nets. *Cognition, 48,* 21–69.

Pollard, C., & Sag, I. (1994). *Head-drive phrase structure grammar.* Center for the Study of Language and Information, Report # CSLI-88-132. University of Chicago.

Reilly, J., Bates, E., & Marchman, V. (1998). Narrative discourse in children with early focal brain injury. In M. Dennis (Ed.), Special issue, Discourse in children with anomalous brain development or acquired brain injury. *Brain and Language, 61* (3), 335–375.

Reilly, J., Klima, E., & Bellugi, U. (1991). Once more with feeling: affect and language in atypical populations. *Developmental Psychopathology, 2,* 367–391.

Rubba, J., & Klima, E.S. (1991). Preposition use in a speaker with Williams Syndrome: Some cognitive grammar proposals. *Center for Research in Language Newsletter Vol. 6*, No. 1. University of California, San Diego.

Shore, C.M. (1995). *Individual differences in language development*. Thousand Oaks, CA: Sage Publications, Inc.

Singer Harris, N., Bellugi, U., Bates, E., Jones, W., & Rossen, M. (1997). Contrasting profiles of language development in children with Williams and Down Syndromes. In D. Thal & J. Reilly (Eds.), Special issue on origins of Communication Disorders, *Developmental Neuropsychology, 13* (3), 345–370.

Slobin, D. (Ed.). (1985–1997). *The crosslinguistic study of language acquisition* (Vols. 1–4). Hillsdale, NJ: Erlbaum.

Tallal, P., Stark, R., & Mellits, D. (1985). Identification of language-impaired children on the basis of rapid perception and production skills. *Brain and Language, 25*, 314–322.

Thal, D. (1991). Language and cognition in late-talking toddlers. *Topics in Language Disorders, 11*, 33–42.

Thal, D., Bates, E., Goodman, J., & Jahn-Samilo, J. (1997). Continuity of language abilities in late- and early-talking toddlers. In D. Thal & J. Reilly (Eds.), Special issue on Origins of Communication Disorders, *Developmental Neuropsychology, 13* (3), 239–273.

Thal, D., Bates, E., Zappia, M.J., & Oroz, M. (1996). Ties between lexical and grammatical development: Evidence from early talkers. *Journal of Child Language, 23* (2), 349–368.

Thelen, E., & Smith, L.B. (1994). *A dynamic systems approach to the development of cognition and action*. Cambridge, MA: MIT Press.

Tomasello, M. (1992). *First verbs: A case study of early grammatical development*. Cambridge, UK; New York: Cambridge University Press.

Tomasello, M., & Merriman, W. (Eds.) (1995). *Beyond names for things: Young children's acquisition of verbs*. Hillsdale, NJ: Lawrence Erlbaum.

Vargha-Khadem, F., Isaacs, E., & Muter, V. (1994). A review of cognitive outcome after unilateral lesions sustained during childhood. *Journal of Child Neurology, 9* (Suppl.), 2S67–2S73.

Vargha-Khadem, F., Watkins, K., Alcock, K., Fletcher, P., & Passingham, R. (1995). Praxic and nonverbal cognitive deficits in a large family with a genetically transmitted speech and language disorder. *Proceedings of the National Academy of Sciences USA, 92*, 930–933.

Vicari, S., Albertoni, A., Chilosi, A., Cipriani, P., Cioni, G., & Bates, E. (2000). Plasticity and reorganization during early language learning in children with congenital brain injury. *Cortex, 36*, 31–46.

Vicari, S., Brizzolara, D., Carlesimo, G.A., Pezzini, G., & Volterra, V. (1996). Memory abilities in children with Williams syndrome. *Cortex, 32* (3), 503–514.

Volterra, V., Pezzini, G., Sabbadini, L., Capirci, O., & Vicari, S. (1996). Linguistic abilities in Italian children with Williams syndrome. *Cortex, 32* (4), 663–666.

Wang, P., & Bellugi, U. (1994). Evidence from two genetic syndromes for a dissociation between verbal and visual-spatial short-term memory. *Journal of Clinical and Experimental Neuropsychology, 16*, 317–322.

Part III

Introduction to Grammatical Development

Introduction to Part III

At the same time they are acquiring their first words children are also acquiring more complex linguistic constructions as kinds of linguistic gestalts. This becomes especially clear as soon as we focus on word learning as something other than the learning of names for objects. Thus, for example, when children learn the word *give*, there is really no learning of the word apart from the participant roles that invariably accompany acts of giving: the giver, the thing given, and the person given to; in fact, we cannot even conceive of an act of giving in the absence of these participant roles. The same could be said of the words *out*, *from*, and *of*, which can only be learned as relationships between two other entities or locations. Therefore, if we are interested in all aspects of children's acquisition of language, we cannot investigate their acquisition of words in isolation, but we must also investigate their acquisition of larger linguistic constructions as meaningful symbolic units, including whole sentence-level constructions (e.g., Wh- questions or passive constructions). Indeed, since children almost never hear individual words in isolation, outside of some larger and more complex utterance, we should probably conceptualize word learning as simply the isolation and extraction of a language's simplest linguistic constructions (Langacker, 1987; Goldberg, 1995).

For various reasons of cognitive and communicative salience, children speaking all the languages of the world choose to talk initially about a delimited set of events and states of affairs. Prominent among these are Manipulative Activity scenes (e.g., someone pushing/pulling/breaking/opening/rolling something) and Figure-Ground scenes (e.g., someone or something coming/going/entering/leaving/being located somewhere) (Slobin, 1985). Children hear adults talking about these scenes using full linguistic constructions, or some partial form appropriate to the discourse context, and so this is what they attempt to reproduce. Importantly, linguistic constructions may be either concrete – based on specific words and phrases – or they may be abstract – based on word-general categories and schemas. Some linguists and psycholinguists believe that young children operate from the beginning with abstract, adult-like, linguistic constructions – because they are born with them (e.g., Pinker, 1994). But others believe that there is simply too much cross-linguistic variability for there to be an innate universal grammar (Comrie, 1990; Dryer, 1997; Croft, 2000; Slobin, 1997), and thus the process is best described as one in which individual children use their species-universal cognitive, social-cognitive, and cultural learning abilities to comprehend and acquire the particular linguistic items and constructions of their particular language (which have evolved historically).

In his paper, Tomasello documents the fact that young children's early multi-word productions are highly concrete. That is to say, they are based on particular words and phrases, not on innate and abstract linguistic categories, schemas, parameters, or rules (see also Bloom, 1991; Braine, 1987). This is seen most clearly when one looks at the distribution of all of a child's utterances and identifies not only patterns in what she does but also patterns in what she does not do. Thus, for example, a child learning a language like French or Spanish might be very good with the first person form of a verb (e.g., as in "Te amo" or "Yo la tengo") but not know the other forms of that same verb. At the same time, this child might know the imperative form of another verb but not the first person form – suggesting that her verb knowledge does not consist of totally abstract and verb-general rules. Tomasello also summarizes experimental studies in which young English-speaking children are given made-up words to see if they can use them in ways suggesting that they possess abstract rules. For example, if a child learns that a novel action is called meeking, can she then say things like "It's meeking" (intransitive construction) or "He's meeking it" (transitive construction) or "He got meeked" (passive construction) – even though she has never before heard this word in this construction? The studies show that it is not until they are three years old or older that young children show creativity of this type – presumably because they have not yet created abstract, verb-general constructions. Cross-linguistic research has shown that this pattern of gradual and word-specific grammatical development is quite widespread, presumably universal, although the details are different in particular languages.

The study reported in the Akhtar paper documents the process of abstraction in action. In this study English-speaking children heard made-up verbs in unusual constructions such as "Ernie the car dacking." When four-year-old children subsequently used this new verb they spontaneously corrected it and said things like "Burt's dacking the chair." However, the two- and three-year-old children often used the new verb in the way they had heard it being used, without correcting it as in "Burt the chair dacking" (although some children of this age corrected it on some occasions as well). The most logical interpretation of these findings is that the younger children – even though they were producing many transitive utterances with familiar verbs in their spontaneous speech – did not yet possess a strong and abstract English transitive construction to which they could assimilate this new verb. They were caught between their tendency to use the new verb as they had heard adults using it and a competing tendency to use the new verb in accordance with the English transitivity patterns that they were in the process of discovering for themselves. Akhtar argues that these results cannot be explained by a parameter-setting approach in which innate and abstract verb-general structures are simply triggered by the environment, since the children treated the new verbs idiosyncratically, that is, differently than other verbs already in their vocabulary.

The paper by Köpcke focuses on morphology. In particular, it investigates how English-speaking and German-speaking children learn to use plural nouns. Some theorists (e.g., Pinker, 1991; Clahsen, 1999) argue that inflectional paradigms invariably have some rule-based members and often have exceptions. The exceptions can only be learned by rote, whereas the rule-based items are assimilated to the rules of universal grammar. Köpcke demonstrates that this dual-process view cannot really account for the data, especially the complex German plural which has nine different forms. Children form schemas in a number of different ways with German plurals – sometimes leading to overgeneralizations analogous to the English "foots" – and none of these functions as a "default," that is, as a special rule-based form different from the others. Köpcke's data thus support a single-process approach in which children hear exemplars and cluster them into "similarity spaces," and in some but not all cases this takes the form of a major pattern with some minor exceptions (see Elman, this volume, for an account for the origins of this debate with respect to the English past tense). Köpcke's account is also very useful in specifying some of the factors that lead young children to make the generalizations they actually make in extending the plural morpheme to novel exemplars, and in so doing introduces important processing notions such as cue reliability, cue strength, etc. Köpcke's schema model is thus broadly compatible with a number of other single-process approaches to the acquisition of grammatical morphology (Bates & MacWhinney, 1989; McLelland & Rumelhart, 1986; Plunkett & Marchman, 1996).

The papers by Budwig and Bloom et al. focus on more complex linguistic constructions. Both papers take a developmental perspective in arguing that young children's understanding and use of these constructions is not totally adult-like. Budwig finds that young children's earliest passive utterances are things like "It got broken" (the get-passive) and "I don't want it to be played with" (the be-passive), in which the agent of the action (the one who broke it or the one who is not supposed to play with it) is not expressed for some reason. Budwig makes the important point that while the discourse function of these two types of passives are similar in that they both serve to background the agent, they are actually somewhat different. Be-passives are typically used to refer to events in which the agent is generic, irrelevant, or unknown; for example, the child doesn't want anyone whomsoever to play with it. Get-passives, on the other hand, are most often used to focus on negative outcomes, where the agent that caused that negative outcome is simply not important; for example, the important fact is that it got broken and we really don't care by whom. This paper thus illustrates clearly that the communicative function of complex linguistic constructions is an integral part of their makeup.

The paper by Bloom et al. describes children's acquisition of verb complements, a set of complex constructions involving two verbs, for example, "I think Mommy's making punch" and "See the train coming." These constructions are especially complex because they contain both a main verb (*think, see*) and an embedded clause that is the object of that main verb (*Mommy's making punch, the train coming*). However, what Bloom et al. demonstrate is that children's earliest utterances of this type all revolve around a very small set of main verbs involving psychological states such as seeing, knowing, thinking, looking, saying, meaning, forgetting, etc. Thus, like simple constructions, these complex constructions also have a clear and delimited set of discourse functions, in this case involving the expression of psychological states or attitudes towards external events. Bloom et al. thus find that there is much item specificity in a particular psychological state and attitude that children find it interesting and important to express.

Slobin's paper, abridged for the current volume, brings a cross-linguistic perspective to the discussion. Slobin first describes a number of theoretical proposals that children are born with a set of concepts destined to be expressed grammatically rather than lexically; that is, concepts destined to be indicated by closed-class function words and grammatical morphology rather than open-class, free-standing words. These privileged notions might involve such things as tense, causation, gender, etc. – which are indeed quite often expressed grammatically in the languages of the world. However, by analyzing a number of different domains in a number of different languages, Slobin shows that there is much too much cross-linguistic variability for the human species to have any preconceived ideas about what kinds of notions will and will not be indicated by grammatical rather than lexical items. In addition, he discusses the historical processes of grammaticalization that create grammatical items (out of lexical items), and shows how these processes can explain both the language-universal and the language-particular aspects of the lexical-grammatical distinction. Slobin argues that grammatical constructions are created to serve specific discourse functions, and thus they are constrained not by innate linguistic structures but rather by basic human processes of cognition, communication, and information processing.

The papers in this section represent a small sample of works on grammatical development, from single morphemes to complex syntactic structures. They represent a coherent theoretical perspective that is broadly compatible with new perspectives in Cognitive-Functional or Usage-Based Linguistics (e.g., Langacker, 1987, 1991; Bybee, 1995; Croft, 2000; see papers in Tomasello, 1998, in press), as well as with new quantitative approaches in corpus-based and computational linguistics (e.g., Biber, 1998; Bod, 1998; see Elman, next section). For approaches based on formal grammars of a different type, the interested reader may consult Radford (1990) and Lust (in press) and the references contained therein.

References

Bates, E., & MacWhinney, B. (1989). Functionalism and the competition model. In B. MacWhinney, & E. Bates (Eds.), *The crosslinguistic study of sentence processing* (pp. 3–76). New York: Cambridge University Press.

Biber, D. (1998). *Corpus linguistics: Investigating language structure and use.* Cambridge: Cambridge University Press.

Bod, R. (1998). *Beyond grammar: An experience-based theory of language.* Stanford, CA: Center for the Study of Language and Information, Stanford University.

Bloom, L. (1991). *Language development from two to three.* Lois Bloom with Joanne Bitetti Capatides. [et al.]. Cambridge; New York: Cambridge University Press.

Braine, M.D.S. (1987). What is learned in acquiring word classes: A step toward an acquisition theory. In B. MacWhinney (Ed.), *Mechanisms of language acquisition.* Hillsdale, NJ: Lawrence Erlbaum.

Bybee, J. (1995). Regular morphology and the lexicon. Language and Cognitive Processes, *10* (5), 425–455.

Clahsen, H. (1999). Lexical entries and rules of language: A multidisciplinary study of German inflection. *Behavioral and Brain Sciences, 22* (6), 991–1013, 1055–1060.

Comrie, B. (1990). (Ed.). *The world's major languages.* New York: Oxford University Press.

Croft, W. (2000). *Explaining language change: An evolutionary approach.* Harlow, England; New York: Longman.

Dryer, M. (1997). Are grammatical relations universal? In J. Bybee, J. Haiman, & S. Thompson (Eds.), *Essays on language function and language type.* Amsterdam: John Benjamins.

Goldberg, A.E. (1995). *Constructions: A construction grammar approach to argument structure.* Chicago: University of Chicago Press.

Langacker, R.W. (1987). *Foundations of cognitive grammar.* Stanford, CA: Stanford University Press.

Langacker, R. (1991). *Foundations of cognitive grammar, Volume 2.* Stanford University Press.

Lust, B. (in press). *The growth of language.* Cambridge: Cambridge University Press.

McClelland, J.L., & Rumelhart, D.E. (1986). *Parallel distributed processing: Explorations in the microstructure of cognition. Volume 2. Psychological and biological models.* Cambridge, MA: MIT Press.

Pinker, S. (1991). Rules of language. *Science, 253,* 530–535.

Pinker, S. (1994). *The language instinct: How the mind creates language.* New York: William Morrow.

Plunkett, K., & Marchman, V. (1996). Learning from a connectionist model of the English past tense. *Cognition, 61* (3), 299–308.

Radford, R. (1990). *Syntactic theory and the acquisition of English syntax.* Oxford: Blackwell.

Slobin, D. (1985). Crosslinguistic evidence for the language-making capacity. In D. Slobin (Ed.), *The crosslinguistic study of language acquisition* (Vol. 2, pp. 1157–1256). Hillsdale, NJ: Erlbaum.

Slobin, D. (1997). On the origin of grammaticalizable notions – Beyond the individual mind. In D.I. Slobin (Ed.), *The crosslinguistic study of language acquisition, Volume 5.* Hillsdale, NJ: Erlbaum.

Slobin, D. (Ed.). (1997). *The crosslinguistic study of language acquisition* (Vol. 5). Hillsdale, NJ: Erlbaum.

Tomasello, M. (Ed.). (1998). *The new psychology of language: Cognitive and functional approaches to language structure.* Mahwah, NJ: Lawrence Erlbaum.

Tomasello, M. (Ed.). (in press). *The new psychology of language: Cognitive and functional approaches to language structure, Volume 2.* Mahwah, NJ: Lawrence Erlbaum.

ELEVEN

The Item-Based Nature of Children's Early Syntactic Development

Michael Tomasello

By all accounts, a major characteristic distinguishing human beings from their nearest primate relatives is the use of language. A central question in this regard is how human beings maintain the conventions of a particular language across generations in a speech community, that is to say, how children acquire a language. Of special interest to many developmental psycholinguists is the question of how children acquire the syntactic structure of a language, because they do not hear an adult speaking in abstract syntactic categories and schemas but only in concrete and particular words and expressions.

The best known answer to this question – first proposed by Chomsky and more recently popularized by Pinker[1] and others – is that children do not have to learn or construct abstract syntactic structures at all, but rather they already possess them as a part of their innate language faculty. This so-called continuity assumption (innate syntactic competence is fundamentally the same at all points in ontogeny[2]) justifies the use of adult-like formal grammars to describe children's early language. In this view, the 5,000 or more natural languages of the world each derive from this same innate universal grammar, differing from one another only in the composition of their lexicons and in a few parametric variations of syntax that are prefigured in the human genome.

Recently, however, a number of empirical findings that challenge this majority view have emerged. Most important is the discovery that virtually all of children's early linguistic competence is item-based. That is to say, children's early utterances are organized around concrete and particular words and phrases, not around any system-wide syntactic categories or schemas. Abstract and adult-like syntactic categories and schemas are observed to emerge only gradually and in piecemeal fashion during the preschool years. These new data are most naturally accounted for by a usage-based model in which children imitatively learn concrete linguistic expressions from the language they hear around them, and then – using their general cognitive and social-cognitive skills – categorize, schematize, and creatively combine these individually learned expressions and structures to reach adult linguistic competence.

Some Recent Findings in Language Acquisition

Most of children's early language is grammatical from the adult point of view, and this fact has been taken by some theorists as support for the hypothesis of an innate universal grammar. But children can also produce "grammatical" language by simply reproducing the specific linguistic items and expressions (e.g., specific words and phrases) of adult speech, which are, by definition, grammatical. To differentiate between these two hypotheses, deeper analyses of children's linguistic competence are needed.

Observational studies

Many researchers believe that young children operate from the beginning with abstract linguistic categories and schemas because they not only follow adult grammatical conventions fairly well, but they also on occasion produce some creative yet canonical utterances that they could not have heard from adults – which means that they must be generating them via abstract linguistic categories or schemas. The most famous example is "*allgone sticky*," as reported by Braine,[3] and indeed such creativity is convincing evidence that the child has some kind of abstract linguistic knowledge. However, recent evidence suggests that, in this example, the only abstract knowledge this child possesses is what kinds of things can be *allgone* – not, for example, what kinds of things may be the subjects or objects of verbs. The general methodological problem is that we can never tell from a single utterance in isolation what is the child's underlying structural knowledge. To determine underlying structural knowledge we must look at *all* of a child's uses – and most especially non-uses – of a whole set of linguistic items or structures.

Using this more systematic method, Tomasello found that although most of his daughter's early language during her second year of life was "grammatical," it was also very limited, uneven, and item-based.[4] The item-based nature of this child's early language was most clearly evident in her use of verbs. Thus, during exactly the same developmental period some semantically similar verbs were used in only one type of sentence frame and that frame was quite simple (e.g., *Cut* ___), whereas other verbs were used in more complex frames of several different types (e.g., *Draw* ___, *Draw* ___ *on* ___, *Draw* ___, *for* ___, ___ *draw on* ___). In addition, morphological marking (e.g., for past tense) was also very uneven across verbs. Within a given verb's development, however, there was great continuity, with new uses almost always replicating previous uses with only one small addition or modification (e.g., the marking of tense or the adding of a new participant role). Overall, by far the best predictor of this child's use of a given verb on a given day was *not* her use of other verbs on that same day, but rather her use of that same verb on immediately preceding days; there appeared to be no transfer of structure across verbs. The hypothesis was thus that children have an early period in which each of their verbs forms its own island of organization in an otherwise unorganized language system (the Verb Island hypothesis), thereby serving to define lexically specific syntactic categories such as "drawer," "thing drawn," and "thing drawn with" (as opposed to subject, object, and instrument).

Using a combination of periodic sampling and maternal diaries, Lieven et al.[5] found some very similar results in a sample of 12 English-speaking children from 2–3 years of age. In particular, they found that children used virtually all of their verbs and predicative terms in one and only one sentence frame early in language development – suggesting that their syntax was built around various particular items and expressions. In fact, 92% of these children's earliest multi-word utterances emanated from one of their first 25 lexically based patterns, which were different for different children. Following along these same lines, Pine and Lieven[6] found that when these same children began to use the determiners *a* and *the* between 2 and 3 years of age, they did so with almost completely different sets of nouns (i.e., there was almost no overlap in the sets of nouns used with the two determiners). This suggested that the children at this age did not have any kind of abstract category of determiner that included both of these lexical items. This general finding of the item-based learning and use of language has now been replicated in a number of different languages of many different types (see Box 11.1).

Box 11.1   Cross-linguistic evidence for item-based patterns

A number of systematic studies of children learning languages other than English have also found many item-based patterns in early language development. For example, Pizzuto and Caselli (Refs a,b) investigated the grammatical morphology used by three Italian-speaking children on simple, finite, main verbs, between the ages of about 18 months to three years. Although there are six forms possible for each verb root (first-person singular, second-person singular, etc.), the findings were that:

- 47% of all verbs used by these children were used in one form only
- an additional 40% were used with two or three forms
- of the 13% of verbs that appeared in four or more forms, approximately half of these were highly frequent, highly irregular forms that could only be learned by rote.

The clear implication is that Italian children do not master the whole verb paradigm for all their verbs at once, but rather they initially master only some endings with some verbs – and often different ones with different verbs.

In a similar study of one child learning to speak Brazilian Portugese at around 3 years of age, Rubino and Pine (Ref. c) found a comparable pattern of results, including additional evidence that the verb forms this child used most frequently and consistently corresponded to those he had heard most frequently from adults. That is, this child produced adult-like subject–verb agreement patterns for the parts of the verb paradigm that appeared with high frequency in adult language (e.g., first-person singular), but much less consistent agreement patterns in low frequency parts of the paradigm (e.g., third-person plural). Similarly, in a study of six Hebrew-speaking children – a language that is typologically quite different from European languages – Berman and Armon-Lotem (Ref. d; see also Ref. e) found that Hebrew children's first 20 verb forms were almost all "rote-learned or morphologically unanalysed" (Ref. d, p. 37). Other similar results have been reported for Hungarian (Ref. f), Catalan, German and Dutch (Ref. g), Inuktitut (Ref. h), Spanish (Ref. i), and Russian (Ref. j).

References

a   Pizutto, E., & Caselli, C. (1992). The acquisition of Italian morphology. *J. Child Lang.*, *19*, 491–557.

b   Pizutto, E., & Caselli, C. (1994). The acquisition of Italian verb morphology in a cross-linguistic perspective. In Y. Levy (Ed.), *Other Children, Other Languages*, pp. 137–188, Erlbaum.

c   Rubino, R., & Pine, J. (1998). Subject–verb agreement in Brazilian Portugese: what low error rates hide. *J. Child Lang.*, *25*, 35–60.

d   Berman, R.A., & Armon-Lotem, S. (1995). How grammatical are early verbs? *Annales Littéraires de l'Université de Franche-Comté*, *631*, 17–56.

e   Berman, R. (1982). Verb-pattern alternation: the interface of morphology, syntax, and semantics in Hebrew child language. *J. Child Lang.*, *9*, 169–191.

f   MacWhinney, B. (1978). The acquisition of morphophonology. *Monogr. Soc. Res. Child Dev.*, No. 43.

g   Behrens, H. (1998). How difficult are complex verbs? Evidence from German, Dutch, and English. *Linguistics*, *36*, 679–712.

h   Allen, S. (1996). *Aspects of Argument Structure Acquisition in Inuktitut*. John Benjamins.

i   Gathecole, V. et al. (1999). The early acquisition of Spanish verbal morphology: across-the-board or piecemeal knowledge? *Int. J. Bilingualism*, *3*, 138–182.

j   Stoll, S. (1998). The acquisition of Russian aspect. *First Lang.*, *18*, 351–378.

Of special note in children's spontaneous speech are so-called overgeneralization errors because the child has presumably not heard such errors from adults. The over-generalizations of most interest in the context of a focus on syntax are those involving basic sentence frames, for example, "*She falled me down*" or "*Don't giggle me*," in which the child uses intransitive verbs transitively (i.e., a verb normally used with a subject only is used with both a subject and an object). Bowerman[7,8] documented a number of such overgeneralizations in the speech of her two English-speaking children, and Pinker[9] compiled examples from other sources as well. The main result of interest was that these children produced very few of these types of overgeneralizations before about 3 years of age. This developmental pattern again provides support for the hypothesis that the construction of abstract linguistic categories and schemas is a gradual process that takes place over many months, and even years, of ontogeny.

Experimental studies

The other main method for studying the nature of children's linguistic knowledge involves teaching them novel linguistic items and seeing what they do with them. The idea is that if the child uses the novel item in creative yet canonical ways, we may infer that she has assimilated it to some kind of abstract category or schema. If she does not use it in any creative ways (despite repeated opportunities), but only in ways she has heard from adults, the inference is that there is no abstract system to take up the new element, and the child is simply imitatively learning a specific linguistic item or structure (assuming that there are no performance limitations, involving limited memory or the like, that prevent the child from demonstrating her syntactic competence in the experiment).

Experiments using novel verbs have demonstrated that by 3–4 years of age most children can readily assimilate novel verbs to abstract syntactic categories and schemas that they bring to the experiment, for example, taking a verb they have heard only in a passive sentence frame and using it in an active sentence frame.[10,11] However, the same is not true for younger children. For example, Tomasello and Brooks[12] exposed 2–3-year-old children to a novel verb used to refer to a highly transitive and novel action in which an agent was doing something to a patient. In the key condition the novel verb was used in an intransitive sentence frame such as "*The sock is tamming*" (to refer to a situation in which, for example, a bear was doing something that caused a sock to "tam" – similar to the verb *roll* or *spin*). Then, with novel characters performing the target action, the adult asked children the question, "*What is the doggie doing?*" (when the dog was causing some new character to tam). Agent questions of this type encourage a transitive reply such as "*He's tamming the car*," which would be creative as the child has previously heard this verb only in an intransitive sentence frame. The outcome was that very few children at either age produced a transitive utterance with the novel verb. As a control, children also heard another novel verb introduced in a transitive sentence frame, and in this case virtually all of them produced a transitive utterance. This demonstrates that children can use novel verbs in the transitive construction when they have heard them used in that way (see figure 11.1).

The generality of this finding is demonstrated by a number of similar studies using different modeled constructions and measurement procedures. These studies have used children of many different ages and have tested for a variety of different constructions (see Box 11.2). Most of the findings concern children's ability to produce a simple transitive utterance (subject–verb–object; SVO), given that they have heard a novel verb only in some *other* sentence frame (e.g., intransitive, passive, imperative, etc.). When all of these findings are compiled and quantitatively compared, we see a continuous developmental progression in which children gradually become more productive with novel verbs during their third and fourth years of life and beyond (see figure 11.2 and Table 11.1). It is clear that this overall pattern is not consistent with the hypothesis that children possess abstract linguistic knowledge early in development, but rather it is consistent with a more constructivist or usage-based model in which young children begin language acquisition by imitatively learning linguistic items directly from adult language, only later discerning the kinds of patterns that enable them to construct more abstract linguistic categories and schemas.

The validity of these findings is further corroborated by two control studies that deal with alternative hypotheses. First, it is possible that young children are simply reluctant to use newly learned words in novel ways. However, when even younger children (22 months) are taught novel nouns, they use them quite freely in novel sentence frames.[13,14] Young children are thus not reticent with all newly learned words, and

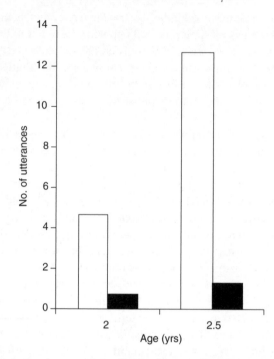

Figure 11.1   Imitative production of novel verbs. The number of utterances children produced with the novel verb in one condition of the Tomasello and Brooks study.[12] Conservative utterances (light gray) were those in which children heard an intransitive use of the novel verb and then reproduced a similar intransitive utterance, even when they were encouraged to produce a transitive utterance. Productive utterances (dark gray) were those in which children used the novel verb (heard in an intransitive utterance) in a transitive utterance. (Adapted from Ref. 12)

indeed they seem to form something like a category of "concrete noun" quite early in development (see also Ref. 15 and related studies for additional evidence.) Second, it might be that children's lack of productivity in the novel verb studies does not have to do with their linguistic knowledge, but only with production difficulties. However, in comprehension tests they perform no better. That is, they are first taught a novel verb in a simple sentence frame (*"Look! Tamming! This is called tamming!*), and they are asked to act out a transitive construction with that verb (*"Show me: the dog's tamming the cat"*). Perhaps surprisingly, children younger than 3 years of age do no better in comprehension than they do in production.[16] (The study of Naigles[17] is sometimes taken to be discrepant with these findings, but in fact it is not relevant because the two sentences that were compared in that study were *"The duck is glorping the bunny"* and *"The bunny and the duck are glorping"* – with one picture depicting the duck doing something to the bunny and the other depicting the two participants engaged in the same parallel action. The problem is that children might very well have been using the word *and* as an indicator of the parallel action picture.[18]

Box 11.2   Other experimental studies of children's early productivity

A number of studies have used the same basic design as Tomasello and Brooks (Ref. a), but with different age children and with the novel verbs presented in different sentence frames. With specific reference to children's ability to generate a novel transitive (subject–verb–object; SVO) utterance:

1   Children were presented with a novel verb in a presentational construction such as "This is called gorping," and encouraged via questions to produce a transitive utterance (Refs b,c,d).

2   Children were presented with a novel verb in an imperative construction such as "*Tam, Anna!*", and encouraged via questions to produce a transitive utterance (Lewis and Tomasello, unpublished data).

3   Children were presented with a novel verb in a passive construction such as "*Ernie's getting meeked by the dog*," and encouraged via questions to produce a transitive utterance (Ref. e).

In all of these studies the overall finding was that children below 3 years of age were very poor at using their newly learned verbs in the transitive construction, with the vast majority of children below this age never producing a single transitive utterance. In most cases we also had control conditions in which those very same children did produce a transitive utterance (using different object names as subject and object) when they had heard a novel verb modeled for them in this way.

It is also noteworthy that the few novel verb studies on languages other than English (although using slightly different syntactic constructions) have found very similar results – a general lack of productivity with novel verbs before 3 years of age (Ref. F, Hebrew; Childers and Tomasello, unpublished data, Childean Spanish).

One other study is of special importance because it did not only show children failing to be creative; it actually succeeded in inducing children to produce non-grammatical English utterances (which should not be possible if certain innate parameters, such as head direction, were already set). Akhtar modeled novel verbs for novel transitive events for young children at 2;8, 3;6, and 4;4 years of age (Ref. g). One verb was modeled in canonical English SVO order, as in "*Ernie meeking the can*," whereas two others were in non-canonical orders, either SOV ("*Ernie the cow tamming*") or VSO ("*Gopping Ernie the cow*"). Children were then encouraged to use the novel verbs with neutral questions such as "*What's happening?*" Almost all of the children at all three ages produced exclusively SVO utterances with the novel verb when that is what they heard. However, when they heard one of the non-canonical SOV or VSO forms, children behaved differently at different ages. In general, the older children used their verb-general knowledge of English transitivity to "correct" the non-canonical uses of the novel verbs to canonical SVO form. The younger children, in contrast, much more often matched the ordering patterns they had heard with the novel verb, no matter how bizarre that pattern sounded to adult ears. Interestingly, many of the younger children vacillated between imitation of the odd sentence patterns and "correction" of these patterns to canonical SVO order. This indicated that they knew enough about English word-order patterns to discern that these were strange utterances, but not enough to overcome completely their tendency to imitatively learn and reproduce the basic structure of what the adult was saying with the novel verb.

References

a   Tomasello, M., & Brooks, P. (1998). Young children's earliest transitive and intransitive constructions. *Cognit. Linguist.*, *9*, 379–395.

b   Olguin, R., & Tomasello, M. (1993). Twenty-five month old children do not have a grammatical category of verb. *Cognit. Dev.*, *8*, 245–272.

c   Akhtar, N., & Tomasello, M. (1997). Young children's productivity with word order and verb morphology. *Dev. Psychol.*, *33*, 952–965.

d   Dodson, K., & Tomasello, M. (1998). Acquiring the transitive construction in English: The role of animacy and pronouns. *J. Child Lang.*, *25*, 555–574.

e   Brooks, P., & Tomasello, M. (1999). Young children learn to produce passives with nonce verbs. *Dev. Psychol.*, *35*, 29–44.

f   Berman, R. (1993). Marking verb transitivity in Hebrew-speaking children. *J. Child Lang.*, *20*, 641–670.

g   Akhtar, N. (1999). Acquiring basic word order: evidence for data-driven learning of syntactic structure. *J. Child Lang.*, *26*, 261–278.

Implications for Theories of Language Acquisition

Combining the results from naturalistic and experimental studies, it is clear that young children are productive with their early language in only limited ways. They begin by learning to use specific pieces of language and only gradually create more abstract linguistic categories and schemas. These findings have important implications for current theories of child language acquisition.

Linguistic nativism

Classically, as espoused by Chomsky for example, linguistic nativism has emphasized that child language acquisition: (1) takes place quickly and effortlessly because children have full linguistic competence at birth and need only to learn to express this competence overtly in performance; (2) relies only indirectly on the language children hear (i.e., "input" only serves to "trigger" innate syntactic structures or to "set parameters"); and (3) is creative from early in ontogeny because it is generated by an abstract grammar. The data just reviewed are clearly at variance with each of these claims, and in addition, the data call into question altogether the use of adult-like grammars to describe children's early language.

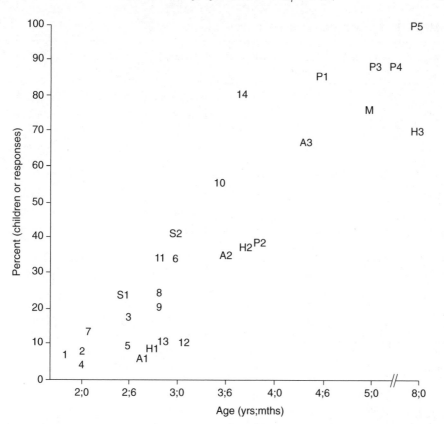

Figure 11.2 Productive transitive utterances in different studies. Percentage of children (or responses in some cases – see Table 1) that produced transitive utterances of a novel verb that was heard in some other sentence frame. The data points correspond to the studies listed in Table 11.1.

The classic response of linguistic nativism to children's syntactic limitations is to invoke hypothesized (but never measured) performance limitations that inhibit the full expression of children's innate linguistic competence (e.g., limited working memory).[19] Many of the control conditions in the above experiments, however, put performance demands on children very similar to those of the experimental conditions, but children experienced no learning difficulties – for example, in using a newly learned noun in novel ways and in using a newly learned verb in a transitive utterance when they had heard it modeled in that way. It is also noteworthy that children's performance was also conservative and item-based in two different comprehension experiments, which place many fewer performance demands on young children.

Recently, some linguistic nativists have also proposed the idea that children are not born with fully adult-like syntactic competence. On this view, children's early language development might be item-based and piecemeal, but the genes for many adult-like syntactic structures begin to "turn on" sometime between 2 and 3 years of age.[20] The problem in this case it that, in the experimental data reviewed, the gradual and piece-

Table 11.1 Research using novel verbs

Reference[a]	Data point in Fig. 2	Age (yrs;mths)	Productivity	Linguistic model	Eliciting question	Scoring
Ref. 14	1	1;10	0.07	Presentational	Neutral	% children
Ref. 12	2	2;0	0.06	Intransitive	Agent	% children
	3	2;6	0.19			
Ref. 43	4	2;0	0.06	Imperative	Neutral	% children
	5	2;6	0.13			
	6	3;0	0.38			
Ref. 18	7	2;1	0.13	Presentational	Neutral	% children
Ref. 39	8	2;10	0.25	Presentational	Neutral	% children
Ref. 40	9	2;10	0.20	Passive	Agent	% children
	10	3;5	0.55			
	11	2;10	0.35			
Ref. 16	12	3;1	0.20	Presentational	Neutral	% children
	13	2;9	0.10			
	14	3;8	0.80			
Ref. 38	1	3;5	0.67	Intransitive (low freq. English verbs)	Agent	% responses
Ref. 11	P1	4;6	0.86	Passive	Agent	% responses (action verbs)
	P2	3;10	0.38			
	P3	5;1	0.88			
	P4	6;1	0.88			
	P5	7;11	1.00			
Ref. 10	M	5;0	0.75	Intransitive	Agent	% children
Ref. 41	A1	2;8	0.08	SOV and VSO	Neutral	% children
	A2	3;6	0.33			
	A3	4;4	0.67			
Ref. 42	H1	2;9	0.09	Intransitive (Hebrew)	Sentence completion	% responses
	H2	3;9	0.38	1st or 3rd person verb (Spanish)	Neutral	% children
	H3	8;0	0.69			
Ref. 44	S1	2;6	0.25			
	S2	3;0	0.38			

[a] Studies investigating children's ability to produce transitive (SVO) utterances as a function of age, given a nonce (made-up) verb modeled in some other sentence frame. Each data point in the table corresponds to one data point in Figure 11.2 (keyed by numbers or letters).

meal developmental process was all within the same syntactic structure, namely, the English transitive construction. Children who can use the simple transitive construction for familiar verbs presumably already have the required genetic bases in place, and so it becomes a mystery why they cannot use these same genetic bases to use novel verbs in transitive utterances in experimental contexts.

Finally, it is also possible to posit that children's early language is item-based, but that after "sufficient" linguistic triggering experiences, it becomes linked with the innate universal grammar.[21] The problem in this case is that there is only one serious theory of how this linking might take place – Pinker's theory of innate linking rules[9] – and this theory does not fit with the empirical data[22,23] (see Ref. 24 on problems of hypothesizing linguistic universals). In general, it is very difficult to envision how an innate universal grammar could be biologically prepared ahead of time to link up its specific categories and schemas to the particular syntactic conventions of the many different languages of the world (e.g., ergative–absolutive versus nominative–accusative systems).

Usage-based accounts

Usage-based approaches to language acquisition attempt to characterize children's language not in terms of innate, adult-like, formal grammars, but rather in terms of the cognitive and communicative processes involved. With respect to the data reviewed above, the hypothesis would be that children's earliest language is based on the specific linguistic items and expressions they comprehend and produce. Children begin to form an abstract category of "concrete noun" quite early, and this allows them to use any symbol categorized in this way productively in a wide range of linguistic contexts. It takes some time for children to categorize or schematize the relational–syntactic structure of their various item-based (verb island) constructions, however, and thereby to become productive with their language in more adult-like ways. The adult endpoint of this developmental process is not an abstract formal grammar, but rather an "inventory of symbolic resources" including everything from words and morphemes to whole grammatical constructions as kind of linguistic gestalts[25] (see papers in Ref. 26). This developmental trajectory depends on cognitive and social-cognitive processes common to all human beings (and, of course, on experiential human universals like growing up in the midst of language users). Three of these processes are especially important.

First in importance is cultural learning or, more specifically, imitative learning in the specific sense used by Tomasello et al.[27] On this view, imitative learning is not simply repeating or mimicking the surface form of adult utterances. Rather, it is the attempt by children to reproduce the language adults produce and for the same communicative function – the reproduction is of both the linguistic form and its conventional communicative function. At one level of analysis, this absolutely must be true because all children learn the language to which they are exposed, and for all non-canonical aspects of language structure – all idioms, lexical items, quirky constructions, and the like – nobody has ever proposed any mechanism other than some form of imitative learning. (For example, only by observing and reproducing particular linguistic symbols can one learn that, in English, "*That won't go down well with him*" means that he won't like that.) The current proposal is simply that, initially, imitative learning is *all* that children do for all linguistic constructions, canonical and quirky alike. This approach thus highlights the role of the language that children hear around them, and it also takes seriously the possibility of individual differences based both on children's potentially different perceptual and cognitive skills and on their potentially different language learning environments.[28,29]

Secondly, children go beyond these early item-based constructions in due course. The only way they can do this is to find patterns in the language they are hearing, and thereby to form some kinds of abstract categories and schemas. Children do this in the case of the category of concrete noun quite early. But in addition they abstract across more complex relational structures as well, for example, whole constructions such as the simple transitive construction. Although there are no good data on how they do this, the work of Gentner on analogy and "structure mapping" provides some interesting hypotheses.[10] The idea is that children must see both the structural and the functional similarities in utterances such as "*I draw trea*," "*She kissed me*," "*I hit Jeffrey*," "*You hug Mommy*," "*Jamie kicking ball*," in terms of their relational structure, independent of the specific words involved. A reasonable assumption is that there must be some "critical mass" of exemplars of particular utterance types necessary for the human cognitive apparatus to be able to make the requisite analogies and subsequent categories and schemas.[31] It may be that the critical factor is the number of different verbs heard in the construction – because verbs are the central organizing element in utterance-level constructions and because many exemplars with only one or a few verbs would seem to be a very inadequate basis for generalizing the construction.[32]

Third and finally, children also combine various kinds of linguistic constructions creatively, involving both concrete and abstract constructions of varying levels of complexity. They combine much more complex structures than just words or word classes. As one example, one child's earliest utterances with three or more words were things like "*See Daddy's car*." But previously this child had said things like "*See ball*" and "*See Mommy*," on the one hand, and also things like "*Daddy's shirt*" and "*Daddy's pen*," on the other. So, the likelihood is that she creatively combined something like a "*See ••*" schema with a "*Daddy's ••*" schema. Note that to do this she had to understand that "*Daddy's car*" as a complex expression was in some sense equivalent to the other things she previously had been talking about seeing (*Ball* and *Mommy*), and so this combination indicates some knowledge of the functional equivalence of these different referring expressions. It should be noted that many different procedures may be used to combine established constructions in these ways. For example, a child might combine an item-based construction with a more abstract construction, or she might combine two item-based or two abstract constructions with one another. Diessel and Tomasello[33]report a further illustration of these processes in more complex constructions (i.e., those with sentential complements; see Box 11.3).

Conclusion

If grammatical structures do not come directly from the human genome, as the above-reported data suggest they do not, and if children do not invent them *de novo*, as they clearly can not, then it is legitimate to ask, Where do grammatical structures come from? The answer is that, in the first instance, they come from processes of grammaticalization in language history. That is to say, at some point in human evolution, *Homo sapiens* evolved the ability to communicate with one another symbolically.[34] When human beings communicate symbolically with one another in extended discourse interactions, the stringing together of symbols begins to become grammaticalized; for

Box 11.3 A more complex example of structure combining

As a more complex example of structure combining, Diessel and Tomasello (Ref. a) looked at the earliest complex sentences with sentential complements of six children. They found that virtually all early complement sentences are composed of a simple sentence schema that the child has already mastered, combined with one of a handful of matrix verbs (see also Ref. b).

These matrix verbs are of two types. First are epistemic verbs such as *think* and *know*. In almost all cases children and *I think* to indicate their own uncertainty about something, and they basically never used the verb *think* in anything but this first-person form (i.e., no examples of "*He thinks* . . . ," "*She thinks* . . . ," etc.). This form was also virtually never negated (no examples of "*I don't think* . . ."), virtually never used in anything other than the present tense (no examples of "*I thought* . . ."), and never with a complementizer (no examples of "*I think that* . . ."). It thus appears that *I think* is a relatively fixed phrase meaning something like *maybe*. The child pieces together this fixed phrase with a full sentence, but this piecing together does not amount to "sentence embedding" as it is typically portrayed in more formal analyses – it is more like simple concatenation because the main verb (*think*) is not really acting as a verb. Second, children also use attention-getting verbs like *look* and *see* in conjunction with full sentences. In this case, they use them almost exclusively in imperative form (again no negations, no non-present tenses, no complementizers). Therefore, these early complex sentences do not appear to be abstract sentence embeddings, but rather concatenations of a formulaic expression and a full sentence.

Examples from Sarah:	Examples from Nina:
I think he's gone	*See* that monkey crying
I think it's in here	*See* Becca sleeping
I think my daddy took it	*See* that go
I think I saw one	*See* my hands are washed
It's a crazy bone, *I think*	*See* he bite me
I think dis is de bowl	*See* him lie down

References

a   Diessel, H., & Tomasello, M. Why complement clauses do not have a *that* complementizer in early child language. *Berkeley Linguistics Society* (in press).

b   Bloom, L. (1992). *Language Development from Two to Three*. Cambridge University Press.

example, content words such as nouns and verbs become function words such as prepositions and auxiliaries, and loosely concatenated symbols acquire syntactic relationships involving constituency and dependency (see Box 11.4). These transformations of linguistic structure occur as a result of social-interactive processes in which (1) speakers try to abbreviate linguistic expression as much as they can, and (2) listeners try to

Box 11.4   Grammaticalization

Each of the 5,000 or more languages of the world has its own inventory of linguistic conventions, including syntactic conventions, which allow its users to share experience with one another symbolically. This inventory of symbolic conventions is grounded in universal structures of human cognition, human communication, and the mechanics of the vocal–auditory apparatus. The peculiarities of particular languages come from differences in the kinds of things that different speech communities think it important to talk about and the ways they think it useful to talk about them – along with various historical "accidents." All of the conventions and constructions of a given language are not invented at one time, of course, and once invented they often do not stay the same for very long, but rather they evolve, change, and accumulate over time as humans use them with one another. This set of processes is called grammaticalization, and it involves such well-attested phenomena as free-standing words evolving into grammatical markers, and loose and redundantly organized discourse structures congealing into tight and less redundantly organized syntactic constructions (see Refs a,b for some recent research). Some examples are as follows:

1   The future tense marker in many languages is grammaticized from free-standing words for such things as volition or movement to a goal. So in English the original verb was *will*, as in "*I will it to happen,*" and this became grammaticized into "*It will happen*" (with the volitional component "bleached" out). Similarly, the original use of *go* was for movement ("*I'm going to the store*") and this was grammaticizied into "*I'm going to die some day*" (with the movement bleached out).

2   The English past perfective, using *have*, is very likely derived from sentences such as "*I have a broken finger*" or "*I have the prisoners bound*" (in which *have* is a verb of possession) into something like "*I have broken a finger*" on which the possession meaning of *have* is bleached out and it only now indicates perfective aspect).

3   English phrases such as "*on the top of*" and "*in the side of*" evolved into "*on top of*" and "*inside of*" and eventually into "*atop*" and "*inside.*" In some languages relator words such as these spatial prepositions have also become attached to nouns as case markers – in this instance as possible locative markers.

4   Loose discourse sequences such as "*He pulled the door and it opened*" may become syntacticized into "*He pulled the door open*" (a resultative construction).

5   Loose discourse sequences such as "*My boyfriend . . . he plays piano . . . he plays in a band*" may become "*My boyfriend plays piano in a band.*" Or, similarly, "*My boyfriend . . . he rides horses . . . he bets on them*" may become "*My boyfriend, who rides horses, bets on them.*"

6 Similarly, if someone expresses the belief that Mary will wed John, another person might respond with an assent "*I believe that*," followed by a repetition of the expressed belief that "*Mary will wed John*" – which become syntacticized into the single statement "*I believe that Mary will wed John.*"

7 Complex sentences may also derive from discourse sequences of initially separate utterances, as in "*I want it . . . I buy it*" evolving into "*I want to buy it.*"

References

a Traugott, E., & Heine, B. (1991). *Approaches to Grammaticalization (Vols 1 and 2)*. John Benjamins.

b Hopper, P., & Traugott, E. (1993). *Grammaticalization*. Cambridge University Press.

make sure that speakers do not go so far in this direction that the message becomes incomprehensible. Grammaticalization processes are well attested in the written records of numerous languages in their relatively recent pasts, and it is a reasonable assumption that the same processes were at work in the origin and early evolution of language, turning loosely organized sequences of single symbols into grammaticized linguistic constructions.[35,36]

Even so, grammaticalization by itself is not enough because it does not account for the abstractness of linguistic structures. Abstractness, as Chomsky recognized in even his earliest writings, must be contributed by the minds of individual children as they acquire the use of particular pieces of particular languages. It is possible – albeit very difficult – to imagine that children make this contribution by simply linking an innate universal grammar with the particular structures of the particular language they are learning. However, it is also possible, and more in accord with recent data, to imagine that children make this contribution in more extended developmental processes in which they apply their general cognitive, social-cognitive, and vocal–auditory processing skills to the historical products of grammaticalization.[37] Overall, then, we may hypothesize that human language originated ultimately from a species-unique biological adaptation for symbolic communication, but the actual grammatical structures of modern languages were humanly created through processes of grammaticalization during particular cultural histories, and through processes of cultural learning, schema formation, and structure combining during particular individual ontogenies.

Outstanding Questions

- When children imitatively learn some complex linguistic expression, how do they come to understand the communicative functions of the different constituents involved?
- On what basis do children make analogies or form schemas as they abstract across their verb island and other relational linguistic schemas?

- What principles govern the ways in which children combine established linguistic constructions with one another creatively?
- How do children select what they need from all the language they hear around them?
- What is the nature of the cross-linguistic and individual differences that can be observed in children acquiring natural languages?

Acknowledgements

The author would like to thank Elena Lieven, Heike Behrens, Holger Diessel, Nameera Akhtar, and Patty Brooks for helping to develop the ideas and the studies reported in this paper.

References

1   Pinker, S. (1994). *The Language Instinct: How the Mind Creates Language.* Morrow.
2   Pinker, S. (1984). *Language Learnability and Language Development.* Harvard University Press.
3   Braine, M.D.S. (1971). On two types of models of the internalization of grammars. In D.I. Slobin (Ed.), *The Ontogenesis of Grammar,* pp. 153–186. Academic Press.
4   Tomasello, M. (1992). *First Verbs: A Case Study in Early Grammatical Development.* Cambridge University Press.
5   Lieven, E. et al. (1997). Lexically-based learning and early grammatical development. *J. Child Lang.,* 24, 187–220.
6   Pine, J., & Lieven, E. (1997). Slot and frame patterns in the development of the determiner category. *Appl. Psycholinguist.,* 18, 123–138.
7   Bowerman, M. (1982). Reorganizational processes in lexical and syntactic development. In L. Gleitman, & E. Wanner (Eds.), *Language Acquisition: The State of the Art,* pp. 319–346. Cambridge University Press.
8   Bowerman, M. (1988). The "no negative evidence" problem: how do children avoid constructing an overgeneral grammar? In J.A. Hawkins (Ed.), *Explaining Language Universals,* pp. 73–101. Basil Blackwell.
9   Pinker, S. (1989). *Learnability and Cognition: The Acquisition of Verb-argument Structure.* Harvard University Press.
10 Maratsos, M. et al. (1987). A study in novel word learning: the productivity of the causative. In B. MacWhinney (Ed.), *Mechanisms of Language Acquisition,* pp. 89–114. Erlbaum.
11 Pinker, S. et al. (1987). Productivity and constraints in the acquisition of the passive. *Cognition,* 26, 195–267.
12 Tomasello, M., & Brooks, P. (1998). Young children's earliest transitive and intransitive constructions. *Cognit. Linguist.,* 9, 379–395.
13 Tomasello, M., & Olguin, R. (1993). Twenty-three-month-old children have a grammatical category of noun. *Cognit. Dev.,* 8, 451–464.
14 Tomasello, M. et al. (1997). Differential productivity in young children's use of nouns and verbs. *J. Child Lang.,* 24, 373–387.
15 Taylor, M., & Gelman, S. (1988). Adjectives and nouns: children's strategies for learning new words. *Child Dev.,* 59, 411–419.

16   Akhtar, N., & Tomasello, M. (1997). Young children's productivity with word order and verb morphology. *Dev. Psychol., 33*, 952–965.

17   Naigles, L. (1990). Children use syntax to learn verb meanings. *J. Child Lang., 17*, 357–374.

18   Olguin, R., & Tomasello, M. (1993). Twenty-five-month-old children do not have a grammatical category of verb. *Cognit. Dev., 8*, 245–272.

19   Valian, V. (1991). Syntactic subjects in the early speech of American and Italian children. *Cognition, 40*, 21–81.

20   Boerer, H., & Wexler, K. (1992). Bi-unique relations and the maturation of grammatical principles. *Nat. Lang. Linguist. Theory, 10*, 147–187.

21   Hyams, N. (1994). Non-discreteness and variation in child language: implications for Principle and parameter models of language acquisition. In Y. Levy (Ed.), *Other Children, Other Languages*, pp. 11–40. Erlbaum.

22   Bowerman, M. (1990). Mapping thematic roles onto syntactic functions: are children helped by innate linking rules? *Linguistics, 28*, 1253–1289.

23   Slobin, D. (1997). On the origin of grammaticalizable notions: beyond the individual mind. In D.I. Slobin (Ed.), *The Cross-linguistic Study of Language Acquisition* (Vol. 5), pp. 119–153. Erlbaum.

24   Dryer, M. (1997). Are grammatical relations universal? In J. Bybee et al., (Eds.), *Essays on Language Function and Language Type*, pp. 115–144. John Benjamins.

25   Langacker, R. (1991). *Foundations of Cognitive Grammar* (Vols 1 and 2). Stanford University Press.

26   Tomasello, M. (Ed.) (1998). *The New Psychology of Language Cognitive and Functional Approaches*. Erlbaum.

27   Tomasello, M. et al. (1993). Cultural learning. *Behav. Brain Sci., 16*, 495–511.

28   Lieven, E. (1997). Variation in a cross-linguistic context. In D. Slobin (Ed.), *The Cross-linguistic Study of Language Acquisition* (Vol. 5), pp. 233–287. Erlbaum.

29   Tomasello, M., & Brooks, P. (1999). Early syntactic development. In M. Barrett (Ed.), *The Development of Language*, pp. 161–190. UCL Press.

30   Gentner, D., & Markman, A. (1997). Structure mapping in analogy and similarity. *Am. Psychol., 52*, 45–56.

31   Marchman, V., & Bates, E. (1994). Continuity in lexical and morphological development: a test of the critical mass hypothesis. *J. Child Lang., 21*, 339–366.

32   Bybee, J. (1985). *Morphology*, John Benjamins.

33   Diessel, H., & Tomasello, M. Why complement clauses do not have a *that*-complementizer in early child language. *Berkeley Linguistics Society* (in press).

34   Deacon, T. (1998). *The Symbolic Species*. Harvard University Press.

35   Traugott, E., & Heine, B. (1991). *Approaches to Grammaticalization* (Vols 1 and 2). John Benjamins.

36   Givón, T. (1995). *Functionalism and Gramma*. John Benjamins.

37   Tomasello, M. (1999). *The Cultural Origins of Human Cognition*. Harvard University Press.

38   Ingham, R. (1993). Critical influences on the acquisition of verb transitivity. In D. Messer, & G. Turner (Eds.), *Critical Influences on Child Language Acquisition and Development*, pp. 19–38. Maximillian Press.

39   Dodson, K., & Tomasello, M. (1998). Acquiring the transitive construction in English: the role of animacy and pronouns. *J. Child Lang., 25*, 555–574.

40   Brooks, P., & Tomasello, M. (1999). Young children learn to produce passives with nonce verbs. *Dev. Psychol., 35*, 29–44.

41   Akhtar, N. (1999). Acquiring basic word order: evidence for data-driven learning of syntactic structure. *J. Child Lang., 26*, 261–378.

42   Berman, R. (1993). Marking verb transitivity in Hebrew-speaking children. *J. Child Lang.*,
     20, 641–670.
43   Lewis, L., & Tomasello, M. Children's ability to generalize novel verbs used in imperatives.
     Unpublisher manuscript.
44   Childers, J., & Tomasello, M. Spanish-speaking children's ability to generalize nonce verbs
     to new constructions. Submitted.

TWELVE

Acquiring Basic Word Order: Evidence for Data-Driven Learning of Syntactic Structure

Nameera Akhtar

Introduction

Natural languages use two grammatical devices to encode the relations among people, objects, and events: case marking inflections and the sequencing of phrasal constituents within the clause (henceforth *basic word order*).[1] Word order is a particularly importance cue to sentence interpretation in English, especially in the case of semantically reversible sentences such as *The girl pushed the boy* (Bates & MacWhinney, 1989). The basic word order of English is subject–verb–object (SVO), but in Japanese it is subject–object–verb (SOV), and in Irish it is verb–subject–object (VSO); object-initial orders also occur, though less frequently (Derbyshire & Pullum, 1981; Pullum, 1981). A child learning the language of a specific community must therefore detect from linguistic input which is the prevailing basic word order in that community. How the child accomplishes this is the subject of some disagreement.

Some theorists describe the acquisition of basic word order as the setting of "parameters" that capture the systematic variation among the world's languages (Pinker, 1984; Mazuka, 1996; Culicover, 1997). On this view, sample utterances act as "triggers" for the setting of these parameters (Lightfoot, 1989; Gibson & Wexler, 1994). Other theorists, however, place more emphasis on linguistic input (data) and on the active role that children play in acquiring grammatical relations (Braine, 1988; Sampson, 1989; O'Grady, 1997). According to these authors, children's acquisition of grammar involves a slower process of inducing general patterns from specific examples. This theoretical approach can be characterized as invoking some form of "data-driven learning" (Pine & Martindale, 1996; Pullum, 1996). A major difference between parameter setting and data-driven learning involves the quantity of linguistic data required by the child to master the basic word order of his/her language (Atkinson, 1987).

---

[1] Although there is some debate over the very notion of "basic word order" (see Mithun, 1987), it will not be addressed here.

Proponents of parameter setting maintain that the acquisition of basic word order may be accomplished quite rapidly (triggered), on the basis of relatively little data. For example, Pinker (1994) states:

> All [children] have to learn is whether their particular language has the parameter value head-first, as in English, or head-last, as in Japanese. They can do that merely by noticing whether a verb comes before or after its object in any sentence in their parents' speech ...Huge chunks of grammar are then available to the child, all at once, as if the child were merely flipping a switch to one of two possible positions. If this theory of language learning is true, it would help solve the mystery of how children's grammar explodes into adultlike complexity in so short a time. They are not acquiring dozens or hundreds of rules; they are just setting a few mental switches.

Support for this view comes from the fact that children do appear to learn basic word order very rapidly; as soon as they begin to produce full sentences, they tend to employ accurate ordering of clausal constituents (Braine, 1976; Pinker, 1984; Bloom, 1991; Tomasello, 1992). Even in comprehension, very young children learning English seem to rely on strategies that indicate a sensitivity to the SVO order of English (Slobin & Bever, 1982; Bates et al., 1984; Hirsh-Pasek & Golinkoff, 1996).

While these facts about acquisition might seem to support parameter setting models, it is important to note that practically all existing studies of word order comprehension and production have examined children's performance with *familiar* verbs. Therefore, the possibility remains that young children do not have a truly *general* understanding of word order, but are being conservative and using only the orders they have heard modeled with individual verbs (Tomasello, 1992). That is, on hearing sentences such as "She gave me a toy," children may form not a general principle such as "SVIO" (subject–verb–indirect object–direct object), but rather a much more specific schema that is centered around the particular verb used. For example, the schema could be as specific as "[phrase denoting donor(s)] – [form of the verb GIVE] – [phrase denoting recipient(s)] – [phrase denoting gift(s)]." Similarly, on hearing multiple sentences containing the verb *push* in sentence-medial position (e.g., "The boy pushed the cat"), children may form the schema "[phrase denoting pusher(s)] – [form of the verb PUSH] – [phrase denoting pushee(s)]."

There is some evidence that very young children acquiring English do show this pattern of verb-specific comprehension; that is, they understand word order with some verbs but not with others. Roberts (1983) showed that a young toddler might be able to correctly enact a transitive sentence containing the verb *tickle*, but not a similar sentence containing the verb *hug*. Older children were able to enact transitive sentences containing a wider range of verbs, leading to the conclusion that children's initial comprehension of word order is "verb specific, gradually expanding, verb by verb, to apply across a wider scope of verbs" (p. 443). Verb-specific formulas such as those outlined above would lead to appropriate performance on tests of production and comprehension of word order with familiar verbs. Consequently, error-free use and comprehension of word order with familiar verbs cannot distinguish between truly general knowledge of basic word order and verb-specific knowledge of word order. What is needed is a test of how general young children's knowledge of word order is.

The only appropriate way to test for general knowledge is to use novel items; that is, it is necessary to assess whether children understand the use of word order with novel (unfamiliar) verbs. If children can use and comprehend word order correctly with verbs they've never heard before, then their understanding is probably general. This approach is inspired by the famous *wug* test designed by Jean Berko (1958) to assess children's morphological productivity. She taught children novel names for novel objects and then tried to elicit plurals from them. The fact that preschoolers could add a plural morpheme to a word they had never heard in the plural form showed that they knew something general about plural formation. The current focus is on whether children learning English understand something general about the use of word order in transitive sentences. So, if, for example, one invented a novel causative action and called it *dacking*, would children know what to do when asked to "Make Bib Bird *dack* Cookie Monster"? Similarly, in producing sentences with the verb to *dack*, would they know that they must place any agent of the action before the verb, and any patient of the action after the verb?

A recent series of studies using this methodology indicates that English-speaking two-year-olds do not have a truly general understanding of SVO order (Akhtar & Tomasello, 1997). In these studies, children were taught novel verbs for novel actions consisting of one toy character acting on another. One verb was modeled without word order (information; i.e., without expressing the agent and patient arguments (e.g., "This is called *dacking*"). Another was modeled with both arguments in a full transitive frame; e.g., "Big Bird's *tamming* Cookie Monster." Children younger than 3;0 were unable to use word order correctly with the verb modeled without arguments. Moreover, they were at chance when asked to act out commands such as "Make Big Bird *dack* Cookie Monster"; that is, half the time they enacted these commands backwards.[2] They were, however, accurate on an identical test of word order comprehension with the novel verb that had been modeled in the full transitive frame (i.e., with word order information). These findings support Tomasello's (1992) *verb island hypothesis* that children learn the appropriate use of grammatical relations (e.g., word order) on a verb-by-verb basis. That is, initially children may rely quite heavily on linguistic input for information about the grammatical properties of specific verbs. Indeed, young children may be paying close attention to patterns in the language they hear and may be constructing generalizations on the basis of recurring patterns (Bates & MacWhinney, 1987; Bowerman, 1988; Braine, 1988; Cartwright & Brent, 1997; Ninio, 1988; Goldberg, 1998).

This possibility was investigated further in the current study by presenting English-speaking children with novel verbs in non-English orders. This unique methodological approach – which essentially involves presenting children with models of ungrammatical input – may provide an avenue for distinguishing between parameter setting and data-driven learning as mechanisms of grammatical development. There are no

---

[2] These children (*M* age = 2;9) were attending to the task and seemed to know that there was a correct response in that they often queried the experimenter "Like this?" as they were preparing to act. The same children performed above chance on tests of comprehension of word order with both a familiar verb and the novel verb they had been taught in a full transitive frame. Therefore, their difficulties with the novel verb presented without arguments are not likely due to performance deficits.

natural languages in which some transitive verbs follow one ordering and some follow another. Consequently, some linguistic have hypothesized that word order (or head direction) is *parameterized*: that is, it is one of those aspects of language that does not have to be learned but rather is triggered by environmental input. A strong version of the parameter setting view therefore predicts that children will establish the basic word order of their language relatively early, and that their grammar will likely be unaffected by subsequent orders they might encounter. More specifically, it predicts that children will use only one word order (within a given language) with *all* transitive verbs. As English-speaking children's linguistic input is very consistent (they generally hear only SVO sentences), the only way to test this hypothesis is to expose children to novel verbs associated with orders not used in their native language.

This was the rationale for the current study. Three groups of children (*M* ages = 2;8, 3;6, and 4;4) were taught three novel verbs, one in each of three sentence positions: sentence-medial (SVO), sentence-final (SOV), and sentence-initial (VSO). Of the six possible orders, these three are by far the most frequently found in the world's languages (Tomlin, 1986). They are also the three used by Bates et al. (1984) in their examination of Italian and American children's comprehension of word order (with familiar verbs). The prediction of parameter setting models is that even the youngest children hearing non-English orders will not acquire the non-SVO orders; that is, they will not be willing to use the SOV or VSO orders because they have already set the head direction parameter. Instead, they may either ignore these verbs or may actively switch to using them in SVO order. Alternatively, if children are forming a generalization based on sample sentences, they will be conservative early in development in that they may acquire word order on a verb-by-verb basis (Roberts, 1983); that is, young children will construct verb-specific formulas such as "[phrase denoting kicker(s)] – [form of verb KICK] – [phrase denoting thing(s) kicked]" before constructing the broader subject–verb–object generalization. From a strong version of the verb island hypothesis, then, the prediction is that the youngest children will be willing to spontaneously use the non-SVO orders. They are not expected to switch these orders to SVO. Older children, on the other hand, will either ignore these orders, or will actively switch them to SVO, as they will have already formed the generalization that English is an SVO language.

Method

Participants

Thirty-six children participated: 12 ranged in age from 2;1 to 3;1 (*M* age = 2;8), 12 ranged in age from 3;2 to 3;11 (*M* age = 3;6), and 12 ranged in age from 4;0 to 4;9 (*M* age = 4;4). There were approximately equal numbers of males and females in each age group.

Materials

Three novel actions were constructed. All involved (pseudo)animate agents (puppet characters familiar to young American children; e.g., Sesame Street and Winnie-the-Pooh characters) acting on inanimate patients (e.g., a toy car, plastic food items). It was thought that this asymmetry in animacy would aid the children in appropriate construal of the scenes described by the verbs as causative actions. The *tamming* action involved a prop on which the inanimate toy was placed; a puppet hitting this prop caused the toy to be catapulted into the air. *Gopping* involved a puppet springing a toy off a platform connected to a metal coil; *dacking* involved a puppet knocking a toy down a curved chute.

Design and procedure

Children in each age group participated in three within-subjects conditions: SVO (e.g., Elmo *dacking* the car), SOV (Elmo the car *gapping*), and VSO (*Tamming* Elmo the car). The assignment of verb–action pair to condition (SVO, SOV, VSO) was counterbalanced across the three age groups; that is, within an age group, each verb was represented an equal number of times in each sentence position. The order of presentation of the conditions was similarly counterbalanced. All children were seen individually in a room in their preschool after becoming familiar with the experimenter (E) and an observer (O) in their classrooms. At the beginning of each session, E ensured that the child knew the names of all the puppets and toys: any puppet or object the child did not readily produce a name for was set aside. Each child participated in two experimental sessions and a free play session. A subset of the children also participated in a Control condition (see below). All sessions were videotaped by O who also transcribed children's use of the novel verbs.

Experimental sessions

In each experimental session, the children were exposed to all three of the novel verbs (consecutively), and they had multiple opportunities to perform and verbally describe the actions. Each verb was modelled with different puppets and toys filling the roles of agents and patients of the action. To ensure appropriate construal of the actions, before each was performed children were told to "Watch what (puppet's name) is going to do to (toy's name)." E then proceeded to describe the action being performed with one of the novel verbs; e.g., *Look! Big Bird the car gopping!* Verbs were modeled in both the present progressive and the past tense; no auxiliaries were used. Language models were given in pairs and after each E performance of the action, the child was given a turn to perform the action as well (with puppets and objects of his/her choosing). For the first 10 trials, E simply told the child "It's your turn now." For the next 10 trials, E asked the child "What's going to happen now?" before the child performed the action or "What happened?" after the child had performed the action. These questions were designed to elicit use of the novel verbs. Both spontaneous and elicited uses of the verbs were transcribed by O and subsequently checked (from videotape) by E. This procedure was followed for each of the three verbs in a preassigned order, and the entire procedure was repeated a day or two later. Thus, each child received a total of 80 models of each verb, and a total of 20 questions per verb that were designed to elicit use of the novel verbs in sentences.

Coding and reliability

The main dependent measure consisted of the frequency of sentences (spontaneous and elicited combined) that children produced with the novel verbs during the experimental sessions. Only non-imitative sentences with both the agent and patient of the action expressed were included in the analyses. Sentences were classified as either matching or mismatching the order in which the verb had been modeled; as will be shown below, virtually all of the mismatches were produced in the non-SVO conditions, and all of these consisted of corrections to SVO order. E initially coded all of the transcripts of the experimental sessions. They were all subsequently coded by an independent coder who achieved 100% reliability with E.

Control condition

The children who used either or both of the non-SVO orders at least once during the experimental sessions were also tested in a control condition. This condition was intended as a control for compliance; it was possible that some of the children might have known that the non-SVO orders were not grammatical but may have used them only to please the experimenter. In this control condition children were exposed to a familiar verb in an ungrammatical order; e.g., *Elmo the car pushing*. The order used for a given child was the one that individual had used most frequently in the experimental phase of the procedure. The procedure was identical to that followed in the experimental conditions. The hypothesis was that, if children acquire word order on a verb-by-verb basis, then they will have already learned the appropriate order to use with the verb *push* (e.g. [phrase denoting pusher(s)] – [form of the verb PUSH] – [phrase denoting pushee(s)]), and will therefore resist using this verb in a novel order. If, however, the children were merely being compliant, they should use the novel order in the control condition as well.

Results

Frequency analyses revealed that older children were far more likely than the younger children to produce sentences containing the novel verbs (see Table 12.1 for the mean frequency of matches and mismatches in the three conditions as a function of age). Therefore a decision was made to graphically display the mean proportion of all sentences containing a given verb that matched the order modeled with that verb. This measure serves to equate baseline performance in the three conditions and three ages. Figure 12.1 depicts the mean proportion of child sentences that matched the order modeled in each condition as a function of age. All statistical analyses reported below were conducted on the frequency data shown in Table 12.1

As expected, all children consistently matched the order modeled in the SVO condition. There were only two utterances (one each from two three-year-olds) that did not match the order of the SVO verb. These exceptions are interesting because they each matched the order modeled with the immediately previous verb, indicating some type of priming effect. It should be noted, however, that any such effect was short-lived as it was seen only once in each of these two children and these same children also frequently matched the SVO order.

Table 12.1 Mean frequency of matches and mismatches as a function of age and condition (standard deviations are in parentheses)

Age		Condition		
		SVO	SOV	VSO
Two years	Matches	5.83 (6.32)	1.67 (2.93)	0.92 (1.44)
	Mismatches	0.00 (0.00)	1.33 (2.81)	1.58 (2.27)
Three years	Matches	8.58 (7.29)	3.17 (4.53)	1.75 (3.52)
	Mismatches	0.17 (0.39)	2.42 (4.03)	4.92 (6.19)
Four years	Matches	14.08 (4.56)	0.42 (0.90)	0.25 (0.62)
	Mismatches	0.00 (0.00)	8.83 (8.43)	9.92 (7.09)

Note. All mismatches in the SOV and VSO conditions were corrections to SVO order.

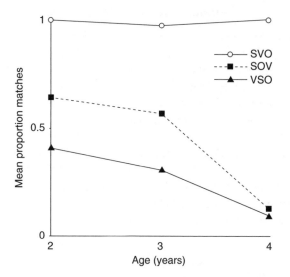

Figure 12.1 Mean proportion of children's sentences matching the order modeled at each age in each condition. All mistakes in the SOV and VSO conditions were corrections to SVO order.

All other mismatches (in the SVO and VSO conditions) consisted of corrections to SVO order. Therefore, the converse of the proportions shown for these two conditions represents the proportion of corrections to SVO order. In the SOV condition, the two younger groups were equally likely to match the modeled structure was to make corrections to SVO order (paired t's (11) both <1), whereas the four-year-olds were far more likely to correct the SOV order to SVO (paired t (11) = 3.47, $p < 0.01$). The same was true in the VSO condition: two- and three-year-olds were equally likely to match as to correct (paired t's (11) = 0.89 and 1.34, p's > 0.20, for the two- and three-year-olds respectively), whereas four-year-olds were more likely to correct than they were to match the VSO order (paired t (11) = 4.61, $p < 0.01$).

Thus, the younger children were clearly willing to *use* the ungrammatical structures with the novel verbs; e.g., they said things like *Tigger the fork dacking* to describe Tigger performing the *dacking* action on a fork. (These children also made several corrections to SVO order – see below for a closer examination of these utterances.) It is important to reiterate that these uses of non-SVO order were not imitative; that is, the children spontaneously used the verbs with different agents and patients than the experimenter had. It is also unlikely the children thought the novel verbs were from another language as the verbs were always presented with English inflections (*-ing, -ed*) in sentences with English lexical items. However, to ensure that their performance was not due to non-linguistic factors such as compliance or simply being agreeable it is necessary: (1) to compare the younger children's performance in Session 1 versus Session 2 (to see whether these children were more likely to match later; i.e., after repeated E models of the non-SVO orders); and (2) to examine children's performance in the control condition.

Session 1 versus Session 2

As the two younger groups were equally like to match the order modeled in the non-SVO conditions as to correct to SVO order, it was important to see if there were any order effects in the data; e.g., did children begin by correcting E's use of the non-SVO orders and only later begin to assume this usage themselves? To address this question, the frequency of matches in Session 1 was compared to the frequency of matches in Session 2. To avoid empty cells, data were collapsed over age (two- and three-year-olds) and over the two non-SVO conditions (SOV and VSO). A paired samples t-test revealed no significant difference in the frequency of matches in Session 1 ($M = 1.75$) and the frequency of matches in Session 2 ($M = 2.00$); $t (23) < 1$. There was also no difference in the mean proportion of matches in Session 1 vs. Session 2; $t (23) = 1.03; p = 0.31$. Apparently children were not more likely to use the non-SVO orders after they had heard more models of these orders.

Control condition

Fifteen children matched a non-SVO order at least once; 11 of them (four two-year-olds, four three-year-olds, and three four-year-olds) participated in the control condition in which a familiar verb (*push*) was modeled in a non-SVO order (the other four children were not available for testing because their families went on vacation). Figure 12.2 depicts the mean proportion of sentences matching the order modeled in the control, SOV, and VSO conditions for this subset of children who matched the non-SVO orders. In the control condition as well as in the two experimental conditions, all mismatches were corrections to SVO order. In the control condition, children were far more likely to correct the experimenter's use of the familiar verb to SVO order, than they were to match it (paired $t (10) = 4.37, p < 0.01$), whereas the same children were equally likely to match as to correct in the non-SVO novel verb conditions (both t's < 1). Indeed, in the control condition, *all* of the children corrected to SVO several times, whereas only three of them occasionally matched this aberrant usage of word order with the familiar verb. Thus, it appears that the younger children were not simply mimicking

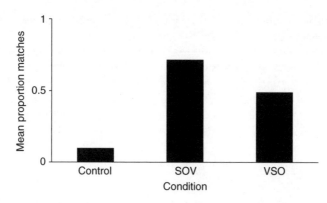

Figure 12.2 Mean proportion of children's sentences matching the order modeled in the control and experimental conditions of the subset of children who matched the non-SVO orders. All mistakes were corrections to SVO order.

the experimenter's use of non-English orders; they did so only when the verbs were novel; that is, verbs for which they had not already developed a specific word order schema to follow (i.e., the SOV and VSO verbs). These same children systematically corrected the E's use of novel word orders to SVO order when the verb being used was familiar to them; that is, a verb for which they had presumably already constructed a schema (e.g., NP_{pusher} – form of the verb PUSH – NP_{pushee}).

Characterizing individual children's performance

The analyses reported above indicate that, as a group, two- and three-year-olds were equally likely to match the non-SVO orders as they were to correct them to SVO order. It is necessary to examine individual children's patterns of performance in the non-SVO conditions to determine whether the group means conceal a bimodal response pattern, such that some children never corrected to SVO and others always did. Table 12.2 presents the number of children in each age group who showed qualitatively different patterns of performance in the non-SVO conditions.

Three of the two-year-olds did not use any of the novel verbs in full sentences; nothing can be said about their knowledge of SVO order. Selectively avoiding use of the non-SVO verbs (that is, using the SVO verb but neither the SOV nor the VSO verb in full sentences) could be considered to be a measure of sensitivity to SVO order; two of the two-year-olds and three of the three-year-olds showed this pattern of performance. Only one two-year-old (along with three three-year-olds and one four-year-old) consistently matched the non-SVO orders. Only one two-year-old consistently corrected the non-SVO orders to SVO, whereas four three-year-olds and eight four-year-olds did so. Five of the two-year-olds showed some mixing of matching and correcting, as did two three-year-olds and three four-year-olds. Recall, however, that the frequency analyses demonstrated that the two-year-olds matched the non-SVO orders about as frequently as they corrected, whereas the corresponding four-year-olds made far more frequent corrections than matches. In combination with the group analyses, then, the

Table 12.2 Number of children in each age group displaying different patterns of performance in the non-SVO conditions

	Two-year-olds	Three-year-olds	Four-year-olds
No sentences	3	0	0
Matched only	1	3	1
Matched & corrected	5	2	3
Avoided use	2	3	0
Corrected only	1	4	8

individual data indicate developmental trends in children's willingness to sponta-neously use the non-SVO orders such that, compared to the four-year-olds, the younger children were: (1) more likely to match these orders; and (2) less likely to consistently correct these orders to SVO. However, as indicated previously, the two younger groups of children were equally likely to correct the non-SVO orders to SVO as they were to use the non-SVO orders. As a strong version of the verb island hypothesis would not predict any corrections to SVO order in the youngest children, it is important to examine more closely the nature of these corrections.

Corrections to SVO order

There are indications from previous studies that children's early grammatical knowl-edge may be organized around any high frequency word or grammatical marker (e.g., case-marked pronouns; Akhtar & Tomasello, 1997), suggesting that children may con-struct syntactic schemas that are structured around lexical items other than verbs. For example, two-year-olds may form schemas of the sort "He-verb-him" in addition to schemas centered around specific verbs (pusher-push-pushee). Examining children's use of pronouns in their corrections to SVO in the non-SVO conditions may provide further support for this more general hypothesis of lexically specific (as opposed to verb-specific) syntactic knowledge. All of the children's corrections to SVO order in the SOV and VSO conditions were collated and coded for number of lexical NP arguments (e.g., *the spoon, Ernie*) and number of pronominal arguments (e.g., *He, him, it*). As E never modelled pronominal arguments with any of the novel verbs, any use of pronouns by the children were, by definition, productive. Data were collapsed over the two non-SVO conditions (SOV and VSO) and are displayed in Table 12.3.

This table presents the number of pronominal and lexical arguments produced in children's matches and mismatches (i.e., corrections to SVO) in the non-SVO condi-tions. The most striking finding is that, with one exception, *none* of the children's matches in the SOV and VSO conditions contained pronominal arguments; in other words, whenever children used a pronoun with the non-SVO verbs, they used SVO order. This is significant because it supports the hypothesis that children may be learn-ing the privileges of occurrence of specific pronouns; that is, some sentence schemas may be structured around pronouns as opposed to verbs (see Pine et al., in press).

Table 12.3 Number of pronominal and lexical arguments produced by children in their matches and mismatches (corrections to SVO) in the non-SVO conditions

Age	Matches		Mismatches (corrections to SVO)	
	Pronominal	Lexical	Pronominal	Lexical
Two years	0	62	33	37
Three years	0	118	82	96
Four years	1	15	233	221

Another possibility is that the young children have some general knowledge of the SVO structure of English; they may know for example that animate agents should come before verbs in sentences and inanimate patients should be placed after the verb (Dodson & Tomasello, in press). It is impossible to assess this hypothesis with the current data because all of the actions used were always enacted with animate patients and inanimate patients; i.e., animacy of the participants was not systematically varied. The important point, however, is that even the youngest children were sometimes able to produce SVO sentences (with both lexical and pronominal arguments) with verbs they had only heard in non-SVO sentences. This finding is not consistent with the strong version of the verb island hypothesis outlined in the introduction. The implications of this finding will be explored in the discussion.

Discussion

In this study, children were exposed to novel (non-SVO) grammatical structures used to describe the actions of an animate agent on an inanimate patient. The main question was whether the youngest children, who presumably do not have a fully general understanding of the SVO order of English (Akhtar & Tomasello, 1997), would acquire these structures. Two-year-olds did use the non-SVO orders with novel verbs; e.g., half of their sentences employing the SOV verb were of the form *Big Bird the grapes gopping* to indicate that Big Bird was performing an action on some grapes. As a group, three-year-olds showed the same pattern. The oldest children tested, however, were resistant to the experimenter's odd usage of word order and, for the most part, tended to correct the non-SVO orders to make them sound like English. Finally, control analyses indicated that the younger children's performance was not simply the result of a tendency to mimic or please the experimenter: children who used non-SVO orders with novel verbs did not do so when a familiar verb was presented in a non-SVO sentence (*Elmo the car pushing*).

These results support the hypothesis that acquisition of a general understanding of the syntactic significance of word order is a gradual process (Akhtar & Tomasello, 1997; Roberts, 1983) and therefore do not fit with strong parameter setting models of acquisition. However, Hyams (1994) has recently proposed that while setting parameters involves discrete changes in the child's grammar, these discrete changes may not necessarily be reflected in the child's use of language. Hyams invokes the distinction between I(nternalized)- and E(xternalized)-language to explain this paradoxical statement. She claims that parameter setting affects I-language (the system of grammatical knowledge the child possesses), whereas E-language (the set of actual or potential utterances) is a result of many interactions between parameters and factors outside of core language. Therefore, one should not expect to see discrete steps in the development of the child's actual speech. If this is true, parameter setting models can be consistent with gradual acquisition of grammatical relations. However, it is important to note that child language researchers only have access to E-language; there therefore appears to be no empirical way to test Hyams's claims. Moreover, it is not at all clear that this view of grammatical development would actually predict that specific characteristics of the input would influence children's E-language in the specific way they obviously did in this study.

Although in general the data do seem consistent with the notion that children's early grammatical development is data-driven, it is important to point out that they also do not support the strong version of Tomasello's (1992) verb island hypothesis that children initially frame their grammatical knowledge around individual verbs. Previous research has shown that young children tend to be quite conservative and use verbs only (or mainly) with the argument structures with which they have heard them used (Akhtar & Tomasello, 1997; Olguin & Tomasello, 1993). Recall, however, that the youngest children in the current study were just as likely to employ SVO order with a verb they had heard only in SOV or VSO order as they were to replicate the order modeled. There are two possible interpretations of this finding.

One interpretation is that two-year-olds have more verb-general knowledge than they have previously been credited with. Perhaps the unique methodology used in the current study (presenting novel verbs in ungrammatical sentences) was better able to elicit this verb-general knowledge than previous methods. The second possibility, not incompatible with the first, is that the young children's corrections to SVO order may be based on knowledge of the privileges of occurrence of the specific lexical items that were used as arguments of the novel verbs (Dodson & Tomasello, in press; Pine et al., in press). For example, by 2;8, children may have formed schemas of the sort "he-verb-him" that allowed them to insert the novel verbs into the appropriate (sentence-medial) position. Knowing that words like *he* and *I* almost always occur in sentence-initial position and that *him* occurs most frequently at the end of sentences would constitute enough information for children to demonstrate the type of productivity exemplified in many of their corrections to SVO order.

The same type of knowledge can also explain children's tendency to place the names of inanimate objects after the verb in their corrections to SVO order: the names of most inanimate objects tend to occur postverbally in transitive sentences. For example, before participating in this experiment, children may have heard the word *grapes* far more frequently in the postverbal position (*I want the grapes; He ate the grapes*). This lexically specific knowledge may have allowed them to form SVO sentences with the non-SVO verbs. As Pine et al. (in press) maintain, this account of children's early grammatical knowledge can explain verb island type effects as well as the limited productivity shown by two-year-olds in the current study. All other things being equal, verbs tend to occur more frequently and in more consistent positions in English input than do the nouns or noun phrases that occur as the arguments of these verbs in sentences: therefore, children should be more likely to construct verb-specific schemas than noun-specific ones.

The current findings thus add to a growing body of literature indicating that young children's grammatical knowledge is initially organized around specific lexical items (Pine & Martindale, 1996; Lieven et al., 1997; Akhtar & Tomasello, 1997; Pine et al., in press; Tomasello & Brooks, in press). They also fit well with a recently proposed computational model of syntax acquisition (Cartwright & Brent, 1997). Cartwright & Brent (1997) describe and provide evidence for a formal model in which children initially form syntactic "templates" on the basis of distributional analyses of linguistic input. These templates (which are analogous to what we have described as sentence schemas) serve as the basis for the formation of syntactic categories and the resulting productivity these categories license. According to this view, children do not have any general knowledge of syntactic categories until they have acquired enough similar templates from which they can abstract a general pattern. This view is consonant with Marchman & Bates' (1994) *critical mass hypothesis* (another specific form of the data-driven learning hypothesis). The essential idea is that children must acquire a sufficient number of exemplars (data) before abstracting general patterns that lead to productivity of the sort demonstrated by the four-year-olds in the present study. In the specific case of word order in transitive sentences, it is probably only after children have acquired many different transitive verbs, and have heard others use word order contrastively with these verbs, that they will be able to form a truly general understanding of SVO order. Before this point, however, they tend to replicate the structures modeled with individual verbs they encounter.

While the current findings provide strong support for data-driven learning of syntactic structure, it should be emphasized that the claim being made is not that English-speaking two-year-olds know nothing about the canonical order of English sentences. Young children clearly attend to word order (even infants do; Mandel et al., 1996); they are also able to respond appropriately in tests of word order with familiar verbs (see recent review by Hirsh-Pasek & Golinkoff, 1996). Even in the current study, the two younger groups of children displayed their sensitivity to SVO order in a number of ways: most of them were more likely to use the SVO verb than the non-SVO verbs, some consistently avoided use of the non-SVO verbs, and, most importantly, some even switched the non-SVO verbs to SVO order. The main point is that there is considerable development taking place between two and four years of age in just how general children's understanding of word order is. Whereas the younger children seem to be in the process of constructing a truly general understanding of the syntactic significance of word order (that all English sentences must employ SVO order), the four-year-olds were simply not willing to use the non-SVO structures. These older children systematically and consistently corrected the experimenter's non-SVO usage to SVO.

The fact that development of this very basic grammatical device is protracted and involves general processes of exemplar-based learning (Chandler, 1993) challenges the notion of a specialized acquisition mechanism dedicated to grammar (O'Grady, 1997). The rationale frequently offered for postulating domain-specific mechanisms for grammatical development is that they account for the rapidity and accuracy with which children acquire language (e.g., Pinker, 1994; Culicover, 1997). However, the current findings indicate that one cannot infer mastery of a given grammatical device from children's appropriate use of that device in their daily speech (Rubino & Pine, 1998). Early correct use of word order with familiar verbs, for example, is most likely the result of lexically specific formulas such as those described above. The current findings therefore highlight the importance of assessing children's linguistic competence with novel items. With this approach, it becomes clear that English-speaking children's mastery of SVO order is a rather gradual process: two- and three-year-olds happily say "Big Bird the ball *gopping*" if that is how they have heard the verb *gopping* used. Four-year-olds, however, have encountered enough English sentences to form a generalization that allows them to actively switch non-English orders to English.

Whereas these specific findings would not have been predicted within most parameter setting models of syntax acquisition, the results are perfectly compatible with theoretical perspectives that grant a larger role to the linguistic environment and to the learning capabilities of the young child (Sampson, 1989; Goldberg, 1995; Lieven et al., 1997; O'Grady, 1997; Tomasello & Brooks, in press). As even infants appear to be armed with powerful abilities to detect statistical regularities in the speech stream (Saffran et al., 1996), the current findings raise the intriguing possibility that many aspects of linguistic structure may be acquired by attention to patterns in linguistic input (Cartwright & Brent, 1997).

References

Akhtar, N., & Tomasello, M. (1997). Young children's productivity with word order and verb morphology. *Developmental Psychology, 33*, 952–965.

Atkinson, M. (1987). Mechanisms for language acquisition: learning, parameter-setting and triggering. *First Language, 17*, 3–30.

Bates, E., & MacWhinney, B. (1987). Competition, variation, and language learning. In B. MacWhinney (Ed.), *Mechanisms of language acquisition*. Hillsdale, NJ: Erlbaum.

Bates, E., & MacWhinney, B. (1989). Functionalism and the Competition Model. In B. MacWhinney, & E. Bates (Eds.), *The crosslinguistic study of sentence processing*. Cambridge: C.U.P.

Bates, E., MacWhinney, B., Caselli, C., Devescovi, A., Natale, F., & Venza, V. (1984). A crosslinguistic study of the development of sentence interpretation strategies. *Child Development, 55*, 341–354.

Berko, J. (1958). The child's learning of English morphology. *Word, 14*, 150–177.

Bloom, L. (1991). *Language development from two to three*. Cambridge: C.U.P.

Bowerman, M. (1988). Inducing the latent structure of language. In F. Kessel (Ed.), *The development of language and language researchers: essays in honor of Roger Brown*. Hillsdale, NJ: Erlbaum.

Braine, M.D.S. (1976). Children's first word combinations. *Monographs of the Society for Research in Child Development, 41* (Serial No. 164).

Braine, M.D.S. (1988). Modeling the acquisition of linguistic structure. In Y. Levy, I. Schlesinger, & M. Braine (Eds.), *Categories and processes in language acquisition*. Hillsdale, NJ: Erlbaum.

Cartwright, T.A., & Brent, M.R. (1997). Syntactic categorization in early language acquisition: formalizing the role of distributional analysis. *Cognition, 63*, 121–170.

Chandler, S. (1993). Are rules and modules really necessary for explaining language? *Journal of Psycholinguistic Research, 22*, 593–606.

Culicover, P. (1997). *Principles and parameters.* Oxford: O.U.P.

Derbyshire, D.C., & Pullum, G.K. (1981). Object-initial languages. *International Journal of American Linguistics, 47,* 192–214.

Dodson, K., & Tomasello, M. (1998). Acquiring the transitive construction in English: the role of animacy and pronouns. *Journal of Child Language, 25,* 555–574.

Gibson, E., & Wexler, K. (1994). Triggers. *Linguistic Inquiry, 25,* 407–454.

Goldberg, A.E. (1995). *Constructions: a construction grammar approach to argument structure.* Chicago: University of Chicago Press.

Goldberg, A.E. (1998). Patterns of experience in patterns of language. In M. Tomasello (Ed.), *The new psychology of language.* Mahwah, NJ: Erlbaum.

Hirsh-Pasek, K., & Golinkoff, R.M. (1996). *The origins of grammar: evidence from early language comprehension.* Cambridge, MA: MIT Press.

Hyams, N. (1994). Nondiscreteness and variation in child language: implications for principle and parameter models of language development. In Y. Levy (Ed.), *Other children, other languages: issues in the theory of language acquisition.* Hillsdale, NJ: Erlbaum.

Lieven, E.V.M., Pine, J.M., & Baldwin, G. (1997). Lexically-based learning and early grammatical development. *Journal of Child Language, 24,* 187–219.

Lightfoot, D. (1989). The child's trigger experience: degree-o learnability. *Behavioral and Brain Sciences, 12,* 321–375.

Mandel, D.R., Kemler Nelson, D.G., & Jusczyk, P.W. (1996). Infants remember the order of words in a spoken sentence. *Cognitive Development, 11,* 181–196.

Marchman, V.A., & Bates, E. (1994). Continuity in lexical and morphological development: a test of the critical mass hypothesis. *Journal of Child Language, 21,* 339–366.

Mazuka, R. (1996). Can a grammatical parameter be set before the first word? Prosodic contributions to early setting of a grammatical parameter. In J.L. Morgan, & K. Demuth (Eds.), *Signal to syntax: bootstrapping from speech to grammar in early acquisition.* Mahwah, NJ: Erlbaum.

Mithun, M. (1987). Is basic word order universal? In Russell S. Tomlin (Ed.), *Coherence and grounding in discourse.* Amsterdam: John Benjamins.

Ninio, A. (1988). On formal grammatical categories in early child language. In Y. Levy, I. Schlesinger, & M. Braine (Eds.), *Categories and processes in language acquisition.* Hillsdale, NJ: Erlbaum.

O'Grady, W. (1997). *Syntactic development.* Chicago: University of Chicago Press.

Olguin, R., & Tomasello, M. (1993). Twenty-five-month-old children do not have a grammatical category of verb. *Cognitive Development, 8,* 245–272.

Pine, J.M., Lieven, E.V.M., & Rowland, C.F. (in press). Comparing different models of the development of the English verb category. *Linguistics.*

Pine, J., & Martindale, H. (1996). Syntactic categories in the speech of young children: the case of the determiner. *Journal of Child Language, 23,* 369–395.

Pinker, S. (1984). *Language learnability and language development.* Cambridge, MA: Harvard University Press.

Pinker, S. (1994). *The language instinct.* NY: W. Morrow & Co.

Pullum, G.K. (1981). Languages with object before subject: a comment and a catalogue. *Linguistics, 19,* 147–155.

Pullum, G.K. (1996). Learnability, hyperlearning, and the Poverty of the Stimulus. To appear in the proceedings of the 22nd annual meeting of the Berkeley Linguistics Society.

Roberts, K. (1983). Comprehension and production of word order in Stage I. *Child Development, 54,* 443–449.

Rubino, R.B., & Pine, J.M. (1998). Subject–verb agreement in Brazilian Portuguese: what low error rates hide. *Journal of Child Language, 25,* 35–59.

Saffran, J.R., Aslin, R.N., & Newport, E.L. (1996). Statistical learning by 8-month-old infants. *Science, 274* (5294), 1926–1928.

Sampson, G. (1989). Language acquisition: growth or learning? *Philosophical Papers, 18,* 203–240.

Slobin, D., & Bever, T. (1982). Children use canonical sentence schemas: a crosslinguistic study of word order and inflections. *Cognition, 12,* 229–265.

Tomasello, M. (1992). *First verbs: a case study of early grammatical development.* NY: Cambridge University Press.

Tomasello, M., & Brooks, P.J. (1999). Early syntactic development: a construction grammar approach. In M. Barrett (Ed.), *The development of language.* London: Psychology Press.

Tomlin, R.S. (1986). *Basic word order: functional principles.* London: Croom-Helm.

THIRTEEN

The Acquisition of Plural Marking in English and German Revisited: Schemata Versus Rules*

Klaus-Michael Köpcke

Introduction

An almost classical debate in linguistics and psychology concerns the question of how morphologically complex words are represented in the grammar and in the lexicon. For a long time the inflectional system for English verbs was seen as a paradigmatic case for the assumption that complex words are formed by rules that concatenate morphemes. With a few exceptions all English verbs form their past tense by adding the morpheme -*ed*. These rule-governed items contrast with those which have to be stored as exceptions in the lexicon, e.g., *go* or *write*.

This polar distinction between the grammar on the one hand and the lexicon on the other was challenged in the last ten to fifteen years by an anti-classical approach to categorization, i.e., prototype theory, a model of categorization inspired by the psychological experiments conducted by Eleanor Rosch since the seventies (see Rosch, 1977, 1978). Rosch assumes that members of natural classes of objects, e.g., *birds* or *furniture*, are organized around "prototypical" examples in the center of the category. The prototypical instances are defined by a maximal number of attributes. Rosch hypothesizes that a category is mentally not represented through abstract attributes but through more concrete typical instances, i.e., "best exemplars" of the category. The category is not characterized by binary contrastive features but rather by a number of properties. Consequently, a distinction has to be made between central and peripheral members of a class. The members of a class are distributed across a continuum. At one pole of this continuum those category members are located which are defined by a maximal number of properties; the opposite pole represents those members which have only one or very few of the relevant properties characterizing the prototype. Such members are thus located at the periphery of the category and they might easily lose their category membership in one class and be reassigned to a contrastive category. The members of a category are not regarded as a homogenous

---

* My thanks are due to David Zubin (Buffalo) for his invaluable ideas and comments on earlier versions of this paper.

Table 13.1   Properties of English strong verbs having /æ/ – /ʌ/ or /ʌ/ – /ʌ/ in past tense and past participle

	/ɪ/ in present tense	Velar as final consonant	Nasal as final consonant
sing	Yes	Yes	Yes
cling	Yes	Yes	Yes
hang	No	Yes	Yes
swim	Yes	No	Yes
stick	Yes	Yes	No
strike	No	Yes	No

set: rather, they are representative of the category as a whole to varying degrees. A model that operates with criterial features requires that every member of a category exhibit all the features of the category whereas the prototype approach only assumes that the members of a category exhibit a lesser or higher degree of "family resemblance" with the prototype.

There is no doubt that linguistic signs belong to "natural" classes in the sense sketched above. The language user is under constant pressure to categorize and classify linguistic items and it is plausible to assume that these categorizations proceed along lines analogous to the principles found in the categorizations of nonlinguistic phenomena. Bybee & Moder (1983: 267) assume that "speakers of natural language form categorizations of linguistic objects in the same way that they form categorizations of natural and cultural objects," consequently, "the psychological principles which govern linguistic behaviour are the same as those which govern other types of human behaviour." Data which were suggestive for this conclusion again came from English verb morphology. There are some strong verbs in English that show the vowel alternation [ɪ/ – /æ/ – /ʌ/ by changing from the present tense to past tense and past participle, e.g., *sing – sang – sung*. The pattern /ɪ/ – /ʌ/ – /ʌ/, e.g., as in *cling*, shows close resemblance with the former. Both patterns were so productive they even attracted members of other classes to switch class membership, e.g., *ring*. It was not even required that /ɪ/ be the stem vowel in the present tense, e.g., *hang*. Table 13.1, which is taken from Taylor (1995, p. 175), shows that the classes exhibit a prototype structure.

By far most of the verbs have a velar nasal as a final consonant, e.g., *spring*. Other verbs share only partial similarity with the central members, e.g., they have a non-velar nasal as a final consonant (*swim*). Even more remote from the prototype are those that end in a non-nasal velar, e.g., *stick*. As a consequence of observations like the one just cited, Bybee (1985, 1988, 1991) has proposed a continuum of schemata extending from irregular to regular morphology. The advantage of such a schema model is that it eliminates the strict division between the grammar on the one hand, which covers regular productive morphology (e.g., how most English verbs and new verbs form their past tense) and the lexicon on the other hand, in which all exceptions to regular processes are stored. If Bybee's position is examined further, then the *rule*, a central theoretical concept of most linguistic theories, is questioned. Bybee's model closely resembles a connectionist model (cf. Rumelhart & McClelland (1986) and McClelland (1988)) since both theories make the assumption that generalizations arise from patterns in an associative network. Rumelhart & McClelland (1986) were able to show that a parallel distributed processing model perfectly simulates acquisitional stages for the past tense form in English, when given input that reflects the type and token frequency of regular and irregular verbs. In the simulation the regularization of the past tense coincides with a sharp increase in the input of regular past tense formations. It must be emphasized here that a parallel distributed processing model does not formulate symbolic rules, rather, just like in Bybee's model, other lexical patterns are accessed, and the strongest of these, which happens to be regarded as being regular in English, at a certain threshold level outnumbers the others.

The counterposition is that the concept of rule is indispensable and that regular inflections are derived by a symbolic rule which operates on an underlying form in order to generate the specifically needed surface form. This position can be found e.g., in Pinker (1991), Marcus et al. (1992), and Marcus et al. (1995). To date, there are two morphological areas from which empirical data have been used to support the two competing models:

1   verb morphology (cf. among others Bybee & Slobin (1982), Bybee & Moder (1983), Clahsen & Rothweiler (1992), and Marcus et al. (1995));
2   plural morphology (cf. among others Köpcke (1988, 1993), Clahsen et al. (1992), and Marcus et al. (1995)).

In what follows, evidence and arguments in favor of the schema model will be presented. I shall concentrate exclusively on acquisitional data of English and German plural morphology.

The acquisition of plural marking in English

In a structural theory of morphology based on an "Item-and-Process" (IP) model (cf. Hockett (1954)) the plural marking system of English seems to be highly transparent and motivated. Consequently, older generative treatments of noun plural formation in English contain simply an abstract plural morpheme "item" (1a) and morphophonemic rewrite "process" rules (1b), producing a set of alternants (cf. also Fromkin & Rodman (1974)):

(1a) (+pl) → {-s}
(1b) alternant   phonological environment   examples
        {-s} → /ɪz/   [+sibilant]____   noises
              → /s/   [−voice]____   books
              → /z/   [+voice]____   boys

Finally, such traditional analyses contain a list of exceptions marked in the lexicon (1c):

(1c) ox: /aks/   → pl: /aksən/
      knife: /nayf/   → pl: /nayvz/
      goose: /gus/   → pl: /gis/
      child: /čayld/   → pl: /čildrən/
      person: /pɛrsən/   → pl: /pipəl/
      deer: /dir/   → pl: -Ø

Such a treatment thus regards the morphological realization of grammatical categories as either categorically regular, as in (1a) and (1b), or as arbitrarily exceptional, as in (1c), resulting in a dichotomy between absolute regularity and irregularity.

The Berko Data

Method and results

It was this IP model of morphological rules that Berko (1958) addressed in her famous "wug" experiment on the acquisition of plural marking in English. Her goal was to test for the extent of internationalization of IP rules. To guarantee "novelty" she used non-sense material for her stimulus items. Berko presented nonce words along with pictures in a task intended to elicit a plural form from her subjects (e.g., "Here is a picture of a 'wug'. Now there are two of them. There are two ___?"). She assumed that if a child could master unfamiliar words in the same consistent way as she or he did real, familiar ones, this would demonstrate that the child had mastered some general morphological rule in order to pluralize nouns, which went beyond the knowledge of those specific plural forms to which the child had been previously exposed.

   Table 13.2 (adapted from Berko's table 2) shows the results for the six/seven-year-olds.[1] The table shows that the subjects performed better with nonce words requiring the {-z} allomorph than those requiring the {-ɪz} allomorph. Only one stimulus (*heaf*) tested the {-s} allomorph, and this was equivocal, since it allowed either /hifs/ or /hivz/ as normative plurals. Berko accounts for this difference by pointing out that {-ɪz} is both phonologically more complex, i.e., the scope of {-ɪz} requires an extra rule, namely vowel epenthesis, and furthermore, less frequent as a plural allomorph than {-z}.

A reanalysis of Berko's results

As a first approximation to a reanalysis of Berko's data consider the pattern of zero responses. In her article Berko does not systematically differentiate zero and non-zero deviant responses, but she does report that the latter are virtually nil. Table 13.2 gives the frequency of deviant responses minus the non-zero responses reported in the text of Berko's article, yielding a very close approximation of the frequency of zero responses. Figure 13.1 shows that the distribution of zero responses is not random, but that the similarity of test items to plural schemata played a crucial role in performing the task.

Table 13.2 Distribution of responses for Berko's (1958) data of the six/seven-year-olds

Nonce word	Expected plural allomorph	Correct (%)	−Ø (%)	Other deviant form (%)
wug	/-z/	97	3	–
lun	/-z/	92	8	–
tor	/-z/	90	10	–
heaf	/-s/, /-z/*	80	16	4
cra	/-z/	86	14	4
tass	/-ɪz/	39	61	–
gutch	/-ɪz/	38	52	10
kazh	/-ɪz/	36	59	5
niz	/-ɪz/	33	67	–

* For the nonce word *heaf* two alternants of the plural morpheme {-s} are scored as correct.

Highest degree of similarity to plural schemata   Lowest degree of similarity to plural schemata

←+ —— + —— + —— + —— + —— + —— + —— + —— +

    niz   tass   kazh   gutch   heaf   cra   tor   lun   wug

Results for six/seven-year-olds

    67   61   59   52   16   14   10   8   3

Figure 13.1 Repetition of stimuli (zero responses) given in percentages and relative similarity to plural schemata.

The aim of the present study is to show that this distribution suggests a cognitive model of morphological representation containing not only IP rules, but also a schematic component in which morphological rules and lexical representations are not separate. In this component, forms (both morphologically simplex and complex) in the lexicon are individually subsumed under *schemata* having a probabilistic, prototype structure (cf. Bybee & Slobin (1982), Lakoff (1982), Bybee & Moder (1983), Köpcke & Zubin (1983), Bybee (1985, 1988), and Köpcke (1993)). This structure is determined by the *cue strength* of the schema's individual components, which is in turn determined by the salience, frequency, and cue validity of these components. The schema model is placed somewhere between traditional IP formulations, in which morphologically complex forms have no independent representations, and the recent position of Bybee (1988), in which all forms are highly associated with one another and form complex networks with membership in particular schemas.

The assumption that plural formation in children is influenced by schemas is not entirely new. Berko herself mentions the idea at various points in her 1958 article, as do Anisfeld & Tucker (1967), but does not develop it. Berko (1958, p. 164) mentions occasionally for example that her subjects repeated the stem as if it were already in the plural and she goes on to suggest that the child's rule for the formation of the plural seems to be "a final sibilant makes a word plural." Furthermore, MacWhinney (1978) seems to have this idea in mind when he remarks that German-speaking children tend to omit plural marking when a given noun in its citation form sounds plural; e.g., *Hammer* "hammer" or *Pfeife* "pipe." The word endings *-er* and *-e* are possible plural markers in German, e.g., *das Kind – die Kinder* "child – children" or *der Tisch – die Tische* "table – tables" (cf. Table 13.5 for further information on the German plural marking system). MacWhinney suggests that children apply an "affix-checking" principle to the noun they retrieve from their lexicon. What this means is simply that the English plural morpheme {-z} is omitted in cases where the nonce word already ends in /z/ or /s/, e.g., *niz* or *tass* respectively (cf. also Solomon (1972), Innes (1974), Derwing & Baker (1979) and Baker & Derwing (1982)). Furthermore, the children's behaviour in the Berko experiment seems to be compatible with observations Linell (1976), Stemberger (1981), Menn & MacWhinney (1984), and Stemberger & MacWhinney (1986) report, namely that many languages of the world avoid repetition of identical morph shapes. Menn & MacWhinney (1984: 529) even propose a weak morphological universal which they term *repeated morph constraint*, formally expressed as follows:

> *XY, where X and Y are adjacent surface strings such that both could be interpreted as manifesting the same underlying morpheme through regular phonological rules, and where either
> (a) X and Y are both affixes, or
> (b) either X or Y is an affix, an the other is a (proper subpart of a) stem.

All this means is that for the child, and to a certain degree also for an adult (cf. Köpcke (1988)), a prototypical singular noun would be one that does not have features of a plural schema. Particular features of singular nouns in English that could be inter- preted as strongly plural-like are the stem-endings /s/, /z/, and /ɪz/. But note that the most common plural morpheme {-z} appears as a stem-final segment in only a handful of cases in singular nouns, e.g., *lens*, whereas /s/ is relatively frequent in singular nouns, e.g., *fox*, and /ɪz/ is extremely rare, e.g., *kermes* (a type of louse). Furthermore, /ɪz/ is iconically suggestive of plurality when compared to /z/ and /s/, since it is an added syllable. These observations lead to hypothesis concerning the degree of similarity of the form of singular nouns to plural morphemes, and corresponding tendencies to reinterpret singular forms as plural. The hypotheses are based on an estimation of the perceptual characteristics of the given plural markers of the language, following psychological principles of categorization, as given in Smith & Medin (1981) and MacWhinney (1989). Table 13.3 elaborates the hypotheses in terms of the *salience, frequency, cue validity,*[2] and *iconicity* of the individual plural markers in English. Each parameter is divided into three levels: high (h), mid (m), and low (l). The term *cue strength* will be used here to refer to the sum effect of these four factors on the func- tional strength of a particular plural marker. Note that this is a first approximation; it is a question of further research to weight the relative sub-strength of each of these factors.

Salience is here understood as a rough estimation of the degree to which a marker is perceptually detectable by a listener, in other words, its acoustic prominence. In the sense of Slobin's (1973) operating principles, all English plural markers are relatively

Table 13.3   Cue strength of plural markers in English

Marker	Salience	(Type) frequency	Cue validity	Iconicity
/-s/	h	m	l	m
/-z/	h	h	m	m
/-ɪz/	h	l	h	h

salient, because they are separable segments in comparison with the corresponding contrast form, i.e., the singular form of a noun, and all of them are suffixes.

Type frequency here refers to the number of nouns that take a particular plural morpheme. The most frequent morpheme is {-z}, less frequent is {-s}, and the least frequent is {ɪz}.

Cue validity is used in its restricted sense as the complement of frequency, i.e., the frequency with which a particular feature occurs in the category which contrasts with the target category. In the context of English plural morphology, {-z} has medium and {-ɪz} has high cue validity, because there are only a few singular nouns that end in /-z/ and nearly none that end in /-ɪz/. The remaining morpheme {-s} has relatively low cue validity, because there are relatively many singular nouns in English that end in /-s/, e.g., *box* /bāks/.

Finally, the principle of *iconicity* suggests that additive morphemes, especially syllabic ones, are evocative of plurality (more in the signal = more in the referent). On this basis {-ɪz} is most evocative of plurality among the English plural allomorphs.

Of the four criteria for determining the cue strength of plural markers in English, {-z} and {-ɪz} rank higher than {-s}. From there, I hypothesize then that {-z} and {-ɪz} are "better" plural markers than {-s}. From this it follows, in the context of a theory of cue strength, that in processing nonce words children should display some tendency to interpret intended singular forms ending in /s/, /z/, and /ɪz/ as acceptable plurals, and to therefore leave them unchanged in an experimental task requiring them to form plurals. Furthermore, they should tend to do so more with /z/ and /ɪz/ than with /s/. This line of reasoning on cue strength can be extended. Stem-final segments which are similar to but not identical with plural allomorphs should show a slight tendency to be taken as plurals in a nonce task, a tendency which should reduce or disappear as the final segment of the nonce word stimuli becomes more dissimilar to actual plural allomorphs. These considerations lead to a rank ordering of Berko's stimuli as presented in Figure 13.2.

Skipping the first three items, stem-final /z/ is identical to the plural allomorph with the highest cue strength, as discussed above.[3] Next, /s/ is identical to the plural allomorph with lower cue strength. For the ranking of the other stem endings the following articulatory features are important: continuancy, friction, and sibilancy. The palatal sibilants /ž/ and /č/ are non-identical but phonetically highly similar to the regular plural allomorphs of English. They are characterized by exactly these three features.[4] The fricative /f/ is still more removed from the regular plural allomorphs: it satisfies the

	Stem shape	Berko's stimuli
Most plural like	/$ɪz/	••*
	/... Cs/z/	••*
	/... Vz/	••*
	/... z/	niz
	/... s/	tass
	/... ž/ and /... č/	kazh, gutch
	/... f/	heaf
	/... V/ and /... r/	cra, tor
least plural like	/... n/ and /... g/	lun, wug

* Berko did not test these stem shapes, but they are of theoretical interest; example stimuli would be /pučɪz/, /pāks/, and /riz/.

Figure 13.2 Rank ordering of Berko's data based on perceptual distance from actual plurals.

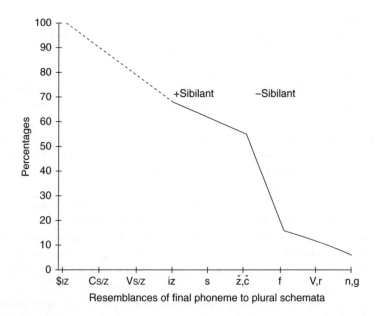

Figure 13.3 Zero responses in percentage of the six/seven-year-olds (based on Table 13.2) according to resemblances of the final phoneme of the test items to plural schemata in English.

features [+continuant] and [+fricative], but it is [−sibilant]. The vowel and the liquid /r/ are both continuant but are negatively specified with regard to friction and sibilancy. Finally, /n/ and /g/ can be grouped together, since they are negatively specified for all three features.

Figure 13.3 represents a reanalysis of zero responses of the six/seven-year-olds in Berko's data. Roughly, the curve shows a clear correspondence between the degree of resemblance to canonical plurals and the extent to which Berko's six/seven-year-old subjects left the stimulus unchanged. This shows that the degree of perceptual similarity to a canonical plural may have affected their responses, and suggests that at some level of their response behavior they perceived some forms as being more plural-like than others in accordance with the cue strength hypothesis.

One could argue, in support of the IP rule hypothesis, that there are two plateaus in the curve, one for stimuli ending in sibilants and the other for stimuli ending in non-sibilants, corresponding to the phonemic conditioning environments for the plural allomorphs {ɪz} and {s; z}, respectively. This plateau effect certainly shows that incomplete acquisition of the plural allomorph {ɪz} plays a role in the subjects' behavior. However, arguing for plateaus fails to account for the consistent drop in the curve from /z/ to /ž, č/, and the consistent drop from /f/ to /n, g/. If perceptual distance from canonical plurals had no effect, then the shape in these plateaus would have been absent. Admittedly, the number of data points is small, but the line of reasoning given is supported by findings from Innes (1974) (cf. the following section).

The three hypothetical points on the curve represent theoretical pivotal predictions about stimuli that Berko did not test. The cue strength hypothesis predicts that a factor complementary to the perceptual distance from canonical plurals will play a role. This is the perceptual distance of the stem from canonical singular forms once the putative plural morpheme has been segmented (cf. Köpcke (1988)). Thus, although the final segments of *niz* and *tass* are identical to canonical plurals, when they are segmented, the resulting stems /nɪ/ and /tæ/ are phonotactically impossible forms in English, and thus maximally distant from canonical singulars. A form such as /riz/ should be more likely interpreted as a plural, since the segmented stem /ri/ is phonotactically possible, although such vowel-final forms have low frequency. A form such as /pãks/ should be even more susceptible to a plural interpretation, since the segmented stem /pãk/ is a high frequency type for monosyllabic singular nouns. Finally, a form like /pučɪz/ should virtually force a plural interpretation since /-ɪz/ has near zero frequency in singular forms, and /puč/ is a canonical singular.

In sum, the results of Berko's experiment do support her conclusion that children learn IP rules for plural formation in English, and, specifically, that the low frequency, phonotactically most restricted allomorph {ɪz} is acquired after the others. But they also point to a learning mechanism in which canonical forms for both singular and plural lexical items are represented, and in which particular words are interpreted as singular or plural depending on their perceptual proximity to or distance from canonical schemata for singular and plural forms, respectively. This mechanism will be referred to as *schema-learning*.

The Baker & Derwing Data

One problem with the Berko data is that the argument is based on a very limited data set. Fortunately, a far more extensive data set is available that puts the model to a more stringent test. From Innes's (1974) data set from 120 children (20 at each age from 2 to 7) and 24 nonce stem-types Baker & Derwing (1982) yield a much more reliable picture of developmental stages children go through when acquiring the English plural morphology. Since the correlation in performance between the subjects in Innes's study and those in Berko's is very high ($r = 0.96$) on comparable stimuli for comparable ages, there is good reason to believe that the reliability between the two studies is quite high. The main advantage of the more recent data set is that it can provide many more test points against which to compare the predictions of the model developed so far.

Method and results

Innes (1974) employed a similar version of the Berko technique to elicit her data. The responses to her 24 items by 120 children were first analyzed in terms of the usual percent correct according to age groups. Almost 97% of the total number of responses were one of the three regular plural allomorphs or zero. A grouping along the lines of correctness and mean age did not reveal very much, except that the children first acquire /z/, then /s/, and last /ɪz/ as plural markers.

In their reanalysis of the Innes data Baker & Derwing (1982) grouped the children by focusing on response profiles. Instead of grouping children by age, those children with an identical or comparable response profile ("response coincidence matrix") were grouped together. In other words, age was not treated as the relevant factor for the analysis, but rather clusters of test items that were treated the same way. On that basis Baker & Derwing divided the total number of subjects into six groups, eliminating two groups from further analysis on the basis of an inclusion criterion specifying that a subject had to leave at least three items and no more than 21 items in conformity with the adult pattern. On the lower end, then, one group of 8 subjects and on the higher end one of 18 subjects were excluded. Contrary to Baker & Derwing I do not eliminate the group on the higher end (18 children), since, even for this group, the reanalysis of the results in light of the schema approach is quite interesting and fits into the theoretical picture.

A reanalysis of Baker's and Derwing's results

In what follows, I focus on the zero responses in order to establish the reliability of the interpretation of the Berko data. Groups I and II in the Baker & Derwing analysis I will treat as one group for several reasons, the main one being that group II contains only 7 subjects, which leads to the assumption that the percentages given might be not very reliable. Furthermore, with regard to the zero responses, which are at issue here, both groups behave fairly identically; and third, the mean age between both groups is very close.

In the following Table 13.4 the zero responses within the 4 groups are given as a function of the final phoneme of the stimuli. Again, as with the interpretation of the Berko data, phonemes are grouped together on the basis of shared phonetic features. Figure 13.4 projects the results given in Table 13.4 onto a scale of decreasing similarity of final phonemes to plural schemata. Figure 13.4 reveals the following: the youngest children seem to have no knowledge of a productive pluralization rule, but they obviously make a distinction between sibilants and, to a certain extent, also fricatives on the one hand and other word endings on the other hand. Sibilants and fricatives share phonetic features with the actual plural markers in English. The more one approaches the prototypical plural marker, the more the children leave the word unchanged, i.e., assign -Ø.

Table 13.4 Distribution of zero responses in percentages to 24 nonce words grouped according to resemblance of the final phoneme

Group	Mean age	z	s	ž, š, č, ʤ	v, f, ð, t	ɔ, i, u	r, l	ŋ, n, m	B, D, G*
II†	4.11	95	90	94	63	48	48	58	54
III	4.22	94	70	68	32	2	4	<1	4
IV	4.92	92	68	54	2	8	0	0	3
V	5.78	33	22	4	0	0	0	0	0

* "B," "D," and "G" refer to the phenomes /b, p/, d, t/,and /g, k/, respectively.
† Group II here is group I and II in Baker & Derwing (1982).

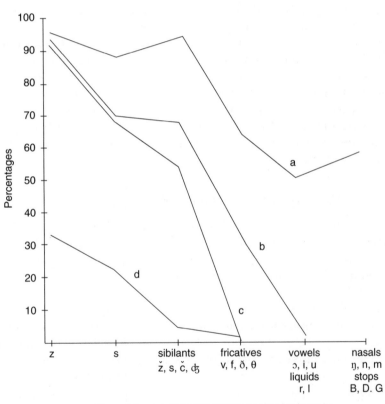

Resemblances of final phoneme to plural schemata

Figure 13.4 Distribution of zero responses in percentages according to resemblances of the final phoneme of the test items to plural schemata in English (line "a" refers to group II, "b" to group III, "c" to group IV, and "d" to group V).

The children belonging to group III still assign -Ø to fricatives and sibilants, but they do this to a lesser extent than the children in group II. Furthermore, they clearly do not confuse vowels, liquids, nasals, and stops in word final position with potential plural endings anymore.

The main difference between group III and IV is that the children belonging to group IV do not treat non-sibilant fricatives as potential plural endings anymore. But they obviously still treat a nonce word ending in /z/ or /s/ or in /ž, š, č, dž/ in the majority of the cases as being already plural. Over all endings they do slightly better than the children in group III, since there is not a single crossing of the curves.

The oldest children (group V) perform best. They do master siblilants, but, surprisingly, they do not do so in all cases with /z/ and /s/. Again, the more one approaches the prototypical plural ending, the more likely it is that the children leave the word unchanged, i.e., from about one-fifth for /s/ up to about one-third for /z/.

Overall then, we get impressive independent support from the Innes (1974) data for our interpretation of the Berko data. But one should keep in mind that in English, plural formation is not an ideal domain in which to study this mechanism of building up schemata for assigning grammatical functions to forms since the distribution of allomorphs in the lexicon strongly invites an IP rule-based learning mechanism. In contrast, German plural formation, as shown by Köpcke (1988, 1993), suggests a schema-learning interpretation in the distribution of forms in the lexicon, an interpretation supported both by the behavior of adult subjects in a nonce word task, and also by historical change. Before elaborating the schema-learning hypothesis more closely I will therefore turn to the organization of the German system and to experimental results with children.

The acquisition of plural marking in German

Plural marking in German differs from English considerably, since it is a complex system composed of several phonologically unrelated alternants and no clearly dominant rule. German has six major plural allomorphs, the occurrence of which correlates with at least the morphological factors given under (2):

(2) *morphological factor*   *examples*
     – the type of the derivational suffix   Frei-*heit* + -*en* "freedoms",
                                                      Jüng-*ling* + -*e* "young men"
     – the final consonant or vowel of the stem   Pizz*a* + -*s* "pizzas"
                                                      Kurv*e* + -*n* "curves"
     – the prefix of the stem noun   Ge-birg-e + -Ø "mountains"
     – the mutability of the stem noun[5]   Vater/Väter "fathers"
     – the gender-assignment of the noun[6]   *der* Tisch/die____-e "tables"
                                                      die Uhr/die____-en "watches"
                                                      das Kind/die____-er "children"
     – the animacy of masculine nouns   der Herr/die____-en "sirs"

The fact that none of these patterns dominates is apparent in Mugdan's (1977) detailed description of plural marking in German: he attempted to set up IP rules for this

Table 13.5 Overview of native nominative plural morphemes in German

Plural morpheme	Masculine	Feminine	Neuter
-e	Fisch/Fische (fish)	Kenntnis/-nisse (knowledge)	Jahr/Jahre (year)
-(e)n	Bauer/Bauern (farmer)	Tür/Türen (door)	Auge/Augen (eye)
-er	Geist/Geister (ghost)	–	Kind/Kinder (child)
-s	Park/Parks (park)	Mutti/Muttis (mom)	Auto/Autos (car)
-Ø	Adler/Adler (eagle)	–	Fenster/Fenster (window)
Umlaut	Vater/Väter (father)	–*	–†
Uml. + -e	Sohn/Söhne (son)	Kuh/Kühe (cow)	–‡
Uml. + -er	Wald/Wälder (wood)	–	Volk/Völker (people)
def. article	der SING/die PLURAL	die SING/die PLURAL	das SING/die PLURAL

* In the entire lexicon there are only two instances, namely *Mutter – Mütter* "mother – mothers" and *Tochter – Töchter* "daughter – daughters."

† Only one instance, namely *Kloster – Klöster* "monastery – monasteries."

‡ Only one instance, namely *Floß – Flöße* "raft – rafts."

complex system and ended up with 15 distinct rules and 21 lists of exceptions. Table 13.5 presents the plural morphemes in more detail.

The first four are suffixes; the fifth is phonetically zero, and is analyzed as a zero morpheme, since it occurs in plural contexts completely parallel to the other plural suffixes. The sixth is an "umlaut" mutation in the stem vowel of the singular form of the word, for example the change from [u] to [y] in *Bruder – Brüder* "brother – brothers." *Umlaut* is the only morpheme which can combine with others, namely -Ø, -e, and -er. Some of the morphemes are limited to two of the three gender classes. Thus while gender does not predict the plural morpheme, it does limit the choice. Although determiners are not viewed in structural analyses as plural markers, they will be included in the present analysis, since, from a perceptual point of view, they are an additional source of information in the NP about number, and when they co-occur with the zero suffix, they are the only source of information. When masculine nouns are marked for plural, the article in the nominative case changes from *der* to *die*, and for neuter nouns from *das* to *die*. From this perceptual perspective it is clear why zero is never used as a plural suffix morpheme for feminine nouns: in this case the singular and plural articles are identical, both *die*, so that some other overt marker is needed. In what follows, we restrict ourselves to the definite article in the nominative case. One might object that the cue validity of the masculine singular nominative *der* is reduced by the fact that it is homophonous with the genitive plural definite article in all genders. However, it has to be borne in mind that children (and many adults) usually use a periphrastic construction with the preposition *von* "of" as a substitute for the genitive.

In Table 13.6 the cue strength of the German plural markers is evaluated. Again, as with the English plural markers it is a question for further research to weight the

Table 13.6   Cue strength of plural markers in German

Marker	Salience	(Type) frequency	Cue validity	Iconicity
-(e)n	h	h	h	h
-s	h	l	h	m
-e	h	m	l	h
-er	h	l	l	h
Umlaut	l	l	m	l

relative sub-strength of each of these factors. The German plural markers -(e)n, -s, -e, and -er can be characterized as salient for the same reason as for the English plural markers. In contrast, *umlaut* is neither a separate segment nor stem final and is thus less salient. The most frequent plural morpheme in German is -(e)n followed by -e. In comparison, -s, -er, and *umlaut* have low frequency. The plural marker -(e)n has high cue validity, because there are relatively few singular nouns that end in /en/.[7] The same holds for -s. In contrast, -e has low cue validity as a plural marker, because there are many -e-stem nouns, most of which are feminine. Low cue validity has to be assigned to -er, since many singular nouns end in /er/. In fact, -er is a productive derivational suffix for agentive nouns just as it is in English. Finally, the situation with *umlaut* is complex: some low-frequency umlauted vowels have moderate cue validity as plural markers, whereas the high frequency vowel "ä" (= /ɛ/) does not. In sum, *umlaut* has mid cue validity as a plural marker. Iconicity holds for all German plural markers except *umlaut*, although -s is less iconic than -(e)n, -e, and -er, since the application of -s never results in a new syllable, whereas the application of the other three plural morphemes frequently does result in a new syllable.

   I hypothesize then that plural marking is output (product) oriented (cf. Zager (1980), Stemberger & MacWhinney (1986)). Consequently, speakers form the plural of a noun by matching it to one (or more) abstract plural schemas residing in the mental lexicon, rather than by blindly generating the plural form with an IP rule applied to the (input) form. Furthermore, speakers must have schematic singular representations, with individual schemas differing in cue strength for singularity and plurality, producing the continuum ranging from prototypical singular to prototypical plural as shown in Figure 13.5 (cf. Köpcke (1988, 1993) for a more detailed discussion of this continuum). Masculine and neuter monosyllabic forms have maximal cue strength for singularity, since monosyllabic stems have high frequency among singulars, and virtually zero frequency among plurals. A mid-point on the scale is provided by polysyllabic forms with final schwa and the article *die*, such as *die Tasse* "cup" and *die Tische* "tables"; this particular schema has approximately equal cue strength for both singular and plural. Anchoring the other end of the scale are polysyllabic forms ending in /-ən/ and occurring with the article *die*. These forms have very high frequency among plurals, and virtually zero frequency among singulars.[8] The decision as to whether a particular form is singular or plural is thus based on the overall structure of the form in question, and not just on the presence or absence of markers. In particular, the language user's deci-

Singular				Plural
+ ——————— +	——————— +	——————— +	——————— +	——————— +
monosyllabic	polysyllabic	polysyllabic	polysyllabic	polysyllabic
final stop	final -er	final -e	final -er	final -en
der/das	der/das	die	die	die

Figure 13.5 Continuum for plural schemas in German.

sion concerning the singularity or plurality of a particular form (X) is, then, based on two factors:

1 Position on the continuum of the schema to which the form (X) conforms.
2 The existence of a (concept-identical) lexical partner (Y) conforming to a schema situated to the right or to the left of (X) on the continuum.

The first factor suggests that a particular schema has an absolute cue strength for signalling singular or plural, while the second suggests that it has a cue strength relative to other schemas on the continuum. In the case of nonce words I assume that mainly factor (1) will be of importance, since no lexical partner exists in the child's lexicon. In other words, then, I hypothesize that the child would tend to treat a given nonce word as being plural the more to the right on the continuum the form is, i.e., the more it matches a plural schema and correspondingly less a singular schema.

Mugdan's Data

Method and results

Mugdan's (1977) nonce word task with 25 German six/seven-year-old preschoolers and first graders (Mugdan does not give the mean age of his subjects) followed exactly the design of Berko's study. Table 13.7 gives the results.[9] The proportion of zero responses was at least 71% ranging up to 100%, suggesting considerable uncertainty in the nonce word task relative to Berko's English data. There was no difference in the behavior between the older and the younger children. Mugdan (1977, p. 172) notes that the children's behavior is not describable on the basis of simple morphological rules. He assumes that his subjects were looking for analogies by using the sound of the test items rather than determining a plural allomorph on the basis of gender assignment or a particular stem ending. The different proportion of zero responses, i.e., the repetition of the test item, is not a topic in Mugdan's analyses.

A reanalysis of Mugdan's results

Figure 13.6 projects the results given in Table 13.7 onto a scale determined by the cue strength hypothesis as detailed in Figure 13.5. Figure 13.6 shows that the perception

Table 13.7 Distribution of responses of 25 children to 16 German nonce words in absolute numbers

Stimuli	Expected plural morpheme	-Ø	-e	-(e)n	-er	-s	Neologism
der /šmirl/	-e/-(e)n	13	9	–	1	–	2
das /getrydə/	-Ø	24	–	1	–	–	–
die /albər/	-(e)n	23	–	1	–	1	–
das /tində/	-(e)n	23	1	–	–	1	–
die /zaːri/	-s	18	–	1	–	5	1
das /gelɛk/	-e	18	7	–	–	–	–
der /nɛːbər/	-Ø	25	–	–	–	–	–
die /rondatš/	-(e)n	22	3	–	–	–	–
das /bros/	-e/-er	17	⁸/₃*	–	–	–	–
die /arl/	-e/-(e)n	19	5	–	–	1	–
der /haːgən/	-Ø	25	–	–	–	–	–
die /neːbə/	-(e)n	17	–	7	–	–	1
das /hɛklain/	-Ø	21	3	–	–	1	–
der /fɛndə/	-(e)n	24	–	1	–	–	–
das /kundər/	-Ø	25	–	–	–	–	–
der /farst/	-e	22	1	2	–	–	–

* In 3 out of 8 cases *-e* was combined with *umlaut*. These are the only cases where the children made use of *umlaut*. This is in accordance with the predictions based on the cue strength of the German plural markers (see Table 13.6).

of forms as possible plurals may have played a role in the response behavior. The prototypically singular monosyllabic stimuli received the lowest number of zero responses, approximately 70%.

Polysyllabic stimuli[10] received a slightly higher number of zero responses, corresponding to the slight increase in plural-likeness of the form, although these specific forms are not possible plurals in the real lexicon. This observation is in accordance with Anisfeld & Tucker (1967, p. 1207/08). They note that children tend to interpret longer forms, such as the nonce word *bipum*, as being plural.

Forms ending in *-er* and *-e* are possible plurals, and receive a still higher number of zero responses. Finally, forms, ending in *-er* or *-en*, for which the normative plural is zero received 100% zero responses. On first sight there seems to be a contradiction between the order of schemas in Figures 13.5 and 13.6. But, for the identical schema [polysyllabicity + -er] mentioned before, the normative plural is *-n* since the stimulus is the feminine nonce word *die/albər/*.

Furthermore, it can be shown that the children were sensitive to the presence of the article *die* (feminine gender or plural) versus the articles *der* and *das* (masculine and neuter singular, respectively) as a component of plural and singular schemas. Monosyllabic *der/das*-items receive zero in 69% of the cases, whereas the number for items classed as *die* is 76%. For polysyllabic items the numbers are 72 and 80%, respectively. Here, only those items are counted, which do not have a particular ending (*-e, -er*, and *-en*) that could be interpreted as a plural marker. Admittedly, the numbers are small, in

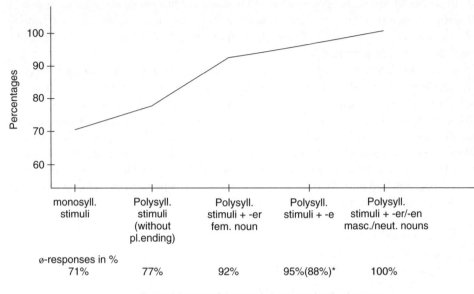

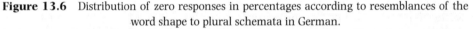

Resemblances of the word shape to plural schemata

Figure 13.6 Distribution of zero responses in percentages according to resemblances of the word shape to plural schemata in German.

* The percentage of φ-responses for pollysyllabic words ending in *-e* goes down to 88% if the stimulus *die/ne:bə/* is taken into consideration. But there are at least two problems involved with this stimulus, both of which lead to the decision to disregard it: (1) *die/ne:bə/* has a partner in the real lexicon, namely *neben* "next to." The presence of such real partners to nonce words was identified as a strong determinant of response behaviour in Köpcke (1988); (ii) a stimulus like *die/ne:bə/* is, because of its structure die [#—e], very provocative for *n*-affixation, since there are literally thousands of feminine nouns ending in Schwa that take *-n* as their plural marker. This is reflected in the children's responses (see Table 13.7).

fact, they are even too small to run a test for significance, but note that they all fit without a single exception the argument developed in this article.

In sum, the reinterpretation of Mugdan's results in light of the schema theory shows that the closer the stimuli approximated plural schemas with greater cue strength, the more German children were inclined to give zero responses.

Spontaneous Data from German

So far, the discussion has focused on the primary goal of this study: the reinterpretation of zero responses in the formation of plurals to nonce words. The schema -theoretic interpretation of zero responses in the Berko (1958), Innes (1974), and Mugdan (1977) experiments suggests that in acquiring plural morphology, children build schematic representations of possible singular and plural lexical items, and attempt to match their growing nominal lexicon to these schemas. The effects of this show up clearly in English-speaking children's acquisition of plural lexical items, which is surprising at first sight, since plural allomorphs are phonemically conditioned, and therefore sorted by phonemic environments as stems are acquired. In German, plural allomorphs are not phonemically conditioned and are therefore much more subject to the schema-building process.

If German children are building schematic representations of possible plurals, then in their expanding lexicon they should show evidence of forms which match plural schemas, but are not the normative (adult) plural of corresponding singular nouns. Veit (1986) provides ample evidence of this type in a Berko-style elicitation of plurals to real nouns, all of which were within the productive vocabulary range of the six-year-old subjects. About 90% of the children's responses were the expected target form. Of the other 10%, less than 2% were zero responses, and virtually all the rest were deviant forms that matched plural schemata. In these deviant responses the children made use of all the plural allomorphs (cf. Table 13.5). Some examples are given under (3):

(3)   *normative plural*   *deviant plural*
      Elefanten "elephants"   Elefänte
      Ärzte "doctors"   Ärzten
      Bälle "balls"   Bäller
      Messer "knives"   Messers

Furthermore, Veit elicited the same words from the children twice. In nine cases the same deviant form was used twice. But in four cases different deviant forms were used in the two trials. This indicates that even with familiar nouns, the children were actively applying plural schemata, but were not sure which schema to apply to a particular noun. Finally, there were a small number of cases of double marking, e.g., *Kleid-er-s* "clothing," *Indianer-n-s* "Indians." In these cases the singly marked plural may not have been perceived as sufficiently plural-like, and so the second marking was added to achieve an unequivocally plural form for the child (cf. the historical double marking of *child-r-en* in English). There are two points in Veit's data I will discuss in more detail, supported by spontaneous tape-recorded data gathered from my daughter Pauline at age 3;0 in play situations. One might argue at this point that the two data sets are from different acquisitional phases; nevertheless, the strategies are strikingly similar and support the theoretical framework developed in this paper.

First, Veit noticed that children overgeneralize the form Umlaut + -*e*. She cites *Elefänte* (normative plural *Elefanten*). As a matter of fact, lots of cases of this kind can be found in Pauline's speech, e.g., *die Pünkte* "points" (normative plural *die Punkte*), *die Büsse* "buses" (normative plural *die Busse*), *die Böte* "boats" (normative plural *die Boote*), etc. The interesting point in light of the schema theory is that in all of these cases the normative plural form matches a plural template, which is not very reliable for the expression of the function of plural in German (cf. Figure 13.5). The schema [die + #____e] only represents the middleground of the continuum for plural schemas in German. The low cue strength of the plural schema based on -*e* is particularly salient in the fact that many children add umlaut for plural forms based on the *e*-schema. Second, Veit noticed overgeneralization of -*s* and -(*e*)*n*. Again, this can be confirmed on the basis of spontaneous data from my daughter. Most masculine and neuter nouns ending in -*er* or -*el* form their normative plural with -Ø, e.g., *das Fenster – die Fenster*,

Table 13.8 The assignment of the German plural markers -s and -(e)n to pseudo-suffixed nouns in -er, -el, and -en by one child over a period of two days

[#__er-s]	[#__el-s]	[#__en-s]	[#__el-n]	[#__el-n]	[#__en-en]
die Ritters "knights"	die Zettels "paper slips"	–	die Räubern "robber"	die Schlüsseln "keys"	–
die Fensters "windows"	die Schlüssels "keys"	–	die Mardern "martens"	die Zetteln "paper slips"	–
die Räubers "robber"	die Esels "donkeys"	–	die Brudern "brothers"	die Stengeln "stems"	–

but the schema [die + #____-er/-el] is not very reliable for the expression of plural, since many feminine nouns resemble the same schema in their singular, e.g., *die Kammer* "chamber" or *die Amsel* "blackbird." It is not surprising, then, that children overgeneralize plural markers in order to achieve a distinctive plural form. Particularly eligible for overgeneralization are plural markers with high cue strength, i.e., -s and -(e)n. However, it is important to note that -s does not show up in all contexts, although it has the least restrictions of all plural markers in German (cf. Bornschein & Butt (1987)). Particularly interesting is the distribution of -s and -(e)n, when the noun ends in a pseudo-suffix, i.e., -er, -el and -en,[11] and when the normative plural marker is -Ø. In Pauline's utterances (recorded over a period of two days) I found the following examples.

Table 13.8 shows that -s and -(e)n are not applied blindly. Both plural markers are applied whenever the schema is not very reliable for marking plural, i.e., word endings in -er or -el.[12] Note that in some cases the same noun shows up with -s and -en, e.g., *Zettel*. On the other hand, however, I did not find a single case where -s or -en was applied to a noun ending in the pseudo-suffix -en; for example, for *der Wagen* forms like **die Wagens* or **de Wagenen* did not occur. This distribution is compatible with the theoretical approach developed in this article since a noun ending in -en resembles a template that has high cue strength for marking plural in German. In exactly those cases the child left the nouns unchanged. These observations strongly support the schema theory and at the same time they are counter-evidence for the assumption of -s being the default plural marker in German (cf. Clahsen et al. (1992) and Marcus et al. (1995)).

Finally, I will discuss longitudinal data on natural L1 acquisition. The data were obtained by Harald Clahsen and his collaborators.[13] Table 13.9 shows all deviant plural marking of 7 monolingual German children at around age 2;6 during 5 to 15 recording sessions. Each recording contains between 200 and 600 utterances. In addition to what Table 13.9 reveals it must be noted that the children produced only a very small number of deviant plural forms in actual speech. A rough estimate is that the children produce only approximately 2–3% deviant plural forms at that age. This is compatible with Marcus et al.'s (1992) finding that overregularization of the regular verb pattern takes place only in a small minority of cases, approximately 2.5%. Probably at age 3;0

Table 13.9   Deviant plural marking in natural L1 acquisition

	No. of recordings and age	(U)+ -en	(U)+ -Ø	-e	-s	-er-n	-er-s	Reduced stem	Others
Antje	8 rec.; 2;3–2;9	1	5	3	1	1	–	1	–
Annelie	6 rec.; 2;4–2;9	–	6	1	–	–	–	–	–
Inga	7 rec.; 2;4–2;9	8	1	–	–	2	1	–	1
Katrin	15 rec.; 2;1–2;6	3	6	1	1	–	–	1	1
Marlis	7 rec.; 2;4–2;10	–	1	–	–	–	–	4	–
Sabrina	6 rec.; 1;11–2;2	–	–	1	–	–	–	–	–
Verena	5 rec.; 2;4–2;8	3	2	1	–	1	–	–	–
Σ		15	21	7	2	4	1	6	2

and younger most of the forms are still learned by rote; a productive pattern of any kind of plural formation does not seem to be established yet, due to the relatively small number of nouns in the active vocabulary of the child. The establishment of other learning mechanisms might be viewed as a function of the expanding lexicon. Taking this into consideration, Table 13.9 clearly shows that -Ø and -(e)n are overgeneralized, less so -e, and only in two cases -s. These findings are reliable, since compatible observations were made by Gawlitzek-Maiwald (1994); the overgeneralization is also noticed by Park (1978) and Mills (1985). Again, these results are not in harmony with the assumption of -s being the default plural marker in German (cf. Clahsen et al. (1992) and Marcus et al. (1995)). One wonders, of course, why -s does not show up more frequently, since the schema theory also predicts its overgeneralization due to its cue strength. An explanation could be that the basis in the children's lexicon at around age 3;0 is too small to develop any kind of generalization for -s. In the child's lexicon are some high-frequency s-plural nouns, like *Mama-s* "mom-s" and *Papa-s* "dad-s," but those are most likely rote learned. Otherwise, in the adult lexicon -s is of low type frequency according to a study by Janda (1990). Marcus et al. (1995) show in their study that -s is restricted to proper names and foreign-sounding nouns. Furthermore, the s-plural is clearly favored in nouns ending in a full vowel, but those are in most cases loanwords, which are usually not accessible to children at age 3;0.

A close look at the overgeneralization of -Ø and -en shows that the children's behavior was far from random. In about two-thirds of the Ø-assignments either the singular form already matched a plural template, e.g., *die Möhre* "carrot" matches the template [die #____UL____e], or the unchanged noun was preceded by a numeral or a scalar particle, e.g., *viele* "many" or *einige* "some." The plural marker -en was assigned 11 out of 15 times when the normative plural was -e. As has been pointed out above, -e is not a very reliable plural marker. In fact, -e is as good a marker of feminine singular as it is of plural.

Double marking, e.g., *Bild-er-n* "pictures," was only observed in cases where the normative plural was -er. In these cases, the singly marked plural may not have been perceived as sufficiently plural-like, and so the second marking was added to achieve an unequivocally plural form for the child. In 4 out of 5 cases -n is used as a second marker and in only one case -*s*. Under the assumption of a default one would have expected the opposite relation.

Finally, a word on reduced plural forms is due. A form such as *die Vöge* is counted as a reduced form, since the normative plural *die Vögel* "birds" is shortened by some phonetic material, in this case the liquid /l/. Again, shortening does not occur arbitrarily. Table 13.9 mentions only 6 cases, but in all of these cases the reduction of the putative plural form leads to a better one. In all cases the shortening takes place with nouns ending in the pseudo-suffix -*el*. As previously indicated, most masculine and neuter nouns ending in -*el* form their plural with -Ø. This results in a very unreliable plural form. More reliable and more to the right of the continuum given in Figure 13.5 would be a gestalt [die #____Umlaut____e], resembled in a word like *die Möhre* "carrot." It is exactly this schema which is matched in all 6 cases: normative *die Vögel* "birds" or *die Fußnägel* "toe-nails" > *die Vöge* and *die Fußnäge*.

Conclusion

The reanalysis of Berko (1958), Mugdan (1977), and Baker & Derwing (1982) suggests that their interpretation of zero responses has only partial validity. Children were clearly sensitive to the extent to which stimuli approximated high cue strength plural schemata, even when this was only a weak approximation (e.g., bi- versus monosyllabic stimuli). This observation is less remarkable with respect to Mugdan's data, since the behavior of German-speaking adults in a nonce word experiment, the actual distribution of plural allomorphs in the German lexicon, and a substantial pattern of historical changes in German plural formation all point to a schema-learning model based on relative cue strength (cf. Köpcke (1988, 1993)). It is worth mentioning, however, that the assumption of more or less reliable plural markers, where reliability is defined as a function of cue strength, is more capable of accounting for the data than the assumption of -*s* being the default marker. In contrast, the observation is all the more remarkable with respect to the English data, since the phonemic conditioning of plural allomorphs in English, as well as the behavior of English-speaking adults with nonce words, point so strongly to an IP model that English plural formation has become a frequently cited radical confirmation of IP rules as the basis of grammatical competence. The English data suggest that underlying the ultimate establishment of IP rules in the speaker's linguistic competence there may be a schema-learning mechanism guiding the sorting out of singular and plural lexical forms, and the acquisition of plural morphology.

Notes

1   The data from Berko's four/five-year-olds also tend to support the new analysis given here, but they are less clear, and thus are not reported for the sake of succinct presentation.

2   MacWhinney, Pleh, & Bates (1985) introduce the terms *detectability, availability,* and *reliability* for *salience, frequency,* and *cue validity,* respectively. Here, I have continued to use the older terms since at the point of writing they seem to be more established in the psychological literature.

3 Berko's experiment did not contain nonce word stimuli with final /ɪz/.

4 The description of the affricate /č/ as a fricative continuant is motivated by the fact that the second part of the phoneme produces audible friction.

5 The morphologization of the vowel harmony process in Old High German known as "Umlaut" has led to vowel alternations which enter into a number of morphological paradigms. In Modern Standard German (spoken) the vowels /a/, /o/, /u/, and /ow/ have alternants, while /i/, /e/, and /ai/ do not. The former will be referred to here as *mutable* ("umlautfähig").

6 The factor "gender-assignment" is probably the most important one for determining the plural marker (see Bittner (1994)).

7 Nominalization of verbs, e.g., *laufen > das Laufen* "to run > running," do not count, because these nouns always have a verbal partner; consequently, the nouns always encode a course of events.

8 A few still exist in southern dialects, such as *die Plunzen* "a type of sausage." Such singulars were gradually eliminated from the language in Middle High German as the cue strength of {en} for plural marking increased (see Köpcke (1988, 1993)).

9 Six of Mugdan's stimuli were eliminated (/mada:t/, /šare:t/, /fore:t/, /gredõ/, /ɛrla:t/, and /kefi:/) because they represent the phonotactics of erudite French loans in German, which are not within the competence of six/seven-year-old children.

10 The polysyllabic stimulus *das /hɛklain/* was eliminated from consideration in Figure 13.6 because it matches a real word in the lexicon, namely *das Hecklein* "little hedge."

11 The term "pseudo-suffix" refers to the frequently occurring but nonsegmentable endings *-el*, *-er*, and *-en*. For example, *-er* is a suffix in *Maler* "painter," since the verb partner *malen* "to paint" with the stem *mal* exists. Cases like *Marder* and *Bruder* look as if *-er* is segmentable, but a partner **Mard* or **Brud* does not exist.

12 Note that *-el* is not a possible plural marker in German and that *-er* is one, but with very low cue strength (see Table 13.6).

13 Here, I would like to thank Harald Clahsen for providing the transcripts of 7 children aged 1;5 to 4;0.

References

Anisfeld, M., & Tucker, G.R. (1967). English pluralization rules of six-year-old children. *Child Development, 38,* 1201–1217.

Baker, W.J., & Derwing, B.L. (1982). Response coincidence analysis as evidence for language acquisition strategies. *Applied Psycholinguistics, 3,* 193–221.

Berko, J. (1958). The child's learning of English morphology. *Word, 14,* 150–177.

Bittner, D. (1994). Die Bedeutung der Genusklassifikation für die Organisation der deutschen Substantivflexion. In K.M. Köpcke (Ed.), *Funktionale Untersuchungen zur deutschen Nominal-und Verbalmorphologie.* Tübingen: Niemeyer.

Bornschein, M., & Butt, M. (1987). Zum Status des *-s*-Plurals im gegenwärtigen Deutsch. In W. Abraham & R. Arthammar (Eds.), *Linguistik in Deutschland*, pp. 135–154. Akten des 21. Linguistischen Kolloquiums, Groningen 1986. Tübingen: Niemeyer.

Bybee, J. (1985). *Morphology: a study of the relation between meaning and form.* Amsterdam: Benjamins.

Bybee, J. (1988). Morphology as lexical organization. In M. Hammond & M. Noonen (Eds.), *Theoretical Morphology*, pp. 119–141. San Diego: Academic Press.

Bybee, J. (1991). Natural morphology: the organization of paradigms and language acquisition.

In T. Huebner & C. Ferguson (Eds.), *Crosscurrents in Second Language Acquisition and Linguistic Theories*, pp. 67–92. Amsterdam: Benjamins.

Bybee, J., & Slobin, D.I. (1982). Rules and schemas in the development and use of English past tense. *Language, 58*, 265–289.

Bybee, J., & Moder, C.L. (1983). Morphological classes as natural categories. *Language, 59*, 251–270.

Clahsen, H., & Rothweiler, M. (1992). Inflectional rules in children's grammars: evidence from the development of participles in German. *Morphology Yearbook*, 1–34.

Clahsen, H., Rothweiler, M., Woest, A., & Marcus, G. (1992). Regular and irregular inflection in the acquisition of German noun plurals. *Cognition, 45*, 225–255.

Derwing, B.L., & Baker, W.J. (1979). Recent research on the acquisition of English morphology. In P. Fletcher & M. Garman (Eds.), *Language Acquisition*, pp. 209–224. Cambridge, Mass.: Cambridge University Press.

Fromkin, V., & Rodman, R. (1974). *An Introduction to Language*. New York: Holt, Rinehart & Winston.

Gawlitzek-Maiwald, I. (1994). How do children cope with variation in the input? The case of German plurals and compounding. In R. Tracy & E. Lattey (Eds.), *How tolerant is universal grammar? Essay on language learnability and language variation*, pp. 225–266. Tübingen: Niemeyer.

Hockett, C.F. (1954). Two models of grammatical description. *Word, 10*, 210–231.

Innes, S.J. (1974). Developmental aspects of plural formation in English. Unpublished master's thesis. University of Alberta.

Janda, R.D. (1990). Frequency, markedness, and morphological change: on predicting the spread of noun plural *-s* in modern High German and West Germanic. *ESCOL' 90*, 136–153.

Köpcke, K.M. (1988). Schemas in German plural formation. *Lingua, 74*, 303–335.

Köpcke, K.M. (1993). *Schemata bei der Pluralbildung im Deutschen. Versuch einer kognitiven Morphologie*. Tübingen: Narr.

Köpcke, K.M., & Zubin, D. (1983). Die kognitive Organisation der Genuszuweisung zu den einsilbigen Nomen der deutschen Gegenwartssprache. *Zeitschrift für germanistische Linguistik, 11*, 166–182.

Lakoff, G. (1982). Categories and cognitive models. Berkeley Cognitive Science Report No. 2.

Linell, Per (1976). On the structure of morphological relations. *Linguistische Berichte, 44*, 1–29.

McClelland, J.L. (1988). Connectionist models and psychological evidence. *Journal of Memory and Language, 27*, 107–123.

MacWhinney, B. (1978). The acquisition of morphophonology. *Monographs of the Society for Research in Child Development, 43*, No. 1.

MacWhinney, B. (1989). Competition and connectionism. In E. Bates & B. MacWhinney (Eds.), *The cross-linguistic study of sentence processing*, pp. 422–457. Cambridge: Cambridge University Press.

MacWhinney, B., Pleh, C., & Bates, E. (1985). The development of sentence interpretation in Hungarian. *Cognitive Psychology, 17*, 178–209.

Marcus, G.F., Pinker, S., Ullman, M., Hollander, M., Rosen, T.J., & Xu, F. (1992). Overregularization in language acquisition. *Monographs of the Society for Research in Child Development, 57* (4, Serial No. 228).

Marcus, G.F., Brinkmann, U., Clahsen, H., Wiese, R., & Pinker, S. (1995). German inflection: the exception that proves the rule. *Cognitive Psychology, 29*, 189–256.

Menn, L., & MacWhinney, B. (1984). The repeated morph constraint: toward an exploration. *Language, 60*, 519–541.

Mills, A. (1985). The acquisition of German. In D.I. Slobin (Ed.), *The cross-linguistic study of language acquisition. Vol. 1: The Data*, pp. 141–254. Hillsdale N.J.: Erlbaum.

Mugdan, J. (1977). *Flexionsmorphologie und Psycholinguistik. Untersuchungen zu sprachlichen Regeln und ihrer Beherrschung durch Aphatiker, Kinder and Ausländer, am Beispiel der deutschen Substantivdeklination.* Tübingen: Narr.

Park, T.Z. (1978). Plurals in child speech. *Journal of Child Language, 5,* 237–250.

Pinker, S. (1991). Rules of language. *Science, 253,* 530–535.

Rosch, E. (1977). Human categorization. In N. Warren (Ed.), *Advances in cross-cultural Psychology,* pp. 1–49. London: Academic Press.

Rosch, E. (1978). Principles of categorization. In E. Rosch & B. Lloyd (Eds.), *Cognition and categorization,* pp. 27–48. Hillsdale, New Jersey: Erlbaum.

Rumelhart, D., & McClelland, J. (1986). On learning the past tenses of English verbs. Implicit rules or parallel distributed processing? In J. McClelland, D. Rumelhart, & the PDP Research Group: *Parallel distributed processing: explorations in the microstructure of cognition.* Cambridge: MIT Press.

Slobin, D.I. (1973). Cognitive prerequisites for the development of grammar. In C. Ferguson & D.I. Slobin (Eds.), *Studies of child language development,* pp. 175–276. New York: Holt, Rinehart & Winston.

Smith, E., & Medin, D. (1981). *Categories and concepts.* Cambridge: Harvard University Press.

Solomon, M.B. (1972). Stem endings and the acquisition of inflections. *Language Learning, 22,* 43–50.

Stemberger, J. (1981). Morphology haplology. *Language, 57,* 791–817.

Stemberger, J., & MacWhinney, B. (1986). Form-oriented inflectional errors in language processing. *Cognitive Psychology, 18,* 329–354.

Taylor, J.R. (1995). *Linguistic categorization. Prototypes in linguistic theory.* Oxford: Clarendon Press.

Veit, S. (1986). Das Verständnis von Plural- und Komparativformen bei (entwicklungs) dysgrammatischen Kindern im Vorschulalter. In G. Kegal et al. (Eds.), *Sprechwissenschaft und Psycholinguistic.* Opladen.

Zager, D. (1980). A real time process model of morphological change. Unpublished dissertation. State University of New York at Buffalo.

FOURTEEN

An Exploration into Children's Use of Passives

Nancy Budwig

The Function of the Passive in English

Research into the function of the passive in English has taken two related directions. Some has focused on when speakers make use of passive constructions in contrast to active sentences. Other research has examined functional distinctions between passive constructions with different auxiliary forms. In this chapter, I review this research and consider implications for children's acquisition of passive constructions.

Several related reasons have been given for why speakers use passive constructions. Jespersen (1965 [1924], p. 167) claims that "we use the active or passive turn accordingly as we shift our point of view from one to the other of the primaries contained in the sentence . . . ." Givón argues more specifically for the relation between the use of the passive and topicality: ". . . the function of passive sentences in language is to code sentences in the context in which the non-agent is more topical" (1979, p. 57). The passive construction provides a way to move nonagent elements into subject position. Another way to view the use of the passive is as a device for moving a less topical agent out of subject position (see Van Oosten, 1985). Of course, the result of the operations suggested by Givón and Van Oosten is the same.

Van Oosten's research on the functions of the passive is particularly relevant to the present study, given our interest in how speakers talk about nonprototypical agency. On the basis of an extensive examination of almost 1,300 passives in a book of edited oral histories (Seifer, 1976) and the Judiciary Committee version of eight of the Nixon conversations (Rodino, 1974), Van Oosten has outlined a variety of semantic, pragmatic, and discursive reasons that lead speakers to use passives. According to several of these, the passive is used when the agent deviates from prototypical agency, for instance, when an agent is general (for example "people") rather than specific or when the action is a corporate act involving no one particular agent. Van Oosten also suggests that speakers switch to passive constructions for pragmatic purposes. The sentence may include a prototypical agent but the speaker prefers to leave the identity of the agent vague. For instance, the speaker may wish to be polite by reducing the assertion of responsibility on the agent's part. Van Oosten also outlines several discursive purposes for which speakers may employ passives. For example, the speaker may want to switch the focus of attention to the patient, or the agent may only be of transitory interest in the discourse (see Bamberg, i.p.).

While Van Oosten has carefully examined the contexts in which passives are used, she has not focused on the relation between choice of auxiliary form and context in which passives appear. Though linguists differ in their proposals about the features linked with *get* and *be* passives, they agree that *get* can act as a passive auxiliary (see Stein, 1979 for review) and suggest that *get* and *be* passives are best viewed as functionally distinct. There is also general consensus that the choice of auxiliary in passive constructions is genre-specific. *Get* passives are disapproved of in formal speech or writing. Thus the selection of passive auxiliary is only at issue in less formal speech and writing (Quirk and Greenbaum, 1973; Standwell, 1981).

Some contemporary grammars of English have attempted to distinguish *get* and *be* passives in terms of whether an animate agent is expressed (Quirk and Greenbaum, 1973). While several researchers have noted that *get* passives rarely occur with an overt agent, this constraint is linked to broader semantic or discursive considerations (Banks, 1986, Lakoff, 1971; Stein, 1979). That is, the nature of the restrictions on *get* passives makes *get* passives with an expressed animate agent rare, although possible. On what basis, then, do speakers choose between the passive auxiliaries? Two broad kinds of suggestions have been proposed: (1) those involving semantic considerations, and (2) those focusing on discursive purpose.

Researchers claiming that *get* and *be* passives are semantically distinct have argued that *get* passives refer to scenes deviating from prototypical agency. Standwell (1981) has suggested that the difference between *get* and *be* passives involves the degree of deliberate planning. Accidental or random events are referred to with *get*, while events that result from deliberate planning involve *be*. In support of such claims Standwell compares the following sentences:

1 George was executed by a firing squad yesterday morning.
2 George got executed by a firing squad yesterday morning.
3 My cat got run over by a bus.

According to Standwell, example 1 sounds appropriate, while example 2 is considered bizarre, since executions generally involve deliberate planning. Conversely, *get* in example 3 is appropriate since the running over of cats is usually accidental. The *get* passive deviates from prototypical agency to the extent that prototypical agents act with a plan in mind.

Other researchers have suggested that *get* passives can be distinguished from *be* passives in that the logical object shares responsibility for the action described. This sharing of responsibility represents a second kind of deviation from prototypical agency. Schibsbye (1970) has suggested that *get* is used when the logical object plays a causal role in the change taking place. Similarly, Barber (1975) claims that the logical object catalyzes the action that is performed by a separate agent.

While many examples of *get* passives can be explained by the semantic accounts reviewed above, other examples suggest that they are insufficient. For instance, sentences like *Our grant got cancelled* cannot be viewed as a random event, nor can we argue that the grant played a causal role in its own cancellation.

Other researchers have attempted to account for the distinction between *get* and *be* passives by appealing to discursive factors. The most convincing theory of this type concerning the distinction between *get* and *be* passives involves the notion of speaker involvement or speaker attitude. One attitude expressed by the speaker in *get* passives is discontent; the process described by the verb is to the detriment of the logical object in question (Banks, 1986; Gee, 1974; Lakoff, 1971). The following comparisons have been offered by Banks (1986):

4 a.   My cache of marijuana was found.
   b.   My cache of marijuana got found.
5 a.   Our grant was cancelled.
   b.   Our grant got cancelled.

It is claimed that 4b and 5b express discontent on the part of the speaker. Banks (1986) has also suggested that parallel examples where there is no question of detriment to the logical object are less acceptable:

6 My car got repaired.

It has also been claimed that the speaker's attitude may be positive as well as negative (Gee, 1974; Hatcher, 1949). Hatcher suggests that in sentences involving animate logical objects, the speaker expresses a positive attitude about the result of action on the logical object. If the logical object is animate, the speaker's attitude is directed toward the animate object; if the logical object is inanimate, the attitude takes into account the consequences for some "other" participant. Examples of happy consequences for an animate logical object include *to get elected, nominated,* or *invited,* etc.; examples of happy consequences in cases involving an inanimate logical object include *to get fixed* or *to get funded.*

This review of the literature on the function of the passive indicates that there is no simple relationship between the passive construction and the function it serves. Research suggests that the passive links up with a constellation of related semantic and discourse factors. The review has highlighted ways the passive functions to demote nonprototypical agents, as well as to topicalize patient arguments. In addition, it has emphasized the importance of examining auxiliary choice. While some suggestions have been made with regard to the semantic and discourse factors that distinguish *get* and *be* passives, little has been said in the literature about the contexts in which *be* passives are used, and how these contexts differ from those in which active sentences are produced.

Developmental considerations

What is the relationship between form and function in English-speaking children's passives? Do children use more than one auxiliary form in passives? If so, are different auxiliary forms linked to different functions? Such questions have not been sufficiently addressed in the acquisition literature.

Although there have been numerous studies of children's comprehension of the passive (for example, Bever, 1970; Maratsos, 1974; de Villiers & de Villiers, 1973), very little research has examined how children use the passive in contrast to the active voice. Turner and Rommetveit (1967) have conducted two experiments in which they attempted to manipulate the voice in which children (ranging from preschool age to 8–9 years old) encoded events. In the first experiment they altered the order in which subjects visually scanned the participants shown in a series of pictures. They predicted that if the actor was scanned first, the children would make use of the active voice, while if the acted-upon element was shown first, a passive would be used. In a second experiment they manipulated "focus of attention" through the type of question they asked about a picture. In both experiments, the use of passive-voice sentences increased when the acted-upon element was highlighted. These experiments could be taken to suggest that young children (like adults) employ passive constructions in order to promote more topical patients. Note, however, that since every picture shown to a subject depicted a clear and visible actor, there was no assessment of whether children employ passives when agents are unknown or generic.

Horgan's study (1978), which was based on experimental elicitation of passives, sheds light on the nature of agency involved in such constructions. Horgan's youngest subjects (2;0–4;2) were asked to describe a series of pictures portraying a variety of agents and objects (animate and inanimate). Pictures were either semantically reversible or irreversible. One participant was highlighted in each picture so as to alter focus. The 5–13-year-old children were asked to tell stories about TAT pictures. First, Horgan concluded that the children in her study (ranging from 2;0 to 13;11) used full and truncated passives differently. The youngest children (between 2;0 and 4;2) relied almost exclusively on truncated passives (no expression of logical subject), and these passives involved stative verbs and inanimate logical objects. In contrast, their occasional full passives involved a wide range of action verbs and had animate logical objects. Second, Horgan claimed that before the age of 11, her subjects made use of either reversible passives to express mutual activity by two animate entities or nonreversible instrumental passives to express nonagent causation. This restriction suggests that Horgan's subjects reserved the use of full passives for talking about nonprototypical agency. In the case of reversible passives, the event described is perhaps viewed in terms of mutual involvement, while in the case of nonreversible passives, the event involves nonagent or instrumental causation. As Pinker et al. (1987) point out, roughly 80% to 90% of all the children below the age of 11 in Horgan's study didn't produce any full passives at all, and, therefore, one must be cautious about generalizing beyond her data.[1]

Maratsos et al. (1985) have offered another hypothesis about semantic restrictions on children's passives, based on a preliminary analysis of passives used by adults interacting with children as well as on results of experiments designed to test children's comprehension of action-verb versus mental-verb passives. Maratsos et al. suggest that children's passive rule may at first apply only to a limited range of verbs, those ranking high in semantic transitivity (such as verbs in clauses involving a volitional agent who carries out a telic kinetic action which affects an individuated object). This hypothesis may appear surprising, given the suggestion above that adults use the passive to talk about nonprototypical agency. I will return to a discussion of this paradox below.

Pinker et al. (1987) offer an alternative hypothesis based on spontaneous production data and data from experiments tapping both comprehension and production. These researchers claim that children should have little difficulty learning to passivize canonical action verbs once they have "picked up the thematic core of the passive construction" (1987, p. 256). But they claim children would have to learn on a class-by-class basis from positive evidence which nonactional verbs can be passivized in English. Here the decision would rest on whether one can construe these verbs as having "abstract" agent and patient arguments.

Clearly there is much overlap in the predictions made by Maratsos et al. and Pinker et al. The major question is why children would passivize sentences involving canonical action verbs involving agent and patient arguments. Slobin (1985), for instance, has argued that children acquiring diverse languages do give special linguistic treatment to scenes involving an agent who brings about a change of state on some object. Nevertheless, children do not seem to use passives for such scenes, but rather *actives*.

Lempert (1989, i.p.), based on the examination of the role of patient animacy on the acquisition of the passive, provides a partial answer to this paradox. Lempert used a passive-sentence training task to test whether preschoolers (mean 3;8) were more likely to imitate passive-sentence descriptions of pictures when the patient was animate rather than inanimate. Children were also probed to produce passives of new pictures depicting animate and inanimate patients. The findings suggest that the children were better able to imitate and produce passives when taught sentences with animate patients. It could be the case that children use the active voice to report scenes involving agents who cause a change of state in physical objects but switch to the passive when the change of state affects an animate patient. While Maratsos et al. did not include inanimate patients in their tasks, Pinker et al. included both inanimate and animate patients. Pinker's findings do not lend support to the claim that passives are restricted to sentences with animate patients. Clearly, what is needed is a more careful analysis of the range of uses of the passive by children, with special attention to whether passive constructions are limited to a narrow range of semantic and discourse functions of the sort outlined by Van Oosten for adult speakers.

While much attention has been given to the issue of factors influencing children's passives in general, a review of the developmental literature reveals that very little attention has been given to the specific issue of auxiliary choice. In examining children's language productions, researchers have almost exclusively focused on *be* passives. There have been scattered reports that children used *get* passives in various experiments (see Pinker et al. 1987; Turner & Rommetveit 1967); however, this has not been relevant to the questions being investigated and so has not been analyzed further.[2]

Although most previous empirical research has not specifically investigated *get* passives, at least three explanations for their use have been put forth in the developmental literature. None of these accounts has attempted to consider functional-semantic distinctions governing the choice of *get* and *be* as auxiliary. Lee (1974) suggested that *get* is a transitional structure derived from predicate-adjective constructions, while

Turner and Rommetveit (1967) claimed that *get* is a "childhood" or colloquial form of the *be* passive. Fraser et al. (1963) argued that children use *get* plus a past participle as a device for distinguishing passive voice from similar sentences in the active voice. What cannot be accounted for by any of these explanations, though, is the basis upon which a particular child chooses an auxiliary form. It seems plausible that *get* and *be* passives are functionally distinct for children, each used in a different context. I will turn now to examine this issue.

Study 1: The Function of Children's Spontaneous Use of Passive Constructions

Subject and materials

In this study, I have examined all instances of passive constructions found in the diary records of Bowerman's two daughters' language development between ages two and ten.[3] As input to the present analysis Bowerman extracted all utterances containing passive constructions from the diary records, as well as limited descriptions of the context. All clauses containing the form Noun Phrase + BE/GET + Past Participle that were not adjectival were included in analysis. Although the distinction between verbal and adjectival passives has been the subject of debate in the literature, there are no well-accepted tests for determining passive type (see Gordon and Chafetz, 1989 for further discussion). In the present analysis, truncated passives (that is, those lacking a *by* phrase) were eliminated if the situation referred to denoted a state. Utterances like *It is broken* or *The barn is locked* were thus excluded from analysis. Only passives with process or dynamic interpretations have been analyzed. While the general context of the utterance was used in attempting to distinguish verbal from adjectival passives, such judgments are not always clearcut, and thus a small amount of coding error may have occurred. Even if a small amount of error occurred, this should not affect the general conclusions. One hundred and forty-two passive constructions were isolated for coding.

Function coding

The goal of the function coding was to assess whether passive constructions co-occurred with particular semantic/pragmatic constellations revealing of their discourse function (see Bamberg, 1987; Budwig, 1986, 1989; Ervin-Tripp, 1987; Gee & Savasir, 1985; Slobin, 1987 for a more complete discussion of this approach). Each passive construction was coded in terms of a multilevel coding scheme that involved six different levels of analysis. The first level specified choice of auxiliary form (for example, all utterances were coded as involving *get* or *be* as auxiliary form). The second level noted whether the passive construction was full or truncated; if full, the form of the preposition was coded. The third level noted characteristics of the patient. The fourth level specified the characteristics of the logical subject. The fifth coding level indicated the semantics of the verb. The final coding level specified whether a modal form occurred.

The present coding scheme focuses more on semantic characteristics of the passives than on pragmatic and discourse features. This restriction reflects the nature of the data

Table 14.1 From characteristics: distribution of passive constructions by auxiliary form: % (n = 142)

	BE	GET	Total
Eva			
under 3;6	58 (7)	42 (5)	(12)
3;6–5	59 (23)	41 (16)	(39)
over 5	80 (16)	20 (4)	(20)
Total	65 (46)	35 (25)	71
Christy			
under 3;6	63 (12)	37 (7)	(19)
3;6–5	61 (23)	39 (15)	(38)
over 5	71 (10)	29 (4)	(14)
Total	63 (45)	37 (26)	71
Combined			
under 3;6	61 (19)	39 (12)	(31)
3;6–5	60 (46)	40 (31)	(77)
over 5	76 (26)	24 (8)	(34)
Total	64 (91)	36 (51)	142

source. Future research should focus on pragmatic factors such as whether children switch to passives to conceal the identity of a known agent for reasons of politeness, etc.

Results

In this section I will show that the passive constructions co-occurred systematically with other features of the clauses in which they were embedded. In addition, I will claim that such co-occurrence patterns are not arbitrary groupings but rather can be linked at a more abstract level of analysis to the kinds of perspectives children take on events when using passive constructions. The discussion will center upon the question of how *get* and *be* constructions co-occur with the other levels coded.

Form considerations

The first level of analysis noted the auxiliary form used in the children's passive constructions. The findings of this analysis are shown in Table 14.1.

Table 14.1 gives the distribution of *get* and *be* passives for each of the two children, with the utterances divided into three age periods. Note that the majority of passives analyzed in this study were produced when the children were under the age of five. The distributional patterns found for the two children are fairly similar. At all age periods, both girls used more *be* passives than *get* passives. This pattern became more pronounced with age. After the age of five, Eva was more likely than Christy to use *be* passives rather than *get* passives.

Type of passive

The second coding level noted whether the children used full or truncated passives. Previous research has led us to expect very few instances of spontaneous full passives in young children's speech. First, we know that full passives occur infrequently in adult discourse. Givón's (1979, pp. 58–59) analysis of various genres indicates that less than 20% of all main-declarative-affirmative clauses contain passives and fewer than 20% of all passives are full passives. Furthermore, we know that full passives are rare in adult input to children. Brown (1973) reports that there were no instances of full passives in the extensive speech samples of parent input he collected. Gordon and Chafetz (1989) in a reanalysis of Brown's data report that an examination of both parent and researcher input revealed only four full passives. In addition, several studies have shown that children rarely produce full passives in experimental settings (see Horgan, 1978).

Table 14.2 lends general support to the claim that children rely primarily on truncated passives, since at all age levels truncated passives occurred more frequently than full passives. Nevertheless, the pattern differs according to the choice of auxiliary. The children were far more likely to use full passives with *get* than with *be* at all ages. In fact, while only 30% of all *be* passives between 3;6 and 5 years were full passives, 48% of all *get* passives were full passives during this age period. These findings suggest that full passives are not as rare as previous experimental research has led us to believe. Nevertheless the question remains: why were the children more likely to use full passives with *get* constructions?

The children's choice of preposition in full passives appears to have been independent of whether the auxiliary was *get* or *be* (see Table 14.2). *By* was the most frequently used form, followed by *from*; *of* and *with* were also used occasionally.

Patient characteristics

Patient characteristics were coded in terms of three related dimensions: (a) animacy – whether the patient was animate or inanimate; (b) self – whether the patient was the speaker or non-speaker; and (c) consequences – whether the consequences of the action could be viewed positively or negatively, or as neutral. Dolls, stuffed animals, and other similar objects were coded as inanimate, since the real issue is one of degree of control or volition of the logical object. While children may treat such objects as if they act with volition, coding of these few instances was conservative.

First, let us consider animacy. Do patients involved in passive constructions tend to be animate or inanimate? Is animacy of patient related to whether *get* or *be* constructions are used? Overall, the children referred to inanimate patients more often than animate ones (see Table 14.3.1). However, closer examination shows that animacy was related to auxiliary form: while only 32% of patients in *be* constructions were animate, 59% of patients in *get* constructions were animate. That is, while *be* passives tended to include inanimate patients (for example *Does the cream of wheat need to be cooled?*; Eva, 2;8), *get* passives often had animate patients (for example *We will get striked by lightening*; Eva, 3;6).

The findings from the analysis of Bowerman's children differ from the experimental findings reported by Lempert (1989, i.p.). I have noted above that Lempert's subjects were more likely to imitate and produce a passive after a probe when the patient was

Table 14.2 Distribution of passives by age according to type: % (raw numbers)

	Passive type		Total
	Full	Truncated	
BE			
under 3;6	11 (2)	89 (17)	(19)
3;6–5;0	30 (14)	70 (32)	(46)
over 5;0	27 (7)	73 (19)	(26)
Total	25 (23)	75 (68)	(91)
GET			
under 3;6	33 (4)	67 (8)	(12)
3;6–5;0	48 (15)	52 (16)	(31)
over 5;0	38 (3)	63 (5)	(8)
Total	43 (22)	57 (29)	(51)

Frequency of use of various prepositions with full passives by age and auxiliary choice (raw numbers)

BE	under 3;6	3;6–5;0	over 5;0	Total
by	(1)	(8)	(5)	(14)
from	(1)	(4)	(2)	(7)
of	(0)	(1)	(0)	(1)
with	(0)	(1)	(0)	(1)
Total	(2)	(14)	(7)	(23)
GET				
by	(0)	(9)	(2)	(11)
from	(2)	(5)	(0)	(7)
of	(2)	(1)	(0)	(3)
with	(0)	(1)	(0)	(1)
Total	(4)	(16)	(2)	(22)

animate. Lempert, though, only used sentences with *be* passives and does not report data in terms of auxiliary choice.

Nineteen percent of all passives involved Self as patient. Given the finding that *get* passives tended to include animate patients more often than *be* passives, it is not surprising that Self occurs as patient in a greater proportion of *get* passives than *be* passives: 26% vs. 15%. The children might have attempted to follow what researchers have labeled the "me first" principle (see Cooper & Ross, 1975), thereby switching to a passive construction when Self is patient. No firm conclusions about this can be drawn from the data analyzed, since we have no way to assess how often children refer to Self as patient in active sentences. It seems reasonable to assume that this principle plays a minor role at best in accounting for children's choice between passive and active sentences in general, and between *get* and *be* passives in particular.

Table 14.3   Characteristics of patient: distribution of passives: % (n)

1.   According to animacy of patient

Form	Animate	Inanimate	Uncoded	Total
BE	32 (30)	65 (59)	3 (2)	(91)
GET	59 (30)	41 (21)		(51)
Combined	42 (60)	56 (80)	2 (2)	(142)

2.   According to relation of patient to speaker (Self, Not self)

Form	Self	Not self	Total
BE	15 (14)	85 (77)	(91)
GET	26 (13)	75 (38)	(51)
Combined	19 (27)	81 (115)	(142)

3.   According to consequences of action (negative, positive, neutral)

Form	Consequence: Negative	Positive	Neutral	Uncoded	Total
BE	18 (16)	3 (3)	74 (67)	6 (5)	(91)
GET	65 (33)	6 (3)	26 (13)	4 (2)	(51)
Combined	35 (49)	4 (6)	56 (80)	5 (7)	(142)

A third aspect of patient characteristics examined involved the notion of consequences of the action. It has been suggested that adult speakers of English use *get* passives to indicate the speaker's attitude about the effects of action on the patient or some
other participant. Since it is not possible to know what perspective the speaker adopted
in the present analysis, I have examined whether the children might use a particular
auxiliary form to talk about consequences by employing the following coding scheme.
I have considered whether the patient could be construed as being (a) negatively
affected, (b) positively affected, (c) neither (neutral), or (d) unclear. The assumption is
that if the patient can be viewed as affected negatively or positively, then a speaker
might express such an attitude.

Utterances like *If Deedee don't be careful, she might get runned over from a car* (Eva, 2;7)
were coded as instances of negative consequences, since the patient could be adversely
affected by the action. The utterance *I want see my bottle getting fix* (Christy, 2;2)
describes a scene in which the patient is positively affected. Utterances such as *Simon?*
He must be the one I've always been heard (= told) about (Christy, 5;2) have been coded as
neutral. Finally, some cases were left uncoded because available contextual notes were
insufficient to draw a conclusion. For instance, an example like *My dolly is scrunched*
from somebody (Eva, 2;8) is ambiguous since it is not clear whether the child sees the
doll's being scrunched as negatively affecting the doll, and the available contextual
notes are insufficient to disambiguate. Using a conservative coding strategy, I was able
to classify 135 or 95% of the passives as positive, negative, or neutral.

The combined analysis shows that over half of the passives (56%) involved neutral
consequences. Once again, though, an analysis considering auxiliary selection reveals
a finer pattern (see Table 14.3.3). Seventy-four percent of all *be* passives occurred with
the expression of neutral consequences, while only 26% of all *get* passives did. In con-

trast, only 18% of all *be* passives referred to negative consequences, while an impressive 65% of all *get* passives encoded this dimension.

To summarize patient characteristics, passive constructions involving *be* tended to involve inanimate patients that were not adversely affected by the action described. In contrast, *get* passives typically involved animate patients that were negatively affected. In one-quarter of the *get* passives, the children referred to themselves as patient. The following examples illustrate these distinctions between patients in *get* and *be* constructions:

7   I want these pancakes to be sugared. (Christy, 4;2)
8   Do you think that flower's supposed to be picked by somebody? (Eva, 2;10)
9   She brought her inside so she won't get all stinked up by the skunk. (Eva, 4;1)
10 I just got pinched from these pointed stuff. (Eva, 3;3)

Logical subjects

The fourth coding category noted aspects of the logical subjects in *get* and *be* passives. Logical subjects were coded to assess whether passive constructions provide a way to talk about nonprototypical agency. The first consideration was whether the logical subject (whether explicit or implicit) was agentive or nonagentive. All agentive logical subjects were further coded as specific agents or general agents. Instances were considered specific agents if the logical subject referred to identifiable agents (as in *I don't want to be splashed by you*, Eva, 4;2; *I guess he is learned how to from his daddy*, Christy, 4;2). Examples coded as general agents were those in which the action referred to would be conducted by an agent but no particular agent need be involved. Most frequently, instances coded as general agents cooccurred with truncated passives (for example *Does the cream of wheat need to be cooled?*, Eva, 2;8; *Hair needs to be brushed*, Christy, 4;2), although a few instances co-occurred with full passives (for example *Do you think that flower's supposed to be picked by somebody?*, Eva, 2;10).

If passives provide a way to talk about nonprototypical agency, passive sentences should involve either nonagentive logical subjects or general agents, but not specific agents. Overall we find support for this claim. As Table 14.4 shows, only 20% of all logical subjects referred to specific agents. *Get* and *be* passives differed, however, in that *get* passives tended to have nonagent entities as logical subjects (45%), while *be* passives typically involved general agents (58%).

Some (41%) of the passives with specific agents deviate from prototypical agency in that they involve actions in which the agent is not fully responsible for the action being brought about. In most cases the speaker or the patient share the responsibility with the agent; for example, *The chicky's getting swinged by his owner because the chicky asked to be swinged by his owner* (Christy, 4;5). This lends further support to the claim that the passive functions as a device for referring to nonprototypical agency.

Verb semantics

The fifth level of analysis looked at the range of verbs occurring in the children's passive constructions (see Table 14.5). Are these highly transitive, as suggested by Maratsos et al. (1985), or, more specifically, do they have agent and patient arguments, either concretely or abstractly, as suggested by Pinker et al. (1987)? An examination of verb

Table 14.4 Proportion of logical subjects that refer to specific agents, general agents, and nonagent entities: % (n)

Form	Non-agent	Specific agent	General agent	Uncoded	Total
BE	12 (11)	21 (19)	58 (53)	9 (8)	91
GET	45 (23)	20 (10)	18 (9)	18 (9)	51
Total	24 (34)	20 (29)	44 (62)	12 (17)	142

Table 14.5 Verb semantics: Eva

Verbs appearing with BE		Verbs appearing with GET	
ashed 1	messed up	bumped	stinked up
bandaided 2	picked/up	burned	striked 12
blowden up 3	pictured on	buried up	untucked
bushed up 4	played with	drowned	usened*
called	putted on	eaten*/aten	washed up
changed	readen to	fastened 7	
cooled	scrunched	floated 8	
cut bald	splashed*	gone out 9	
descripted	stepped on	hurt	
dried/up	sticked on	kill	
eaten*/up	throwed up/off	lightninged 10	
fired 5	throwned away	losed	
glued	tooken away/out/down	pinched	
goened in 6	used*/up	pricked	
ground	voted	sent (to jail)	
hided	whipped toppinged	splashed up*	
invaded	written	staled 11	

* Indicates verb appears with both auxiliary forms.
Key: 1 = cremated; 2 = bandaid applied; 3 = inflated; 4 = overgrown, said of bushes; 5 = caused to erupt, said of volcano; 6 = urinated in, said of toilets; 7 = affected by a cold sensation; 8 = caused to float imagining the effects of a flood on a house; 9 = spilled, said of pegs; 10 = struck by lightning; 11 = caused to become stale; 12 = struck by lightning.

semantics supports previous research that suggests that production and comprehension of the passive is limited to action verbs (Maratsos et al., 1985; Pinker et al., 1987). Bowerman's children did not passivize mental-state verbs. Rather, many of the verbs shown in Table 14.5 ranked high in transitivity, in that they referred to kinetic actions brought about by an agent who causes a change of state in a patient.

Some of the verbs in Table 14.6 that do not at first glance seem highly transitive can be viewed as expressing a relationship between an agent and a patient at a more

Table 14.6 Verb semantics: Christy

Verbs appearing with BE		Verbs appearing with GET	
bloomed 1	lost*	burn*	spanken
breaked/breaken	made	caught	splashed
broken out	mummied 5	cut	sucked
brush	paint	dressed	swinged*
burn*	plugged out	feeded*	unsnapped
chewed off	put in/putten on*	fired 6	washed*
cut	shoelaced	fix*/fixed*	
died 2	spank/spanked	gone 7	
eaten	stayed open	hitten	
feeded*	sugared	hurt*	
filled/fulled	surrounded	knocked over	
fix*/fixed*	swinged	learned 8	
gone 3	take caren of	losen*	
heard about 4	taught	mixed up	
hurt*	tied up	punished	
invented	tooken	putten on*	
leaved	treated for	scratched	
	washed*		

* Indicates verb appeared with both auxiliaries.
Key: 1 = caused to bloom; 2 = killed; 3 = taken; 4 = told about; 5 = made into mummy; 6 = caused to catch on fire; 7 = said of object about to be eaten; 8 = taught.

abstract level. For instance, *punish* in example 11 below can be given a high transitivity rating if *punish* is viewed as a social action.

> 11   And he got punished with the teacher – by the teacher spanking him hard.
>   (Christy, 4;2)

The presence of verbs of this sort supports Pinker et al.'s (1987) claim that children can passivize noncanonical action verbs as long as these verbs can be construed as having abstract agent and patient argument. Other examples are less clear:

> 12   I don't want it to be played with. (Eva, 3;10)
> 13   Eva is take caren (= taken care) of by a farmer. (Christy, 9;4)
> 14   If you won't Christy will get readen to and I won't. (Eva, 3;6)
> 15   I am described (= described) as a four-year-old girl. (Eva, 8;3)

Examples 12 and 13 could possibly be construed as having agent and patient arguments, although for 14 and 15 this is more difficult.

While both *be* and *get* passives seem to be restricted to canonical action verbs and a restricted range of extensions via processes of analogy (see Budwig, 1986; Pinker et al., 1987; Talmy, 1985 for further details about such processes), the verbs found in *get* and *be* passives are distinct. Only a few of the verbs used by each child appeared with both *be* and *get* as auxiliary (6% for Eva, 17% for Christy). As can be gleaned from Table 14.5 verbs appearing with *get* typically encode an action with undesirable or negative consequences (such as *get runned over, pinched, struck by lightening,* etc.), whereas those with *be* do not (for example *blow up, cool, pick,* etc.).

Modal forms

The final coding level examines the use of modals in passive constructions. It has been claimed that modals mitigate the degree of control exercised by the agent, in that an appeal is made to broader, often psychosocial, factors controlling the situation described (see Gerhardt, n.d.; Talmy, 1985 for further discussion). Compare, for instance, the following two sentences:

16   a.   John throws the ball.
     b.   John must throw the ball.

In 16b, John's action is not performed simply due to John's personal desire but instead is related to some larger force – for instance, rules of the game.

Given that modals can mitigate the degree of agency expressed, and given the claim that passives provide a way to demote agents, one might expect modals to appear in passive constructions. In particular, modals could provide a way to play down a particular agent's involvement in an event in which focus is placed on controlling factors that are beyond an agent's personal volition. The question of present concern is whether modals appear more frequently in *get* or *be* passives. It has been claimed that modals express a subjective attitude toward the situation that the proposition describes (Lyons, 1977; Palmer, 1986). Since it is also argued, as noted earlier, that *get* passives differ from *be* passives in that they signal speaker attitude, one might expect modal markers to appear more frequently in *get* passives than *be* passives. A further question is whether different modals are used in *get* and *be* passives, and, if so, whether this difference is informative about the nature of *get* and *be* constructions. The findings are presented in Table 14.7.

Contrary to the prediction about frequency, modal forms were not more likely to occur with *get* passives. In fact, there was even a slight preference for modals in *be* passives. Inspection of the range of modal forms found in *get* and *be* passives suggests a reason why modals co-occur with both types of passives. As Table 14 6 shows, *be* passives were most likely to occur with *can* and *gonna*, while *get* passives were most likely to occur with *will*. While the overall numbers are not large, the following speculations seem worth pursuing in future research.

Both passive constructions involve a speaker attitude about the relationship between the action described and the patient, but the nature of the relationship described differs. The speaker attitude found in *get* passives with *will* focuses on likely effects on the patient, often negative; for example, *Mommy will get lightninged* (Eva, 5;2). In contrast, the speaker attitude involved in the use of *be* passives focuses on the potential for action to be carried out on patients. Consider the following examples:

Table 14.7 Percentage of passives with and without modal forms (n)

Form	With modal	Without modal	Total
BE	26 (23)	75 (68)	91
GET	20 (10)	80 (41)	51
Combined	23 (33)	77 (109)	142

Rank order and frequency of modal forms in BE and GET passives
BE passives (n = 23)
  can (7)
  gonna (5)
  need (4)
  will (4)
  hafta (1)
  should (1)
  supposed to (1)
GET passives (n = 10)
  will (5)
  gonna (1)
  can (1) (negative)
  should (1)
  might (1)
  would (1)

17   Also it can be putten on your foot. (Christy, 3;6)
18   This can be thrown away. (Eva, 4;4)
19   My room gonna be paint. (Christy, 2;5)
20   Does the cream of wheat need to be cooled? (Eva, 2;8)

These examples appeal to norms or conventions, procedures for ways things are done without a focus on the agent.

With both auxiliary forms, passives with modals express a kind of speaker attitude that mitigates agency by focusing on the action–patient relationship. This contrasts with the meaning of related active sentences like *Someone can put it on your foot; Someone can throw it away*. In such examples the modals express the speaker attitude toward the agent–action relationship. Thus the subjective involvement of the speaker may not be limited to *get* passives, as has been suggested in the linguistic literature (see previous discussion of Banks, 1986; Gee, 1974; and Lakoff, 1971). Speaker involvement may also be characteristic of *be* passives that contain modal forms. Clearly, further research should consider the distinction between various modal forms and their role in *get* and *be* passives.

Summary

This naturalistic study of the early use of the passive provides evidence that before the age of five, children acquiring English use the passive productively. In keeping with previous research, the present study suggests that children primarily passivize action verbs. The present findings go beyond previous research by suggesting that characteristics of passive sentences differ according to which auxiliary form is used.

Be passives, which occurred more frequently than *get* passives, tended to be truncated and to involve inanimate patients. The logical subjects were often generic agents. Modal forms that co-occurred with *be* passives referred to norms and conventions. *Get* passives were also frequently truncated, although when full passives were used they most frequently occurred with *get* passives. In contrast to *be* passives, *get* passives typically involved animate patients. Neither *get* nor *be* passives tended to have specific agents as logical subjects, but their subjects differed: those of *get* passives tended to be nonagent entities, whereas those of *be* passives were typically general agents. Self as patient was more frequent in *get* passives. *Get* passives also expressed more often an attitude about negative consequences. Get passives involved verbs describing adverse actions, while *be* passives did not.

Discussion

Are the various dimensions that distinguish *get* and *be* passives related, or are they simply an arbitrary array of co-occurrence patterns? I will argue that the co-occurrence patterns noted at each level can be integrated into an overarching activity type that guides the use of the two constructions. The claim is that *get* and *be* passives reflect two distinct ways of talking about actions without taking an agentive perspective.

The analysis of logical subjects suggests that *be* passives refer to events in which the agent is generic, irrelevant, or unknown. In general it is not important *who* is performing the action. These sentences fall into several subcategories, as follows: (1) instances describing "ways things are done" or rules of conduct (for example *Does the cream of wheat need to be cooled?*, Eva, 2;8; *Sometimes Eva needs to be feeded with you because she doesn't eat* (= by you), (Christy, 4;3); (2) recurrent happenings where the agent may change but the result is the same (for example *Both are going to be goened in*, Eva, 3;7; *Yes but it can be blowden up like the other one's blowed up*, Eva, 3;0 with reference to a blow-up toy); (3) hypothetical happenings with no specific agent (for example *I'm gonna have a will and it's gonna say that I wanna be ashed*, Eva, 6;7).

The *get* passives do not have the normative, generic quality of the *be* passives. How, then, can we account for the various co-occurrence patterns found in *get* passives? I would argue that *get* passives are reserved for the expression of a particular kind of speaker attitude. Children employ *get* passives as a perspective-taking device to focus on actions that have painful or negative outcomes. Often the event described deviates from a prototypical agentive perspective in that the agent may not have volitionally carried out the action described, or is an inanimate causal source, as in *They got all scratched up of rock* (Christy, 4;3), *I just got pinched from those pointed stuff* (Eva, 3;3). Even when animate agents are involved, as in utterances like *No one would get sent to jail from by putting a june bug in a jar would they?* (Eva, 5;1) or *They got spanken* (Christy, 3;9), the agent deviates from what DeLancey (1984) and others have referred to as prototypical agency in that the ultimate cause is not clearly located within the implied agent. Notice that those who get sent to jail and those who receive the spankings typically play a causal role in the actions taking place.

A comparison of the children's *get* passives with literature on adult's *get* passives reveals that the children focus primarily on the expression of an attitude about negative consequences of action, while adults use *get* passives when expressing both negative and positive consequences. Savasir (1983) has found that the early passives in the speech of young Turkish children are restricted in form (for example, negative, third-person, present tense) and limited to the context of reporting on objects that are resisting the child's manipulations (for example "it doesn't open"). Future cross-linguistic research should examine whether children acquiring other languages give special linguistic treatment to this scene.

One of my central claims has been that the different distributional patterns found at the various levels of analysis can be related at a more abstract level to broader activity types. If so, then one would need to account for not only the finding that the two kinds of passive constructions appear in conjunction with different features, but also how the findings at a specific level of analysis relate to the broader activity type suggested.

For example, let us consider two levels of analysis for which it might not seem clear at first glance why the findings went in the direction they did. First, why do we find that full passives more frequently have *get* than *be* as their auxiliary? Given the finding that *be* passives typically involved an agent that was unknown, irrelevant, or generic, it would be expected that full passives would occur less frequently with *be* as their auxiliary. Second, why do the implicit or explicit logical subjects of *get* and *be* passives encode distinct semantic notions? Although *get* and *be* passives differed in the relations encoded, neither tended to occur with specific agents. The implicit or explicit logical subjects of *get* passives were nonagent sources, while the logical subjects of *be* passives were general agents. Given the normative, generic quality noted for *be* passives, this pattern is not surprising.

Overall the specific direction of the distributional regularities follows from what one would expect if the *get* and *be* passives expressed two distinct activity types of the sort proposed.

The question can be raised, where do the children's meaning associations come from? A preliminary consideration is whether children perhaps do not in fact draw semantic distinctions between *get* and *be* passives. Instead they might simply learn on a verb-by-verb basis from the input which verbs take *be* and which take *get* (see Brown, 1973; Kuczaj, 1978 for consideration of this possibility with respect to which verbs can take progressive *-ing*, or Gordon and Chafetz i.p. for a discussion of verb-by-verb learning for passives, in general). At best however, verb-by-verb learning can account only for the earliest passives. By the age of 3;6 both of Bowerman's children used passivized novel verbs.

General Discussion

At this point we can relate the findings from the study presented here with the research summarized in the first section of this article. I have noted that a central function of the passive in English is to promote nonagent elements into subject position. In particular, Van Oosten (1985) notes that adult speakers of English also use passives to emphasize the result of an action on the patient or, more generally, to focus attention on the patient. I have found that the children studied in the research reported above also used the passive to place emphasis on patients. However, the children limited their use of patient-topicalizing passives to scenes in which the action negatively affected the patient.

Van Oosten (1985) has also stressed that another central function of the English passive is to demote the agent. She claims that agents that are demoted often deviate from prototypical agency or are not relevant to the discourse. The present studies suggest that preschool children acquiring English also use the passive to indicate that the agent deviates from prototypical agency or is irrelevant to the discourse.

There is an overlap between the findings of the present research and the linguistic literature discussed earlier on the relationship between the use of *get* and *be* passives. In previous literature, it has been claimed that *get* passives mark extra meaning in adult speech. Although different investigations have highlighted slightly different meaning nuances, many agree that *get* passives convey a greater degree of speaker involvement, based on positive or negative consequences of the action carried out. *Be* passives, in contrast, are taken to be the unmarked case: their meaning is implicitly assumed to be similar to that expressed by the active voice. The findings from the present research suggest that children, like adults, are sensitive to distinct form–function pairings. In particular, they associate the use of *get* passives with an activity scene in which an action brings about negative consequences. Children also appear to limit *be* passives to a particular activity scene involving a generic or unknown agent, or one who is irrelevant to the discourse. This specific linkage of *be* passives to such a function has not been discussed in previous literature.

The present research agrees with previous developmental studies but goes beyond them to add three important specifications. First, it has suggested that agent demotion plays as much a role in passives as does patient promotion. In addition, it has highlighted the importance of examining distinctions between passives involving different auxiliaries. *Get* and *be* passives were used contrastively by the children in the present studies. Finally, it suggests the importance of analyzing not only the semantic class of verbs passivized by children but also the kinds of agent and patient arguments referred to. The verbs the children passivized tended to rank high in transitivity (Maratsos et al., 1985) and could be construed as having agent/patient arguments (Pinker et al., 1987). However, the children limited the passive to scenes involving particular kinds of agents (for example, generic, unknown, or irrelevant to the discourse) or patients (for example, those in sentences in which the speaker focuses on the consequences of the action received).

The suggestion that children use passives with particular agent or patient arguments provides a partial answer to the question raised earlier in connection with Maratsos et al.'s and Pinker et al.'s hypotheses about semantic restrictions. Why do children at times passivize action verbs when they could also use the active voice? The paradox to be accounted for relates to the claims that *both* actives and passives are associated with highly transitive verbs. My claim is that the children do so for discursive purposes: they use the passive as a way to talk about an event from a nonagentive perspective. For instance, they switch to the passive to talk about an event in which the agent is unknown, generic, or irrelevant to the discourse, or when they wish to downplay agency and emphasize the consequences of a particular action for a patient.

The present research illustrates a way in which researchers interested in examining form–function relationships can integrate analysis of naturalistic data with experimental design. While this procedure is straightforward, most research makes use of either one or the other design (see Clark and Carpenter, 1989 for a similar point). The advantages of such an integration are that one can (1) empirically test the robustness of predictions based on an analysis of spontaneous productions of a limited number of children, and (2) assure that experimental tasks are sensitive to the form–function relationships they are designed to examine. For instance, most of the previous experimental studies of the passive involve tasks in which a picture is provided of a specific agent or in which the child is requested to act out scenes involving a specific agent. These designs are at odds with the major function of *be* passives in English-speaking children's spontaneous speech – to talk about an event in which the agent is unknown, generic, or irrelevant to the discourse. A major challenge for future research is to design experiments testing nonprototypical instances of agency.

Future research should consider the present findings from a cross-linguistic perspective. Slobin (1985) suggests that children around the world give special linguistic attention to scenes involving prototypical agency. The question remains whether children acquiring other languages attempt to linguistically mark a scene involving nonprototypical agency, and, if so, whether passive constructions fulfill this function. Cross-linguistic research will not only provide a better understanding of the function of the passive in child language, but will also enable us to draw conclusions about whether children use voice contrasts to shift perspective away from the prototypical agentive scene.

References

Bamberg, M. (1987). *The Acquisition of Narratives: Learning to Use Language*. Berlin: Mouton de Gruyter.

Bamberg, M. (i.p.). Narrative as perspective taking: the role of emotionals, negations, and voice in the construction of the story realm. *Journal of Cognitive Psychotherapy*.

Banks, D. (1986). Getting by with get. *La Linguistique*, 22 (1), 125–130.

Barber, E. (1975). Voice – beyond the passive. In *Proceedings of the First Annual Meeting of the Berkeley Linguistics Society*, pp. 16–24. Berkeley, CA: Berkeley Linguistics Society.

Bever, T. (1970). The cognitive basis for linguistic structure. In J.R. Hayes (Ed.), *Cognition and the Development of Language*. New York: Wiley.

Brown, R. (1973). *A First Language: The Early Stages*. Cambridge, MA: Harvard University Press.

Budwig, N. (1986). Agentivity and control in early child language. Unpublished dissertation, University of California, Berkeley.

Budwig, N. (1989). The linguistic marking of agentivity and control in child language. *Journal of Child Language*, 16, 263–284.

Clark, E., & Carpenter, K. (1989). On children's uses of *from*, *by* and *with* in oblique noun phrases. *Journal of Child Language*, 16, 349–364.

Comrie, B. (1981). *Language Universals and Linguistic Typology*. Chicago: University of Chicago Press.

Cooper, W., & Ross, J. (1975). World order. In R.E. Grossman, L.J. San, & T.J. Vance (Eds.), *Functionalism*. Chicago: Chicago Linguistic Society, University of Chicago.

DeLancey, S. (1984). Notes on agentivity and causation. *Studies in Language*, 8, 181–213.

de Villiers, J.G., & de Villiers, P.A. (1973). Development of the use of word order in comprehension. *Journal of Psycholinguistic Research, 2,* 331–341.

Frvin-Tripp, S. (1987). Speech acts and syntactic development: linked or independent? Keynote address. Twelfth Annual Boston University Conference on Language Development, October.

Fraser, C., Bellugi, U., & Brown, R. (1963). Control of grammar in imitation, comprehension, and production. *Journal of Verbal Learning and Verbal Behavior, 2,* 121–135.

Gee, J.P. (1974). "Get passive": on some constructions with "get". Bloominton: Indiana University Linguistics Club.

Gee, J., & Savasir, I. (1985). On the use of WILL and GONNA: towards a description of activity-types for child language. *Discourse Processes, 8* (2), 143–175.

Gerhardt, J. (n.d.). The language of accountability: children's expression of different reasons for their actions through the use of the catenative system. Unpublished manuscript.

Givón, T. (1979). *On Understanding Grammar.* New York: Academic Press.

Givón, T. (1984). *Syntax: A Functional-Typological Introduction.* Amsterdam: Benjamins.

Gordon, P., & Chafetz, J. (1989). Verb-based vs. class-based accounts of actionality effects in children's comprehension of the passive. *Cognition.*

Harris, F., & Flora, J. (1982). Children's use of *get* passives. *Journal of Psycholinguistic Research, 11,* 297–311.

Hatcher, A. (1949). To get/be invited. *Modern Language Notes, 64* (7), 433–434.

Hopper, P., & Thompson, S. (1980). Transitivity in grammar and discourse. *Language, 56,* 251–299.

Horgan, D. (1978). The development of the full passive. *Journal of Child Language, 5,* 65–80.

Jespersen, O. (1965 [1924]). *The Philosophy of Grammar.* New York: Norton.

Kuczaj, S. (1978). Why do children fail to produce the progressive inflection? *Journal of Child Language, 5,* 167–171.

Lakoff, G. (1977). Linguistic gestalts. In W. Beach, S. Fox, & S. Philosoph (Eds.), *Papers from the Thirteenth Regional Meeting.* Chicago: Chicago Linguistic Society, University of Chicago.

Lakoff, R. (1971). Passive resistance. In *Papers from the Seventh Meeting of the Chicago Linguistic Society.* Chicago: Chicago Linguistic Society, University of Chicago.

Lee, L. (1974). *Developmental Sentence Analysis: A Grammatical Assessment Procedure for Speech and Language Clinicians.* Evanston, IL: Northwestern University Press.

Lempert, H. (1989). Animacy constraints on pre-school children's acquisition of syntax. *Child Development, 60,* 237–245.

Lempert, H. (i.p.). Acquisition of passives: the role of patient animacy, salience, and lexical accessibility. *Journal of Child Language.*

Lyons, J. (1977). *Semantics,* Vol. 2. Cambridge: Cambridge University Press.

Maratsos, M. (1974). Children who get worse at understanding the passive: a replication of Bever. *Journal of Psycholinguistic Research, 3,* 65–74.

Maratsos, M., Fox, D., Becker, J., & Chalkley, M. (1985). Semantic restrictions on children's passives. *Cognition, 19,* 167–191.

Palmer, F. (1986). *Mood and Modality.* Cambridge: Cambridge University Press.

Pinker, S., Lebeaux, D., & Frost, L. (1987). Productivity and constraints in the acquisition of the passive. *Cognition, 26,* 195–267.

Quirk, R., & Greenbaum, S. (1973). *A Concise Grammar of Contemporary English.* New York: Harcourt Brace Jovanovich.

Rodino, P.W. (1974). Transcripts of eight recorded presidential conversations. Hearings before the Committee on the Judiciary, House of Representatives, Ninety-Third Congress. Second Session, May–June 1974, Serial No. 34.

Savasir, I. (1983). How many futures? Unpublished masters thesis, University of California. Berkeley.

Schibsbye, K. (1970). *A Modern English Grammar.* Oxford: Oxford University Press.

Seifer, N. (1976). *Nobody Speaks for Me! Self-Portraits of American Working-Class Women.* New York: Simon and Schuster.

Slobin, D. (1981). The origins of grammatical encoding of events. In W. Deutsch (Ed.), *The Child's Construction of Grammar.* London: Academic Press.

Slobin, D. (1985). Crosslinguistic evidence for the language making capacity. In D. Slobin (Ed.), *The Crosslinguistic Study of Language Acquisition.* Hillsdale, NJ: Erlbaum.

Slobin, D. (1987). Frequency reflects function. Paper presented at Conference on the Interaction of Form and Function in Language, University of California at Davis.

Standwell, G. (1981). The get-passive and the be-passive. *British Journal of Languages Teaching, 19* (3), 163–164.

Stein, G. (1979). *Studies in the Function of the Passive.* Tübingen: Narr.

Talmy, L. (1985). Force dynamics in language and thought. In *Parasession on Causatives and Agentivity.* Chicago: Chicago Linguistic Society, University of Chicago.

Turner, E., & Rommetveit, R. (1967). Experimental manipulation of the production of active and passive voice in children. *Language and Speech, 10,* 169–180.

Van Oosten, J. (1985). The nature of subjects, topics and agents: a cognitive explanation Bloomington: Indiana University Linguistics Club.

FIFTEEN

Acquisition of Complementation

Lois Bloom, Matthew Rispoli, Barbara Gartner,
and Jeremie Hafitz

Introduction

The study reported here is part of a larger investigation into the acquisition of complex sentences by four children between two and three years of age. We have defined *complex sentences* in child speech as sentences with two verbs that express two propositions (Bloom et al., 1980). *Complementation* is the special instance of complex sentences in which one proposition serves as an argument *within* another proposition (see also the definitions in Quirk et al., 1972). Those complement-taking verbs that take the *to*-complementizer (e.g., *want to* and *have to*) were the subject of an earlier report (Bloom, et al., 1984). For the purposes of the present study, all the remaining complement-taking verbs that this same group of children learned in this period were examined. Verbs were identified as complement-taking verbs if (1) they could take sentential complements (e.g., *I* THINK *I can put him in a house*) or (2) they could take *Wh*-complementizers with null arguments (e.g., LOOK *at what the little bear's eating*).

All the complement-taking verbs in the children's speech are listed in Table 15.1 along with the number of children who used those verbs productively. Productivity was defined as three different sentences with a particular matrix verb. The verbs are categorized here according to their superordinate meaning. Four verbs were chosen for analysis in the present study (*think, know, see,* and *look (at)*[1]) because these were the only matrix verbs that were productive in the speech of all the children (except the volition/intention verbs that take *to* complements, reported in Bloom et al., 1984). These same four verbs were also reported in descriptions of the acquisition of complementation in child speech by Limber (1973) and Pinker (1984).

Complement-taking verbs are developmentally interesting for both linguistic and psychological reasons. Linguistically, they provide the first forms of complex sentences in child speech after the acquisition of simple sentence and question frames (Limber, 1973; Bloom et al., 1980; Pinker, 1984). Psychologically, these verbs name internal, mental states rather than actions and, moreover, the mental states they name are directed toward actions or other internal states. The emergence of complementation in child speech is, then, a qualitative development in both linguistic and psychological

Table 15.1   Lexical categorization of complement-taking verbs[a]

	Perception	Epistemic	Volition/Intention	Communication	Causative
Four children	see look (at)	think know	want like go have	–	–
At least two children	watch show	–	got try	say tell	let make
One child	–	forget wonder remember bet mean afraid	need	–	help get

[a] The productivity criterion for inclusion here was the occurrence of at least three different sentences with a particular verb in one observation session. The volition/intention verbs are the same as those taking *to*-complements and are reported in Bloom et al. (1984).

complexity. The purpose of this study was to investigate factors that contribute to this development.

Procedure

Transcripts of naturally occurring child speech, annotated with descriptions of context and relevant activity, were examined for evidence of (1) the developing productivity of complement-taking verbs, (2) their discourse contexts, and (3) the surface structures of sentences with matrix verbs, including complement type and complementizer connectives.

Subjects and methods

The speech of four children – Eric, Gia, Kathryn, and Peter – was studied longitudinally from two to three years of age and provided the data we present here. The children were first-born, of college-educated parents, and lived in university communities in New York City. The children were observed in their homes during routine activities of daily living and while playing with a group of toys in interaction with an investigator or their mothers.

For the present study, data are reported for three of the children from five observation sessions, each lasting approximately eight hours, at six-week intervals. For the fourth child, Peter, observation sessions were shorter (approximately five hours), with one-month intervals between sessions, and data are reported from seven observation

Table 15.2 Age and mean length of utterance for two developmental times

	Times[a]	Number of sessions	Age		MLU	
			Range	Mean	Range	Mean
Eric	1	3	2;1.1–2;5.3	2;3.1	2.63–3.45	2.97
	2	2	2;9.0–3;0.0	2;10.2	3.49–4.21	3.85
Gia	1	3	2;1.2–2;4.2	2;3.2	2.30–3.07	2.71
	2	2	2;6.0–2;10.2	2;8.1	3.64–3.71	3.68
Kathryn	1	3	2;0.2–2;5.1	2;2.3	2.83–3.35	3.16
	2	2	2;8.1–2;11.1	2;9.3	3.70–4.23	3.97
Peter	1	3	2;3.0–2;6.0	2;4.2	2.63–2.90	2.75
	2	4	2;7.2–3;2.0	2;10.2	3.05–3.58	3.37

[a] Times 1 and 2 are the result of grouping data, with Time 1 = MLU < 3.5, and Time 2 = MLU > 3.5.

sessions. A summary description of the children in terms of age and mean length of utterance (MLU) is presented in Table 15.2. In this and subsequent tables and figures, Times 1 and 2 represent a grouping of the data on the basis of MLU, for the purpose of identifying developmental trends. The MLU criterion for distinguishing between Times 1 and 2 was 3.5 morphemes (or its closest equivalent).

The sentences analyzed for this study represented only 0.007 of all the utterances that the children produced in these sessions between two and three years of age. The four children produced approximately 79,000 utterances altogether. All instances of verbs that could take complements were extracted from the corpus whether or not they occurred with complements and/or complementizer connectives. In all, over 6,000 sentences with such verbs occurred. The acquisition of those verbs that take *to* complements was described in another study (Bloom et al., 1984). The remaining verbs that could take *S-* or *Wh*-complements and were used in the speech of all four children are the subject of this study: *think, know, see,* and *look* (at). Approximately 2,600 sentences occurred with these verbs, and in 577 of these sentences the verbs occurred as matrix verbs with complements.

Results

The first result is the distribution of the epistemic and perception verbs, with and without complement structures, in the child data. The subsequent results concern only the sentences with complementation and consist of (1) their discourse contingencies and (2) the subcategorization of complement types, complementizer connectives, and co-occurrence restrictions. As will be seen, these subcategorization phenomena in the course of the children's acquisition were not always consistent with the target language they were learning.

Table 15.3 Frequencies of complement and non-complement sentences

		Perception		Epistemic	
		see	look	know	think
Eric					
Time 1	+COMP	15	13	6	12
	−COMP	349	161	4	2
Time 2	+COMP	53	8	27	42
	−COMP	96	119	68	5
Gia					
Time 1	+COMP	1	9	1	7
	−COMP	115	27	4	3
Time 2	+COMP	23	10	11	5
	−COMP	77	58	14	1
Kathryn					
Time 1	+COMP	23	7	7	30
	−COMP	174	40	1	4
Time 2	+COMP	45	4	9	44
	−COMP	223	37	4	41
Peter					
Time 1	+COMP	17	3	20	3
	−COMP	165	63	6	5
Time 2	+COMP	30	8	49	35
	−COMP	87	89	16	4
Totals	+COMP	207	62	130	178
	−COMP	1286	594	117	65

Distribution of verbs

The frequency with which each verb occurred, both with and without complementation, is presented in Table 15.3. The perception verbs occurred with complements, on average, 12.5% of the time (*see* 14%, *look* 10%). Examples of perception verbs without complements were:

1   Eric: Doggie is looking up.
2   Kathryn: And nobody can see him.

Examples of these verbs with complements were:

3   Gia: Look *what my mommy got me.*
4   Kathryn: I'll see *where it is.*

See was the most frequent of these verbs overall; although *see* occurred only 14% of the time with a complement, it was the most frequent matrix verb with complements in the corpus.

Epistemic verbs appeared with complements, on average, 64% of the time (*know* 44%, *think* 83%). Examples of epistemic verbs without complements included routine phrases like *I don't know*, *You know?*, *I think so*, and *Think so?*, but also:

    5   Eric: I don't know that part.
    6   Kathryn: I think up on this bed.

Examples of these verbs with complements were:

    7   Peter: Know *what the other ones do?*
    8   Gia: I think *the children go to bed.*

Thus, except for their routine phrases (e.g., *I don't know*), these children used the epistemic verbs largely as complement-taking verbs.

Discourse environment

All sentences with complement clauses were examined for evidence of textual contingency. *Textual contingency* was defined as the adult having said something within five prior speaker turns that included either the matrix verb or part of the complement of the child utterance. These two sources of contingency were not mutually exclusive. A sentence could have been said by a child when the adult had already said a sentence with that matrix verb, or some part of the adult's sentence could have become a part of the complement in the child's sentence, or both these things could have happened.

For example, the children's sentences were textually contingent when an adult utterance introduced a verb or argument that appeared subsequently in the complement of the child sentence, for example:

    9   Adult: Let's see how this one *works*.
        Kathryn: You know how it *works?*

The frequency with which the complement in the children's sentences included something from a prior adult utterance is presented in figure 15.1. Complements with *think* repeated something from a prior utterance most often (66% on average); sentences with *look* (*at*) did so the least (16% on average).

Textual contingency also included the child's use of a matrix verb when the matrix verb had been used by an adult in a prior utterance, for example:

    10   Adult: I *think* that lamb is cold.
        Eric: He is very cold/I *think* I can put him in a house.

(Range and mean)

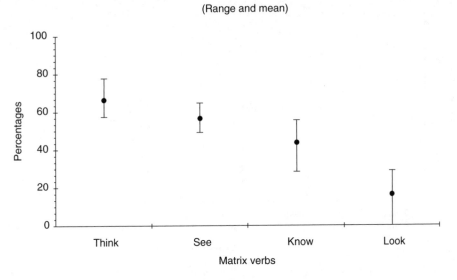

Figure 15.1   Complement contingency.

The matrix verb *think* was repeated from a prior adult utterance more often than any other matrix verb. On average, *think* had prior adult introduction into discourse 32% of the time and *see* 11%, while *know* and *look* (*at*) had prior adult use only occasionally.

We interpret these results to mean that *think* was most likely maintain the discourse topic while *look* (*at*) was most likely to introduce a new topic. However, this conclusion is not independent of a second conclusion, that hearing the matrix verb and/or some part of what the child would say also made it more likely that the child would use a matrix verb with complementation. *Think*, the verb that was most frequently contingent, was also the matrix verb with the highest proportion of complementation.

Complementation structure

Complement type subcategorization

The two complement types were (1) sentential complements (*S*-complements), for example:

11   Kathryn: I see *Mommy washing her hands*.

and (2) *Wh*-complements, for example:

12   Kathryn: Let's go see *where Mommy is*.

The average frequency of Verb + Complement types is presented for each verb in figure 15.2. The development of complementation in this period of time is apparent: except

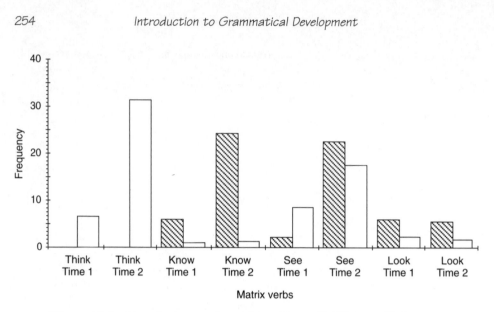

Figure 15.2 Mean frequency of complement types. ▨, *Wh*-comp; ☐, *S*-comp.

for sentences with *look*, complementation was more frequent in Time 2 than in Time 1. However, the production of particular complement types was not independent of the matrix verbs.

Think appeared only with *S*-complements (as expected). *S*-complements occurred more frequently with *think* than with any other verb for all the children in both time periods. The other epistemic verb, *know*, appeared almost exclusively with *Wh*-complements, for example:

13   Gia: You know *what's in this bag?*

and rarely with *S*-complements, for example:

14   Eric: I know *I open it up.*

Both complement types were used with *see*. Before MLU reached 3.5 (in Time 1) the most frequent complement type with *see* was sentential, while *Wh*-complement sentences were less frequent. Once MLU exceeded 3.5 (in Time 2) the balance was reversed and *Wh*-complements were more frequent than *S*-complements. However, this reversal was due almost entirely to one child, Eric. At Time 1 Eric produced 14 *S*-complements with *see*, for example:

15   Eric: I see *two bus come there.*[2]

and one *Wh*-complement sentence. At Time 2 he produced only eight sentences with *see* and *S*-complements, and 45 sentences with *see* and a *Wh*-complement, for example:

16   Eric: Let's see *what's in the train house.*

Table 15.4 Average age of emergence for *Wh*-question words and *Wh*-complement words

Wh-Q[a] words	Average age	Number of children[b]	*Wh*-COMP words	Average age	Number of children[c]
what	2; 2	7	–	–	–
where	2; 2	7	–	–	–
who	2; 4	7	–	–	–
–	–	–	what	2; 6	4
–	–	–	where	2; 7.2	3
how	2; 9	7	how	2; 9.2	3
–	–	–	(if)	2; 10	4
why	2; 11	7	who	2; 11	3

[a] The results for *Wh*-question words are from Bloom et al. (1982).
[b] $n = 7$.
[c] $n = 4$.

S-complements appeared with *look at* (15 instances among the four children), for example:

17   Peter: Look at *that airplane coming out the airplane home.*

However, in both developmental periods, *Wh*-complements with *look* (as in example 3 above) were more frequent.

In sum, the two epistemic verbs took different complement types: *S*-complements occurred with *think* and *Wh*-complements occurred with *know*. Overall, *Wh*-complementation was more frequent than *S*-complements with the perception verbs, especially in Time 2, and *S*-complements were more frequent with *see* than with *look (at)*.

Acquisition of complementizer connectives

Wh-complements were not expected with *think* and were not observed. Otherwise, the complementizers these children learned with *know*, *see*, and *look (at)* were the same words, except for *if*, that they had acquired earlier in their *Wh*-questions (Bloom et al., 1982). *If*, which is not a *Wh*-question word, was the last of the complementizers they acquired in this period. The order of emergence of *Wh*-complementizers resembled the earlier emergence order of *Wh*-questions. The two emergence orders are compared in Table 15.4.

The emergence age for *Wh*-questions in Table 15.4 is the average for seven children (from Bloom et al., 1982); the emergence age of the complementizers is an average for four of the same children. Consistent with Bloom et al. (1982), emergence was considered the beginning of productivity and was defined as at least three different complements used with a particular *Wh*-complementizer. As can be seen, these children asked *what* and *where* questions four months (on average) before they used *what* and *where* as complementizers. Two complementizers, *where* and *how*, reached productivity for three children. *How* did not become productive in questions until approximately

Table 15.5 Distribution, order of emergence and number of children using the different connectives

---

Distribution of connectives

see-what (4)[a]	know-what (4)	look-what (4)
see-if (4)	know-where (3)	
see-how (2)	know-how (1)	
see-where (1)		

Order of emergence of connectives

$\left|\begin{matrix} \text{know-what} \\ \text{see-what} \end{matrix}\right| > \text{look-what (3)}$

know-what > see-what > look-what (1)

know-where > see-where (1)

see-if > know-if (1)

---

[a] Number of children in parentheses.

seven months after *what* and *where* questions, but unlike *what* and *where*, *how* emerged as both a question word and a complementizer at about the same time. The last *Wh*-word to become productive in the children's questions, *why*, was not acquired as a complementizer in the time period covered by this study.

Wh-words are not perceptually salient as complementizers because they occur in the middle of a sentence between the matrix verb and the complement. Their acquisition for complementation may have depended, in part, upon prior segmentation in the more salient, sentence-initial position as *Wh*-question words, much as the complementizer *to* was learned after the preposition *to* (Bloom et al., 1984; Pinker, 1984).

Use of the different complementizer connectives was verb specific. This result is presented in Table 15.5. Of the three verbs with *Wh*-complementizers, only *see* was productive with all four connectives; *know* was productive with three; and *look (at)* was productive only with *what*. The only *Wh*-complementizer acquired with all the matrix verbs (except *think*) was *what*, and *what* was used by all the children with each of the three verbs that took complementizers. However, the different connectives did not appear at the same time with the different matrix verbs. The order of emergence is presented in Table 15.5. *What* was acquired with *look (at)* only after it had become productive with *know* and *see*. *Where* was productive with *know* before *see*, while *if* was productive with *see* before *know*. These results mean that the acquisition of a complementizer did not promptly generalize to all of the children's matrix verbs that could take that complementizer. Rather, these children acquired the complementizer connectives verb by verb.

That was rare as a complementizer in these sentences. A total of 179 complement sentences with *think* were said by all the children, but only three of these included *that* as a connective, for example:

18   Gia: I think *that* he wanna eat this.

These children certainly knew the word; demonstrative pronouns were among the earliest forms in their simple sentences (Bloom, 1970). In addition, *that* appeared with other functions in the complements. *That* appeared 14 times as the subject of the complement verb, in the same deictic sentence frame which had been productive from the beginning of these children's multiword speech, for example:

19   Kathryn: I thought *that was a snacktime.*
20   Eric: I think *that is a porkypine.*

In addition, 35 complement sentences occurred with the copula as the matrix verb (not considered in the study reported here), and 25 of these included *that* as a deictic subject, for example:

21   Eric: *That* where the butterfly live.
22   Peter: *That's* how get them out.

Although *this* was frequent as a determiner in the complement subject, only one instance of *that* occurred in the same position:

23   Kathryn: I think *that* girl is going to dust that that paper away.

(Note also that Kathryn stumbled on the subsequent use of *that* in the same sentence.)

Three factors could have contributed to *that* not being acquired for complementation in the period studied here. First, the plurifunctionality of *that* may have inhibited its acquisition as a complementizer. Since an item with more than one function *within* a sentence presumably increases perceptual difficulty (Bever, 1970), we might expect an item with several functions in different sentences to be more difficult to acquire. In this instance, then, the prior acquisition of *that* with other functions did not facilitate its acquisition as a complementizer, as had been suggested for the acquisition of the plurifunctional *to* and the *Wh*-forms (both of which have only two possible functions). A second factor is, of course, input frequency. We do not know how often these children heard *that* as a complementizer with *think*, *know*, or *see* in this time period.

In addition, Jespersen pointed out that complementation without *that* is especially frequent after such verbs as *think*, *know*, and *see*, but in these cases "it is historically wrong to say that the conjunction *that* is omitted" (1956, p. 32). Complementation with and without *that* evolved out of independent sentences, for example, (1) *I think that S* and (2) *I think S*. Originally *that* in (1) was a demonstrative pronoun object of the verb (i.e., *I think that*). The distinction in this historical argument is relevant to these children's development inasmuch as they did not say sentences like *I think that* or *I know that* and also did not use *that* as a complementizer.

Co-occurrence restrictions on matrix and complement verbs

Two features distinguished the surface syntax of the matrix and complement clauses. First, the matrix subjects were hightly restricted while the subjects of complement verbs were varied. Second, matrix verbs were rarely inflected whereas the subordinate verb in the complement was often either inflected or marked for modality.

Subject restrictions

Certain restrictions would be expected on the matrix verbs studied here. For example, only animate subjects can see, look, think, and know. However, the differences in variety of subjects of the subordinate and matrix verbs were greater than would be predicted by the target language.

Subjects of subordinate verbs.   The subordinate complement clauses were copular constructions, with pronominal subjects, in an average of 48% of the sentences with *know*, 35% with *think*, 31% with *see*, and 8% with *look (at)*, for example:

24   Kathryn: I think *it's* big enough.
25   Eric: Know *what's* in here?
26   Gia: I'm going to see if *there's* any more.

Otherwise, a full variety of first-, second-, and third-person subjects occurred in the complements, both nominal, for example:

27   Eric: Look at *that donkey* carrying baskets.

and pronominal, for example:

28   Kathryn: I think *we* can put it side of him.

Subjects of matrix verbs.   In contrast, the subjects of matrix verbs were highly restricted. To begin with, no subjects were expressed with *look*; all were null second person (as in 27). The matrix verb *think* occurred only with *I* in the speech of three of the children. Only Peter, whose earliest and latest sentences with *think* included only *I*, produced *think* sentences in the interim without *I*. Most of these were null first person, but several were null second person and one second-person subject was expressed:

29   Peter: *You* think it don't belongs to me.

The subjects of sentences with *know* and *see* were only somewhat more varied, and the order of acquisition differed for the different children. Both Gia and Eric began saying sentences with these two matrix verbs first with first-person *I*, and then with second-person *you* both expressed and null. Kathryn and Peter both began to say sentences with *know* and *see* with null second-person subjects (Kathryn also expressed second-person *you*) before they used these matrix verbs with *I*. Neither Gia, Kathryn, nor Peter used any of their matrix verbs with third-person subjects. Only Eric eventually used both of these matrix verbs with third-person subjects, for example:

30   Oh *the bunny rabbit* doesn't know what to do.

In sum, this group of matrix verbs were verbs that named internal mental states and they were acquired to express these states of the child and, to a lesser extent, of the child's discourse partner. They were not used to express the child's attributions of such states to others who were not participants in the discourse (in contrast to the data reported by Shatz et al., 1983). On the one hand, the use of these verbs in the children's speech was consistent with accounts that have described limitations on the preschool child's awareness of the mental states of other persons (e.g., Piaget, 1955; Wellman, 1985). On the other hand, the fact that these children did not talk about what third persons see, look at, think, or know is not by itself evidence that they could not attribute these internal states to other persons. By the age of three years children are able to attribute seeing and looking to other persons (Flavell, 1977). Mothers of children in the same age-range as the children studied here have reported that their children use perception words (and significantly more often than epistemic words) in talking about other persons (Bretherton & Beeghly, 1982). Nevertheless, the differences between matrix and subordinate subjects were not entirely predicted by the target language.

Coreference

The children's sentences were examined to determine the coreference of the subject of the complement verb. A total of 332 complements occurred with nominal or personal pronoun subjects, and in only 46 (14%) was the subject of the complement verb coreferent with an expressed subject of the matrix verb. Of these coreferent subjects, 61% occurred with *think*, 28% with *see*, 11% with *know*, and none with *look* (*at*). Thus when coreferent subjects did occur, these were with *think* most often, for example:

31   Kathryn: *I think I*'ll pull the other side.

Sentences with such volition/intention verbs as *want*, *like*, and *go* were productive with *to*-complements in these children's speech about two months earlier than complementation with epistemic and perception verbs (reported in Bloom et al., 1984). In sentences with *to*-complements the subject of the matrix verb was also the subject of the complement verb. The children were most often talking about what it was that they wanted to do or were going to do. Non-coreferent subjects appeared in sentences with *to* after MLU 3.5, and this was after non-coreferent subjects appeared with the epistemic and perception verbs. This sequence of development (from Bloom et al., 1984 together with the present study) was the same sequence that Pinker (1984) also observed. Complementation with subject coreference (with *to*-complement verbs and then with *think*) occurred before complementation with non-coreferent subjects.

Morphological marking

Matrix verbs and subordinate complement verbs also differed in the extent to which they were inflected and/or marked for modality. Again, this difference was not entirely predicted by the target language.

Matrix verbs.   The restrictions on subjects of matrix verbs and the fact that these verbs were state rather than process verbs limited the opportunities for matrix verb inflection.

No inflections occurred with *look* (*at*) but none was expected since *look* (*at*) occurred only with second-person subjects in the imperative. *Know* was limited to either first- or second-person subjects and used frequently with generic copular statements in the complement. *Know* was never inflected. *Think* was used almost exclusively with first-person *I* but only Kathryn used *think* with past tense (6 instances, e.g., (19) above).

See was used with only first- and second-person subjects. It was never infected. However, *see* was the one matrix verb that occurred with adverbial or modal marking with any regularity. Twenty-four percent of the sentences with *see* as a matrix verb also included an adverb (e.g., *now*) or modal, for example:

32   Peter: *Wanna see* I make a ball with my gum?

The children differed in the matrix adverbials and modals used with *see*. Eric used only *let's* (16 above) and *now*; Gia used *gonna* and *wanna*; Kathryn used *let's* (12 above); and Peter used *wanna* (32 above). While the modals would not be expected with *think*, they might have occurred with *know* and *look*, but did not.

Subordinate verbs.   In contrast to the matrix verbs, the subordinate verbs in the complement were inflected or occurred with marked modality more than 50% of the time. However, subordinate verbs were used with modals primarily in sentences with *think* and *see* (65% of the modals in complement sentences occurred after *think* and 29% after *see*), for example:

33   Eric: I *think* we *should* put this in a house.

Except for Gia, the children used modals with subordinate verbs after *see* and most of these (64% of the modal complement sentences with *see*) were *can* after the complementizer *if*, for example:

34   Kathryn: *See if* it *can* make some sound.

Together, these results lead to the same conclusion offered above with respect to discourse function, complement type, and selection of complementizer connectives: the syntax of sentences with complements was matrix verb specific. Different co-occurrence restrictions on verb inflections, modality, and subjects were observed with the different matrix verbs. In addition, the matrix verbs, as a group, were more restricted in their co-occurrence than were the subordinate verbs in the complement.

Discussion

The results presented here together with the results reported in Bloom et al. (1984) document the beginning of the acquisition of complementation in the year between the ages of two and three. We will discuss these results in terms of two aspects of the acquisition of complementation with perception and epistemic verbs: the use of developmentally prior linguistic forms for acquiring the syntax of complementation, and the meaning function that these complement-taking verbs served in the mental life of the child.

The origin of the structures of complementation

Both complementizers and complement types were based upon structures previously acquired. The children were ready to produce both *S*-complement and *Wh*-complement structures in the first developmental period of this study because they already knew their basic surface structures from earlier learned sentence frames. As observed originally by Limber, "complex sentences will be formed from the child's repertoire of simple sentences" (1973, p. 184).

S-complementation was essentially the addition of a simple sentence frame after a matrix verb. Sentences with *Wh*-complements consisted of a *Wh*-question word and a sentence with elision of the element corresponding to the question word. The syntax of *Wh*-complements was the same as in children's early questions. When children first begin to ask *Wh*-questions, they often start the question with a *Wh*-word and add a simple sentence (e.g., *What you doing?* and *Where the ball go?*). Similarly, when these children began to produce *Wh*-complements, they added the matrix verb to a *Wh*-question (e.g., *See what you doing* and *Know where the ball go*). Interestingly, "errors" like *I don't know what's his problem* are found even among adults (Fay, 1980, p. 117). Thus the developmental origins of both *S*-complements and *Wh*-complements were in the structures acquired at an earlier time for simple sentences and asking *Wh*-questions.

However, this process of acquisition consisted of more than the simple addition of forms. For example, while certain co-occurrence restrictions on matrix verbs could have been expected (e.g., lack of tense inflections with second-person subjects in the imperative), others were not (e.g., the lack of modals with subordinate verbs after *know* and *look*, or the occurrence of adverbs and modals in the matrix only with *see*, or the limitations on the subjects of all the matrix verbs). Two factors could explain this pattern of results. One explanation might have been found in the input that the children received, and this is a subject for future research. In addition, however, evidence from psycholinguistic studies of sentence processing has suggested that complement-taking verbs are inherently more difficult than simple transitive verbs for adults to process (Fodor et al., 1968). Children might therefore be expected to have greater difficulty in learning co-occurrence restrictions with complement-taking verbs than with the earlier learned transitive and intransitive verbs that appeared as subordinate verbs in complements.

The acquisition of complementation builds on prior acquisition of simpler structures in yet another way. The acquisition of *Wh*-complementizers followed their prior segmentation in the more salient sentence-initial question frames. To acquire a word as a complementizer requires that "the word in question must be isolated as a word beforehand" (Pinker, 1984, p. 227). Thus *Wh*-complementizers appeared originally as *Wh*-question words. Similarly, the complementizer *to* was segmented first as a preposition before it was acquired as a complementizer (Bloom et al., 1984). When *to* did appear as a complementizer, with volition/intention verbs, it was not semantically empty. Rather, *to* had the meaning "direction toward" which derived historically from the prepositional meaning. A related analysis to demonstrate that the "complementizers (*for*, *to*) [are] identical to prepositions" has since been reported with *for*, which was first used as a complementizer only with purposive meaning (Nishigauchi & Roeper, 1987).[3] The categorization of a word as a complementizer may be "given" along with its categorization as a preposition (Pinker, 1984, p. 226). However, we would suggest instead that the knowledge that a word can also be a complementizer is acquired from observing the distributional regularities of matrix verbs with relevant complementizer connectives in the input. Thus one reason why *that*, which was one of the children's earliest and most frequent words, was not acquired as a complementizer in the period studied here was its perceptual confusability. *That* was learned with several different functions in sentences with matrix verbs.

In sum, the acquisition of complementation began for the four children whom we have studied between their second and third birthdays. This acquisition no doubt continued well into their school years as they learned more different verbs that take complements and more of the lexical, discourse, and syntactic functions of those verbs.

The meaning function of complement-taking verbs

These children acquired the structures of complementation with only a handful of the possible verbs that take complements in adult English (Rosenbaum, 1967). Moreover, the majority of the verbs acquired (in Table 15.1) expressed two superordinate meanings; they were epistemic verbs (e.g., *think* and *know*) and perception verbs (e.g., *see* and *look* (*at*)).

A pattern of lexicalization for the verbs of perception in a sample of 53 languages has been reported by Viberg (1984). Lexical differentiation of the five sensory modalities, sight, hearing, touch, taste, and smell, was hierarchically organized in this typology. The hierarchy is manifested in the extent to which different words name the *activity* and *experience* dimensions in each modality. The modalities of sight and hearing have different lexicalizations for activity and experience most often in these languages. In English, for example, the activity verbs are *look* and *listen* and the experience verbs are *see* and *hear* for sight and hearing, respectively. The modalities of touch, taste, and smell show differentiation between activity and experience much less often, English being an example of a language that does not lexicalize these distinctions (e.g., *taste* in English names both the activity and the experience).

Languages that differentiate activity and experience for only one of the modalities of sight and hearing do so in the sight modality rather than hearing. Sight verbs, then, are at the top of the lexicalization hierarchy for perception verbs, and correspondingly the children in this study differentially lexicalized only sight verbs with complementation. The sight verbs in the speech of all four children were the two basic sight verbs cited by Viberg, *look* (activity) and *see* (experience). Although one or more of the children also acquired other complement-taking perception verbs (in Table 15.1), these were also sight verbs (i.e., the activity verbs *watch* and *show*). The acquisition of complement-taking verbs was thus consistent with the lexicalization hierarchy found for the languages studied by Viberg (1984).

While a similar typology is not available, to our knowledge, for epistemic verbs, the two epistemic verbs the children acquired also distinguished between the activity (*think*) and the experience (*know*). *Think* and *know* were also the most frequent epistemic verbs by far in the longitudinal data reported by Shatz et al. (1983).

While few studies have looked at the uses of such verbs in spontaneous speech, several experimental studies of the comprehension of epistemic verbs have been reported with children as young as three years of age (e.g., Johnson & Maratsos, 1977; Abbeduto & Rosenberg, 1985). The conclusion in these studies was that three-year-olds do not present evidence in comprehension tasks that they understand the differences in the psychological meaning entailments in the terms *think* and *know*. Such under-standing was not reported in these studies until age four. However, in the pattern of results presented here, the two-year-old children whom we studied used these two verbs differently. Moreover, the differences in use suggested that they used these verbs to express an assessment of the "degree of reliability" (Chafe, 1986) of the proposition expressed in the complement of their sentences with *think* and *know*.

These children seemed to have learned *think* and *know* in order to qualify the degree of "certainty/uncertainty" of the complement propositions in their sentences. The expression of uncertainty with *think* was suggested by the following findings. (1) *Think* was most often contingent on prior discourse, suggesting that the children were expressing new information from the prior discourse that they had not yet fully assimilated (Choi, 1986). (2) The frequent use of modals (e.g., *should, can*) with the verbs in complements of *think* expressed a lack of definiteness in the complement. (3) The complementizer *that*, which indicates certainty with *think* (Jespersen, 1956; Quirk et al., 1972), was almost entirely absent from the children's sentences with *think*. Likewise, Limber (1973, p. 185) citing Urmson (1963), observed that *think* was "used parenthetically, especially in the first person, *I*, with the sense of *perhaps* or *maybe*."

A pattern of certainty for *know* was suggested by other findings. (1) Less contextual and textual contingency occurred with *know* than with *think*, indicating that sentences with *know* expressed what the children already had in mind and were prepared to intro-duce into the discourse. (2) *Know* occurred most often with the copula as the subordi-nate verb in the complement, suggesting talk about attributions and generic events. These children, then, differentiated the epistemic verbs with respect to their assessment of the degree of certainty regarding the complement propositions.

Similar attitudinal distinctions could be attributed to the use of the perception verbs *look* and *see*; and *see* was similar to *think* in expressing uncertainty. *See* was second only to *think* in the extent to which the children's sentences repeated something from the prior discourse. *See* was second only to *think* in the frequency of modals in the com-plement and the only one of the matrix verbs used with modals and adverbs. And, finally, *see* occurred with the conditional connective *if* and never with the definite *that*. *Look*, in contrast, suggested an attitude of definiteness or certainty; it was used exclusively with second-person subjects as an imperative, and was contingent on prior discourse least often among all the matrix verbs.

The attitudinal distinctions expressed through the different matrix verbs are best rep-resented by *think* and *look*, the two matrix verbs that were the most clearly differenti-ated: (1) in their superordinate meaning (epistemic/perception), (2) in their functions (first-person statements/second-person imperatives), and (3) the extent to which they incorporated elements from the prior discourse. *Think* expressed the child speaker's uncertainty and continued a topic introduced into the discourse by someone else most

often. *Look* expressed a directive to the hearer and introduced a new topic that originated with what the child had in mind. *Know* and *see* were intermediate between these
two verbs, with *know* closer to *look* in expressing certainty and *see* closer to *think* in
expressing uncertainty. This lexical patterning suggests an intricacy in the emerging
verb lexicon, derived from the child's view of the world, that has both discourse and
syntactic manifestations. It also supports the suggestion that the acquisition of internal state verbs begins with an effort to modify the reliability of statements before the
truly cognitive meanings of the terms are acquired (Johnson, 1982).

Conclusions

The conclusions we draw from these results are consistent with those we have drawn
in other studies of these children's language development: learning the structure of the
language is verb dependent (e.g., Bloom et al., 1975; Bloom, 1981). The study reported
here, together with the study of *to*-complements, revealed developments in the subcategorization of complement structures by matrix verbs. The earlier learned
volition/intention verbs have the inherent meaning "direction toward" and take complements with *to* (Bloom et al., 1984). Epistemic and perception verbs, learned later,
take *S*- and *Wh*-complements. The acquisition of the syntax of complementation was
lexically specific. Rather than learning a general rule for complementation per se, or
even separate rules for *Wh*-complements, *S*-complements, *to* complements, *if* complements, and so forth, the children's grammatical knowledge was specific to the matrix
verbs. The matrix verbs determined whether a complementizer occurred, and if a
complementizer occurred, which one. In the period studied here the children learned
this for each matrix verb separately.

   This developmental account is consistent with the procedures Pinker proposed for
the acquisition of Lexical Function Grammar, whereby children learn that "matrix
verbs specify the formal properties of their complements, such as being finite or infini-
tival, and whether and which complementizers must be present in the complements"
(1984, p. 213). However, in addition, we have proposed that procedures for acquisition
are influenced by the psychological attitudes that children have towards the propositions they express. In sum, the acquisition of complementation depends upon the child
being able to hold in mind two propositions, where one of the propositions is express-
ible in a simple sentence frame and the other is the mental attitude directed toward the
contents of that proposition.

Acknowledgments

The research reported here was funded by research grants from the National Science
Foundation and the National Institutes of Health, for which we are grateful. The results
of this study were originally presented to the Fifth Annual Boston University Conference on Language Development, October 1980. We thank Patsy Lightbown and Lois
(Hood) Holzman for their contribution to the study of these children's language development over a period of several years. We owe a particular debt of gratitude to the chil-

dren – Eric, Gia, Kathryn and Peter – who, although they are now entering their adult years, have always been two-year-olds to us. In their words and the details of that year of their lives, they unwittingly provided us with much to ponder. We thank Richard Beckwith and Margaret Lahey for their helpful comments on earlier drafts of this manuscript.

Notes

1 Sentences with *look* were not included in the analyses reported here if (1) they were spoken with segmentation prosody to indicate a sentence break after the matrix verb, and/or (2) the sentence complement was a complete sentence with no null constituents (e.g., *Look my truck got a top*). In both instances, the data were equivocal as to complementation inasmuch as *look* was potentially a separate sentence.
2 In the absence of AUX, an alternative argument could be made for considering the subordinate verb phrase in sentences like this a reduced relative clause (see also 17 and 21).
3 We thank Richard Beckwith for calling this analysis to our attention.

References

Abbeduto, L., & Rosenberg, S. (1985). Children's knowledge of the presuppositions of *know* and other cognitive verbs. *Journal of Child Language, 12,* 621–641.

Bever, T. (1970). The cognitive basis for linguistic structures. In J. Hayes (Ed.), *Cognition and the development of language.* New York: Wiley.

Bloom, L. (1970). *Language development: form and function in emerging grammars.* Cambridge MA: M.I.T. Press.

Bloom, L. (1981). The importance of language for language development: linguistic determinism in the 1980s. In H. Winitz (Ed.), *Native language and non-native language acquisition.* New York: New York Academy of Sciences.

Bloom, L., Lahey, M., Hood, L., Lifter, K., & Fiess, K. (1980). Complex sentences: acquisition of syntactic connectives and the meaning relations they encode. *Journal of Child Language, 7,* 235–261.

Bloom, L., Merkin, S., & Wootten, J. (1982). *Wh*-questions: linguistic factors that contribute to the sequence of acquisition. *Child Development, 53,* 1084–1092.

Bloom, L., Miller, P., & Hood, L. (1975). Variation and reduction as aspects of competence in language development. In A. Pick (Ed.), *Minnesota symposia on child psychology.* Minneapolis: University of Minnesota.

Bloom, L., Tackeff, J., & Lahey M. (1984). Learning *to* in complement constructions. *Journal of Child Language, 11,* 391–406.

Bretherton, I., & Beeghly, M. (1982). Talking about internal states: the acquisition of an explicit theory of mine. *Developmental Psychology, 18,* 906–921.

Chafe, W. (1986). Evidentiality in English conversation and academic writing. In W. Chafe & J. Nichols (Eds.), *Evidentiality: the linguistic coding of epistemology.* Norwood NJ: Ablex.

Choi, S. (1986). Pragmatic analysis of Korean modal markers in children's speech. Paper presented to the Annual Meeting of the Linguistic Society of America, New York.

Fay, T. (1989). Transformational errors. In V. Fromkin (Ed.), *Errors in linguistic performance: slips of the tongue, ear, pen and hand.* New York: Academic Press.

Flavell, J. (1977). The development of knowledge about visual perception. In C. Keasey (Ed.), *Nebraska symposium on motivation: social cognitive development*. Lincoln/London: University of Nebraska.

Fodor, J., Garrett, M., & Bever, T. (1968). Some syntactic determinants of sentential complexity. II. Verb structure. *Perception and Psychophysics, 3*, 453–461.

Jespersen, O. (1956). *A modern English grammar*, Vol. 3. London: Allen & Unwin.

Johnson, C. (1982). Acquisition of mental verbs and the concept of mind. In s. Kuczaj (Ed.), *Language development*, Vol. 1. Hillsdole NJ: Erlbaum.

Johnson, C., & Maratsos, M. (1977). Early comprehension of mental verbs: *think* and *know. Child Development, 48*, 1743–1747.

Limber, J. (1973). The genesis of complex sentences. In T. Moore (Ed.), *Cognitive development and the acquisition of language*. New York: Academic Press.

Nishigauchi, T., & Roeper, T. (1987). Deductive parameters and the growth of empty categories. In T. Roeper & E. Williams (Eds.), *Parameter setting*. Dorrecht: Reidel.

Piaget, J. (1955). *The language and thought of the child*. Cleveland OH: World Publishing. (Originally published in 1923.)

Pinker, S. (1984). *Language learnability and language development*. Cambridge MA: Harvard University Press.

Quirk, R., Greenhaum, S., Leech, G., & Svartvik, J. (1972). *A grammar of contemporary English*. London: Longman.

Rosenbaum, P. (1967). *The grammar of English predicate complement constructions*. Cambridge MA: M.I.T. Press.

Shatz, M., Wellman, H., & Silber, S. (1983). The acquisition of mental verbs: a systematic investigation of the first reference to mental state. *Cognition, 14*, 301–321.

Urmson, S. (1963). Parenthetical verbs. In C. Caton (Ed.), *Philosophy and ordinary language*. Urbana IL: University of Illinois.

Viberg, A. (1984). The verbs of perception: a topological study. In B. Butterworth, B. Comrie, & O. Dahl (Eds.), *Explanations for language universals*. Berlin: Mouton.

Wellman, H. (1985). The child's theory of mind: the development of conceptions of cognition. In S. Yussen (Ed.), *The growth of reflection in children*. San Diego: Academic Press.

SIXTEEN

Form/Function Relations: How Do Children Find Out What They Are?

Dan I. Slobin

Human languages, broadly speaking, provide two kinds of meaningful elements, using both to create grammatical constructions. On the one hand, there are morphemes that make reference to the objects and events of experience, and on the other, there are morphemes that relate these bits of experience to each other and to the discourse perspectives of the speaker. Linguistic theories of all stripes honor this duality, using such distinctions as "material content" vs. "relation" (Sapir, 1921, 1949), "lexical item" vs. "grammatical item" (Lyons, 1968), or, most commonly, "content word" vs. "function word" (or, to include both free and bound morphemes, "functor"). Typically, the first class includes nouns and verbs, and usually also adjectives; the second class includes free morphemes such as conjunctions and prepositions, and bound morphemes, such as affixes marking such categories as number, case, tense, and so forth. It has generally been claimed that: (1) functors express a limited and universal set of meanings ("grammaticizable notions"), and (2) functor classes are small and closed, while content word classes are large and open. The first claim has led to proposals that the set of meanings is, in some sense, "prespecified" for language; the second has led to proposals that this collection of morphemes plays a critical role in both the acquisition and processing of language. Furthermore, many attempts have been made to relate these two "design features" of language:

- Theorists with a nativist bent – including both generative and cognitive linguists – equip the mind/brain with predispositions to relate particular types of meaning to grammatical elements and syntactic constructions. Such predispositions make it possible for the child to crack the code and for expert language-users to successfully parse sentences. (This position, for example, can be found in Bickerton, 1981, Pinker, 1984, and Slobin, 1985.) On such accounts, the relations between the two design features – limited sets of meanings and limited sets of functors – are facts about the language module or language-making capacity, perhaps in relation to other modules or capacities, but not in need of developmental explanation.

- Theorists more concerned with language *use* – functionalists – point to recurrent diachronic processes that inevitably result in small, closed classes of grammatical morphemes with their characteristic meanings across languages. On these accounts, this design feature of language cannot be attributed to the mental structure of the individual alone.

Regardless of theoretical position, however, everyone agrees that grammaticizable notions are "special." Here I want to examine the consequences for acquisition theory that flow from taking grammaticizable notions as special in one way or another. If it is supposed that the mental lexicon consists of two classes of items, with two distinct kinds of meanings, then there are two separate semantic tasks for the learner. Further, if one class draws on prespecified meanings, its acquisition consists of procedures of look-up and elimination, while the acquisition of meanings in the other class requires some kind of more general learning abilities. I will propose, however, that such theorists – including myself – have erred in attributing the origins of structure to the mind of the child, rather than to the interpersonal communicative and cognitive processes that everywhere and always shape language in its peculiar expression of content and relation. As Sapir put it: "language struggles towards two poles of linguistic expression – material content and relation"; but he went on to add: "these poles tend to be connected by a long series of transitional concepts" (1921/1949, p. 109). I will argue that the cline between the two poles, when properly understood, makes it unlikely that the child comes to the task of language acquisition prepared with the relevant distinctions – either semantic or syntactic – thereby challenging my own previous assumptions and those of both generative and cognitive linguists. But first, some necessary preliminaries.

Grammatically Specified Notions

It is clear from an examination of even a single language that grammatical morphemes and constructions encode specific types of notions. In English, for example, nouns can be marked for *plural*, relations of *possession*, and *definiteness*. In other languages, these particular notions may be left unmarked, while shape or substance of objects may be grammatically expressed. Looking across many languages, it is evident that there is a great deal of variation both in the categories that are grammaticized and in their boundaries. At the same time, however, it seems that the set of such notions is not vast.

This problem has been explored in depth by Leonard Talmy (1978, 1983, 1985, 1988). He has been struck by the finding that many notions seem to be excluded from grammatical expression. Thus no known language has grammatical morphemes indicating the color of an object referred to by a noun; nor are there verb inflections indicating whether an event occurred in the daytime or at night, or on a hot or a cold day. In his most extensive study, Talmy (1985) lists conceptual domains which are typically realized as verb inflections or particles, and contrasts this list with a collection of domains which are apparently not amenable to grammaticization.[1] For example, (1a) lists domains that are typically expressed by grammatical elements associated with verbs (inflections, particles), whereas the domains listed in (1b) are apparently excluded from such expressions.[2]

1a   **Grammaticizable domains typically marked on verbs**
tense (temporal relation to speech event)
aspect and phase (temporal distribution of an event)
causativity
valence/voice (e.g., active, passive)
mood (e.g., indicative, subjunctive, optative)
speech act type (e.g., declarative, interrogative, imperative)
personation (action on self vs. other)
person (1st, 2nd, etc.)
number of event participants (e.g., singular, dual, plural)
gender of participant
social/interpersonal status of interlocutors (e.g., intimate, formal)
speaker's evidence for making claim (e.g., direct experience, hearsay)
positive/negative status of an event's existence

1b   **Conceptual domains *not* amenable to grammaticization as verbal inflection**
color of an event participant
symmetry of an event participant
relation to comparable events (e.g., "only," "even," "instead")
spatial setting (e.g., indoors, outside)
speaker's state of mind (e.g., bored, interested).

We are faced here with the first major question about grammaticizable notions: why are some conceptual domains apparently excluded from grammatical expression? Talmy goes on to raise a second major issue: within any particular grammaticizable domain, there are striking restrictions in the number and type of distinctions that are grammatically marked. He has explored this question most fully with regard to restrictions on the notions that can be *conflated* in a single grammatical morpheme. The most widely cited examples concern locative terms, and these will figure in some of the acquisition issues discussed later. For example, an English preposition like *through* indicates motion that proceeds in some medium (*through the grass/water/crowd*), but does not indicate the shape or contour of the path (e.g., zigzag, direct, circling), the nature of the medium, or the precise extent of the path. Another type of restriction suggests that grammar is concerned with *relative*, rather than quantified, distinctions. For example, the deictic demonstratives *this* and *that* are neutral with regard to magnitude. One can just as well compare "*this* leaf and *that* leaf" as "*this* galaxy and *that* galaxy." Talmy (1988, p. 171) summarizes across numerous examples to conclude that the notions excluded from grammatical expression "involve Euclidean-geometric concepts – e.g., fixed distance, size, contour, and angle – as well as quantified measure, and various particularities of a quantity: in sum, characteristics that are absolute or fixed." By contrast, grammaticizable notions are "topological, topology-like, or relativistic." He offers the following two lists. (For details, see the cited references.) I will call them *qualities* to distinguish them from *domains* such as those listed in (1a, b).

2a **Non-topological and non-grammaticizable qualities:** material, motion, medium, precise or quantified space or time

2b **Topological/topology-like and grammaticizable qualities:** point, linear extent, locatedness, within, region, side, partition, singularity, plurality, same, different, "adjacency" of points, one-to-one correspondence, pattern of distribution

Finally, Talmy (1988) notes a series of restrictions that impose a limited schematization of semantic content for any grammatically specified notion. These restrictions apply to both nouns and verbs. For example, Talmy introduces the term "plexity" to characterize the distinction of number. Thus a "uniplex" noun becomes "multiplex" by pluralization (e.g., *bird/birds*) and a uniplex verb can become multiplex by verbal inflection and/or auxiliary (e.g., *sigh/keep sighing*). Talmy calls these *categories of grammatically specified notions*. In the course of a lengthy analysis (Talmy 1988, pp. 173–192), he lists the following types of distinction:

3 **Categories of grammatically specified notions**
dimension (continuous/discrete)
plexity (uniplex/multiplex)
boundedness (unbounded/bounded)
dividedness (particulate/continuous)
disposition (combinations of the above)
extension (point, bounded extent, unbounded extent)
distribution (one-way non-resettable, one-way resettable, full-cycle, multiplex, steady-state, gradient)
axiality (relation to border)
perspectival mode (long-range/close-up; moving/static)
level of synthesis (Gestalt/componential)
level of exemplarity (full complement/single exemplar)

Putting together the various parts of Talmy's analysis – *domains, qualities*, and *categories* of grammaticizable notions – we can more precisely characterize the meanings of grammatical morphemes. To take just one example, consider the sentence **The** boy-s were runn-ing **in-to the** house. The grammatical elements in boldface point to particular domains and categories within those domains, while the lexical items *boy, run*, and *house* provide the items of content that are related by the grammatical frame. The article *the*, together with the plural *-s*, categorizes *disposition* of the actors as *multiplex* and *particulate* (as opposed to *boys were running*, where the absence of the article categorizes the actors as *multiplex* and *continuous*). The plural past-tense *were* categorizes the reported event in the domains of *tense (past)* and *number (plural)*, while the progressive *-ing* categorizes *aspect (progressive)*. The form *in-to* schematizes *path* and *ground of movement* as directed across a border into an extent. The quality of the path is topological: simply movement across a partition to within a region. (The two uses of *the* also situate the sentence in a discourse context of presupposed information – that is, the speaker assumes that the listener has specific referents in mind for *boys* and *house*. Talmy's analysis does not include the pragmatic functions of grammatical morphemes.

The interpersonal domain must also figure heavily in any account of the origins and functions of these items.)

To return to the guiding question: why should precisely *these* types of notions receive grammatical expression across the languages of the world? Talmy offers two kinds of accounts. One is presented in cognitive terms: "The grammatical specifications in a sentence . . . provide a conceptual framework or, imagistically, a skeletal structure or scaffolding, for the conceptual material that is lexically specified" (1988, p. 166). That is, the grammatical elements – functors and syntactic construction types – provide a schematization of experience. The cognitive argument is that this particular schematization is a consequence of schematization at a nonlinguistic conceptual level. For example, Talmy (1978, 1983, 1988) proposes parallels between structuring in visual perception and in language. Landau & Jackendoff make a similar proposal, tying the limited set of locative prepositions to a "submodule" of the brain specialized for object location: "Our hypothesis is that there are so few prepositions because the class of spatial relations available to be expressed in language – the notions prepositions can mean – is extremely limited" (1993, p. 224).

Such parallels between cognitive domains, however, do not explain the linguistic division of labor between content words and functors, nor all of the peculiarities of grammaticizable notions. For Talmy, and other linguists, the division of labor is apparently taken as given, as is the set of grammaticizable notions. Talmy refers to "an innate inventory of concepts available for serving a structuring function in language" (1985, p. 197). Such innate knowledge, of course, would facilitate the acquisition task. Bickerton includes a version of the inventory in his bioprogram, equipping the acquisition mechanism with "a very short list of semantic primes" that serve the child as "grammatically-markable semantic features" (1981, p. 205).

Whether or not the "inventory" is innate, it has been assumed to play a key role in the child's entry into the linguistic system. In 1979 I presented Talmy's analysis as part of the child's "initial assumptions" about grammar. And in later work on "operating principles" for acquisition, I suggested "that such notions must constitute a privileged set for the child, and that they are embodied in the child's conceptions of 'prototypical events' that are mapped onto the first grammatical forms universally" (Slobin, 1985, p. 1173f.). The proposal was that the division between the two classes of grammatical morphemes reflected a cognitive division between concrete and relational concepts, and that the relational concepts were, to some extent, already in place at the beginning of grammatical acquisition (whether on the basis of an "innate list" or arising from prior cognitive development). A similar position was taken by Pinker, in his proposal that "the child can extract . . . the potentially grammatically relevant semantic features of the sentence participants (their number, person, sex, etc.) and of the proposition as a whole (tense, aspect, modality, etc.)" (1984, p. 30). He, too, was agnostic about the prelinguistic origins of such features: "the theory is, of course, mute as to whether these cognitive distinctions are themselves innate or learned, as long as the child is capable of making them" (1984, p. 363). The position continues in *Learnability and cognition*, with a clear statement of the learning task (Pinker, 1989, p. 254f.):

> Consider the target in the learning of an inflection, namely, a list of features . . . The features are drawn from a finite universal set of possible grammaticizable features. Each one

has a conceptual or perceptual correlate: the child can determine, for example, whether the referent of a noun in a particular context is singular or plural, human or nonhuman. When attempting to learn a given inflection from its use in a given utterance, the child samples a subset of features with their currently true values from the universal pool.

The purpose of these proposals was to clear the way for "operating principles" or "procedures" to work out inflectional paradigms and other form-function mappings. However, such procedures also run into the problem that the set of grammaticizable features, although limited, is still large; and many of the features are not relevant to the particular language being acquired. The solution here was to appeal to a preestablished ranking of notions with regard to their applicability to grammar. With the addition of an innate "accessibility hierarchy" (Talmy, 1988, p. 197) or a "weighting of hypotheses" based on "cognitive saliency" (Pinker, 1984, p. 170), the child is spared the task of initially scanning the entire inventory of grammaticizable notions.[3]

In my work on operating principles, I called upon cognitive and processing variables to account for differences in the accessibility of grammaticizable notions, rather than building the hierarchy into a grammar module. My solution was to attempt to ground the accessibility hierarchy in the child's cognitive development. On this account, the first notions to receive grammatical marking in a child's speech are those that correspond to the child's conceptions of "prototypical events." For example, I proposed that the salience of hands-on action on objects – the "Manipulative Activity Scene" – provided the starting point for the acquisition of such forms as accusative or ergative inflections. Much empirical work remains to be done before we can specify the range of such starting points. I expect that some will be universal, whereas others will show cross-linguistic variation. Pioneering research, such as the work of Bowerman, Choi (Choi & Bowerman, 1991; Bowerman, 1993, 1994, 1996a, 1996b), Clark (1995), and others, places the conceptual origins of grammaticizable notions in domains of cognitive development, tempered by the semantic organization inherent in the exposure language.

It is important, however, to distinguish between the course of development of grammaticizable notions *in the child* and explanations for their existence *as linguistic phenomena*. On closer inspection, cross-linguistic diversity in patterns of grammaticization points to adult communicative practices as the most plausible source of form-function mappings in human languages, rather than prototypical events in infant cognition. The following sections of the chapter explore the roles of grammaticizable notions in ontogeny and diachrony, drawing on recent findings in cognitive linguistics and grammatic(al)ization theory.

The Learning Task

This historical and theoretical introduction sets the stage for defining the task that the child faces in determining the meanings of grammatical morphemes. The standard definition of the task assumes the following linguistic conditions to be true:

Condition 1: there is a distinct and identifiable collection of grammatical morphemes, arranged in small, closed classes.

Condition 2: these morphemes map onto a universal, limited set of semantic
entities (grammaticizable notions).

Condition 3: grammaticizable notions are arranged in a universal accessibility
hierarchy.

According to standard accounts, acquisition occurs on the basis of assumptions about
biology and cognition:

Assumption 1: conditions 1, 2, and 3 exist because of the structure of the
mind/brain (in modules for aspects of language, perhaps in conjunction with
other modules).

Assumption 2: the role of linguistic input is to allow the relevant mental capacities to organize themselves in terms of the exposure language.

Assumption 3: the child learns the meaning of a grammatical form by isolating
and identifying a particular stretch of speech as instantiating a grammatical form
and attempting to map it onto a relevant grammaticizable notion.

I propose that Conditions 1, 2, and 3 are only partly true, and that therefore Assumption 1 must be seriously modified or abandoned. Assumption 2 remains, but with a shift
of emphasis to structures inhering in the exposure language. Assumption 3 must be
seriously modified – and this is the challenge to learning theory in my title.

Synchronic Evidence for Modifying the Linguistic Conditions on Learnability

What is a grammatical morpheme?

Prototypical grammatical morphemes are affixed to content words, are general in
meaning, phonologically reduced, and not etymologically transparent. Familiar examples are elements like plural markers on nouns and tense/aspect inflections on verbs.
Another obvious type of grammatical morpheme is represented by "little worlds" like
prepositions and auxiliaries, which consist of small sets of items occurring in syntactically fixed positions. But there are also items that are not so obvious. Consider several
examples that demonstrate the lack of clear boundaries of syntactic categories defined
as "functors," "grammatical morphemes," or "closed-class elements."

English modals and equivalents

English has a grammatical class of modal auxiliaries that fit in the frame, SUBJECT
MODAL VERB, such as *You **should/must/can/might** . . . go*. This is a prototypical
small, closed class: *can, could, shall, should, will, would, may, might, must*. The forms do
not function as normal verbs; rather, they have a number of grammatical peculiarities
– e.g., they don't have normal past tenses (**you shoulded go*) or person inflections (**he*

shoulds go), they can take a contracted negative clitic (*shouldn't*), and they "move" under certain syntactic conditions (e.g., *Should you go?*). However, there are other items that can occur in the same slot, such as *You* **hafta/needa** . . . *go*. These function as normal verbs – e.g., PAST: *You had to go*; PERSON: *you* **hafta**, *he hasta*; QUESTION: **Do** *you* **hafta** *go?*; NEGATIVE *You don't hafta go*. Nevertheless, they, too, are part of a small, closed, and specialized set, with phonological reduction in some contexts. Therefore some linguists refer to them as "quasi-modals." Nonverbs can also fall in the specialized slot of medals and quasi-modals, but with other syntactic constraints. Consider *You better go*, which (in American English) has no obvious past tense or question form. It is negated like an auxiliary, but only in the uncontracted form (compare *you should not go/you better not go; but you shouldn't go/you *betterr'n't go*). Looking across contexts of use, *better* is another sort of specialized "modal-like" element in American English. If you are a child learning this dialect, you can identify a set of full auxiliaries on syntactic grounds, and find that it maps onto a restricted set of grammaticized meanings in the domain of modality. This knowledge is adequate for the *comprehension* of modals; however, when you are concerned with speech *production*, and access the set of modal notions from your mental set of grammaticizable notions in this domain, you find that there is, indeed, a small closed set – but that it does not have a clear or unitary syntactic definition. The slot in declarative sentences that is reserved for expressing categories within the grammaticizable domain of modality can be filled with a heterogeneous collection of modal auxiliaries, semi-modals, and an adjective/adverb *better* that does not act like a normal adjective or adverb in this function. The semantic and syntactic tasks do not seem to run in parallel as neatly as in the textbook cases, which take only well-defined grammatical morphemes into account in their expositions.

This is, in fact, a widespread problem in acquisition – only coming to light when we consider production, rather than comprehension. Consider several more examples of the fuzziness of the category "grammatical morpheme" or "closed-class element."

Spanish modal verbs and auxiliaries

In Spanish the equivalents of English modal verbs do not have syntactic peculiarities. That is, they function just like normal, full verbs, using the standard paradigms for person/number and tense/aspect. Yet they, too, are a small closed set, performing similar functions. The set, however, can only be defined on semantic grounds, listing those verbs – such as *poder* "can," *deber* "should," and the like – that perform a modal function. For example, *puedo ir* "I can go," *debo ir* "I should go" have the same morphosyntactic characteristics as constructions with nonmodal verbs. Lacking the peculiar morphosyntactic definition of English modals, however, the corresponding Spanish verbs are a small closed set *within the "open" class*. (I will argue that, in fact, the "open class" of verbs is better conceived of as a collection of closed classes.) There is also a small class of about twenty-four "semiauxiliaries" (Green, 1982) which have restricted meanings in particular semantic/syntactic contexts. These are verbs that can function both as main verbs and semi-auxiliaries – again, making it difficult to draw a clear boundary around "grammatical morphemes." In their grammatical function, such verbs have restricted meanings in comparison to their uses as fully lexical verbs. For example, the verb *llevar* "carry," in construction with a participle, takes on an auxiliary aspectual meaning: *Juan* **lleva** *entendido que X* "Juan **carries** understood that X" predicates an established state of understanding in Juan that X; *la diferencia* **viene** *motivada por X* "the difference comes motivated by X" means that the difference can be accounted for by X. Green notes that some of the twenty-four semi-auxiliaries are more special- ized and limited in their functions than others. He observes that a semantic examina- tion of these verbs "strongly favours a gradient analysis . . . At one extreme of the gradience would be verbs like *haber* [have] which have lost virtually all trace of lexical meaning, and at the other, verbs like *mostrarse* [show self] and *notarse* [note] which have lost virtually none of theirs" (p. 127). A critical feature is thus the "fullness" versus "abstractness" of lexical meaning of an item. This is not a criterion that a child could use to identify an item as belonging to either the lexical class or the gramma- tical class. Looked at in diachronic perspective, some are more "grammaticized" than others (as I will discuss later in more detail). Some may remain on the borderline between lexical and grammatical item for centuries, and may never become fully grammaticized.

The Spanish "modal" and "semi-auxiliary" verbs attract our interest because their semantic and discourse functions parallel the more highly grammaticized auxiliaries of English. This leads one to wonder whether Spanish-speaking children are using their prespecified "grammatical acquisition device" or their more general "lexical acquisition device" in learning such forms.

Many more examples could be adduced, underlining the point that there is no clear dividing line between "content words" and "functors." Rather, there is a continuum with clearly lexical items on one end (nouns like *computer, couch, zebra*, verbs like *tackle, broil, sneeze*) and grammatical inflections on the other (such as English progressive-*ing*, Turkish accusative-*l*, Warlpiri ergative-*ngku*). In between, there are lexical items that play more or less specialized roles, sometimes on their way to becoming grammatical morphemes over time. What, then, is a grammatical morpheme? It depends on the purposes of the analysis. In any event, it would be difficult to preprogram the child with an adequate definition.

What is a closed-class item?

One way of getting the child started in the task of grammatical form-function mapping has been to equip the language acquisition device with a special detector for members of the "closed class." The terminology is deceptive here, however. Obviously, the child cannot define a class as "closed" before having acquired all of its members and finding that there are no more to acquire. Therefore this can't be part of early acquisition. Lila Gleitman and her associates have proposed an acoustic rather than a semantic or syn- tactic cue to closed-class membership (Gleitman & Wanner, 1982; Landau & Gleitman, 1985; Gleitman et al., 1988). On this model, the child eventually comes to pay atten- tion to elements in the speech stream that are unstressed or otherwise perceptually non-salient. They propose that "the distinction between open and closed class may play a role in the child's discovery of linguistic structure. This is because, though this dis- tinction may be discovered through a physical property (i.e., stress), it is well correlated with syntactic analyses the child will have to recognize to recover the structure of sen- tences" (Gleitman & Wanner, 1982, p. 23). However, this analysis obliterates both the syntactic and semantic characteristics of closed classes, as well as their statistical distribution. That is, grammatical morphemes are high-frequency elements, occurring in fixed syntactic positions. The child must be sensitive to these factors, along with prosodic features. An acoustic definition of the class leads Gleitman and her associates to define stressed grammatical inflections, paradoxically, as open class. For example, when discussing the fact that grammatical morphemes are acquired earlier in Turkish than in many other languages, they argue: "According to Slobin, the relevant inflectional items in Turkish . . . are a full syllable long, are stressed, do not deform the surrounding words phonetically, and do not criticize. Thus these items are OPEN CLASS not CLOSED CLASS, under phonological definitions of this partitioning of the morphological stock" (Gleitman et al., 1988, p. 158). On this account, agglutinative languages like Turkish and Japanese have no closed-class morphemes, thus exempting children acquiring such languages from the learning task defined above. This solution clearly throws out the baby with the bath water.

In other formulations, Gleitman and her associates rely on the traditional definition of the two classes. Landau & Gleitman (1985, p. 44ff.) define the closed class on *distributional* grounds alone, including such items as auxiliaries, prepositions, and determiners, which are full syllables and can receive stress. On this model, the child must have some means of identifying members of these grammatical categories. The only possible cues are meaning, syntactic position, and statistical distribution – the traditional cues used in all models of language acquisition. Thus there is no evident definition of "closed-class morpheme" that can give the child a solution to the learning task.[4] Gleitman's solution, at best, suggests that some kind of "prosodic bootstrapping" might help children learning particular types of languages to identify particular types of grammatical morphemes. But this leaves open the question of how grammatical morphemes in general are discovered, and how they are mapped onto linguistically relevant notions.

The original motivation behind the definition of "closed" classes comes from the observation that some types of words are rarely added to a language; as a consequence, it is unlikely that speakers will encounter new instances of such words during their lifetimes. Languages are most free in adding new nouns over time, as new artifacts are created and new phenomena are categorized and labeled. It is my impression that verbs are hardly ever invented "out of whole cloth," as nouns are; rather, they tend to be derived from nouns by morphological or phrasal means – e.g., *to xerox, to skateboard, to privatize, to test drive, to do a number*.

The verb lexicon of a language can be subdivided into many limited, fairly closed classes that provide the language's analysis and categorization of a given conceptual domain. Consider, for example, the set of English verbs of manner of talking (*shout, scream, whisper, mumble, mutter* . . .), posture (*sit, stand, lie, crouch* . . .), or cooking (*bake, fry, roast, boil* . . .). Within such a subclass it is possible to find systematic sets of semantic components in quite the same fashion as componential analyses of grammatical morphemes. A good example is the domain of object destruction, which is quite elaborated in the English verb lexicon. We make distinctions of the nature of the object to be destroyed (e.g., *break, tear, smash*), force dynamics (e.g., *tear* vs. *rip*), the degree of destruction or deformation (e.g., *cut* vs. *shred*), the texture or constituency of the object (e.g., *crumple, crumble, shatter*), and so forth. In learning this "closed-class' set of verbs, the English-speaking child has acquired a language-specific set of linguistically relevant notions, and will not go on learning more and more such verbs throughout life. This process is, in principle, no different than the acquisition of a "closed-class" set such as the English spatial prepositions.

Organization of the verbal lexicon into classes also has profound syntactic consequences. As Beth Levin (1993) has documented in detail in her recent book, *English verb classes and alternations*, "verbs in English and other languages fall into classes on the basis of shared components of meaning" (p. 11), and the members of a class "have common syntactic as well as semantic properties" (p. 7). This pioneering attempt to characterize the "open class' of verbs as a collection of linguistically definable subclasses poses another type of challenge to theories that postulate a special psycholinguistic module devoted to the acquisition and processing of the "closed class."

What makes a notion grammaticizable?

The other side of the coin is to equip the child with grammaticizable notions that can be mapped onto the specialized morphemes of the "closed lass," however defined. When we look across languages, though, we find that the same notions are often also used to delimit the meanings of *content* words – members of the open class – depending on the language and the type of analysis chosen. Simply identifying a notion as grammaticizable does not allow the child to determine *whether* it is actually grammaticized in the exposure language or *how* it is grammaticized. (That is, cross-linguistic diversity precludes a preestablished table of correspondences between grammatical forms and semantic meanings, as in Pinker, 1984.) Again, there are many possible examples.

How are grammaticizable notions organized?

Up to this point I have treated grammaticizable notions as a universally specified collection, applicable across languages. However, it has become more and more evident in research since the late 1980s or so that there is considerable cross-linguistic variation in the meanings of closed-class categories, including both functors and small, closed verb classes. Melissa Bowerman has been a pioneer in arguing that "the way in which languages organize meaning . . . [is] an integral part of their structure" (1985, p. 1313), with consequences for patterns of acquisition. Her work has demonstrated that children can be guided by language-specific form–meaning relations – perhaps from the earliest phases of acquisition – in establishing categories appropriate to the exposure language (Choi & Bowerman, 1991; Bowerman, 1994, 1996a, b; Bowerman et al., 1995). This work has stimulated others to find similar patterns (e.g., Slobin, 1991, 1996; Berman & Slobin, 1994; Choi, 1997). Cross-linguistic variation in types of "conceptual packaging" in a semantic domain poses another serious challenge to learning models, because there is no set of prelinguistic categories that can be directly mapped onto the meanings of linguistic elements. (See Bowerman, 1996a for a recent and cogent exposition of this problem in the domain of spatial concepts and language.) Four types of problems must be faced by learning theories: (1) languages differ in how finely they divide up a conceptual continuum and in where they place cuts for grammatical purposes; (2) languages differ in the combinations of semantic components that are packaged into grammatical morphemes in common conceptual domains; (3) languages differ in the overall division of a semantic domain into linguistically relevant categories; (4) the array of concepts relevant to a particular domain is distributed across several types of linguistic elements in any given language, and the patterns of distribution also vary across languages. I will give examples of the first two of these problem types.

Dividing a continuum into linguistically relevant categories

Izchak Schlesinger has long argued for a distinction between cognitive and semantic levels of categorization (1982, 1988). In a broad cross-linguistic study he offers evidence for the proposal that "conceptually, the instrumental and comitative are really only two extreme points on what is a conceptual continuum" (1979: 308). This continuum is marked by a single preposition in English – *with* – as shown in the following ten sentences that Schlesinger used in his study:

1　The pantomimist gave a show with the clown.
2　The engineer built the machine with an assistant.
3　The general captured the hill with a squad of paratroopers.
4　The acrobat performed an act with an elephant.
5　The blind man crossed the street with his dog.
6　The officer caught the smuggler with a police dog.
7　The prisoner won the appeal with a highly paid lawyer.
8　The Nobel Prize winner found the solution with a computer.
9　The sportsman hunted deer with a rifle.
10　The hoodlum broke the window with a stone.

English speakers were asked to rank these sentences on a continuum from the meaning of "together" (as in "He went to the movie with his friend") to the meaning of "by means of" (as in "He cut the meat with a knife"). The respondents agreed, at a high level of statistical significance, on the ranking given above. Schlesinger then presented these sentences to speakers of languages that use distinct grammatical forms for parts of this continuum. Speakers of twelve different languages divided the continuum at different points and agreed in treating it as a continuum.[5] In general, wherever they may have made a division they did not violate the ranking. For example, sentences 1–8 received the same form in Iraqi Arabic, while 9–10 received a different form; Swahili, by contrast, required a separate form for 7–10. Schlesinger concludes that "the finding that languages differ widely in their cutoff points runs counter to the hypothesis that the instrumental and comitative are two disparate categories in our cognitive structures ... [Rather], there seems to be a continuum in our cognitive system, which each language segments in its own way" (1979, p. 313).

　More recently, Bowerman & Pederson (1992) report a similar pattern in the spatial domain. They found that it was possible to rank pictured situations of locative relations between two objects on a continuum from *containment* to *support*, with differences between languages in their division of the continuum. Thus, even if the child were equipped with predefined conceptual continua, it would not be evident how many linguistically relevant cuts to make on a continuum, or even whether it is divisible at all, since some languages use a single term for an entire continuum such as *comitative–instrumental* (e.g., English *with*) or *containment–support* (e.g., Spanish *en*).

Packaging components into linguistically relevant categories

Languages differ in terms of the "granularity" of their division of conceptual material into linguistically relevant categories. For example, one language may have a simple *continuative* aspect for any temporally unbounded situation, while others may subdivide this aspect to distinguish between *habitual* and *iterative* events, or between *progressive* events and *states*. Further, events can be cross-classified on different dimensions: one language may mark such distinctions only in the past, for example, while another might mark them in other tenses as well. It is the hope of cognitive linguists such as Jackendoff (1983, 1987, 1990) that there is a universal set of conceptual components underlying cross-linguistic diversity in the semantics of lexical items. I share this hope, but even if the child had a definitive set of such components, the task of packaging them into the linguistically relevant categories of the particular exposure language would remain. In some learning theories such packages are given in advance, as in Pinker's (1984, p. 41) table of correspondences between grammatical and conceptual categories. On closer inspection, however, considerable diversity remains to be accounted for.

As one example, consider the grammatical category *accusative*, which appears in various languages in the form of case affixes or particles associated with nouns, or as verb affixes, or as special construction types. In Pinker's table, "Accusative" is linked with "Patient of transitive action."[6] However, in many languages this semantic category is subdivided – and in different ways. That is, it is not a unitary notion, nor does it lie on a one-dimensional continuum with other case categories, because the subdivisions cut across different types of categories. Here are just a few examples of the many possibilities:

> *Some factors influencing choice of grammatical marking of patient:*
> definite patient only (Turkish case inflection)
> masculine animate vs. other, whole vs. partial patient, singular vs. plural patient, affirmative vs. negative clause (Russian case inflections)
> whole vs. partial patient, completed vs. non-completed action (Finnish case inflections)
> direct physical action on patient only (Mandarin particle)
> patient marking (direct and indirect conflated) in present tense only (Georgian)
> one marker for patient, goal, recipient, beneficiary (English personal pronouns)

This is just a very brief and simplified list, but it makes it clear that the notion of "patient," or "direct object," conflates with various other notions from language to language, including such categories as tense, aspect, definiteness, nature of effect, and so forth. It may well be that some packagings are more accessible to the child than others, and that children across languages begin with similar notions of patient (e.g., the prototypical event of direct physical manipulation proposed in my "Manipulative Activity

Scene" [Slobin, 1985]). This is, of course, an empirical question. But however children may break into the mapping of such grammaticizable notions, our learning theories will have to account for the selective fine-tuning required for arriving at language-specific patterns of grammaticization. That is, regardless of a child's starting point in grammaticizing a particular notion, a developmental account is needed because the endpoints vary so much across languages.

Summary

Let us briefly summarize the answers to the questions posed in the preceding four sub-sections before moving on to the diachronic evidence.

What is a grammatical morpheme?

There is a cline of linguistic elements from fully lexical content words to fully special-ized grammatical morphemes, but there is no obvious place to draw a line between lexical and grammatical items.[7]

What is a closed-class item?

The lexicon is made up of a number of classes, ranging from almost entirely open (pro-totypically nouns) to almost entirely closed (prototypically grammatical morphemes such as clitics and inflections).

What makes a notion grammaticizable?

At present there is no useful answer to this question beyond an empirically based list of the notions that receive grammatical expression in the languages of the world. The same notions are found repeatedly in the analysis of both lexical and gramma-tical items, as has been noted frequently by linguists working in various traditions (e.g., Lyons 1968, p. 438). A modem statement of this position can be found in Pinker's (1989) analysis of the acquisition of argument structure. He suggests that a single "Grammatically Relevant Subsystem" of concepts (derived from Jackendoff and Talmy) provides the "privileged gramantic machinery" (p. 166) needed *both* to specify the meanings of closed-class morphemes and to organize verbs into subclasses that are sensitive to various types of lexical rules and patterns of syntactic alternation.

How are grammaticizable notions organized?

There is great diversity across languages in the level of granularity, the number and positions of cuts on semantic continua, the types of semantic components employed, and the balance between different parts of the linguistic system in expressing gram-maticizable notions. This diversity has not yet been sufficiently systematized to make claims about its conceptual or developmental underpinnings. At the present state of our knowledge, it is premature to attribute a particular organization of grammaticiz-able notions to the child at the beginning of language acquisition (*pace* Slobin, 1985). It would seem more plausible to endow the child with sufficient flexibility to discern and master the particular organization of the exposure language.

Diachronic Evidence for Modifying the Linguistic Conditions on Learnability

All of the dominant accounts of learnability attempt to relate the structure of the mind with the structure of language, as if these were the only two factors to consider. When the social factor is considered, it is only as a source of data: the "input" language, perhaps with some attention to the interactive speech contexts in which the input is situated. Accordingly, when there is not enough information in the input to account for the structure of language, it must be sought in the individual mind. The end result is always some kind of nativism, whether of syntactic form, semantic content, or some interaction between form and content, perhaps with various cognitive prerequisites added in. This argument has been re-stated thousands of times since Chomsky first proposed it in the 1960s. Of the many formulations, the following representative summary by Jackendoff (1987, p. 87) is useful in clearly revealing the limited options that flow from this conception of the problem:

> The claim, then, is that some aspects of our language capacity are not a result of learning from environmental evidence. Aside from divine intervention, the only other way we know of to get them into the mind is biologically: genetic information determining brain architecture, which in turn determines the form of possible computations. In other words, certain aspects of the structure of language are *inherited*.
>
> This conclusion, which I will call the *innateness hypothesis*, provides a potential solution to the paradox of language acquisition by appealing to evolution. The child alone does not have enough time to acquire all the aspects of language that linguists are struggling to discover. But evolution has had more time at its disposal to develop this structure than linguists will ever have . . .

Note a jump in the argument: it begins by discussing "some aspects of our language *capacity*," but ends up with the claim that "certain aspects of the *structure* of language are inherited" (emphasis added). There can be no disagreement that aspects of the capacity to acquire and use language are inherited: this is a general truth about species-specific behavior. But the *structure* of language arises in *two* diachronic processes: biological evolution and ever-changing processes of communicative interaction. The structure of language could not have arisen in the genetically determined brain architecture of an individual ancestor alone, because language arises only in communication between individuals. That is, after all, what language is for. As soon as we free ourselves of this confusion of levels of analysis – the individual and the social – many of the puzzles of language structure appear to have solutions beyond divine intervention or genetic determinism. The traditional attempt to account for linguistic structure is rather like trying to locate the law of supply and demand in the minds of the individual producer and consumer, or the shape of a honeycomb in the genetic structure of the individual bee.

Since the late 1970s there has been a rapidly growing interest in the *historical*, rather than the evolutionary processes that shape language – particularly with regard to the ways in which languages acquire and modify grammatical elements and constructions. A field calling itself "grammaticization" or "grammaticalization" (see note 1) has revived longstanding interest in language change, using a wealth of new typological, historical, and psycholinguistic data and theory.[8] As I have suggested, this field helps to explain the nature and origins of grammaticizable notions.

A central phenomenon of language change was already identified at the beginning of the twentieth century by the French linguist Antoine Meillet. In 1912, in a paper "L'évolution des formes grammaticales," he introduced the term *grammaticalisation* to designate the process by which a word develops into a grammatical morpheme ("le passage d'un mot autonome au rôle d'élément grammatical"). This process provides an explanation of why it is impossible to draw a line between lexical and grammatical items, as well as why grammatical morphemes have their peculiarly restricted and universal semantics. Hopper & Traugott (1993, p. 7) define a cline of linguistic elements from a "lexical area" to a "grammatical area, with no firm boundaries between the categories:

content item > grammatical word > clitic > inflectional affix

Diachronically "a given form typically moves from a point on the left of the cline to a point further on the right" (1993, p. 7).

The literature is full of examples of the lexical origins of grammatical items. Familiar English examples are the development of the verb *go* from a full verb of motion to a reduced future marker *gonna*, and the development of modals from verbs of cognition and ability – e.g., *can* originally meant "know how to," *may* and *might* developed from a verb meaning "have the (physical) power to." The English contracted negative, *n't*, began in Old English as an emphatic form, *ne-a-wiht* "not-ever-anything," used to reinforce another negative form, *ne*. By the time of Middle English it had contracted to *nat* and eventually replaced the nonemphatic *ne*, becoming the new nonemphatic negative and finally contracting (Traugott, 1972, p. 146f.). This is the typical progress along the cline from full, stressed form with a more specific meaning, to reduced, unstressed form with a more general meaning. When such processes are traced out in full, the nature of grammatical morphemes – unstressed and general in meaning – is no longer mysterious.

Towards a Solution

The problem of constraints on hypotheses: what is "economy"?

My very brief overview of a few problems to do with the grammatical marking of semantic and pragmatic categories makes it evident that the child could be prey to many false starts and dead-end attempts. This fact alone has led to the proliferation of "constraints," "predispositions," "parameter settings," "operating principles," and the like in the theoretical literature of recent decades. But there are no obvious constraints on the constraints, because we have no plausible metric of what makes a task "too hard" for a child learner. We know that children do acquire the manifold and subtle complexities of language. And we realize that this is a hard task for conscious, problem-solving adults (even linguists). Therefore we try to make the task "easier" for children by providing bootstraps that they can use pull themselves up (an unclear metaphor at best). The list of grammaticizable notions was intended to provide an aid – intended to prevent the child from making too many false hypotheses. But, I would propose, we really have no way of knowing how many false hypotheses it takes to overburden the vastly complex human brain, or how quickly and efficiently they can be revised or dismissed. It is unsettling to realize how many of our theories are aimed at the simplistic criterion of "economy," when we have no rational measure of that economy.

What is "reasonable"?

Having voiced these qualms about the soundness of our endeavor, I will return to the attempt to give the child some guidelines for the task. Our theories are haunted by the risk that children might think that everything might be relevant to everything. Our data, however, suggest that children are more "reasonable" than that. As developmental psychologists have pointed out, children are at work constructing "intuitive theories" of domain of experience (e.g., Keil, 1989; Gopnik & Meltzoff, 1996). Hypotheses about the meanings of linguistic forms occur in the context of such general theorizing, which provides the child with "reasonable" factors to consider when encountering, say, verbs of motion or locative particles or casemarkers. Recall the diachronic processes of grammaticization (and, I would add, the processes of forming small sets of specialized verbs). The only available items are those which occur again and again in talking about a great range of experiences. They occur so frequently because they are applicable so generally. Therefore it should be no surprise that children find these notions salient. For example, the factors that apply to many instances of moving and placing objects include the force-dynamic and motoric aspects of picking up an object, moving it, and placing it in another location. It is "reasonable" for grammatical items and small verb sets dealing with these actions to be sensitive to such factors as characteristics of figure and ground objects, direction of movement, and relation of the two objects at the endpoint of the action (e.g., tight fit, located near the bottom of another object, etc.).[9] The color of the objects or the time of day are not *relevant* to this type of scene, given the kind of social world in which we live at present. In part, then, children are reasonable because languages are reasonable. It has been assumed in the literature that it is odd that systems of grammatical meaning, and children acquiring such systems, seem to be indifferent to "non-grammaticizable" notions such as those listed by Talmy. However, if we look carefully at the communicative contexts in which language is used – both on the diachronic and ontogenetic planes – the situation seems much less odd. I suggest that the same factors that keep certain notions from becoming grammaticized also keep children from postulating them as the meanings of grammatical forms.

There are several parts to this argument. One part is social-pragmatic, as has been eloquently and elegantly advanced by Tomasello (e.g., 1992, 1995, this volume). That is, the child is at work figuring out adults' intentions, aided both by social knowledge and by the cooperative communicative behavior of adults. Another factor is what might be called "the texture of experience." For example, particular colors do not occur frequently in association with the linguistic encoding of particular event types. The child is not likely to encounter one set of object placement events that consistently occur with red objects and another with black ones. Even a simple model of statistical sampling, not to mention a connectionist network, would quickly drop color as a determining factor in choice of linguistic form. And a third factor can be found in the nature of form–function mappings themselves. It has long been noted by linguists that grammatical morphemes are placed in association with the content words with which they have the most conceptual affinity – e.g., tense is marked on verbs rather than nouns, shape classifiers are placed in relation to object nouns or verbs of handling, and so forth. A classic formulation of this principle was offered by the German linguist Behaghel (1932, p. 4): "What belongs together mentally is placed close together syntactically."[10] Bybee (1985) has refined the principle, showing not only that particular notions are relevant to verb stems, but that grammatical morphemes reflecting such notions are ordered in a reasonable way, with those meanings that are most relevant to the meaning of the stem occurring closest to the stem, and often phonologically fusing with the stem. Bybee's analysis is part of a series of discoveries of the "iconicity" of form–function mappings in language (e.g., Haiman, 1985a, b). To the extent that the arrangement of linguistic items is a "diagram" or "icon" of the arrangement of mental items, the child may be aided by "iconic bootstrapping." There are many examples of iconicity in children's early grammars, across languages, summarized in Slobin (1985). Putting these various sorts of factors together – social-pragmatic, environmental, linguistic – reduces the need to posit *a priori* constraints in form–function relations.

Typological bootstrapping

In the process of concept formation, children build up and revise "explanatory systems" that are relevant to classes of phenomena. As the child develops a successful explanatory structure for part of the exposure language, other parts become more accessible – that is, a coherent theory of the language begins to emerge. This is true, in part, because the language really *is* a fairly coherent system – as a result of constant balancing out of competing forces. Over time, each language acquires a typological character resulting from the particular interplay of forces in its history. (There is a small number of language types, but this is not because there is a small number of innate parameter settings; rather, there is a small number of solutions to the kinds of competing forces which shape language in use.) At the risk of overburdening the child's shoe-rack, I propose yet another kind of bootstrapping: *typological bootstrapping*. For example, Korean uses verbs to express paths of motion, while English uses particles; and each language uses particular semantic features in categorizing location and movement. As a Korean child learns more linguistic constructions describing motion events, the lexicalization patterns and grammaticized notions of the language become an established pattern. She comes to expect that paths will be lexicalized in verb stems, that caused-motion verbs are sensitive to properties of the objects involved, and so forth. The English-speaking child comes to expect verb particles to structure domains in terms of locative and temporal relations, and finds that certain locative and temporal notions occur again and again. That is, to some extent, the language structures itself as it is learned. Certain patterns of semantic and formal organization become more and more familiar, and, to use an old term, habits are established. This is possible because of the fact that languages naturally develop into coherent systems of various types. In the process of learning various pieces of the system, they come to interrelate because of inherent typological factors. In Karmiloff-Smith's (1992) terms, "representational redescription" occurs – in this case aided by the systematicity inherent in the language that is being learned.

An intriguing consequence of typological bootstrapping is that children come to formulate experience for linguistic expression in quite different ways, depending on the type of language they are learning. I have suggested that each type of language fosters its own modes of "thinking for speaking" (Slobin, 1991, 1996). Because of the systematic cross-linguistic diversity in selection and patterning of grammaticizable notions, different patterns of online mental organization result. In cross-linguistic work on narrative development, Ruth Berman and I (Berman & Slobin, 1994) have identified a number of ways in which children come to structure discourse in terms of the typological characteristics of the particular language. By school age, children have acquired typologically distinct ways of describing events and constructing connected texts. From this point of view, grammaticizable notions have a role in structuring language-specific mental spaces, rather than being there at the beginning, waiting for an input language to turn them on.

I am aware that this formulation still leaves open the mechanisms that a child might use to detect and "representationally redescribe" the systematicity of the exposure language. Various sorts of "operating principles" and "procedures" will be needed in order to give substance to the formulation. However, the very fact that form–function relations become systematically patterned in the course of acquiring a particular language points to an important learning mechanism. As suggested above, in the course of development the child comes to attend to particular types of meanings and to expect them to be expressed by particular types of forms. Such a combination of thinking for speaking and typological bootstrapping seems to guarantee that language-specific form–function patterns will be established and maintained by learners.

Notes

I have benefited from many long discussions of these topics with Melissa Bowerman, and she will find her influence obvious in the revisions of my earlier position. I also owe much to Joan Bybee, Alison Copnik, Len Talmy, David Wilkins, the many colleagues in Nijmegen who have provided stimulation and (re-)education, and the participants in the 1995 conference on "Language acquisition and conceptual development." Thanks also to Paul Bloom, Steve Levinson, Marianne Mithun, Izchak Schlesinger, Elizabeth Traugott, and Tania Kuteva for valuable correspondence on topics raised here. A longer version of this chapter has been published as "The origins of grammaticizable notions: beyond the individual mind" (Slobin, 1997).

1   At present there are two roughly synonymous terms in the literature: "grammaticization" and "grammaticalization." I prefer the former, shorter form, but nothing hangs on the difference. Theorists working within the same overall theoretical framework have not agreed. It seems that American researchers prefer "grammaticization" (e.g., Wallace Chafe, Marianne Mithun, Joan Bybee, and her associates), while those of European origin prefer "grammaticalization" (e.g., Elizabeth Traugott, Paul Hopper, Bernd Heine, and his associates).

2   This is a partial listing, extracted from Talmy (1985, pp. 126–138). The domains listed in

1a can be expressed by bound morphemes (inflections), suggesting that they are more highly grammaticized than other domains that Talmy lists as being realized as satellites to the verb. The important distinction for present purposes is between 1a and 1b. For details, see Talmy (1985).

3 Various investigators have proposed that the hierarchy corresponds to the frequency of occurrence of grammaticized notions in the languages of the world (e.g., Pinker, 1984, p. 171; Bowerman, 1985, p. 1306). This suggestion has at least two major problems: (1) we tack an adequate sample of the world's existing languages, and can never have a full sample of all of the languages that have been used by human beings; (2) on this hypothesis, languages using "rare" forms should pose problems of acquisition and processing – but there is no evidence for such problems. (For discussion of these issues, see the longer version of this chapter [Slobin, 1997].)

4 There is also a long tradition in aphasiology that has sought to find a neurological basis for grammatical morphology in syndromes of telegraphic speech. The classical claim has been that closed-class items are lost, thus proving that they reside in a distinct module. However, by now there is ample evidence against the view that agrammatism is simply an impairment of linguistic structure. Grammatical morphology is often preserved in judgments of grammaticality and in tasks that reduce online time pressure; cross-linguistic studies of aphasia show differential loss of grammatical morphemes, depending on both their "functional load" in the language and their acoustic salience (e.g., Bates & Wulfeck, 1989). All of these findings remove any basis for a neurological definition of the closed class as a linguistic subsystem. What remains is a congeries of factors which lie outside the various attempts to distinguish the two classes on linguistic grounds, including "the sonorance hierarchy, the status of an affix with respect to derivational or inflectional morphology, the lexical status of a root or stem, the salience of a lexical item, attentional and control processes" (Caplan 1992, p. 340).

5 The languages were Slovak, Serbo-Croatian. Iraqi Arabic, Polish, Luo, Akan Alur, Finnish, Swahili, Japanese. Korean, and Tamil. This ordering of languages reflects the division point on the continuum, from mainly comitative to mainly instrumental. For example, Slovak uses a distinct instrumental only for sentence 10 ("with a stone"), whereas Tamil uses a special comitative form only for sentences 1 and 2 ("with the clown," "with an assistant").

6 Pinker attempts to deal with the typology of Nominative/Accusative and Ergative/Absolutive languages by linking "Patient of transitive action" with "Accusative or Absolutive," and "Agent of transitive action" with "Nominative or Ergative." this leaves the child with the problem of determining the typology of the exposure language, with problems such as those spelled out by Van Valin (1992) for ergative languages.

7 Note that the existence of clines wreaks havoc with parameter-setting theories, which rely on discrete categories and principles that are applicable throughout a language.

8 Two recent overviews, both with the title Grammaticalization, have been provided by Heine, Claudi, & Hünnemeyer (1991) and Hopper & Traugott (1993). An early and insightful approach was developed by Bybee (1985), elaborated in successive papers with various collaborators, and most recently presented as *The evolution of grammar* (Bybee, Perkins, & Pagliuca 1994). Two volumes of conference papers, *Approaches to grammaticalization*, have been edited by Traugott & Heine (1991) and published in the John Benjamins Series, "Typological Studies in Language," which includes many books dealing with diachronic linguistic issues. The journal *Language Variation and Change* is a forum for diachronic research using statistical methods. The closely related field of "typology and universal," places diachronic issues in a synchronic framework; see textbooks by Comrie (1981) and Croft (1990), and the new journal Typology, of the recently established Association for Linguistic Typology.

9   What was in retrospect, not "reasonable was my Platonic hope that all children would start with the same semantic notions – the "Basic Child Grammar" of Slobin (1985).

10 "Das oberste Gesetzist dieses, daB das geistig eng Zusammengehörige auch eng zusammengestellt wird."

References

Bates, E., & Wulfeck, B. (1989). Crosslinguistic studies of aphasia. In E. Bates & B. MacWhinney (Eds.), *The crosslinguistic study of sentence processing*, pp. 328–374. Cambridge: Cambridge University Press.

Behaghel, O. (1932). *Deutsche syntax: eine geschichtliche Darstelling*, vol. 4: *Worstellung. Periodenbau*, Heidelberg: Carl Winters.

Berman, R.A., & Slobin, D.I. (Eds.) (1994). *Relating events in narrative: a crosslinguistic developmental study*. Hillsdale, NJ: Lawrence Erlbaum.

Bickerton, D. (1981). *Roots of language*. Ann Arbor, MI: Karoma Publishers.

Bowerman, M. (1985). What shapes children's grammar? In D.I. Slobin (Ed.), *The crosslinguistic study of language acquisition*, vol. 2: *The data*, pp. 1257–1319. Hillsdale, NJ: Lawrence Erlbaum.

Bowerman, M. (1993). Typological perspectives in language acquisition: do crosslinguistic patterns predict development? In E.V. Clark (Ed.), *The proceedings of the Twenty-fifth Annual Child Language Research Forum*, pp. 7–15. Standard, CA: Center for the Study of Language and Information.

Bowerman, M. (1994). From universal to language-specific in early grammatical development. *Philosophical Transactions of the Royal Society of London B, 346*, 37–45.

Bowerman, M. (1996a). Learning how to structure space for language: a crosslinguistic perspective. In P. Bloom, M.A. Peterson, L. Nadel, & M.F. Garrett (Eds.), *Language and space*. Cambridge, MA: MIT Press, 385–436.

Bowerman, M. (1996b). The origins of children's spatial semantic categories: cognitive versus linguistic determinants. In J.J. Gumperz & S.C. Levinson (Eds.), *Rethinking linguistic relativity*. Cambridge: Cambridge University Press, 145–176.

Bowerman, M., de León, L., & Choi, S. (1995). Verbs, particles, and spatial semantics: learning to talk about spatial actions in typologically different languages. In E.V. Clark (Ed.), *The proceedings of the Twenty-seventh Annual Child Language Research Forum*. Stanford, CA: Stanford University Center for the Study of Language and Information, 101–110.

Bowerman, M., & Pederson, E. (1992). Crosslinguistic perspectives on topological spatial relationships. Paper presented at the annual meeting of the American Anthropological Association, San Francisco, CA, December.

Bybee, J.L. (1985). *Morphology: a study of the relation between meaning and form*. Amsterdam/Philadelphia: John Benjamins.

Bybee, J.L., Perkins, R., & Pagliuca, W. (1994). *The evolution of grammar: tense, aspect, and modality in the languages of the world*. Chicago: Chicago University Press.

Caplan, D. (1992). *Language: structure, processing, and disorders*. Cambridge, MA: MIT Press.

Choi, S. (1997). Language-specific input and early semantic development: evidence from children learning Korean. In D.I. Slobin (Ed.), *The crosslinguistic study of language acquisition*, vol. 5: *Expanding the contexts*, pp. 41–133. Mahwah, NJ: Lawrence Erlbaum.

Choi, S., & Bowerman, M. (1991). Learning to express motion events in English and Korean: the influence of language-specific lexicalization patterns. *Cognition, 41*, 83–121.

Comrie, B. (1981). *Language universals and linguistic typology: syntax and morphology*. Chicago: University of Chicago Press.

Craig, C. (Ed.) (1986). *Noun classes and categorization.* Amsterdam/Philadelphia: John Benjamins.

Croft, W. (1990). *Typology and universals.* Cambridge: Cambridge University Press.

Erbaugh, M.S. (1986). Taking stock: the development of Chinese noun classifiers historically and in young children. In Craig 1986, pp. 399–436.

Gleitman, L.R., Gleitman, H., Landau, B., & Wanner, E. (1988). Where learning begins: initial representations for language learning. In F.J. Newmeyer (Ed.), *Linguistics: the Cambridge survey,* vol. 3: *Language: psychological and biological aspects,* pp. 150–193. Cambridge: Cambridge University Press.

Gleitman, L.R., & Wanner, E. (1982). Language acquisition: the state of the state of the art. In E. Wanner & L.R. Gleitman (Eds.), *Language acquisition: the state of the art,* pp. 3–48. Cambridge: Cambridge University Press.

Gopnik, A., & Meltzoff, A.N. (1996). *Words, thoughts, and theories.* Cambridge, MA: MIT Press.

Green, J.N. (1982). The status of the Romance auxiliaries of voice. In N. Vincent & M. Harris (Eds.), *Studies in the Romance verb,* pp. 97–138. London/Canberra: Croom Helm.

Haiman, J. (Ed.) (1985a). *Iconicity in syntax.* Amsterdam, Philadelphia: John Benjamins.

Haiman, J. (Ed.) (1985b). *Natural syntax: iconicity and erosion.* Cambridge: Cambridge University Press.

Heine, B., Claudi, U., & Hünnemeyer, F. (1991). *Grammaticalization: a conceptual framework.* Chicago: University of Chicago Press.

Hopper, P.J., & Traugott, E.C. (1993). *Grammaticalization.* Cambridge: Cambridge University Press.

Jackendoff, R.S. (1983). *Semantics and cognition.* Cambridge, MA: MIT Press.

Jackendoff, R.S. (1987). *Consciousness and the computational mind.* Cambridge, MA: MIT Press.

Jackendoff, R.S. (1990). *Semantic structures.* Cambridge, MA: MIT Press.

Karmiloff-Smith, A. (1992). *Beyond modularity: a developmental perspective on cognitive science.* Cambridge, MA: MIT Press.

Landau, B., & Gleitman, L.R. (1985). *Language and experience: evidence from the blind child.* Cambridge, MA: Harvard University Press.

Landau, B., & Jackendoff, R. (1993). "What" and "where" in spatial language and spatial cognition. *Behavioral and Brain Sciences, 16,* 217–265.

Levin, B. (1993). *English verb classes and alternations: a preliminary investigation.* Chicago: University of Chicago Press.

Levinson, S.C. (1994). Vision, shape and linguistic description: Tzeltal body-part terminology and object description. *Linguistics, 32,* 791–855.

Lyons, J. (1968). *Introduction to theoretical linguistics.* Cambridge: Cambridge University Press.

Meillet, A. (1912). L'évolution des formes grammaticales. *Scientia (Rivista di scienza), 12* (26). Reprinted in Meillet, A. [1982]. *Linguistique historique et linguistique générale,* pp. 130–148. Geneva: Slatkine/Paris: Champion.

Pinker, S. (1984). *Language learnability and language development.* Cambridge, MA: Harvard University Press.

Pinker, S. (1989). *Learnability and cognition: the acquisition of argument structure.* Cambridge, MA: MIT Press.

Sapir, E. (1921/1949). *Language: an introduction to the study of speech.* New York: Harcourt Brace.

Schlesinger, I.M. (1979). Cognitive and linguistic structures: the case of the instrumental. *Journal of Linguistics, 15,* 307–324.

Schlesinger, I.M. (1982). *Steps to language: toward a theory of language acquisition.* Hillsdale, NJ: Lawrence Erlbaum Associates.

Schlesinger, I.M. (1988). The origin of relational categories. In Y. Levy, I.M. Schlesinger, & M.D.S. Braine (Eds.), *Categories and processes in language acquisition,* pp. 121–178. Hillsdale, NJ: Lawrence Erlbaum Associates.

Slobin, D.I. (1985). Crosslinguistic evidence for the Language-Making Capacity. In D.I. Slobin (Ed.), *The crosslinguistic study of language acquisition*, vol. 2: *Theoretical issues*, pp. 1157–1256. Hillsdale, NJ: Lawrence Erlbaum.

Slobin, D.I. (1991). Learning to think for speaking: native language, cognition and rhetorical style. *Pragmatics, 1,* 7–25.

Slobin, D.I. (1996). From "thought and language" to "thinking for speaking." In J.J. Gumperz & S.C. Levinson (Eds.), *Rethinking linguistic relativity*, pp. 70–86. Cambridge: Cambridge University Press.

Slobin, D.I. (1997). The origins of grammaticizable notions: beyond the individual mind. In D.I. Slobin (Ed.), *The crosslinguistic study of language acquisition*, vol. 5: *Expanding the contexts*, pp. 265–323. Mahwah, NJ: Lawrence Erlbaum.

Talmy, L. (1978). The relation of grammar to cognition – a synopsis. In D. Waltz (Ed.), *Proceedings of TINLAP-2 (Theoretical Issues in Language Processing)*, pp. 1–11. New York: Association for Computing Machinery.

Talmy, L. (1983). How language structures space. In H. Pick & L. Acredolo (Eds.), *Spatial orientation: theory, research and application*, pp. 181–238. New York: Plenum Press.

Talmy, L. (1985). Lexicalization patterns: semantic structure in lexical form. In T. Shopen (Ed.), *Language typology and semantic description*, vol. 3: *Grammatical categories and the lexicon*, pp. 36–149. Cambridge: Cambridge University Press.

Talmy, L. (1988). The relation of grammar to cognition. In B. Rudzka-Ostyn (Ed.), *Topics in cognitive linguistics*, pp. 166–205. Amsterdam/Philadelphia: John Benjamins.

Tomasello, M. (1992). The social bases of language acquisition. *Social Development, 1,* 67–87.

Tomasello, M. (1995). Pragmatic contexts for early verb learning. In M. Tomasello & W.E. Merriman (Eds.), *Beyond names for things: young children's acquisition of verbs*, pp. 115–146. Hillsdale, NJ, and Hove: Lawrence Erlbaum.

Traugott, E.C. (1972). *The history of English syntax*. New York: Holt, Rinehart & Winston.

Traugott, E.C., & Heine, B. (Eds.) (1991). *Approaches to grammaticalization*, vol. 1: *Focus on theoretical and methodological issues*; vol. 2: *Focus on types of grammatical markers*. Amsterdam/Philadelphia: John Benjamins.

Van Valin, R.D., Jr. (1992). An overview of ergative phenomena and their implications for language acquisition. In D.I. Slobin (Ed.), *The crosslinguistic study of language acquisition*, vol. 3, pp. 15–38. Hillsdale, NJ: Lawrence Erlbaum.

Part IV

Brains, Genes, and Computation in Language Development

Introduction to Part IV

The readings in Parts I–III were selected to provide a perspective on basic phenomena in language development, from speech perception, through first words, to the development of grammar. Of the many papers that we might have chosen from this extraordinary rich and active field, we focused on works that emphasize learning and change, including both quantitative (gradual, continuous) change as well as qualitative (discrete, discontinuous) change. This decision was motivated by theoretical as well as empirical concerns: to provide coherence, and to prepare the interested reader for reading and research in child language development within the framework of 21st-century Cognitive Science.

To preserve coherence, we decided against the "one of everything" strategy, a democratic approach but one that often results in books that resemble a small-town zoo, with one animal from every major species. In the field of language development, which has more than its share of controversy, the one-of-everything strategy can lead to a collection that is less like a zoo and more like a jungle, with the warring factions of nativism and empiricism all given equal time to fight today's battles. A book of that kind might leave our readers well informed about those battles, but it is not clear that it would prepare them for tomorrow's science. The papers in Parts I–III present an array of solid facts that must be explained regardless of one's theoretical framework. But by focusing on papers that emphasize learning and change, we have also made a carefully considered judgment about the future of the field.

In our view, the Nature–Nurture debate is over. Indeed, it is increasingly clear that this debate was based on a series of false oppositions, between learning and maturation, and between social and biological constraints. To prepare our readers for research on child language in the future, we end this volume with three tutorials on biological and computational approaches to language learning – papers that will (we hope) clarify why the Nature–Nurture debate has come to an end at last. The chapter by Clancy and Finlay reviews key aspects of brain development before and during the period in which language is acquired. The chapter by Elman reviews computational models of learning in neural networks, with special reference to language. Finally, the paper by Karmiloff-Smith describes the course of language, cognitive, and social development in children with genetic disorders, yielding insights into the complex and indirect route by which genes influence behavioral outcomes.

All three papers underscore why the opposition between learning and maturation is so misleading. Behavioral evidence (and there is now a great deal of it) clearly shows that language develops across an extended period of time, drawing on powerful learning mechanisms that are up and running at birth (indeed, well before birth), and that are sensitive to the fine-grained structure and statistics of the input. However, this result in no way constitutes a victory of Nurture over Nature. Instead, it is a discovery about the nature of Nature. Learning is a biological process; the human brain evolved to acquire information, just as the lungs evolved to breathe air, and the heart to pump blood. Furthermore, as Clancy and Finlay show in their paper, the neural mechanisms that are used to set up the cortex in the first place (i.e., the ones that most people have in mind when they use the term "maturation") are largely the same mechanisms that are used to acquire new knowledge about the world (the processes that are usually grouped under "learning"). Neural elements sprout, die away, or fortify their connections to other units in response to patterned input, conditioned by their immediate context (including the neuron next door) and by the larger neurochemical and structural environment. These processes are the same, whether that input comes from another part of the child's own body (including other parts of the brain) or from the face and voice of another human being.

In his chapter, Elman reviews some relatively simple rules of learning in neural networks, showing how the nonlinear dynamical properties of these "brain-like" systems can lead to profiles of learning and change that simulate many of the phenomena that characterize language learning in children. Many of the 20th-century claims about the "unlearnability" of language (especially grammar) need to be re-examined in light of these discoveries (Elman et al., 1996). This does not mean, however, that language learning is an unconstrained process by which the environment stamps itself upon an empty brain. The human brain is already exquisitely structured at birth (due in part to learning from its own body), and it is biased to learn in particular ways. Entirely different outcomes (e.g., whether or not a grammar with long-distance dependencies can be learned at all) can rise or fall depending on small changes in the timing, speed, and nature of the learning device itself. Without building in innate knowledge of any kind (in the usual sense of the term), evolution can act to guarantee widely different outcomes just by twiddling with the dials on the learning machine.

This brings us to the false choice between biological and social constraints. From or before birth, healthy human children are strongly biased to learn from the people around them (Tomasello, 1999). Statistical learning is extremely fast and powerful (see Gómez & Gerken, Part I), and perhaps for that reason, evolution had to assure that it would not be applied promiscuously; apparently typing it to social processes is one way to do this. During our protracted period of gestation, "The brain is the captive audience of the body" (as Anthony Damasio has put it). Through patterned sensory and motor activity in utero, the brain is gradually and thoroughly colonized by the body, organized along sensorimotor dimensions that will influence the way we think and how we feel for the rest of our lives. As a crucial dimension of this initial sensorimotor organization, healthy children are also born looking and listening especially intently for social signals, clues about where and how they should learn from that point on. Human infants are thus biologically prepared to learn about people, to solve problems and manipulate objects, to watch how other people solve problems and manipulate objects, and to do what they can to be like other persons. Human biology is social (or, if you prefer, human sociality is a product of biology). By binding our powerful capacity for learning to an equally powerful capacity for sociality, humans became the only species capable of language, culture, and technology. In her paper on the role of development in developmental disorders, Karmiloff-Smith shows how small perturbations in the "starting state" of the human infant (due to defective genes) can lead to deviant outcomes in the normal process.

In the new century, the study of language development will (we believe) take place within the larger interdisciplinary community of Cognitive Science and Neuroscience, and it will emphasize not only the empirical facts of language development (of the sort that are illustrated in Parts I–III), but also the biological and computational mechanisms for learning and change that permit language development to take place. The three tutorials in the final part of this volume are designed to place research on language development within this larger context, emphasizing the neural substrates of learning (Clancy & Finlay), computational models of learning (Elman), and genetic contributions to this learning process (Karmiloff-Smith).

References

Elman, J.L., Bates, E., Johnson, M., Karmiloff-Smith, A., Parisi, D., & Plunkett, K. (1996). *Rethinking innateness: A connectionist perspective on development.* Cambridge, MA: MIT Press/Bradford Books [paperback edition published 1998].

Tomasello, M. (1999). *The cultural origins of human cognition.* Cambridge, MA: Harvard University Press.

SEVENTEEN

Connectionism and Language Acquisition
Jeffrey L. Elman

Metaphors play a far more important role in science than many people realize. We are not only fascinated when we discover resemblances between phenomena that come from wildly different domains (atoms and solar systems, for example); these similarities often shape the way we think. Metaphors both extend but also limit our imagination.

Until recently, the metaphor that dominated the way we thought about the human brain was the digital computer. This is no coincidence: During the early days of what we now call computer science, in the 1940s and 1950s, engineers and mathematicians were very impressed by work by neuroscientists that suggested that the basic process-ing elements of the brain – neurons – were nothing more than binary on/off units. The first computers were actually designed to mimic with vacuum tubes what neuro-scientists thought brains were doing. Thus, the metaphor of the brain-as-computer actually started the other way around: the computer-as-brain.

This metaphor has had an enormous impact on the theories that people have devel-oped about many aspects of human cognition. Cognitive processes were assumed to be carried out by discrete operations that were executed in serial order. Memory was seen as distinct from the mechanisms that operated on it. And most importantly, processing was thought of in terms of symbolic rules of the sort that one finds in computer pro-gramming languages. These assumptions underlay almost all of the important cogni-tive theories up through the 1970s, and continue to be highly influential today.

But as research within this framework progressed, the advances also revealed short-comings. By the late 1970s, a number of people interested in human cognition began to take a closer look at some of basic assumptions of the current theories. In particu-lar, some people began to worry that the differences between digital computers and human brains might be more important than hitherto recognized. In part, this change reflected a more detailed and accurate understanding about the way brains work. For example, it is now recognized that the frequency with which a neuron fires – an essen-tially analog variable – is more important than the single on/off (or digital) pulse from which spike trains are formed. But the dissatisfaction with the brain-as-computer metaphor was equally rooted in empirical failures of the digitally based models to account for complex human behavior.

In 1981, Geoff Hinton and Jim Anderson put together a collection of papers (*Parallel Associative Models of Associative Memory*) that presented an alternative computational framework for understanding cognitive processes. This collection marked a sort of watershed. Brain-style approaches were hardly new. Psychologists such as Donald Hebb, Frank Rosenblatt, and Oliver Selfridge in the late 1940s and 1950s, mathematicians such as Jack Cowan in the 1960s, and computer scientists such as Teuvo Kohonen in the 1970s (to name but a small number of influential researchers) had made important advances in brain-style computation. But it was not until the early 1980s that connectionist approaches made significant forays into mainstream cognitive psychology. Then, in 1981, David Rumelhart and Jay McClelland published a paper that described a model of how people people read words. The model did not look at all like the traditional computer-based theories. Instead, it looked much more like a network of neurons. This paper had a dramatic impact on psychologists and linguists. Not only did it present a compelling and comprehensive account of a large body of empirical data, but laid out a conceptual framework for thinking about a number of problems which had seemed not to find ready explanation in the Human Information Processing approach. The publication, in 1986, a two-volume collection edited by Rumelhart and McClelland, and the PDP Research Group, called *Parallel Distributed Processing: Explorations in the Microstructure of Cognition*, served to consolidate and flesh out many details of the new approach (variously called PDP, neural networks, or connectionism).

This approach has stimulated a radical re-evaluation of many basic assumptions throughout cognitive science. One of the domains in which the impact has been particularly dramatic – and highly controversial – is in the study of language acquisition. Language is, after all, one of the quintessentially human characteristics. Figuring out just how it is that children learn language has to be one of the most challenging questions in cognitive science. But before turning to some of these new connectionist accounts of language acqusition, which is the main subject of this chapter, let us briefly define what we mean by connectionism.

What Is Connectionism?

The class of models that fall under the connectionist umbrella is large and diverse. But almost all models share certain characteristics.

Processing is carried out by a (usually large) number of (usually very simple) processing elements. These elements, called nodes or units, have a dynamics that is roughly analogous to simple neurons. Each node receives input (which may be excitatory or inhibitory) from some number of other nodes, responds to that input according to a simple activation function, and in turn excites or inhibits other nodes to which it is connected. Details vary across models, but most adhere to this general scheme. One connectionist networks is shown in figure 17.1. This network is designed to take visual input in the form of letters, and then to recognize words – that is, to read.

There are several key characteristics that are important to the way these networks operate. First, the response (or activation) function of the units is often *nonlinear*. This means that the units may be particularly sensitive under certain circumstances but relatively insensitive under others. This nonlinearity has very important consequences for

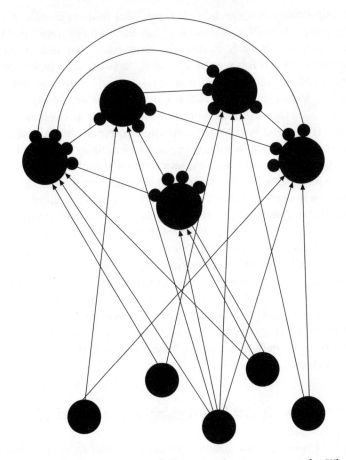

Figure 17.1 A neural network that reads letters and recognizes words. When a letter is detected, the corresponding letter node activates all words that contain it (lines with arrows). Since only one word can be present at a time, word nodes compete with inhibitory connections (lines with filled circles).

processing. Among other things, networks can sometimes operate in a discrete, binary-like manner, yielding crisp categorical behavior. In other circumstances, the system is capable of graded, continuous responses.

Second, what the system "knows" is, to a large extent, captured by the pattern of connections – who talks to whom – as well as the weights associated with each connection (weights serve as multipliers).

Third, rather than using symbolic representations, the vocabulary of connectionist systems consists of patterns of activations across different units. For example, to present a word as a stimulus to a network, we would represent it as a pattern of activations across a set of input units. The exact choice of representation might vary dramatically. At one extreme, a word could be represented by a single, dedicated input unit (thus acting very much like an atomic symbol). At the other extreme, the entire ensemble of input units might participate in the representation, with different words having different patterns of activation across a shared set of units.

Given the importance of the weighted connections in these models, a key question is, What determines the values of these weights? Put in more traditional terms, Who programs the networks? In early models, the connectivity laid out by hand, and this remains the case for what are sometimes called "structured" connectionist models. However, one of the exciting developments that has made connectionism so attractive to many was the development of algorithms by which the weights on the connections could be learned. In other words, the networks could learn the values for the weights on their own – they could be self-programming. Moreover, the style of learning was through induction. Networks would be exposed to examples of a target behavior (for example, the appropriate responses to a set of varied stimuli). Through learning, the network would learn to adjust the weights in small incremental steps in such a way that over time, the network's response accuracy would improve. Hopefully, the network would also be able to generalize its performance to novel stimuli, thereby demonstrating that it had learned the underlying generalization that related outputs to inputs (as opposed to merely memorizing the training examples).

(It should be noted that the type of learning described above – so-called "supervised learning" – is but one of a number of different types of learning that are possible in connectionist networks. Other learning procedures do not involve any prior notion of "correct behavior" at all. The network might learn instead, for example, the correlational structure underlying a set of patterns.) Now let us turn to some of the interesting properties of these networks and the ways in which they offer new accounts of language acquisition.

Learning the Past Tense of English: Rules or Associations?

The study of language is notoriously contentious, but until recently, researchers who could agree on little else have all agreed on one thing: that linguistic knowledge is couched in the form of rules and principles. (Pinker & Prince, 1988)

We have, we believe, provided a distinct alternative to the view that children learn the rules of English past-tense formation in any explicit sense. We have shown that a reasonable account of the acquisition of past tense can be provided without recourse to the notion of a 'rule' as anything more than a description of the language. (Rumelhart & McClelland, 1986)

In 1986, Rumelhart and McClelland published a paper that described a neural network that learned the past tense of English. Given many example of the form "walk → walked," the network not only learned to produce the correct past tense for those verbs to which it had been exposed, but for novel verbs as well – even including novel irregular verbs (e.g., "sing/sang"). Impressively, the network had not been taught explicit rules, but seemed to have learned the pattern on which the English past tense is formed through an inductive process based on many examples. Rumelhart and McClelland's conclusion – that the notion of "rule" might help *describe* the behavior of children as well as netowrks, but play no role in generating that behavior – generated a storm of controversy and has given rise to hundreds of experiments (with children) and simulations (with neural networks) as these claims and the counter-claims (e.g., by Pinker & Prince, in the above citation) have been refined and tested.

The particular example of the past tense was particularly significant, because the pattern that many children display in the course of learning the past tense of English verbs had long been interpreted as evidence that children were learning a rule. Cazden (1968) and Kuczaj (1977) were among the first to notice that at very early stages of learning, many children are relatively accurate in producing both the "regular" (add +ed to make the past) and "irregular" ("sang," "came," "made," "caught") verbs. Subsequently, as they learn more verbs, some children appear to go through a stage where they indiscriminately add the "+ed" suffix to all verbs, even irregulars that they have previously produced correctly (e.g., "comed" or "camed"). A reasonable interpretation is that at this point, the child has discovered the rule "add +ed." The errors arise because learning is incomplete and they have failed to note that there are some verbs to which the rule does not apply. So they overgeneralize the "+ed" pattern inappropriately. Ultimately, of course, the children do then pass to a third stage in which these exceptions are handled correctly. Voilà: a rule caught in the process of being learned.

But is this really what is happening? Rumelhart and McClelland's model also demonstrated a similar U-shaped performance as it learned the past tense. Yet their network did not seem to be learning a rule per se. Instead, the network was using analogy to discover patterns of behavior. During the very early stages, the network did not know enough verbs for this process to be very effective, and so its performance was very conservative – almost a matter of rote learning. As more verbs were acquired, the pattern of "add +ed" that was common to the majority of verbs took hold, and the network started generalizing that pattern across the board. It was only with additional learning that the network was able to learn both the general pattern as well as the sub-patterns ("sing/sang," "ring/rang," etc.) and outright exceptions ("is/was," "have/had").

This alternative account does not, of course, prove anything about what real children do. But it does provide an alternative and very different account of what had been taken to be the paradigm example of rule-learning by children. So it is no surprise that this model generated a storm of controversy. Steven Pinker and Alan Prince wrote a detailed and highly critical response in which they questioned many of the methodological assumptions made by Rumelhart and McClelland in their simulation, and challenged Rumelhart and McClelland's conclusions. This then spurred many others to develop connectionist models that corrected some of the weaknesses of the original model, and also to help provide a better understanding for the underlying principles that guide learning in connectionist networks (e.g., Daugherty & Seidenberg, 1992; Hare et al., 1995; Plunkett & Marchman, 1991, 1993: to name but a few).

In response, proponents of the symbolic rule account have argued that perhaps children might employ something like a connectionist system to learn irregular verbs, but that the regular verbs are produced be a distinct rule-based mechanism (e.g., Marcus et al., 1993; Marcus, 1995; Prasada et al., 1990). This has become known as the "dual mechanism" account. Furthermore, researchers cite neurological and genetic data that they say argues for two such separable systems in humans (Jaeger et al., 1996; Gopnik

& Crago, 1991). Connectionists, who favor a single mechanism approach, argue that a network can in fact produce the full range of behaviors which characterize regular and irregular verbs (Marchman et al., 1997; Nakisa & Hahn, 1996; Plunkett & Nakissa, 1997) – including historical changes in the way the English past tense was formed (Hare & Elman, 1995), as well as the neurological data (Elman & Hare, 1997; Joanisse & Seidenberg, 1999).

This debate continues today, and although the acrimony is at times excessive, there is no question that the issues have been sharpened through this debate, and we have developed a far more detailed picture of this corner of language than we had before.

Learning the Concept "Word": Studies with Infants and Networks

Clearly, knowledge of vocabulary cannot be innate: A child born in Singapore must be able to learn a different word for "milk" than a child born in Tibet. But how do infants even know that there are such things as words in the first place? After all, spoken language rarely brackets words with signposts that say "here is a word." In fluent speech, for example, words are not separated by pauses or silence, and all the infant hears is a continuous stream of unsegmented noise. But many theories of acquisition depend crucially upon prior knowledge of such primitive concepts as word, or morpheme, or more abstract categories such as noun, verb, or phrase (e.g., Berwick & Weinberg, 1984; Pinker, 1984). Rarely is it asked how a language learner knows about these concepts in the first place. Often, it is assumed they are innate.

Yet in fact, there is considerable debate among linguists and psycholinguists about what are the basic representations that are used in language. It is commonplace to speak of basic entities such as phoneme, morpheme, or word. Surprisingly, these constructs have no clear or uncontroversial definition. Furthermore, in what are called polysynthetic languages (e.g., many Inuit languages) things that might in those languages be called a word would, in English, be considered a phrase or even entire sentence. Thus, there is a fundamental question about how even the concept word might be learned – let alone the vocabulary of a language itself.

One connectionist model that investigated this question began by making two simple assumptions. First, the architecture of the network would have feedback loops so that the network had a basic kind of memory (memory not for the literal past, but for the network's only internal prior states). Such a network (called a "simple recurrent network") is shown in figure 17.2. Second, the network would be given a sequence of encoded stimuli, and after each new stimulus, asked to predict what might come next.

The encoded stimuli were actually numeric codes that stood for letters, and the whole series of stimuli were drawn from a children's story. But instead of seeing "Many years ago, a boy and a girl lived by the sea . . . ," the network saw a continuous stream of numbers (each number standing for a different letter). There were no breaks (spaces) between words. And the network wasn't told what letters the codes stood for.

Of course, short of memorizing the story – which was too long for memorization to be a feasible strategy – one would not expect the network to perform perfectly in its prediction. On the other hand, consider what a person would do if confronted with the

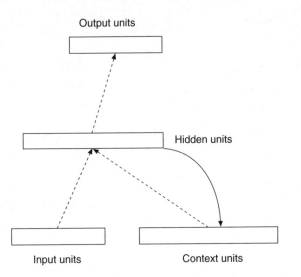

Figure 17.2 Simple recurrent network. Groups of nodes are shown as rectangles. The feedback connection between Hidden Units and Context Units provides the network with memory.

first two letters of a word, for example, "Ma__," and asked to predict what came next. She would know that there is a limited range of possibilities. The next letter is almost certainly a consonant, and "n," "t," "s" are far more likely than "v," given the vocabulary of English. And this turns out to be exactly what the network learns. It discovers the distributional properties of these encoded stimuli (which, remember, it doesn't know are letters) and then it predicts stimuli in a way that reflects their conditional probabilities, given the context. If one graphs the network's performance, measuring its error when predicting each letter, the result looks something like what is shown in figure 17.3.

An immediate pattern is obvious here: The network's ability to predict letters depends on where in the word the letter is. Word-initial letters are difficult to predict (because virtually any letter might occur), whereas after a few letters, the constraints limit the possible letters and the network's predictions improve.

As far as the network is concerned, of course, it doesn't need to know about things such as letters or words. The network is merely trying to anticipate what could come next, and is taking advantage of the statistical regularities in the sequence. However, the fact that there are some sequences (letters internal to a word) that are more predictable than otherss (letters between words) provides evidence that the network could then use this to infer the existence of the basic units we call words. All that is needed is that the network is aware of its own performance, and notices that there are strings of sequences which seem to go together, and others that don't. The strings that go together are, of course, what we know to be words. (Notice that in the above example, "aboy" would be segmented as a single word. This is because this phrase is very common and the network has not yet broken the sequence into two words. Interestingly, young children also make similar errors, treating common sequences as if they were units.)

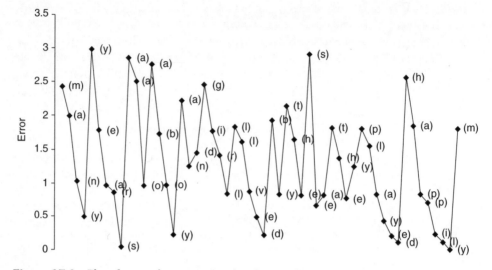

Figure 17.3 Plot of network error in "predict the next letter" task, using a simple recurrent network (after Elman, 1980).

This simulation suggests a strategy that infants might use to learn the basic units of their language. In 1996, empirical evidence was reported that suggested that infants in fact do use such a strategy (Saffran et al., 1986). In the Saffran et al. study, 8-month-old infants were exposed to nonsense speech made up of three-syllable "words" that were strung together with no breaks (e.g., "bidakupadotigo-labubidaku"). After listening to this sequence for only a few minutes, infants were able to discriminate between two new sequences, one of which was made up of a new combination of these "words" vs. another that used the same syllables permuted in a different order. The behavior of these infants is very much like what one would expect if they were using statistical regularities in a way similar to the prediction network above.

More recently, other researchers have found that young infants are able to learn regularities in artificially generated sequences that are even more complex – as if the rudiments of simple grammar might be learned through statistical induction (Gómez & Gerken, 1999; Marcus et al., 1999). The interpretation of these data are quite controversial. Marcus and his colleagues, for example, argue that the results show that infants are using algebraic, symbol-processing (Gómez and Gerken, on the other hand, make no such claims). But Seidenberg and Elman (1999a, 1999b) have demonstrated that neural networks show exactly the same kind of performance as the infants, and clearly are not using symbolic machinery to learn the patterns.

Learning the Unlearnable: Recursion and "the Importance of Starting Small"

The last example of connectionist models of language acquisition to be discussed concerns a phenomenon that many have held provides unequivocal evidence for innate knowledge of linguistic structure – yet which we now know from connectionist modeling is learnable. The phenomenon is what has been called "recursion," and it turns up in virtually every sentence we produce that has more than a few words.

Consider the phrases such as "John," "the old man," "the curious yellow cat," or "the mouse that ate the cheese." These are all examples of what are called noun phrases. Notice in this last example, "the cheese" itself is a noun phrase. Thus, noun phrases may contain other noun phrases (if you remember from high school English, "who ate the cheese" is called a "relative clause") and in fact, there is no principled limit to how far this process can be carried (e.g., "the mouse that ate the cheese that the child dropped on the floor . . ."). Such embedding of one linguistic unit inside another is called "recursion," and refers to the possibility that a category may be defined in terms of itself.

The Rumelhart and McClelland verb learning simulation that we began with dealt with issues in morphology (e.g., verb inflections), but soon other connectionist simulations were developed which modeled syntactic and semantic phenomena. All of those simulations, however, involved sentences of pre-specified (and limited) complexity. In 1988, Jerry Fodor and Zenon Pylyshyn wrote a paper in which they called attention to this shortcoming, and argued that the deficiency was not accidental. They claimed that connectionist models were in principle unable to deal with this kind of unbounded recursion or to represent complex structural relationships (constituent structure) in an open-ended manner.

In a simple recurrent network, the internal (or "hidden") units feed back on themselves (see Figure 17.2). This provides the network with a kind of memory. The form of the memory is not like a tape recorder, however; it does not literally record prior inputs. Instead, the network itself has to learn how to encode the inputs in the internal state, such that when the state is fed back it will provide the necessary information to carry out whatever task is being learned.

In 1991, Servan-Schreiber et al. demonstrated that such a network could be trained on an artificial language which was generated by something called a Finite State Automaton (FSA; an FSA is the simplest possible digital computer; the most powerful type of computer is a Turing Machine). The recurrent network's task was simply to listen to each incoming symbol, one at a time, and to predict what would come next. In the course of doing this, the network inferred the more abstract structure of the underlying artificial language.

The FSA language, however, lacked the hierarchical structure shown in Figure 17.2. In another set of simulations, Elman (1991, 1993) showed that simple recurrent networks could also process sentences containing relative clauses, which specifically involve hierarchical/compositional relations among different sentence elements. Weckerly and Elman (1992) showed that these networks also exhibit the same performance asymmetry in processing different types of embedded sentences that humans do. Their networks, like people, find sentences such as (1) more difficult than sentences such as (2a and 2b).

1   The mouse the cat the dog scared chased ran away.
2a   The dog scared the cat that chased the mouse that ran away.
2b   Do you believe the report the stuff they put in coke causes cancer is true?

Understanding exactly how such networks work is an interesting problem in its own right, and there are strong connections between their solutions and the dynamical systems we discuss below. What was interesting from the viewpoint of language acquisition, however, was something entirely unanticipated.

Initial attempts to train simple recurrent networks on an artificial language that contained sentences with recursion did not in fact succeed. Dismayingly, the network's performance was far worse than would have been expected given prior results with simple sentences. In order to see where the problem might lie (perhaps the network might deal with a limited form of recursion, for example), a new training regime was tried in which the network was given only simple sentences. This network did fine. So the same network was then given additional sentences to learn, a small number of which were complex (i.e., contained recursion). Again, the network did fine. In fact, as the complexity of the sentences was gradually increased, the network easily assimilated the new examples. By the end, the network was able to process the original set of complex sentences that it had failed to learn from when they were the initial dataset. The crucial difference was that when the network was hand-fed simple sentences prior to the complex ones, it was then – and only then – able to progress to the more complex forms later.

But it's not necessary to spoon-feed the network in this way. In a second simulation, at the outset of training, artificial noise was injected into the network every few words, simulating the effect of having a very limited working memory. The network, however, was exposed from the start to complex sentences. Over time, the noise was gradually decreased, as if the network's working memory were gradually improving with age. By the time the network had "grown up" (had adult-like working memory), it was able to fully process the complex sentences. The key to both simulations (described in greater detail in Elman, 1993) turned out to be that by focusing on the simple sentences first, the network was able to learn basic facts about language, such as grammatical category, noun–verb agreement, etc., that provided the necessary scaffolding for learning about more complex sentences. The problem with starting with those more complex sentences is that, lacking knowledge of the fundamentals, the patterns that are created by recursion were too difficult for the network to identify.

This result is interesting from several points of view. First, the fact that the network was able to learn complex grammar shows that these kinds of structures can be learnable by example, and without need for symbolic rules. Innate knowledge that is specifically linguistic is not necessary. Second, the networks demonstrate "the importance of starting small." This strategy suggests that what may be special about children's ability to learn languages may not be due to any special mechanism that they possess as children (e.g., a "Language Acquisition Device" of the sort hypothesized by Chomsky). The starting small hypothesis, which is similar to Newport's (1990) "less is more" proposal, is that children's language learning abilities are rooted in something entirely different. It is children's processing limitations that make language learning possible. By having a restricted working memory, children may be able to process only simple patterns; these patterns then provide a crucial foundation for learning subtler generalities. Viewed this way, what is "innate" that makes language possible has nothing to do specifically with language. Instead, it is – paradoxically – a maturational limitation on working memory that interacts with a general purpose learning mechanism that makes it possible to learn complex sentences.

Of course, the language that the networks described here have learned is still quite limited, and there are clearly many other aspects of human cognitive and social development that are necessary to learn language. The lesson of the connectionist models that have been described here is just that rather simple learning algorithms may be far more powerful than were previously recognized. And what makes human language possible may turn out not to be the evolution of a separate Language Organ, as envisaged by Chomsky, but rather a number of fairly small tweaks and twiddles in the cognitive capacities (including things such as the developmental timetable for working memory) that we share with our non-human cousins. It is from the complex interaction of these many small changes that language emerges.

References

Berwick, R.C., & Weinberg, A.S. (1984). *The grammatical basis of linguistic performance.* Cambridge, MA: MIT Press.

Cazden, C.B. (1968). The acquisition of noun and verb inflections. *Child Development, 18,* 21–40.

Daugherty, K., & Seidenberg, M. (1992). *The past tense revisited.* Paper presented at The Proceedings of the 14th Annual Meeting of the Cognitive Science Society, Princeton, N.J.

Elman, J.L. (1990). Finding structure in time. *Cognitive Science, 14,* 179–211.

Elman, J.L. (1991). Distributed representations, simple recurrent networks, and grammatical structure. *Machine Learning, 7,* 195–224.

Elman, J.L. (1993). Learning and development in neural networks: The importance of starting small. *Cognition, 48,* 71–99.

Elman, J.L., & Hare, M.L. (1997). *Single mechanism = single representation.* Hillsdale, NJ: Erlbaum.

Fodor, J.A., & Pylyshyn, Z.W. (1988). *Connectionism and cognitive architecture: A critical analysis.* Cambridge, MA: MIT Press/Bradford Books.

Gomez, R.L., & Gerken, L. (1999). Artificial grammar learning by 1-year-olds leads to specific and abstract knowledge. *Cognition, 70* (2), 109–135.

Gopnik, M., & Crago, M.B. (1991). Familial aggregation of a developmental language disorder. *Cognition, 39,* 1–50.

Hare, M.L., & Elman, J.L. (1995). Learning and morphological change. *Cognition, 56,* 61–98.

Hare, M.L., Elman, J.L., & Daugherty, K.G. (1995). Default generalization in connectionist networks. *Language and Cognitive Processes 10* (6), 601–630.

Hinton, G.E., & Anderson, J.A. (Eds.). (1981). *Parellel models of associative memory.* Hillsdale, NJ: Erlbaum.

Jaeger, J.J., Lockwood, A.H., Kemmerer, D.L., Van Valin, R.D., Murphy, B.W., & Khalak, H.G. (1996). Positron emission tomographic study of regular and irregular verb morphology in English. *Language, 72* (3), 451–497.

Joanisse, M.F., & Seidenberg, M.S. (1999). Impairments in verb morphology after brain injury: A connectionist model. *Proceedings of the National Academy of Sciences of the United States of America, 96* (13), 7592–7597.

Kuczaj, S.A., II. (1977). The acquisition of regular and irregular past tense forms. *Journal of Verbal Learning and Verbal Behavior, 16,* 589–600.

Marchman, V.A., Plunkett, K., & Goodman, J. (1997). Overregularization in English plural and past tense inflectional morphology: a response to Marcus (1995). *Journal of Child Language, 24* (3), 767–779.

Marcus, G.F. (1995). Children's overregularization of English plurals: A quantitative analysis. *Journal of Child Language, 22* (2), 447–460.

Marcus, G.F., Brinkmann, U., Clahsen, H., Wiese, R., Woest, A., & Pinker, S. (1993). *German inflection: The exception that rpoves the rule* (Occasional Paper 47). Cambridge, MA: Center for Cognitive Science, MIT.

Marcus, G.F., Vijayan, S., Rao, S.B., & Vishton, P.M. (1999). Rule learning by seven-month-old infants. *Science, 283* (5398), 77–80.

Nakisa, R.G., & Hahn, U. (1996). *Where defaults don't help: the case of the German plural system.* Paper presented at the 18th Annual Conference of the Cognitive Science Society, San Diego.

Newport, E.L. (1990). Maturational constraints on language learning. *Cognitive Science, 14,* 11–28.

Pinker, S. (1984). *Language learnability and language development.* Cambridge, MA: MIT Press.

Pinker, S., & Prince, A. (1988). On language and connectionism: Analysis of a parallel distributed processing model of language acquisition. *Cognition, 28,* 73–193.

Plunkett, K., & Marchman, V. (1991). U-Shaped learning and frequency effects in a multi-layered perceptron–implications for child language acquisition. *Cognition, 38* (1), 43–102.

Plunkett, K., & Marchman, V. (1993). From rote learning to system building – acquiring verb morphology in children and connectionist nets. *Cognition, 48* (1), 21–69.

Plunkett, K., & Nakisa, R.C. (1997). A connectionist model of the Arabic plural system. *Language and Cognitive Processes, 12,* 807–836.

Prasada, S., Pinkder, S., & Snyder, W. (1990). *Some evidence that irregular forms are retrieved from memory but regular forms are rule generated.* Paper presented at the Psychonomic Society meeting.

Rumelhart, D.E., & McClelland, J.L. (1981). *Interactive processing through spreading activation.* Hillsdale, NJ: Erlbaum.

Rumelhart, D.E., & McClelland, J.L. (1986). *On learning the past tenses of English verbs.* Cambridge, MA: MIT Press.

Saffran, J.R., Aslin, R.N., & Newport, E.L. (1996). Statistical learning by 8-month-old infants. *Science, 274* (5294), 1926–1928.

Seidenberg, M.S., & Elman, J.L. (1999a). Do infants learn grammar with algebra or statistics. *Science, 284,* 434–435.

Seidenberg, M.S., & Elman, J.L. (1999b). Networks are not 'hidden rules'. *Trends in Cognitive Sciences, 3* (8), 288–289.

Servan-Schreiber, D., Cleeremans, A., & McClelland, J.L. (1991). Graded state machines: The representation of temporal contingencies in simple recurrent networks. *Machine Learning, 7,* 161–193.

Weckerly, J., & Elman, J.L. (1992). *A PDP approach to processing center-embedded sentences.* Hillsdale, NJ: Erlbaum.

EIGHTEEN

Neural Correlates of Early Language Learning

Barbara Clancy and Barbara Finlay

The course of language development is exceedingly complex, characterized by massive variability across children and by multiple bursts and plateaus within individual children. This complexity is well illustrated in other chapters in this reader and in an extensive review from which this chapter is excerpted (Bates et al., in press). Learning plays an extremely important role throughout the development of language, beginning even in utero when children start to pick up language-specific preferences. Across development, language can be "tuned" in various directions depending on the nature of the input. This is not the original view of language development. Language milestones were previously believed to timed by a "biological clock" that also governed motor milestones like crawling and walking (Lenneberg, 1967). However, this notion of lockstep development (based on average onset times across different samples of children) implies a set of correlations that should hold up within individual children as well.

Doubts about such a lockstep process were raised when Bates et al. (1979) looked for such correlations in their longitudinal study of language and communication in a sample of healthy, normal children aged 9–13 months. They found no significant links between motor and language milestones, and, if anything, the non-significant correlation between walking and talking seemed to run in the wrong direction, as if there were a slight tendency for children to make some kind of choice about where to invest their energies among the various skills that are starting to emerge around this time. And yet we know that the nervous system continues to develop after birth in our species. Surely it ought to be possible to find neural correlates (and perhaps neural causes?) for the dramatic changes that characterize language development in the first few years of human life.

During a previous search for such correlates (Bates et al., 1992), two candidates appeared promising. First, the period between 8 and 10 months is a behavioral watershed, characterized by marked changes and reorganizations in many different domains including speech perception and production, memory and categorization, imitation, joint reference and intentional communication, and of course word comprehension. It seemed plausible that this set of changes (which *are* correlated within individual children) might be related to patterns of connectivity and brain metabolism. Second, the period between 16 and 30 months encases a series of sharp nonlinear increases in expressive language, including exponential increases in both vocabulary and grammar. A link seemed possible between this series of behavioral bursts and a marked increase in synaptic density and brain metabolism that was estimated to take place around the same time.

However, the search for neural correlates of language learning has turned out to be vastly more complex than previously thought. Although brain maturation undoubtedly plays a role in language learning, we now are somewhat wary of summaries or tables that imply any simple form of cause and effect. There are three main reasons for this new skepticism.

First, it has become increasingly clear that learning itself plays a massive role in language development. Of course this has to be true in some trivial sense, because we know that English children learn English and Chinese children learn Chinese. However, there has been a long tradition of suspicion about learning in the child language literature, because language development is characterized by so many funny-looking events, including long plateaus interrupted by exponential shifts, with occasional steps backward. These nonlinearities led many investigators to underplay the role of "garden-variety" learning in favor of a maturational view in which discontinuities at the behavioral level were caused by discontinuities in the nervous system (Pinker, 1994; Wexler, 1996). As it turns out, that simply isn't true. Artificial neural networks (Elman et al., 1996) have shown us that simple structures can be very good at learning, even simulating in considerable detail many of the discontinuities that characterize language development. Moreover, in "real life," we now have compelling evidence that even very young infants are capable of rapid and powerful forms of statistical learning (e.g., Bates & Elman, 1996; Elman & Bates, 1997; Saffran et al., 1996).

Second, we know much more than we used to know about human brain development, before and after birth. Some years ago, it seemed plausible that prenatal development was characterized primarily by *additive* events (e.g., neural tube formation, cell proliferation, the first wave of connectivity). Postnatal development seemed to be characterized primarily by *regressive* events (e.g., cell death, axon pruning) perhaps occurring under the guidance of experience. We now know it's not that easy – certainly it does not happen in any simple two-stage form. In fact, the picture of human brain development that we present here is one that is quite compatible with the burgeoning literature on early (even prenatal) learning, because so many of the events required to create a learning machine take place within the first two trimesters of prenatal human life. Everything that happens after that is really a matter of degree – maturational changes at every level of the system, in multiple overlapping gradients. There is little evidence for the old-fashioned notion of modular brain systems that "turn on" at a particular time, like successive levels in a computer game.

Third, it has become increasingly clear that the relationship between brain development and behavior is bi-directional. Although that was understood some years ago (Bates et al., 1992 underscored the role of experience in subtractive events, yielding the metaphor of experience as a sculptor working away in the studio of life), recent advances in developmental neurobiology have shown that the bi-directional dance between brain development and experience occurs at many more levels of the system, including additive events throughout the lifetime of the organism (Kempermann et al.,

1998; Kornack & Rakic, 1999). Even in adulthood, learning induces striking new morphological changes in brain regions related to a new task (Kleim et al., 1996; Kleim et al., 1997). As a result of all this new information, we can no longer assume that correlated changes in brain and behavior reflect a causal flow in one direction. It could just as easily be the other way around.

With these lessons in mind, we will attempt to replace the conventional notion of a lock-step version of language milestones and neural development, replacing it with a more dynamic, challenging, and ultimately more hopeful story. We are now able to offer support for a complex neural/language relationship that is actually quite forgiving in its very complexity. Dynamics of neural interactions, gradients, and overlapping events impart flexibility and plasticity, underscoring the value of remedial strategies and intervention training.

Here we will provide an overview of basic events in human brain development that precede, prepare, parallel, and (perhaps) participate in the language-learning process (for a comprehensive review of the literature on the language learning process and more detail on neural development, see the chapter from which this section is excerpted, Bates et al., in press). We will review neural events globally rather than concentrating on those areas conventionally viewed as "language areas" in the adult. In fact, it is more accurate to think of language acquisition and production as an interactive process involving auditory, visual, somatosensory, motor, memory, emotional, and associative functions.

First we will briefly review some basic neural terminology. Our discussion focuses primarily, but not exclusively on the brain region called the *isocortex* (a synonym for *neocortex* that neuroanatomists prefer because it does not make false assumptions about how "new" in phylogeny the cortex is). This is the convoluted sheet of layered neurons that appears on surface views of the brain (gray matter). Visual, somatic, language, all sensory/motor processing is accomplished here, associated with input relayed via the *thalamus*. The thalamus is a subcortical "relay-station" that transmits virtually all sensory input from the body surface and special sense organs (except olfaction) to the isocortex. Even during development, the thalamus maintains the "packaging" that separates one kind of input from another (e.g., visual, auditory, somatosensory). We will also briefly discuss the *limbic* system, a circuit of widely distributed neural structures that includes the hippocampal formation (associated with memory and spatial learning) as well as neural regions associated with olfaction and emotion.

On a basic level, these and all neural regions are made up of two types of cells, *neurons* (or nerve cells) and *glial* cells. A typical neuron has three divisions: a cell body (*soma*), an *axon*, which transmits chemoelectrical signals, and several branch-like *dendrites* that contain *receptors*, the receiving units of the neuron. Small currents of positively or negatively charged chemical ions cause a signal (or action potential) to travel down an axon. Glial cells are supporting cells for neurons. Some form white fatty sheaths, *myelin* (white matter), which insulate axons and so increase the speed and efficiency with which the signals can be transmitted. Chemical data (neurotransmitters or neuromodulators) are passed between cells at a gap where an axon from one cell almost, but not quite, meets a dendrite or cell body of another neuron. This point is called a *synapse*. Information transfer, or *synaptic transmission*, occurs when chemicals stored in a signaling neuron are released across the synapse onto receptors of another neuron. On some neurons, especially during development, the gap is even smaller than normal and the transmitting and receiving cells are almost contiguous. These points are called *gap junctions* or *electrical* synapses. Neural cells are formed in a process called *neurogenesis*, while the formation of the connections between neurons is called *synaptogenesis*. These types of formative events are considered additive events. The elimination of cells, axons, or synapses are considered regressive events.

   With these defininitions in hand, we will now address our attention to three main topics.

1   *Prenatal neural events: fundamental brain scaffolding*: What is the state of the brain at or before birth when language learning begins?
2   *Postnatal neural events*: What types of neurodevelopmental events take place after birth and across the period in which languages are learned?
3   *Interactions of neural patterns and events with language learning*: Do any neurodevelopmental events seem placed or ordered in such a way as to constrain when events in language learning might occur? Alternately, does language learning itself alter the course of brain development?

Prenatal Events: Fundamental Brain Scaffolding

Fixing the timing of events

There are no experimental studies directly relating language and cognitive development to brain maturation, and there are only a handful of studies that have tried to relate disorders of brain and behavioral development to fundamental cellular processes. As a result, our estimates of maturational timing in the human brain must be based on correlational and comparative approaches. We are aided by recent investigations showing that the schedule of human brain development can be mapped with some precision onto the maturational schedules of other animals (Clancy et al., 2000; Darlington et al., 1999; Finlay & Darlington, 1995). In fact, the order and relative spacing of brain development is remarkably stable across all mammalian species, permitting use of a regression equation to generate predictions of dates for events that are not able to be empirically measured in humans. This analysis has shown that primates (including humans) differ systematically from other mammals in the timing of neurogenesis in two key neural regions, the limbic system and the isocortex. Neurogenesis of the limbic regions is abbreviated in primates, resulting in uniformly smaller limbic structures when compared to similar areas in nonprimates. In contrast, the isocortex in primates has a relatively protracted neurogenesis, and a consequently increased relative size (Clancy et al., 2000; Finlay & Darlington, 1995). A very simple principle underlies this difference in the relative size and shape of brain systems: if a species gains extra cycles of neurogenesis across the course of evolution, the greatest relative enlargement occurs in the parts of the brain that develop relatively late.

   With this fact about primate variability factored into the statistical model we are able to produce reliable predictions for the dates of several aspects of neurogenesis, pathway formation, and various regressive events across brain systems which would typically require invasive procedures for accurate determination (discussed in more detail in Clancy, et al., 2000). Unless indicated, all statements in the following text about the time of occurrence of maturational events in human neural development are drawn from data produced using this comparative mammalian model.

First trimester

It is startling to realize how much of fundamental brain morphology and organization is already laid down by the end of the first three months of life (before many mothers even know that they are pregnant). A region of the embryo called the neural tube generates stem cells which give rise to almost the entire brain in the first trimester (the last layers of the isocortex and the external granular layer of the cerebellum are born during the second trimester). Two exceptions are the hippocampal dentate gyrus and the olfactory bulb, which are (as far as we now know) the only regions in which neurons are generated throughout life (Bayer, 1982, 1983; Kornack & Rakic, 1999; Kuhn et al., 1996; Luskin, 1998). One of the first activities of the early-generated neurons is to lay down the basic axonal pathways of the brainstem (Easter et al., 1993). There is no simple lockstep plan for all neurons like "Migrate; become electrically excitable; produce axon; produce dendrites; make neurotransmitter, fire away." To take the case of axons alone, axons can be produced while neurons are migrating; not produced until the terminal site is reached; may show growth of multiple stages and types (branching or not, for example); may be produced and then retracted; or may show prolonged periods of no apparent growth (waiting periods).

Two more critical processes are virtually complete by the end of the first trimester: the differentiation of cells into different subtypes (also called cell specification) and the migration of cells from their birthplace to their ultimate destinations in the isocortex. Neurons begin to express various complements of neurotransmitters and neuromodulators even before migration (Lidow & Rakic, 1995) and continue to develop in the following months. Although there are many different kinds of neurochemicals within and across cell types, there seems to be a general developmental principle at work: during development, neurons will often co-express multiple transmitters and modulators whereas single cells in the mature brain exhibit much less diversity.

Second trimester

This is the period in which the basic wiring of the brain takes place, i.e., large patterns of connectivity develop between neural regions, including the isocortex (Honig et al., 1996). From a developmental point of view, one of the most important events is the establishment of connections from the thalamus to all regions of the isocortex. These connections are set up in the second trimester in a pattern that very much resembles the adult pattern from the start, with animal studies showing that visual, somatosensory, auditory, and limbic areas of cortex all receive projections fairly exclusively from those thalamic nuclei that will project to them in adulthood (Miller et al., 1993; Molnar et al., 1998; O'Leary et al., 1994). This is particularly important for theories of development, because it means that the brain is "colonized" by the body long before birth and well before the outside world has a chance to instruct the brain. Intracortical pathways (i.e., connections from one cortical region to another) also begin to establish their mature connectivity patterns in the second trimester. The connections start to communicate (produce synapses) in their target structures in short order, although the bulk of synaptogenesis will occur later (Antonini & Shatz, 1990; Bourgeois & Rakic, 1993).

A particular kind of regressive event called apoptotic neuronal death begins in the second trimester (*apoptosis*, a type of cell death associated with an orchestrated program, not a disorganized dissolution of the cell). Overall, this early neuronal death seems to serve to grossly fix cell numbers in interconnecting populations and to fine-tune topographic projections between structures (Finlay, 1992), but does not con-tribute to the kind of fine-tuning of connectional anatomy associated with learning from the extra-uterine environment in the isocortex.

The second trimester is also the period in which something akin to learning or self-instruction begins, a process of activity-dependent self-organization of the nervous system. While the physiological and cellular consequences of this phenomenon have been best studied in the visual system, it seems like such a useful developmental mecha-nism for organizing spatially distributed systems that it is likely to be utilized else-where. For example, the first motor activity of the fetus begins at 2–3 months post conception and continues through intrauterine life, and although the neuroanatomi-cal consequences of this activity are not known, the pattern of activity that it gener-ates in the nervous system is structured and phasic (Robertson et al., 1982). At a time corresponding to the second trimester in humans, "waves" of activity begin to be propa-gated across the surface of the retina of cats and ferrets, beginning after basic con-nectivity is established and stopping before eye opening (reviewed in Wong, 1999). This organized activity can be the basis for a kind of primitive categorization, a process in which similar (correlated) inputs hang together while dissimilar (uncorrelated) inputs dissociate. This self-organizing process has some very interesting theoretical implica-tions for developmental psychologists because it seems to occupy a middle ground in the nature–nurture debate. Similar organizing mechanisms will be used later for learn-ing from the outside world, but they begin in utero to help set up the basic functional architecture of the brain.

Third trimester

By the beginning of the seventh month of gestation, a remarkably large number of neural events are complete. The human fetus has matured to the point where the eyes move and remain open for measurable periods of time. Reciprocal connectivity from higher-order cortical areas to primary areas has also begun (Burkhalter, 1993). Path-ways exhibit the initial process of myelination (Yakovlev & Lecours, 1967). Large descending pathways from the cortex are also in the process of development. Aside from the more obvious role of descending pathways in motor control, the appearance of descending pathways also means that the brain has started to "talk back" to the body, a form of interaction found in all sensory and motor systems.

In the eighth and ninth months, a massive and coordinated birth of connections (synaptogenesis) begins in the neurons of the isocortex and related structures. (This mass production will extend postnatally and is discussed in more detail below.) It is fair to say that the infant arrives in the world with a nervous system whose working components are in place and organized. All cells are generated, major incoming sensory pathways are in place and have already gone through a period of refinement of their total number of cells, connections, and topographic organization. Intracortical and connectional pathways are well developed, though output pathways lag behind. This brain is up and running by birth, ready to learn (or rather, ready to keep on learning).

Postnatal neural events.   Now we turn to a consideration of events that extend past birth, with special emphasis on the neural events that surround language learning.

Myelination

In the central nervous system, increases in the fatty sheaths around axons tend to occur earlier in sensory areas than in motor areas. This sequence of myelination has previously been offered as a possible contributor to a word comprehension/production disparity observed in some children. And since myelination of some neural regions continues well into maturity (Yakovlev & Lecours, 1967), there have also been speculations about its involvement in behavioral development (Parmelee & Sigman, 1983; Volpe, 1987). However, there are no clear-cut transitions in myelination and "undermyelinated" connections in the young human brain are quite capable of transmitting information. Interest in the role of myelination has waned in favor of other events in early brain development that are influenced by interactions of maturation and experience, such as synaptogenesis.

Synaptogenesis

An event that occurs within the critical time window for early language development is synaptogenesis. Synapse formation seems optimally placed for the rapid statistical learning infants show in both the visual and auditory realms during this time (Saffran et al., 1996). There are some interesting features to the formation of synapses and their restructuring and elimination within the perinatal period that seem quite closely related to early language acquisition.

Synapses are actually made up of several regions which we will briefly describe because some are altered during the same time period when language develops. On the transmitting side of the synapse, the axon contains the metabolic machinery to produce neurotransmitters and package them in vesicles. It also includes a *pre-synaptic specialization*, a thickening of the cellular membrane that helps transfer the contents of vesicles to the receiving neuron. The receiving *post-synaptic* cell also has a visible thickening of the membrane and includes the machinery to take up, and perhaps degrade the neurotransmitter, and to cause a reaction in the post-synaptic cell. Most, but not all, excitatory synapses have *asymmetric* synapses, in which the pre-synaptic specialization is thicker and denser than the post-synaptic one; most inhibitory synapses are *symmetric*, with pre- and post-synaptic thickenings of equal density. The location of the synapse is significant to its function – a synapse can be located on the cell body of the neuron itself, on the shafts of dendrites, or on small spikes appropriately called dendritic spines. This placement has consequences for how effectively the pre-synaptic input can induce changes in the post-synaptic cell.

A primary mode of learning in the nervous system (though not the only mode) takes place when the synaptic juncture is formed or modified as a function of experience, a "strengthening" or "weakening" referred to as *Hebbian* learning. If we ask ourselves where the nervous system stores its "knowledge" (assuming that this term is useful at all), most neuroscientists would agree that synaptic connectivity is a primary means by which knowledge is represented in the brain (Elman et al., 1996). This is why there is so much interest in the role of synaptogenesis and synaptic connectivity in behavioral development.

In cognitive science, the number of synapses is often thought of as an index for the amount and complexity of information transfer in a structure. Even though synaptic number might be used as such a metric in some comparisons (for example, after certain kinds of experience (Greenough, 1984), it is misleading to understand synaptic numbers in development in only this way. More in development does not necessarily mean better, more complex, or more mature. To take an extreme case, sudden infant death syndrome (SIDS) is associated with an excess number of persisting synapses in the medulla (O'Kusky & Norman, 1994, 1995). This point is important for understanding a high-profile controversy about synaptogenesis and the peak of synaptic numbers in the isocortex of primates and humans. Briefly, in work with rhesus macaques, Rakic and colleagues described a rapid increase in the number of synapses that seemed to take place almost simultaneously across a number of cortical areas, reaching a peak at around the same time in frontal, cingulate, somatosensory, and visual cortical areas (Bourgeois et al., 1994; Granger et al., 1995; Rakic et al., 1986; Zecevic et al., 1989; Zecevic & Rakic, 1991). In contrast, Huttenlocher, working with human material, showed that the peak of synaptic density varies between visual, auditory, and somatosensory regions, with the frontal regions not reaching their peak until 3–4 years after birth, while the visual and auditory regions peak more closely to birth (Huttenlocher & Dabholkar, 1997).

A closer examination proves that the story these two investigators tell is not very different after all. Rakic and Huttenlocher have both shown that the number of synapses accelerates wildly beginning just before birth, in both the macaque and the human, and across a wide variety of cortical areas. In macaques, the peak of synaptic density across cortical areas is reached two to four months after birth (Figure 18.1a – replotted from Bourgeois et al., 1994; Granger et al., 1995; Rakic et al., 1986; Zecevic et al., 1989; Zecevic & Rakic, 1991). In humans, the curves are very similar, with a marked perinatal increase in synaptic density that begins around birth and flattens postnatally across all cortical areas (Figure 18.1b – from Huttenlocher & Dabholkar, 1997).

The synapse counts may, or may not, vary across different cortical regions. In the graph, for example, synapse counts in human auditory cortex appear to outnumber those in other human and macaque cortical regions. However, for many methodological and technical reasons (reviewed in Bates et al., in press), absolute values of synapse counts should be considered somewhat conditional, especially in human tissue. Moreover, in the graph, we have attempted to normalize the data by plotting synapse numbers as a percent of the total at puberty, which we arbitrarily defined as 12 years in human and 3 years in macaque. The take home message from the graph lies not in the absolute numbers, but rather in the pattern of *relative* changes. The most interesting feature in both the macaque and the human data lies in the strikingly similar timing of acceleration and deceleration.

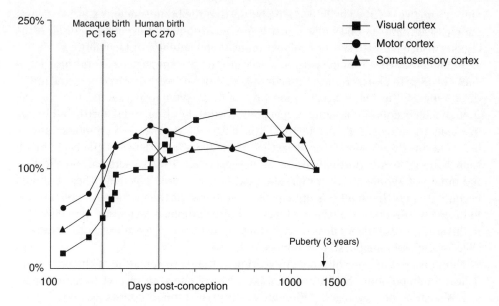

Figure 18.1A Macaque synaptogenesis. PC 112d – puberty.

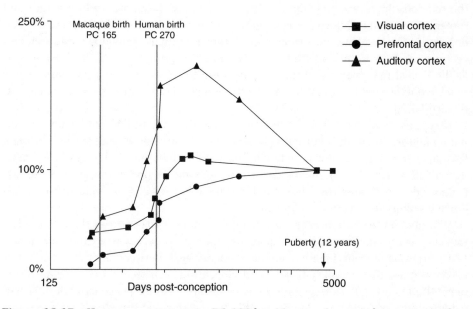

Figure 18.1B Human synaptogenesis. PC 192d – 12 years (converted to macaque days PC 146d – puberty).

We can safely conclude that the generation of synapses in the entire isocortex of humans accelerates around birth, overshoots by a substantial proportion in the first six months or so, and then declines to its adult value. Where the exact peak lies is probably not too important, as it will be influenced by any number of co-occurring additive and subtractive events. The important point is that the brain suddenly starts to generate massive numbers of synapses just before environmental experience, in all of its regions associated with sensory, motor, motivational, and linguistic ability.

What causes the dramatic perinatal acceleration of synaptogenesis? In this case, it does not seem to be experience. When monkeys and cats were deprived of visual input, the timing of the initial acceleration and peak of synaptogenesis did not change, though later events of changing proportions, cortical layering and so forth, did change markedly (Bourgeois & Rakic, 1996; O'Kusky, 1985). Moreover, when monkeys were delivered three weeks prematurely, so that a barrage of experience would begin much sooner than it would normally occur (Bourgeois et al., 1989), there was no effect on the timing of synapse acceleration and peak – it occurred precisely when it should occur, based on the monkey's anticipated gestational birthdate, not the prematurely induced one. Secondary effects on types and distributions of synapses were also seen in this study, so experience does matter. However, experience doesn't seem to be responsible for the perinatal burst in synaptogenesis.

Humans present an evolutionary experiment that is the opposite of the premature delivery manipulation, because we are born rather late with respect to neural milestones such as neurogenesis. Although we think of human infants as being behaviorally immature at birth (compared to monkeys for example), there are many aspects in which the human brain is unusually mature at birth. When we look at the relationship between synaptogenesis and birth in humans, we find a rare and rather exciting exception to the general laws of neural development that create such orderly similarities between humans and other mammals: synaptogenesis seems to occur much later in humans than it occurs in other primates. If humans were born at the neural maturational stage corresponding to the stage when macaques show rapid synaptogenesis, human birth would occur at about 7 months post-conception (Figure 18.1b).

Recent work has shown that it is a signal from the fetus that initiates labor, coordinating maturation in the fetus with physiology in the mother. It would be interesting if this same signal might also initiate wholesale neuroanatomical changes in the fetus itself (Nathanielsz, 1998). In any case, the bottom line for present purposes is this: experience does not cause the initial burst in synaptogenesis instead evolution has coordinated synapse production with birth.

Why does nature bother to produce so many elements just to throw them away? The massive overproduction and subsequent pruning of synapses is a expensive neural tactic in terms of neural components and energy cost. Between ages 2 and 5, it has been estimated that 5,000 synapses are disappearing each second in the visual cortex alone (Bourgeois, 1997), and similar recessions are most likely occurring in all cortical areas that participate in language. What purpose could this steady decline serve, especially occurring as it does in a period when details of language (including complex grammar) are mastered? The strategy of excess production followed by pruning has been documented in other neural areas, notably in callosal axonal connectivity, where it has been proposed to permit the neural adjustments that favor evolutionary changes (Innocenti, 1995). Certainly flexibility is a primary outcome of such a system, but refinement, defined in terms of accuracy and speed despite complexity, may be another important consequence of these regressive stages.

Empirical studies are limited to observed descriptions of gross synapse counts, but computer simulations have been run that yield interesting information about the computational consequences of this peculiar strategy of overproduction and pruning (Elman et al., 1996). For one thing, in adaptively constructed neural networks that employ overproduction and removal of synapses, input information is more reliably preserved than it is in simple feed-forward networks (Adelsberger-Mangan & Levy, 1993, 1994). Networks constructed using adaptive synaptogenesis also manage to "sculpt" connections that permit quicker transformations of complex data when compared to networks constructed with conventional non-adjustable connective mechanisms. Moving away from machines back to humans, it is true that the net numbers of synapses are decreasing during adolescence; however, new ones are still sprouting, resulting in constant and co-occurring processes of production and trimming that could also serve to adjust and improve on initial connections.

So now let's take a closer look at the various kinds of synaptogenesis that occur before and after birth, and also consider some of the local and global events that affect the learning potential (and perhaps the learning style) within and across brain regions. A summary of the timetable of synaptic stages can be found in Figure 18.2, in which milestones of language acquisition and production are mapped alongside sequences of some of the human neural events that are discussed in this section.

Developmental differences in synapse morphology and distribution

The sequence of synaptogenesis can be classified into five stages (reviewed in Bourgeois, 1997). In the initial stage, synapses are present in a region of cortex called the "pre-plate" which comprises the earliest-generated cortical neurons. This is followed by a secondary stage in which synapses are generated in the cortical plate itself, initially following a gradient corresponding to that of the developing cortical neurons. Phase III of synaptogenesis is the synchronized global perinatal burst phase described above; at its peak in the infant macaque, it is estimated that 40,000 synapses are formed each second in the visual cortex alone (Bourgeois, 1997). Phase IV is a stabilized high level that lasts from late infancy until puberty, while in the last phase, which extends from puberty to adulthood, synapses steadily decline in density and absolute number.

Variations in morphological characteristics of the third stage of proliferating synapses make it clear that the complexities of the synaptogenic peak extend beyond sheer numbers. There are also interesting development changes in the kinds of synaptic connections that are being made. This includes a change in the ratio of asymmetric to symmetric synapses during the perinatal period – recall that asymmetric synapses are more likely to be excitatory and symmetric inhibitory. During Phase III of synaptogenesis, the asymmetric (putative excitatory) connections decline in number while the numbers of symmetric (putative inhibitory) synapses remain about the same (Bourgeois & Rakic, 1993; Zecevic & Rakic, 1991). Functionally, this means that there may be a developmental shift from a high proportion of excitatory activation toward a more tempered balance between excitation and inhibition, which seems a plausible account of the increasingly better coordination of perception and action.

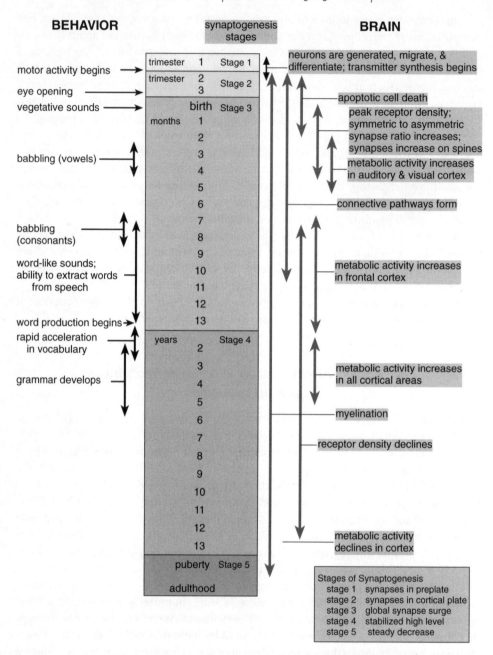

Figure 18.2   Neural events and language development.

The sites of synaptic innervation are also altered over development (Zecevic & Rakic, 1991). Early in development (in the more exuberant phase), large numbers of connections are made (or attempted) on the shafts (the trunks and branches) of dendrites. Later there is a shift in contact site, with more connections on dendritic spines. Because

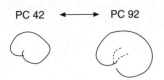

A   Relative birthdate of cortical neurons   B   Relative birthdate fo corresponding thalamic neurons

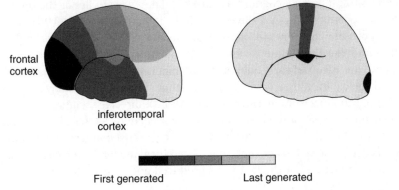

First generated   Last generated

Figure 18.3   Gradients of neurogenesis.

spine contact may allow neurotransmitter release to be localized with more specificity than shaft contact (Harris & Stevens, 1989), this shift in site might reflect an increase in connectional efficiency during the early learning process. Theoretical models, as well as imaging experiments which can track ion flow in single cells, also support the role of spine contact in the induction of the plasticity associated with learning (reviewed in Koch & Zador, 1993). Overall, the significance of these changes in the constellations of the types and forms of synaptic interaction is just beginning to be understood.

We will now turn to other, larger-scale changes in brain structure and function that start prenatally but extend well into the postnatal period.

Maturational gradients of the isocortex in the early postnatal period

There is not a single dimension called maturational state that any area of the isocortex can be retarded or advanced on (which makes it less likely there could be a moment when a region turns on). Rather, each isocortical area is best viewed as an assembly of different features, including neurogenesis, process and axon extension, neurotransmitter inclusion, type and rate of synaptogenesis. (The simultaneous perinatal peaking of synaptogenesis across all cortical areas, supporting the notion of a global signaling process, is an exception to this general rule.) Figure 18.3 contrasts the gradients that are observed in two critically different aspects of cortical development: the timing of neurogenesis in different cortical areas compared to similar timing in their corresponding thalamic nuclei, superimposed on the cortex of a schematized human brain. Because different areas of the brain follow maturational gradients that don't match in order, interesting temporal asynchronies are produced – for example, in some areas, intracortical connections will be relatively more mature than thalamic connections (the frontal cortex), and in others, the reverse will hold (primary visual cortex).

Intrinsic cortical gradients

The isocortex has its own gradient of maturation that is quite conserved across all mammals. Bayer, Altman and colleagues have produced detailed studies of the timing of neurogenesis in rodents (Altman & Bayer, 1979a,b, 1988; Bayer et al., 1993) and we are able to apply the comparative mammalian model of Finlay and Darlington (1995) to predict a similar time sequence for humans. Neurogenesis begins at the front edge of the cortex where frontal cortex abuts inferotemporal cortex and proceeds back to primary visual cortex, framing a period of genesis that can last over 50 days during the first trimester of human gestation. However, there is little direct association between the time of a neuron's genesis and when it makes its connections as this also depends heavily on the maturational/trophic status of the regions it must connect to. Paradoxically, the frontal cortex, viewed in conventional hierarchical models as the last maturing cortical area, is in fact one of the first to be produced and thus quite "mature" in some features.

Imposed thalamic gradients

Each area of cortex receives a thalamic input by maturity, but as depicted in Figure 18.3, the order of thalamic development in no way resembles the intrinsic cortical gradient. If intrinsic cortical gradients and imposed thalamic gradients occur in different orders, then we have a dissociation with potentially very interesting consequences. It is the thalamic order of neurogenesis that gives rise to the hierarchical notion of cortical development (e.g., visual matures early; frontal matures late), although this gradient is really not a general rule. This difference in developmental gradients might mean that frontal cortex, the area that bears so much weight in speculation about human evolution (e.g., Deacon, 1997) is primed for higher-order associative function from the start.

General modulatory cortical input

In addition to the thalamus, there are other subcortical structures that project to the cortex that are deeply implicated in systems of arousal, attention, and emotion in adulthood, and in modulation of plasticity and growth in development. In general, *cholinergic* fibers arise from the basal forebrain, *norpinepherine* fibers from the locus coeruleus, *serotonin* fibers from the raphe nuclei, and *dopamine* fibers originate in the cells of the substantia nigra. During development, these long-range systems are focused throughout the entire isocortex with the exception of the less diffuse dopamine system which focuses more specifically on limbic and prefrontal cortical regions. Unlike the precocious thalamic afferents, cholinergic and aminergic innervation begins relatively late in development, with much elaboration after birth, and even extending into adulthood (Dori & Parnavelas, 1989; Kalsbeek et al., 1988; Lidov & Molliver, 1982). We really don't know what these systems are for developmentally, except that disturbance of them disturbs normal development. Because we can reasonably conclude that the timing of this innervation, like other neural events, is conserved across species, we can extrapolate these innervation dates to begin in the second or third trimesters of human gestation, likely extending well into the first postnatal year and, for some, even into the adolescent years.

What might the protracted and largely postnatal innervation of these neural fibers mean to a human infant or toddler in the process of learning so many behaviors, including language? We know that that these connections transmit substances that are highly implicated in mechanisms of arousal and reward, but they also have multiple functions in many distributed systems. It would seem that the progressive innervation of these substances into the developing brain is timed so that they can optimally influence learning behaviors, but much additional research will be needed to tease out a distinct role for each.

Neurochemicals and receptors

The transmitters used in the systems described above are just a small number of the chemicals that can be set in motion from the presynaptic (transmitting) side of the synapse. About 20 neurotransmitters (which have rather strict classification criteria) have already been identified (glutamate and GABA are high-profile examples) and many more are under investigation. Upon maturity, the neural areas subserving functions associated with language will contain unique combinations of neural transmitters and modulators in distribution patterns distinctive to each area, a form of neural fingerprint. The synthesis and distributions of these neural substances change over the course of maturity (Goldman-Rakic & Brown, 1982; Hayashi et al., 1989; Hornung & Fritschy, 1996) making them strong candidates for roles in development. Although much research remains to be done, it is certainly likely – given the timing of the fluctuations and combinations – that these variations in neural substances may play a functional role in maturing behaviors such as language learning.

Neural receptors are the receiving side of the synapse – the part of the postsynaptic complex where neurotransmitters and modulators can exert influence on the cells they contact. One developmental alteration has been consistently documented regardless of the species, the cortical area under investigation, or the related neurosubstance: there is a dramatic overproduction of virtually every type of receptor which occurs around the time of birth (Gremo et al., 1987; Herrmann, 1996; Hornung & Fritschy, 1996; Lidow et al., 1991), similar to – and simultaneous with – the perinatal surge of synaptogenesis. The receptor surge greatly supports the notion that the synapses are functional since the necessary transmitter docking mechanisms appear to be produced concurrently. Similar to the many other events we have described in the developing brain, interactions between receptor formation, neurosubstance synthesis, and synaptogenesis are likely to be more complicated than any simple cause-and-effect mechanism.

Interactions of Neural Events and Language Learning

The picture of human brain development that we have provided here leaves little room for a lockstep table of correlates between language milestones and neural events, but it does provide some useful constraints on how we should conceive of this complex bi-directional relationship, with implications for both normal and abnormal development. We close with four conclusions, or better yet, four working hypotheses to guide future research in this area: (1) readiness for learning, (2) experience-driven change, (3) rethinking two specific postnatal correlates of language, and (4) sensitive periods.

Readiness for learning

There was a period in developmental psychology when the capacities of the newborn infant for perception and learning were vastly underestimated. Much-needed correctives to this misunderstanding have come in two waves: research demonstrating rich perceptual skills in the first few weeks of life (e.g., Bertenthal & Clifton, 1998; Johnson, 1998; Kellman & Banks, 1998), and research demonstrating at least some learning in utero, as well as a capacity for rapid learning of arbitrary statistical patterns (including language-specific phonetic details) in the first months of life. With the first wave, there was extensive speculation in the literature on infant development regarding the stock of innate knowledge that infants must possess in order to perform so well in (for example) tasks that require response to complex transformation of objects, including their disappearance and reappearance (Spelke, 1994; Spelke et al., 1992; Spelke & Newport, 1998). With the second wave, it has become increasingly evident that we have underestimated the power and speed of learning even in very young infants, forcing a revaluation of the extent to which infant performance is influenced by learning vs. innate perceptual, motor, and perhaps even conceptual biases about the nature of the physical and social world (Elman & Bates, 1997; Seidenberg, 1997; Thelen & Smith, 1994, 1998). The material that we have reviewed in this chapter provides support for the idea that the infant brain is up and running at or before birth. We see no evidence for the hypothesis that whole bounded regions of the brain are pre-functional, quiescent, inactive, or waiting for some key maturational event before they can "turn on" in the postnatal period.

However, even though the relevant neural systems may be in place and ready to work from the beginning, that does not mean that they are being used in an adult manner, nor that they are being used in all the tasks for which they will eventually be relevant. Recent neural imaging studies of human adults have shown that the configuration of highly active areas changes markedly across a 20-minute period as the subject attains expertise in a new task (Petersen et al., 1998). If that is true for mature and sophisticated adults, over a very short period of time, it will undoubtedly prove true for children who are in the process of acquiring language.

Experience-driven changes

It is now clear that learning itself contributes to the structure of the developing brain, in infants and in adults. Particular clear examples of an experience-dependent increase can be found in a series of experiments by Greenough and colleagues examining the effects of enriched housing and/or skill learning on morphological changes in rodent brain. These studies have consistently documented significant increases in dendritic fields and in the ratio of synapses per neurons in rats exposed to complex environments or involved in learning tasks when measured against handled controls (Black et al., 1990; Greenough et al., 1985; Turner & Greenough, 1985). Experience-based synaptogenesis is also accompanied by increases in populations of glial cells (Sirevaag & Greenough, 1987), as well as by increases in metabolic activity (Sirevaag et al., 1988; Sirevaag & Greenough, 1987). We may reasonably conclude that similar reactive neural changes accompany learning in the developing human brain.

Hence, if we do eventually find evidence for neuroanatomical and neurophysiological events that correlate with milestones in language development, we must be open to the possibility that these correlations are the product rather than the cause of language learning. In the same vein, if we find evidence of neuroanatomical and/or neurophysiological differences between children who are developing normally and children who are substantially delayed in language learning, we should not assume that this neural indicator has caused a language delay. The brain may still be in a relatively immature state because the relevant experience-driven events have not yet taken place. This insight certainly applies to the burgeoning literature on neural correlates of Specific Language Impairment and/or congenital dyslexia, and it may apply to other disorders as well.

Rethinking two postnatal correlates of language

We noted earlier two previously proposed postnatal correlates of major language milestones: changes in frontal lobe activity that seemed to coincide with the 8–10-month watershed in comprehension, communication, imitation, and reasoning, and changes in synpatic density that seemed to coincide with bursts in vocabulary and grammar between 16 and 30 months.

However, the idea that behavioral events late in the first year of life are correlated with changes in frontal lobe function rested primarily on two sources of evidence. The first was a positron emission study (PET) of human infants suggesting that there is a marked increase in frontal lobe metabolism starting between 9 and 12 months postnatal age (Chugani et al., 1987) that did not occur in response to any particular stimulus or task. It was suggested that this sharp increase in glucose metabolism might be caused by a burst in synaptogenesis. The second source of evidence came from lesion studies showing that infant monkeys with bilateral frontal lobe lesions behave very much like age-matched normal controls but only until a critical point in development (roughly equivalent to 8–12 months in postnatal human life) when normal animals learn to solve short-term memory tasks that are failed by the lesioned animals and by adults with frontal lobe pathology (Diamond & Goldman-Rakic, 1989; Goldman-Rakic, 1987; Pennington, 1994). Findings like these led to a previous hypothesis that the frontal lobes "come on line" around 9 months of age, coinciding in humans with dramatic changes in many aspect of language, cognition, and social interaction. However, it now seems very clear that the frontal lobes are functional (though still immature) by the end of the second trimester, and may actually be *more* mature than other areas in terms of their intracortical connectivity.

How can we reconcile these apparently contradictory claims? The resolution may lie in the difference between *absolute functionality* (i.e., whether or not an area is working at all) and *task-specific functionality* (i.e., whether the organism has reached a state in which that area is recruited and activated for a given task). Evidence for the latter view comes from a study by Jacobs, Chugani and colleagues (Jacobs et al., 1995), a PET study of infant monkeys that shows high levels of frontal lobe metabolism at birth, well before the point at which monkeys solve the short-term memory tasks that have been associated with frontal lobe function. These authors do find a further increase in metabolism later on, in many regions of the brain including the frontal lobes, compatible with the idea that metabolism and synaptogenesis increase together after birth. However, the amount of activity seen in the frontal lobes of newborn monkeys is not compatible with the standard view that frontal lobes develop especially late. If Goldman-Rakic's classic findings are not "caused" by the sudden appearance of mature frontal cortex, how can we explain the sudden relevance of frontal lesions for memory tasks around the human equivalent of 8–10 months of age? We suggest that these results can be reinterpreted within the bi-directional framework that we have recommended here, in which areas are *recruited* into complex tasks across the course of learning. On this argument, normal infants (humans and monkeys) cannot succeed in so-called frontal lobe tasks until they have made enough progress (perceptual, motor, mnemonic) to realize that a new set of strategies is required – strategies that are, in turn, only possible with the involvement of the frontal lobes. We tentatively suggest that the 8–10-month behavioral watershed in human infants may involve a learning-dependent change in social and cognitive systems that have developed in parallel because they began in parallel (at or before birth), are roughly similar in complexity, and are likely in communication with each other. As a result, all of these systems reach a certain critical level of organization around the same time (approximately 8–10 months).

The hypothesized parallel between synaptogenesis and the correlated burst in vocabulary and grammar that are observed from 16–30 months requires more recharacterization still. It is now reasonably clear that the initial burst in synaptogenesis itself is independent of experience, arranged to coincide with the barrage of experience that will arrive at birth. It is certainly intriguing that the peak and plateau of synaptogenesis in humans brackets the primary events in early language development (from word comprehension to the mastery of fundamental aspects of grammar), but we still need to learn much more about these events.

Is there any possibility that we should rule out? In our view, it would be wise to rule out the idea that the "vocabulary burst" and the "grammar burst" depend entirely on synaptogenesis for their shape and size, because such bursts are also observed when learning occurs in a non-linear dynamical system with a stable architecture (Elman et al., 1996). Such exponential bursts are characteristic of learning, and are observed whether or not they are superimposed on a burgeoning brain. Hence the compelling parallel between the language burst and the synapse burst may represent a mutually beneficial relationship, but not a crucial and direct relationship of cause and effect.

Sensitive periods

The term sensitive period is preferred by neurobiologists over the widely used and widely misunderstood term critical period, because the former term implies a softer and more plastic set of developmental constraints and transitions. The term critical period is still used in the literature on language development, and it is often used to imply hard boundaries and a crisp dissociation in the mechanisms that are responsible for language learning in children vs. adults (for discussions, see Bates, 1999; Bialystok & Hakuta, 1994; Elman et al., 1996; Johnson & Newport, 1989; Oyama, 1992; Weber-Fox & Neville, 1996). The notion of a critical period for language has been invoked to explain differences between first- and second-language learning, and to account for age-related changes in recovery of language abilities following left-hemisphere injury. It has been shown that adults and children perform at similar levels in the early stages of second-language learning when learning conditions are controlled (Snow & Hoefnagel-Hohle, 1978). The one compelling exception to this general rule is the ability to learn a second language without an accent, which seems to elude all but a very rare subgroup of talented adults. However, studies that focus on the later stages of language learning have shown that adults tend to "fossilize" at a level below native speakers, while children generally go on to acquire full competence (Johnson & Newport, 1989). Results like these provide support for the idea that there is an age-related decrease in plasticity for language learning, but there is no consensus about the shape of this function or its cause. Some investigators (e.g., Johnson & Newport, 1989) conclude that there is no single moment when the window of linguistic opportunity slams shut, but rather, a series of gradients that vary with task difficulty and other poorly understood parameters.

The literature on brain development may also shed light on this issue. In the well-studied primate visual system, multiple overlapping sensitive periods have been identified (Harwerth et al., 1986) and it is likely that human language acquisition is affected by similar complex receptive intervals. Although these learning periods were once thought to be fixed in time, it is now clear that the temporal windows when adequate experiences is necessary for proper development are more flexible than previously assumed, and may be retarded or advanced by natural or empirical means (e.g., Stryker & Harris, 1986; Kroodsma & Pickert, 1980).

We are by now quite prepared to accept that learning itself affects the subsequent ability of the brain to learn something new. Brain maturation affects experience, but experience returns the favor, altering the very structure of the brain. Hence the putative critical period for language (which really comprises many overlapping sensitive periods) may be one more example of the bi-directional events that have been a focus of this chapter.

The search for a neuroanatomical basis for language learning has, at this time, no unequivocal conclusion. We have noted here some neural developmental alterations that accompany language milestones. These neural events may drive, or alternatively, reflect, developmental behaviors such as language learning – although the complexity of the interactions remains to be researched. What is clear is that time-tables for human neural developmental events cannot be simply mapped onto sequences of language acquisition and production. As depicted schematically in Figure 18.3, the human brain develops as an overlapping and interconnected series of multimodal additive and regressive neural events, many of which are completed prior to birth. Although certain cortical events, especially developmental modifications in the numbers, components, and locations of synapses, may contribute somewhat more directly, all pre- and postnatal events should perhaps be considered essential to the language-learning process.

References

Adelsberger-Mangan, D.M., & Levy, W.B. (1993). Adaptive synaptogenesis constructs networks that maintain information and reduce statistical dependence. *Biological Cybernetics, 70* (1), 81–87.

Adelsberger-Mangan, D.M., & Levy, W.B. (1994). The influence of limited presynaptic growth and synapse removal on adaptive synaptogenesis. *Biological Cybernetics, 71* (5), 461–468.

Altman, J., & Bayer, S.A. (1979a). Development of the diencephalon in the rat. IV. Quantitative study of the time of origin of neurons and the internuclear chronological gradients in the thalamus. *Journal of Comparative Neurology, 188* (3), 455–471.

Altman, J., & Bayer, S.A. (1979b). Development of the diencephalon in the rat. VI. Re-evaluation of the embryonic development of the thalamus on the basis of thymidine-radiographic datings. *Journal of Comparative Neurology, 188* (3), 501–524.

Altman, J., & Bayer, S.A. (1988). Development of the rat thalamus: II. Time and site of origin and settling pattern of neurons derived from the anterior lobule of the thalamic neuroepithelium. *Journal of Comparative Neurology, 275* (3), 378–405.

Antonini, A., & Shatz, C.J. (1990). Relationship between putative neurotransmitter phenotypes and connectivity of subplate neurons during cerebral cortical development. *European Journal of Neuroscience, 2*, 744–761.

Bates, E. (1999). Plasticity, localization and language development. In S. Broman, & J.M. Fletcher (Eds.), *The Changing Nervous System: Neurobehavioral Consequences of Early Brain Disorders*, pp. 214–253. New York: Oxford University Press.

Bates, E., Benigni, L., Bretherton, I., Camaioni, L., & Volterra, V. (1979). *The Emergence of Symbols: Cognition and Communication in Infancy*. New York: Academic Press.

Bates, E., & Elman, J. (1996). Learning rediscovered. *Science, 274*, 1849–1850.

Bates, E., Thal, D., Finlay, B.L., & Clancy, B. (in press). Early language development and its neural correlates. In I. Rapin, & S. Segalowitz (Eds.), *Handbook of Neuropsychology, Vol. 6, Child Neurology (2nd edn)*. Amsterdam: Elsevier.

Bates, E., Thal, D., & Janowsky, J. (1992). Early language development and its neural correlates. In I. Rapin, & S. Segalowitz (Eds.), *Handbook of Neuropsychology, Vol. 7: Child Neuropsychology*, pp. 69–110. Amsterdam: Elsevier.

Bayer, S.A. (1982). Changes in the total number of dentate granule cells in juvenile and adult rats: a correlated volumetric and 3H-thymidine autoradiographic study. *Exp. Brain Res., 46* (3), 315–323.

Bayer, S.A. (1983). 3H-thymidine-radiographic studies of neurogenesis in the rat olfactory bulb. *Exp. Brain Res., 50* (2–3), 329–340.

Bayer, S.A., Altman, J., Russo, R.J., & Zhang, X. (1993). Timetables of neurogenesis in the human brain based on experimentally determined patterns in the rat. *Neurotoxicology, 14* (1), 83–144.

Bertenthal, B.I., & Clifton, R.K. (1998). Perception and action. In W. Damon (Series Ed.), D. Kuhn, & R. Siegler (Vol. Eds.), *Handbook of Child Psychology: Vol. 2. Cognition, Perception and Language* (5th edn), pp. 51–102. New York: Wiley.

Bialystok, E., & Hakuta, K. (1994). *In Other Words: The Science and Psychology of Second-Language Acquisition*. New York: BasicBooks.

Black, J.E., Isaacs, K.R., Anderson, B.J., Alcantara, A.A., & Greenough, W.T. (1990). Learning causes synaptogenesis, whereas motor activity causes angiogenesis, in cerebellar cortex of adult rats. *Proceedings of the National Academy of Sciences USA, 87* (14), 5568–5572.

Bourgeois, J.P. (1997). Synaptogenesis, heterochrony and epigenesis in the mammalian neocortex. *Acta Paediatrica Supplement, 422*, 27–33.

Bourgeois, J.P., Goldman-Rakic, P.S., & Rakic, P. (1994). Synaptogenesis in the prefrontal cortex of rhesus monkeys. *Cerebral Cortex, 4* (1), 78–96.

Bourgeois, J.P., & Rakic, P. (1993). Changes of synaptic density in the primary visual cortex of the macaque monkey from fetal to adult stage. *Journal of Neuroscience, 13* (7), 2801–2820.

Bourgeois, J.P., & Rakic, P. (1996). Synaptogenesis in the occipital cortex of macaque monkey devoid of retinal input from early embryonic stages. *European Journal of Neuroscience, 8* (5), 942–950.

Bourgeois, J.P., Jastreboff, P.J., & Rakic, P. (1989). Synaptogenesis in visual cortex of normal and preterm monkeys: Evidence for intrinsic regulation of synaptic overproduction. *Proceedings of the National Academy of Sciences USA, 86* (11), 4297–4301.

Burkhalter, A. (1993). Development of forward and feedback connections between areas V1 and V2 of human visual cortex. *Cerebral Cortex, 3* (5), 476–487.

Chugani, H.T., Phelps, M.E., & Mazziotta, J.C. (1987). Positron emission tomography study of human brain functional development. *Annals of Neurology, 22*, 487–497.

Clancy, B., Darlington, R.B., & Finlay, B.L. (2000). The course of human events: Predicting the timing of primate neural development. *Developmental Science.*

Darlington, R.B., Dunlop, S.A., & Finlay, B.L. (1999). Commentary: Neural development in metatherian and eutherian mammals: Variation and constraint. *Journal of Comparative Neurology.*

Deacon, T. (1997). *The Symbolic Species: The Co-Evolution of Language and the Brain.* New York: Norton.

Diamond, A., & Goldman-Rakic, P.S. (1989). Comparison of human infants and rhesus monkeys on Piaget's AB task: Evidence for dependence on dorsolateral prefrontal cortex. *Experimental Brain Research, 74*, 24–40.

Dori, I., & Parnavelas, J.G. (1989). The cholinergic innervation of the rat cerebral cortex shows two distinct phases in development. *Experimental Brain Research, 76* (2), 417–423.

Easter, S.S. Jr., Ross, L.S., & Frankfurter, A. (1993). Initial tract formation in the mouse brain. *Journal of Neuroscience, 13* (1), 285–299.

Elman, J.L., & Bates, E. (1997). Letters, *Science, 276*, 1180.

Elman, J.L., Bates, E., Johnson, M., Karmiloff-Smith, A., Parisi, D., & Plunkett, K. (1996). *Rethinking Innateness: A Connectionist Perspective on Development.* Cambridge, MA: MIT Press/Bradford Books.

Finlay, B.L. (1992). Cell death and the creation of regional differences in neuronal numbers. *Journal of Neurobiology, 23* (9), 1159–1171.

Finlay, B.L., & Darlington, R.B. (1995). Linked regularities in the development and evolution of mammalian brains. *Science, 268* (5217), 1578–1584.

Goldman-Rakic, P.S., & Brown, R.M. (1982). Postnatal development of monoamine content and synthesis in the cerebral cortex of rhesus monkeys. *Brain Research, 256* (3), 339–349.

Goldman-Rakic, P.S. (1987). Development of cortical circuitry and cognitive function. *Child Development, 58*, 601–622.

Granger, B., Tekaia, F., Le Sourd, A.M., Rakic, P., & Bourgeois, J.P. (1995). Tempo of neurogenesis and synaptogenesis in the primate cingulate mesocortex: Comparison with the neocortex. *Journal of Comparative Neurology, 360* (2), 363–376.

Greenough, W.T. (1984). Structural correlates of information storage in the mammalian brain: A review and hypothesis. *Trends in Neurosciences, 7*, 229–233.

Greenough, W.T., Hwang, H.M., & Gorman, C. (1985). Evidence for active synapse formation or altered postsynaptic metabolism in visual cortex of rats reared in complex environments. *Proceedings of the National Academy of Sciences USA, 82* (13), 4549–4552.

Gremo, F., Palomba, M., Marchisio, A.M., Marcello, C., Mulas, M.L., & Torelli, S. (1987). Heterogeneity of muscarinic cholinergic receptors in the developing human fetal brain: Regional distribution and characterization. *Early Human Development, 15* (3), 165–177.

Harris, K.M., & Stevens, J.K. (1989). Dendritic spines of CA 1 pyramidal cells in the rat hippocampus: Serial electron microscopy with reference to their biophysical characteristics. *Journal of Neuroscience, 9* (8), 2982–2997.

Harwerth, R.S., Smith, E.L., Duncan, G.C., Crawford, M.L., & von Noorden, G.K. (1986). Multiple sensitive periods in the development of the primate visual system. *Science, 232* (4747), 235–238.

Hayashi, M., Yamashita, A., Shimizu, K., & Oshima, K. (1989). Ontogeny of cholecystokinin-8 and glutamic acid decarboxylase in cerebral neocortex of macaque monkey. *Experimental Brain Research, 74* (2), 249–255.

Herrmann, K. (1996). Differential distribution of AMPA receptors and glutamate during pre- and postnatal development in the visual cortex of ferrets. *Journal of Comparative Neurology, 375* (1), 1–17.

Honig, L.S., Herrmann, K., & Shatz, C.J. (1996). Developmental changes revealed by immuno-histochemical markers in human cerebral cortex. *Cerebral Cortex, 6* (6), 794–806.

Hornung, J.P., & Fritschy, J.M. (1996). Developmental profile of GABAA-receptors in the marmoset monkey: Expression of distinct subtypes in pre- and postnatal brain. *Journal of Comparative Neurology, 367* (3), 413–430.

Huttenlocher, P.R., & Dabholkar, A.S. (1997). Regional differences in synaptogenesis in human cerebral cortex. *Journal of Comparative Neurology, 387* (20), 167–178.

Innocenti, G. (1995). Exuberant development of connections, and its possible permissive role in cortical evolution. *Trends in Neurosciences, 18* (9), 397–402.

Jacobs, B., Chugani, H.T., Allada, V., Chen, S., Phelps, M.E., Pollack, D.B., & Raleigh, M.J. (1995). Developmental changes in brain metabolism in sedated rhesus macaques and vervet monkeys revealed by positon emission tomography. *Cerebral Cortex, 3,* 222–233.

Johnson, J., & Newport, E. (1989). Critical period effects in second language learning: the influence of maturational state on the acquisition of English as a second language. *Cognitive Psychology, 21,* 60–99.

Johnson, M.H. (1998). The neural basis of cognitive development. In W. Damon (Series Ed.), D. Kuhn, & R. Siegler (Vol. Eds.), *Handbook of Child Psychology: Vol. 2 Cognition, Perception and Language,* 5th edn, pp. 1–50. New York: Wiley.

Kalsbeek, A., Voorn, P., Buijs, R.M., Pool, C.W., & Uylings, H.B. (1988). Development of the dopaminergic innervation in the prefrontal cortex of the rat. *Journal of Comparative Neurology, 269* (1), 58–72.

Kellman, P.J., & Banks, M.S. (1998). Infant visual perception. In W. Damon (Series Ed.), D. Kuhn, & R. Siegler (Vol. Eds.), *Handbook of Child Psychology: Vol. 2 Cognition, Perception and Language,* 5th edn, pp. 103–146. New York: Wiley.

Kempermann, G., Brandon, E., & Gage, F. (1998). Environmental stimulation of 129/SvJ mice causes increased cell proliferation and neurogenesis in the adult dentate gyrus. *Current Biology, 8,* 939–942.

Kleim, J.A., Lussnig, E., Schwarz, E.R., Comery, T.A., & Greenough, W.T. (1996). Synaptogenesis and Fos expression in the motor cortex of the adult rat following motor skill learning. *Journal of Neuroscience, 16,* 4529–4535.

Kleim, J.A., Swain, R.A., Czerlanis, C.M., Kelly, J.L., Pipitone, M.A., & Greenough, W.T. (1997). Learning-dependent dendritic hypertrophy of cerebellarstellate neurons: Plasticity of local circuit neurons. *Neurobiology of Learning and Memory, 67,* 29–33.

Koch, C., & Zador, A. (1993). The function of dendritic spines: Devices subserving biochemical rather than electrical compartmentalization. *Journal of Neuroscience, 13* (2), 413–422.

Komack, D.R., & Rakic, P. (1999). Continuation of neurogenesis in the hippocampus of the adult macaque monkey. *Proceedings of the National Academy of Sciences USA, 96* (10), 5768–5773.

Kroodsma, D.E., & Pickert, R. (1980). Environmentally dependent sensitive periods for avian vocal learning. *Nature, 288,* 477–479.

Kuhn, H.G., Dickinson-Anson, H., & Gage, F.H. (1996). Neurogenesis in the dentate gyrus of the adult rat: Age-related decrease of neuronal progenitor proliferation. *Journal of Neuroscience, 16* (6), 2027–2033.

Lenneberg, E. (1967). *Biological Foundations of Language.* New York: Wiley.

Lidov, H.G., & Molliver, M.E. (1982). Immunohistochemical study of the development of serotonergic neurons in the rat CNS. *Brain Research Bulletin, 9* (1–6), 559–604.

Lidow, M.S., Goldman-Rakic, P.S., & Rakic, P. (1991). Synchronized overproduction of neurotransmitter receptors in diverse regions of the primate cerebral cortex. *Proceedings of the National Academy of Sciences USA, 88* (22), 10218–10221.

Lidow, M.S., & Rakic, P. (1995). Neurotransmitter receptors in the proliferative zones of the developing primate occipital lobe. *Journal of Comparative Neurology, 360* (3), 393–402.

Luskin, M.B. (1998). Neuroblasts of the postnatal mammalian forebrain: Their phenotype and fate. *Journal of Neurobiology, 36* (2), 221–233.

Miller, B., Chou, L., & Finlay, B.L. (1993). The early development of thalamocortical and corticothalamic projections. *Journal of Comparative Neurology, 335* (1), 16–41.

Molnar, Z., Adams, R., & Blakemore, C. (1998). Mechanisms underlying the early establishment of thalamocortical connections in the rat. *Journal of Neuroscience, 18* (15), 5723–5745.

Nathanielsz, P.W. (1998). Comparative studies on the initiation of labor. *European Journal of Obstetrics, Gynecology and Reproductive Biology, 78* (2), 127–132.

O'Kusky, J.R. (1985). Synapse elimination in the developing visual cortex: A morphometric analysis in normal and dark reared cats. *Brain Research, 354* (1), 81–91.

O'Kusky, J.R., & Norman, M.G. (1994). Sudden infant death syndrome: increased synaptic density in the central reticular nucleus of the medulla. *Journal of Neuropathology and Experimental Neurology, 53* (3), 263–271.

O'Leary, D.D., Schlaggar, B.L., & Tuttle, R. (1994). Specification of neocortical areas and thalamocortical connections. *Annual Review of Neuroscience, 17,* 419–439.

Oyama, S. (1992). The problem of change. In M. Johnson (Ed.), *Brain Development and Cognition: A Reader,* pp. 19–30. Oxford: Blackwell Publishers.

Parmelee, A.H., & Sigman, M.D. (1983). Perinatal brain development and behavior. In M.M. Haith, & J. Campos (Eds.), *Infancy and the Biology of Development: Vol. 2. Handbook of child psychology.* New York: Wiley.

Pennington, B.F. (1994). The working memory function of the prefrontal cortices: Implications for developmental and individual differences in cognition. In M. Haith, J. Benson, R. Roberts, & B. Pennington (Eds.), *The Development of Future-Oriented Processes,* pp. 243–289. Chicago: The University of Chicago Press.

Petersen, S.E., van Mier, H., Fiez, J.A., & Raichle, M.E. (1998). The effects of practice on the functional anatomy of task performance. *Proceedings of the National Academy of Sciences of the United States of America, 95* (3), 853–860.

Pinker, S. (1994). *The Language Instinct: How the Mind Creates Language.* New York: William Morrow.

Rakic, P., Bourgeois, J.P., Eckenhoff, M.F., Zecevic, N., & Goldman-Rakic, P.S. (1986). Concurrent overproduction of synapses in diverse regions of the primate cerebral cortex. *Science, 232,* 232–235.

Robertson, S.S., Dierker, L.J., Sorokin, Y., & Rosen, M.G. (1982). Human fetal movement: spontaneous oscillations near one cycle per minute. *Science, 218* (4579), 1327–1330.

Saffran, E.M., Aslin, R.N., & Newport, E.L. (1996). Statistical learning by 8-month-old infants. *Science, 274,* 1926–1928.

Seidenberg, M.S. (1997). Language acquisition and use: Learning and applying probabilistic constraints. *Science, 275* (5306), 1599–1603.

Sirevaag, A.M., Black, J.E., Shafron, D., & Greenough, W.T. (1988). Direct evidence that complex experience increases capillary branching and surface area in visual cortex of young rats. *Brain Research, 471* (2), 299–304.

Sirevaag, A.M., & Greenough, W.T. (1987). Differential rearing effects on rat visual cortex synapses. III. Neuronal and glial nuclei, boutons, dendrites, and capillaries. *Brain Research, 424* (2), 320–332.

Snow, C., & Hoefnagel-Hohle, M. (1978). The critical period for language acquisition: Evidence from second language learning. *Child Development, 49,* 1114–1128.

Spelke, E.S. (1994). Initial knowledge: Six suggestions. *Cognition, 50,* 431–445.

Spelke, E.S., & Breinlinger, K., Macomber, J., & Jacobson, K. (1992). Origins of knowledge. *Psychological Review, 99* (4), 605–632.

Spelke, E.S., & Newport, E.L. (1998). Nativism, empiricism, and the development of knowledge. In W. Damon (Series Ed.), R.M. Lerner (Vol. Ed.), *Handbook of Child Psychology: Vol. 1. Theoretical Models of Human Development,* 5th edn, pp. 275–340. New York: Wiley.

Stryker, M.P., & Harris, W.A. (1986). Binocular impulse blockade prevents the formation of ocular dominance columns in cat visual cortex. *Journal of Neuroscience, 6* (8), 2117–2133.

Thelen, E., & Smith, L.B. (1994). *A Dynamic Systems Approach to the Development of Cognition and Action.* Cambridge, MA: MIT Press.

Thelen, E., & Smith, L.B. (1998). Dynamic systems theories. In W. Damon (Series Ed.), D. Kuhn, & R. Siegler (Vol. Eds.), *Handbook of child Psychology: Vol. 1. Theoretical Models of Human Development,* 5th edn, pp. 563–634. New York: Wiley.

Turner, A.M., & Greenough, W.T. (1985). Differential rearing effects on rat visual cortex synapses. I. Synaptic and neuronal density and synapses per neuron. *Brain Research, 329* (1–2), 195–203.

Volpe, J.J. (1987). *Neurology of the Newborn,* 2nd edn. Philadelphia: Saunders.

Weber-Fox, C.M., & Neville, H.J. (1996). Maturational constraints on functional specializations for language processing: ERP and behavioral evidence in bilingual speakers. *Journal of Cognitive Neuroscience, 8* (3), 231–256.

Wexler, K. (1996). The development of inflection in a biologically based theory of language acquisition. In M.L. Rice (Ed.), *Toward a Genetics of Language,* pp. 113–144. Mahwah, NJ: Erlbaum.

Wong, R.O. (1999). Retinal waves and visual system development. *Annual Review in Neuroscience, 22,* 29–47.

Yakovlev, P., & Lecours, A. (1967). The myelinogenetic cycle of regional maturation of the brain. In A. Minkowski (Ed.), *Regional Development of the Brain in Early Life.* Philadelphia: Davis Co.

Zecevic, N., Bourgeois, J.P., & Rakic, P. (1989). Changes in synaptic density in motor cortex of rhesus monkey during fetal and postnatal life. *Developmental Brain Research, 50* (1), 11–32.

Zecevic, N., & Rakic, P. (1991). Synaptogenesis in monkey somatosensory cortex. *Cerebral Cortex, 1* (6), 510–523.

NINETEEN

Development Itself Is the Key to Understanding Developmental Disorders

Annette Karmiloff-Smith

All scientists studying normal and atypical development – from the staunchest Chomskyan nativist to the most domain-general empiricist – agree that development involves contributions from both genes and environment. The gulf between the theories lies in how genes and environment are claimed to contribute to developmental outcomes. At some level, of course, we all concur in the existence of some degree of innate specification. The difference in positions concerns how rich and how domain-specific the innately specified component is, whether development is the result of predetermined epigenesis[1] (mere triggering) or probabilistic epigenesis,[1] and what happens when things go wrong. These differences in position influence the focus of the questions asked (nature or nurture, on the one hand, versus the mechanisms of progressive developmental change, on the other) and the way in which developmental disorders are studied.

Let's briefly take the example of language. For the staunch nativist, a set of genes specifically targets domain-specific modules as the end product of their epigenesis (e.g., a syntactic module,[2] a morphological module,[3] or a more narrowly pre-specified module for, say, canonical linkage rules in grammar[4]). Under this non-developmental view, the environment simply acts as a trigger for identifying and setting (environmentally derived) native-tongue realizations of (pre-specified) parameters of universal grammar. The child is born innately expecting nouns, verbs, canonical linking rules, agreement between asymmetrical sentence elements, and so forth, but not yet knowing how they are realized in her/his native tongue.[5] The deletion, reduplication, or mispositioning of genes is assumed to result in very specific impairments in the endstate.[3–6] For the empiricist, by contrast, much of the structure necessary for building language and the rest of the human mind is discovered directly in the structure of the physical and social environment.

These two extremes are not the only options, however. The neuroconstructivist approach to normal and atypical development fully recognizes innate biological constraints but, unlike the staunch nativist, considers them to be initially less detailed and less domain-specific as far as higher-level cognitive functions are concerned. Rather, development itself is seen as playing a crucial role in shaping phenotypical outcomes, with the protracted period of postnatal growth as essential in influencing the resulting domain specificity of the developing neocortex.[7,8] A clearer way to capture this idea is to specify that the interaction is not in fact between genes and environment. Rather, on the gene side, the interaction lies in the outcome of the indirect, cascading effects of interacting genes and their environments and, on the environment side, the interaction comes from the infant's *progressive* selection and processing of different kinds of input. For both the strict nativist and the empiricist, the notion of "environment" is a static one, whereas development (both normal and atypical) is of course dynamic. The child's way of processing environmental stimuli is likely to change repeatedly as a function of development, leading to the progressive formation of domain-specific representations.

Most nativists interested in language argue that what is innately specified are *representations* of universal grammar. Other theorists recognize that knowledge representations per se are unlikely to be pre-specified in neocortex (although see Ref. 9 for an alternative, selectionist view of pre-specified representations). Rather than representational innateness, they opt for dedicated domain-specific mechanisms within innately specified modules, the presumed absence of which in a developmental disorder will inform about their specific function in normal development.[10,11] Such arguments seem to be heavily influenced by so-called evolutionary psychology.[12] According to this view, phylogenesis has led to increasing pre-specification for ontogenesis, such that there are genetically coded responses to evolutionary pressures, leading, through relatively predetermined epigenesis, to hardwired circuitry for language, theory of mind, and other specific forms of higher-level cognitive processing. In this "Swiss army knife" view of the brain, domain specificity is the starting point of ontogenesis, with development relegated to a relatively secondary role. A different view is that although evolution has pre-specified many constraints on development, it has made the human neocortex increasingly flexible and open to learning during postnatal development. In other words, evolution is argued to have selected for adaptive outcomes and a strong capacity to learn, rather than prior knowledge.[7] Within such a perspective, it is more plausible to think in terms of a variety of what one might call domain-relevant mechanisms that might gradually *become* domain-specific as a result of processing different kinds of input.

What does such a distinction entail? First we need to draw a distinction between domain-specific and domain-general mechanisms. Take, for example, inhibition. For the domain-general theorist, when the inhibitory mechanism is impaired, it will affect all systems across the board. By contrast, for the domain-specific theorist, the infant brain will contain, say, an inhibitory process *A* for theory-of-mind computations, an inhibitory process *B* for language-relevant computations, and yet another for sensorimotor development, and so forth. For this position, when the theory-of-mind inhibitory process is impaired, it will affect solely theory-of-mind computations, but leave intact linguistic, sensorimotor, and other domains. It is a subtly different distinction that I wish to draw between domain-relevant and domain-specific mechanisms. Unlike the domain-general theorist, this position does not argue for domain-general mechanisms simply applied across all domains. Rather, it suggests that biological constraints on the developing brain might have produced a number of mechanisms that do not start out as strictly domain-specific, that is, dedicated to the exclusive processing of one and only one kind of input. Instead, a mechanism starts out as somewhat more relevant to one kind of input over others, but it is usable – albeit in a less efficient way – for other types of processing too. This allows for compensatory processing and makes development channelled but far less predetermined than the nativist view. Once a domain-relevant mechanism is repeatedly used to process a certain type of input, it becomes domain-specific as a result of its developmental history.[7,13] Then, in adulthood, it can be differentially impaired. For example, a learning mechanism that has a feedback loop will be more relevant to processing sequential input than to processing static, holistic input. With time such a mechanism would become progressively dedicated to processing, say, sequentially presented linguistic input. In other words, rather than evolution providing pre-specified representations, this change in perspective places the mechanisms of progressive ontogenetic change on centre stage.

The Implications for Developmental Disorders

The neuroconstructivist modification in perspective crucially influences the way in which atypical development is considered. In this approach, the deletion, reduplication, or mispositioning of genes will be expected to subtly change the course of developmental pathways, with stronger effects on some outcomes and weaker effects on others. A totally specific disorder will, *ex hypothesis*, be extremely unlikely, thereby changing the focus of research in pathology. Rather than solely aiming to identify a damaged module at the cognitive level, researchers are encouraged to seek more subtle effects beyond the seemingly unique one, as well as to question whether successful behavior (the presumed "intact" part of the brain) is reached by the same processes as in normal development. This change in perspective means that atypical development should not be considered in terms of a catalogue of impaired and intact functions, in which non-affected modules are considered to develop normally, independently of the others. Such claims are based on the static, adult neuropsychological model which is inappropriate for understanding the dynamics of developmental disorders[14,15] (see Box 19.1).

The neuroconstructivist approach highlights how tiny variations in the initial state could give rise to domain-specific differences in endstates[7,13,15] (see Box 19.2). With a shift in focus from dissociations to cross-syndrome associations, disorders might turn out to lie on more of a continuum than commonly thought. Thus, two very distinct phenotypical outcomes could start with only slightly differing parameters but, with development, the effects of this small difference might be far reaching. This contrasts with the notion that a whole cognitive module is initially impaired. Rather, phenotypical outcomes could stem from small differences in one or more of the following parameters: developmental timing, gene dosage, neuronal formation, neuronal migration, neuronal density, biochemical efficiency affecting firing thresholds, variations in transmitter types, dendritic arborization, synaptogenesis, and pruning. The effects of alterations in these initial parameters might also vary in strength at different developmental periods.[14] Furthermore, some problems might stem from lack of connections between brain regions or between the two hemispheres.[16,17] In some cases, like Down syndrome, cognitive problems could stem from a failure to progressively specialize or modularize

Box 19.1   The postulates of the static adult neuropsychological model and its application to developmental disorders

- The method of double dissociation is used to identify specialized functions: Patient 1 has function A intact and function B impaired, whereas for Patient 2 the opposite obtains.
- This leads to the conclusion that the brain is organized into specialized circuits or modules which can be differentially damaged.

Thus far, the argument might be valid with respect to the fully formed adult brain (although for arguments against the reduction of double dissociation to autonomy of modules, see Refs a.b; and for those against modularity of adult processing, see Ref. c). The subsequent conclusions are, in my view, open to serious challenge:

- Similar dissociations are found in certain developmental disorders.
- This leads to the conclusion that modules are innately specified in the human brain, with impaired genes mapped to impaired modules, alongside otherwise normal brain development.
- Developmental disorders are then explained in terms of the juxtaposition of damaged and intact sets of modules.

This ignores both the probabilistic dynamics of gene expression during embryogenesis and of progressive brain development during postnatal growth. When one considers the dynamics of development, the notion of the juxtaposition of spared and impaired higher-level cognitive processes is challenged, suggesting that in some developmental disorders, ostensibly "intact" performance might turn out to be achieved through different cognitive processes (see Box 19.5).

References

a   Plaut, D. (1995). Double dissociations without modularity: evidence from connectionist neuropsychology *J. Clin. Exp. Neuropsychol. 17*, 291–331.
b   Van Orden, G.C., Jansen op de Haar, M., & Bosman, A.M.T. (1997). Complex dynamic systems also predict dissociations, but they do not reduce to autonomous components *Cognit. Neuropsychol., 14*, 131–165.
c   Marslen-Wilson, W.D., & Tyler, L.K. (1987). Against modularity, in J.L. Garfield (Ed.), *Modularity in Knowledge Representations and Natural Language Understanding*, pp. 37–62. MIT Press.

as a function of development, whereas in others specialization might occur too rapidly leaving less opportunity for environmental constraints to play a role in shaping the developmental outcome. These are all indirect and at a much lower level than the notion of direct damage to innately specified cognitive modules invoked by strict

Box 19.2   Single and multiple gene disorders, but no Swiss army knives

A report in the press recently heralded the discovery of a specific gene for hearing. The Science article on which it was based, however, illustrates how indirect the effects of the gene are. Geneticists studying eight generations of a Costa Rican family found a 50% incidence of acquired deafness, with onset around age 10 and complete deafness by age 30. A single gene mutation was identified, with the last 52 amino acids in the gene's protein product misformed, and the first 1,213 amino acids formed correctly. This gene produces a protein that controls the assembly of actin. Actin organizes the tiny fibres found in cell plasma which determine a cell's structural properties, such as rigidity. Because the genetic impairment is tiny and the protein functions sufficiently well to control the assembly of actin in most parts of the body, no other deficits are observable. However, it turns out that hair cells are especially sensitive to loss of rigidity, such that even this tiny impairment has a huge effect on them, resulting in deafness. In other words, what might look like a specialized gene for a complex trait like hearing is, on closer examination, very indirect – hearing is dependent on the interaction of huge numbers of genes, one of which affects the rigidity of hair cells and has cascading effects on the others. A "gene for hearing" might be a convenient shorthand, but it could be a very misleading one, impeding the researcher from seeking to understand the probabilistic dynamics of development.

A second illustration comes from a computational model of the development of the ventral and dorsal pathways of visual cortex. There are several things we know about these pathways. First, they operate on somewhat different time schedules in early infancy: infants track novel objects (dorsal pathway) before they can categorize them (ventral pathway). Second, double dissociations exist in adult brain damage, such that patients can locate objects without being able to identify them, or vice versa.[b] This has led some neuropsychologists to argue that the two pathways must be innately specified. But is this conclusion necessary? Their specialization in adulthood could have emerged from development itself. A computational model illustrates how this might occur.[c] A simple three-layer feed-forward network was used. At the hidden layer, two channels were fed with identical input (see figure 19.1). The only difference was the speed with which activation levels changed (channel A rapidly, channel B slowly). Despite processing identical inputs, channel A progressively came to represent where objects were (mimicking the dorsal pathway in the brain), whereas channel B came to represent what each object was (ventral pathway). These functions were not pre-specified in the network but emerged from its developmental history, caused by a small difference in a starting state parameter. Thus, when neuropsychologists find dissociations in brain-damaged adults in visual form agnosia, this does not mean that the "where" and "what" pathways are necessarily pre-specified in the infant neocortex for spatio/temporal information versus form/color/shape information. A small difference simply in firing thresholds (which might be innate) could give rise to such specialized functions indirectly, via the gradual processing during

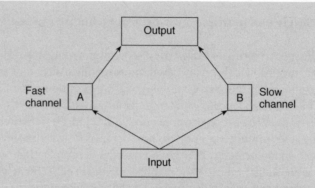

Figure 19.1   A simple three-layer feed-forward network model of specialization in neural pathways. (See text for details.)

early infancy of differences between moving versus static stimuli. And a lack of such a difference in firing thresholds could result in domain-specific abnormality in one of these pathways. Again, the shorthand of talking about innate "where" and "what" pathways could be seriously misleading. They might only *become* what they are after processing the input. This leads to an important speculation: domain-specific outcomes might not even be possible without the process of development itself.

These two examples highlight the importance of giving serious consideration to very indirect causes of albeit very specific outcomes.

References

a   Lynch, E.D. et al. (1997). Nonsyndromic deafness DFNA1 associated with mutation of a human homolog of the *Drosophila* gene *diaphanous*. *Science*, *278*, 1315–1318.

b   Goodale, M.A., & Milner, A.D. (1992). Separate visual pathways for perception and action. *Trends Neurosci.*, *15*, 20–25.

c   O'Reilly, R.C., & McClelland, J.L. (1992). The self-organization of spatially invariant representations. *Technical Report PDP.CNS.92.5*, Carnegie Mellon University.

nativists to explain developmental disorders. It is these subtle differences that are likely to explain the range of phenotypical outcomes that atypical development can display. Such differences might affect the resulting organism at multiple levels.

These multiple levels – brain volume, regional anatomy, brain chemistry, hemispheric asymmetry, the temporal patterns of brain activity, physical characteristics, and cognitive/behavioral outcome – have recently been studied in some detail with respect to one neurodevelopmental disorder, Williams syndrome (see Boxes 19.3, 19.4 and 19.5). Consideration of the multiple two-way mappings from the biological to the cognitive levels leads to different hypotheses about so-called "intact" abilities; that is, even where normal *behavioral* levels are found in a developmental disorder in a given domain, they might be achieved by different *cognitive* processes. This turns out to

Box 19.3   Williams syndrome: genetic and brain levels

Williams syndrome (WS) is caused by a microdeletion on the long arm of chromosome 7 at q.11,23 (Refs a,b). The genes on the deleted area have not all been identified, but they include:

- the elastin gene (*ELN*), not expressed in the brain, and thought to cause the vascular abnormalities;
- the *Limkinasel* gene (*LIMK1*) expressed in the brain, and claimed to cause the spatial deficits;
- the gene for DNA replication factor C2 (*RFC2*), and syntaxin1A (*STX1A*) which affects the way chemicals are released in the brain;
- the *frizzled* gene (*FZD3*), affecting the way in which cells signal to one another during development.

All patients with classic WS are hemizygous for *ELN*, *LIMK1*, *STX1A*, and *RFC2*. While these discoveries seem to offer a neat mapping between genes and particular phenotypical outcomes, our recent study challenges these conclusions.[c] Three patients were identified with hemizygotic *ELN* and *LIMK1* deletions, two of whom also had *RFC2* deletions and one the *STX1A* deletion. However, none had the facial dysmorphology, the mental retardation, or the specific spatio-constructive problems typical of people with Williams syndrome. The explanation of the WS phenotype clearly cannot be sought in simple gene/outcome mappings, but lies at the level of developmental timing and downstream effects of the complex interaction between all the deleted genes and the rest of the developing organism.

At the brain level, WS has been mainly described in terms of adult brains.[d] No work has yet been done on the developing infant brain. Some important discoveries about the fully formed adult brain include:

- the WS brain is 80% of normal volume;
- the total cerebral grey matter is significantly reduced;
- there is abnormal layering, orientation, clustering, and size of neurones;
- the anterior regions are smaller than in normal controls but larger than in Down syndrome brains;
- the dorsal hemispheres show cortical malformation;
- the cerebrum is particularly small;
- the limbic structures of the temporal lobe are small but proportionally similar to normal controls;
- the frontal cortex displays a near normal proportional relation with posterior cortex, although both are reduced in size.

Although limbic structures and frontal cortex are both proportionally similar in WS compared with normal brains, their functions show very different levels of impairment, with socio–affective behavior being relatively good[e] and executive functions being particularly impaired.[f] Thus, the existence of normal anatomical proportions cannot be used to infer normal functions in the domains that they subserve in normal adults.

Our study using magnetic resonance spectroscopy has shown that brain biochemistry is also atypical in people with WS (Ref. g). Significant correlations were found between abnormal brain chemistry in the cerebellum and various neuropsychological tests, including Verbal and Performance IQ, British Picture Vocabulary Scale, and Ravens Progressive Matrices. The strongest correlation was with very poor results on a task measuring speed of processing, suggesting decreased neuronal efficiency in WS.

Finally, several studies have investigated brain activation in WS, particularly with respect to their domains of relative proficiency (language and face processing; see Box 19.5).[h] Event-related potentials of individuals with WS show abnormal patterns for both face processing and language. More importantly, such patterns are found at no age across normal development, suggesting aberrant rather than delayed development in WS (Ref. h). Neither do people with WS show the progressive hemispheric asymmetries typical of normal development.[h] Furthermore, infants with WS spend far more time than controls focused on faces and language,[i] suggesting that more of the developing brain might be devoted to processing such inputs.

In sum, brain volume, brain anatomy, brain chemistry, hemispheric asymmetry, and the temporal patterns of brain activity are all atypical in people with WS. How could the resulting cognitive system be described in terms of a normal brain with parts intact and parts impaired, as the popular view holds?[j,k] Rather, the brains of infants with WS develop differently from the outset, which has subtle, widespread repercussions at the cognitive level (see Box 19.5).

References

a   Frangiskakis, J.M. et al. (1996). *LIM-kinase1* hemizygosity implicated in impaired visuospatial constructive cognition. *Cell, 86,* 59–69.
b   Tassabehji, M.K. et al. (1996). LIM-kinase detected in Williams syndrome. *Nat. Genet., 13,* 272–273.
c   Tassabehji, M.K. et al. (1997). Genotype–phenotype correlations in Williams Syndrome. *Am. J. Hum. Genet., 61,* 11.
d   Galaburda, A.M. et al. (1994). Cytoarchitectonic anomalies in a genetically based disorder: Williams syndrome. *NeuroReport, 5,* 753–757.
e   Karmiloff-Smith, A. et al. (1995). Is there a social module? Language, face processing and theory-of-mind in subjects with Williams syndrome. *J. Cogn. Neurosci., 7,* 196–208.
f   Wang, P.P. et al. (1992). The specific neurobehavioral profile of WS is associated with neocerebellar hemispheric preservation. *Neurology, 42,* 1999–2002.
g   Rae, L. et al. Brain biochemistry in Williams syndrome: evidence for a role of the cerebellum in cognition? *Neurology* (in press).
h   Neville, H.J., Mills, D.L., & Bellugi, U. (1993). Effects of altered auditory sensitivity and age of language acquisition on the development of language-relevant neural systems:

preliminary studies of Williams syndrome, in S. Broman, & J. Grafman, (Eds.), *Cognitive Deficits in Developmental Disorders: Implications for Brain Function*, pp. 67–83. Erlbaum.

i   Mervis, C.B. et al. Williams syndrome: findings from an integrated program of research, in H. Tager-Flusberg, (Ed.), *Neurodevelopmental Disorders: Contributions to a New Framework from the Cognitive Neurosciences*. MIT Press (in press).

j   Pinker, S. (1994). *The Language Instinct*. Harmondsworth: Penguin.

k   Bickerton, D. (1997). Constructivism, nativism and explanatory adequacy. *Behav. Brain Sci.*, *20*, 557–558.

Box 19.4   Clinical characteristics of the Williams syndrome phenotype

Williams syndrome (WS) is a rare genetic disorder that occurs in 1 in 20,000 live births. Its clinical features[a] include dysmorphic faces (see figure 19.2 A–C), congenital heart and renal disorders due to a narrowing of the large arteries, musculo-skeletal abnormalities, growth retardation, hyperacusis, and infantile hypercalcemia. The physical abnormalities are accompanied by moderate to

M.S., aged 2yrs

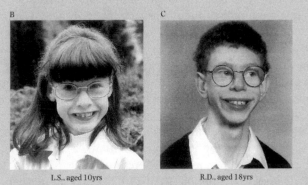

L.S., aged 10yrs   R.D., aged 18yrs

Figure 19.2   The typical facial dysmorphology in WS, illustrated in three patients (photographs reproduced with permission of parents), aged 2 years, 10 years, and 18 years, respectively. To be noted are the full cheeks, flared nostrils, wide mouth, full lips, pointed ears, and dental irregularities.

severe mental retardation, a specific personality profile, very poor visuospatial constructive skills, and relatively good language and face processing abilities (see Box 19.5).

Reference

a   Udwin, O., & Dennis, J. (1995). Williams syndrome, in G. O'Brien, & W. Yule, (Eds.), *Clinics in Developmental Medicine No. 138: Behavioural Phenotypes,* pp. 201–204. London: MacKeith Press.

Box 19.5   Williams syndrome: the resulting cognitive-behavioral phenotype

Classic Williams syndrome (WS) has been characterized along the following lines (for more details, see Refs a–c):

- IQs mainly in the 50s (range: 45–87);
- serious deficits in spatio-constructive skills, but spatio-perceptual skills as would be predicted by Mental Age;
- serious deficits in numerical cognition;
- serious deficits in problem solving and planning;
- intact syntactic capacities alongside aberrant semantics;
- intact face-processing capacities;
- relatively spared social cognition skills.

The above conclusions stemmed mainly from standardized tests used to assess intact and impaired functions, and approach inspired theoretically by the adult neuropsychological model of deficit. However, even in cases where behavioral scores are equivalent to chronologically matched controls, it is essential to go beyond behavioral success and study the underlying cognitive processes in detail.[d,e] For example, our study of face-processing capacities of people with WS (Ref. e) showed that, although their scores were equivalent to normal controls, the way in which they solved the task was different. Whereas normal controls used predominantly configural (holistic) processing, the subjects with WS reached their good scores by using predominantly componential (feature-by-feature) processing. In other words, different *cognitive* processes led to similar *behavioral* outcomes. The notion that WS displays a normal, intact face-processing module is thereby challenged. None the less, the neuroconstructivist view could accept that people with WS might have developed a face-processing module. However, it would be argued that, rather than simply being triggered, such a module – like the normal face-processing module – is the result of a developmental process of modularization, but emerging in this case from an atypical ontogenetic pathway.

A similar story obtains for WS language acquisition. Several studies now suggest that neither syntax nor semantics is entirely normal in WS, despite earlier claims to the contrary. First, there is a discrepancy between vocabulary Mental Age (MA) and syntactic MA, the former being considerably higher.[f] Second, high vocabulary scores in WS patients camouflage the fact that they learn the lexicon in a somewhat different way from normally developing children.[g] Third, they show dissociations within syntax itself, with problems in forming agreement between elements in phrase structure, difficulties in processing embedded relative clauses and subcategorization frames (the distinction between transitive and intransitive verbs), and so forth.[f,h,i] Furthermore, even when language is fluent, Williams syndrome cannot be used to claim, as some have,[j] that syntax develops independently of cognition. The use of IQ scores is very misleading in this respect. To state that a person has fluent language but an IQ of 51 indeed appears theoretically surprising and could lead to the conclusion that syntax develops in isolation from the rest of the brain. But to state that the same person has fluent language and an MA of 7yrs changes the conclusion. In other words, those people with WS who have relatively fluent language might indeed have low IQs, but their MAs in non-verbal cognition, although seriously behind their chronological age, are usually well over 5, the age at which most language has been acquired in normally developing children.

In sum, not only are brain anatomy, brain chemistry, and temporal brain processes atypical, but Williams syndrome also displays an abnormal cognitive phenotype in which, even where behavioral scores are equivalent to those of normal controls, the cognitive processes by which such proficiency is achieved are different.

Our ongoing longitudinal behavioral and brain-imaging studies of atypical infants (with Janice Brown, Sarah Paterson, Marisa Gsödl, Michelle de Haan, Mark Johnson, and others) already point to important differences in the initial state of WS patients compared with controls. The atypical groups' patterns are not one of juxtaposition of intact and impaired functions, as different end states might suggest. Interestingly, too, although WS linguistic performance ends up resembling normal language far more than Down syndrome performance, our preliminary results with infants show how important it is to distinguish the cognitive level from the behavioral level (see Box 19.6). Fluent linguistic behavior might stem from different processes at the cognitive level of description. Our initial results suggest that Down syndrome language comprehension has a delayed but relatively normal developmental pathway in infancy, whereas WS language development seems to be deviant from the outset. It is only by focusing studies of developmental disorders at their roots in early infancy that we will ultimately be able to chart longitudinally the varying developmental pathways that progressively lead to different phenotypical outcomes.

References

a　Udwin, O., & Yule, W. (1991). A cognitive and behavioural phenotype in Williams syndrome. *J. Clin. Exp. Neuropsychol., 13,* 232–244.

b　Bellugi, U., Wang, P., & Jernigan, T.L. (1994). Williams syndrome: an unusual neuropsychological profile, in S. Broman, & J. Grafman, (Eds.), *Atypical Cognitive Deficits in Developmental Disorders: Implications for Brain Function,* pp. 23–56. Erlbaum.

c　Mervis, C.B. et al. Williams syndrome: findings from an integrated program of research, in H. Tager-Flusberg, (Ed.), *Neurodevelopmental Disorders: Contributions to a New Framework from the Cognitive Neurosciences.* MIT Press (in press).

d　Pennington, B. (1997). Using genetics to dissect cognition. *Am. J. Hum. Genet., 60,* 13–16.

e　Karmiloff-Smith, A. (1997). Crucial differences between developmental cognitive neuroscience and adult neuropsychology. *Dev. Neuropsychol., 13,* 513–524.

f　Karmiloff-Smith, A. et al. (1997). Language and Williams syndrome: how intact is 'intact'? *Child Dev., 68,* 246–262.

g　Stevens, T., & Karmiloff-Smith, A. (1997). Word learning in a special population: do individuals with Williams syndrome obey lexical constraints? *J. Child Lang., 24,* 737–765.

h　Karmiloff-Smith, A. et al. (1998). Linguistic dissociations in Williams syndrome: evaluating receptive syntax in on-line and off-line tasks. *Neuropsychologia, 6,* 342–351.

i　Volterra, V. et al. (1996). Linguistic abilities in Italian children with Williams syndrome. *Cortex, 32,* 67–83.

j　Bickerton, D. (1997). Constructivism, nativism and explanatory adequacy. *Behav. Brain Sci., 20,* 557–558.

be then case for Williams syndrome, in which face processing and language are particularly proficient alongside other serious impairments, but the proficiency seems to be achieved through different cognitive processes (see Box 19.5).

Are Some Developmental Disorders Truly Specific?

Despite the arguments in the previous section, some developmental disorders (e.g., autism,[18,19] Asperger syndrome,[20] dyslexia,[21] Turner's syndrome,[22] Specific Language Impairment[14]) appear at first sight to involve very specific deficits at the cognitive level. Autism, for example, is argued to be the result of impairment of the domain-specific mechanism of metarepresentation, dedicated solely to the processing of social stimuli[10,19] – a deficit in the so-called "theory-of-mind" module. When other, non-social impairments are noted, they are explained either in terms of secondary effects[10] or of an additional, unrelated cognitive impairment,[23] with other parts of the brain assumed to be intact. A similar approach has been taken with respect to Specific Language Impairment (SLI). This phenotype suggests, by its very name, a specific linguistic deficit alongside otherwise intact intelligence, as if grammar developed in total isolation of the rest of the growing brain. Researchers differ as to what they claim the specific deficit to be: the inability to make canonical links from grammar to semantics,[4] feature blindness with respect to morphology,[3,24] and so forth (for comprehensive reviews, see Refs 14, 25). The common suggestion, however, is that there is a specific genetic underpinning to the derivation of certain grammatical rules, which is impaired in these forms of SLI but leaving the rest of development intact.

It is clear that disorders like autism and SLI have a genetic origin and that evolutionary pressures have contributed to whatever is innately specified. This is a truism. The question is whether, on the one hand, the deficit results from damage to a domain-specific starting point at the cognitive level, as a result of evolution specifying dedicated processing systems for grammar, theory of mind and so forth, or whether, on the other hand, evolution has specified more general constraints for higher-level cognition and there is a more indirect way for genetic defects to result in domain-specific outcomes as a function of development.

The case of SLI (Ref. 14) shows how this second alternative might hold. Developmental timing plays a crucial role. If, early on, the infant's processing of fast auditory transitions is even slightly delayed in maturation, then certain aspects of grammar might, with development, emerge as more impaired than others. Grammatical disorders would then be the indirect, developmental effect of a subtle, initial acoustic deficit. Such a position is supported by the fact that training solely at the acoustic level has been shown to have positive repercussions at the grammatical level.[26] However, some adolescents and adults with SLI do not display a processing deficit.[3,4,25] It is none the less possible that by later childhood or adulthood, an initial deficit in acoustic processing which had a huge effect at one point in development might no longer be detectable (owing, for example, to subsequent long-term compensation or to ceiling effects and the lack of sufficiently subtle measures; S. Rosen, pers. commun.), but its early effects could continue to have a significant impact. This stresses the importance of developmental timing in understanding developmental disorders. Although atypical processing of fast auditory transitions might not turn out to be the final cause of SLI, this view aptly illustrates how a less pre-specified approach to language can result in a language-specific representational impairment through the process of development itself. This is why a truly developmental approach is so crucial.

The neuroconstructivist account modifies the way a developmental disorder like SLI will be studied. It suggests that focus must be placed on at risk populations in early infancy, before the onset of language, and longitudinally thereafter, to ascertain whether the timing of subtle developmental processes is out of synchrony and grows in importance as the child starts to process more complex linguistic input. Furthermore, the neuroconstructivist approach predicts that because of the way genes interact in their developmental expression, we should seek co-occurring, more subtle impairments which might have nothing to do with language. In fact, it has been shown that people with language-related deficits, such as SLI or dyslexia, often display an impairment (albeit lesser) in various forms of motor control such as balance.[27] This indicates that we might not be dealing with an initially language-specific impairment, but a deficit that turns out to be more detrimental to spoken and/or written language over developmental time (i.e., caused by an earlier language-relevant deficit), but that also gives rise to (weaker) problems in other areas. There is unlikely to be such a thing as impaired "genes for reading" or "genes for grammar." Rather, genetic impairments lead to a disruption in probabilistic epigenesis pushing individuals onto different developmental pathways which eventually result in reading or grammatical deficits.[26–28]

The neuroconstructivist approach would seek the initial disruption in innate mechanisms such as level of firing thresholds, differences in inhibition, and so forth. These are clearly at a lower-level, less richly domain-specific form than is commonly invoked by strict nativists who argue for innately specified representations of universal grammar. Neuroconstructivists would seek domain-relevant computational biases and the effects of differential developmental timing.[7] This is because we hypothesize that, rather than bringing greater pre-specialization to neocortex, evolution has provided the human neocortex with a greater and more varied capacity to learn via the process of development itself.[29] This clearly requires innate constraints but, because of the unusually slow period of human postnatal brain development, the child's gradual processing of different types of input is likely to have a strong influence on the way in which neocortex structures itself.

Conclusions

One of the major problems with very specific accounts of developmental disorders of higher-level cognition is that so far no gene (or set of genes) has been identified that is expressed solely in a specific region of neocortex (see Ref. 30 for discussion). Yet, such theories claim that neocortex is pre-specified for functions such as theory of mind or language and that this is why they can dissociate in adulthood. This is the basis for most brain imaging studies. Some authors go as far as claiming that epigenetic selection acts on preformed synaptic substrates and that to learn is to stabilize pre-existing synaptic combinations and to eliminate the surplus.[31] By contrast, current knowledge suggests that genes that are expressed in neocortex tend to do so throughout most regions, resulting in a similar six-layer structure and a similar overall pattern of intrinsic connectivity.[30] Combinations of neuroanatomical features, cortical layers, and brain cytoarchitectural regions are found to be remarkably similar in all regions of the brain from birth to 72 months. In other words, for quite some time the developmental patterns of different cytoarchitectural regions are indistinguishable from one another.[32] A single set of instructions might structure the different areas of neocortex, leaving the interaction with different environmental inputs to influence specific forms of synaptogenesis and dendritic arborization. In fact, neocortical specialization has already been shown to be very progressive across developmental time.[33] So if there is early genetic impairment, then it could be relatively widespread in the developing neocortex, even though its effects might be surprisingly differential in outcome. To be biologically and developmentally plausible, we must go beyond the more obvious deficit to seek far subtler effects on other aspects of the developing system. Even if future research were to uncover a specific regional pattern of neocortical gene expression – which is not ruled out by the position developed in this paper – the neuroconstructivist approach would force a reinterpretation of the meaning of localized gene expression, encouraging researchers to take serious account of the developmental time course. The systemic properties of ontogenesis and the developmental effects of the interconnectedness of brain regions, together with a structuring rather than merely triggering role for environmental input, would still be likely to result in a cascade of subtle deficits rather than a single, higher-level one.

Because both normal and abnormal development is progressive, a change of focus is essential in future research into pathology. Rather than concentrate on the study of disorders solely at their end state in school-aged children and adults, which is most commonly the case, it becomes essential to study disorders in early infancy, and longitudinally, to understand how alternative developmental pathways might lead to different phenotypical outcomes. Furthermore, if we accept that behavioral outcomes could stem from different cognitive processes, then matching control groups on the basis of behavioral scores, rather than underlying processes, might also be open to challenge.

One essential step towards a deeper understanding of developmental disorders is to model their various manifestations. In an important contribution to the field, Morton and Frith devised a structural framework for causal modelling within which to explore a variety of theories concerning different abnormal phenotypes.[34] Work of this nature is crucial in developing more constrained theories of developmental disorders. The authors present their discussion in terms of a framework rather than the embodiment of a particular theory. However, the 55 different models that they explore are all unidirectional in their causal chains, and so do not capture the basic assumptions of the neuroconstructivist approach. The figure in Box 19.6 illustrates how the neuroconstructivist approach differs from both the nativist and empiricist approaches to developmental psychopathology. It pinpoints the various theoretical assumptions discussed in this paper and the different research strategies to which they lead.

The complex dynamics of both normal and atypical development indicate, in my view, that the neuroconstructivist approach is the most viable theoretical framework within which to explore developmental disorders. These must be approached from early infancy onwards, and simultaneously at multiple levels: the genetic, the brain in its spatial and temporal dynamics, the cognitive, the environmental and the behavioral, as well as stressing the multiple two-way rather than unidirectional chains that interact all the way from genetic causes through to ultimate behavioral outcomes. This is because the dynamics of development itself are the key to understanding developmental disorders.

Outstanding Questions

- Some argue that evolution has provided the human cortex with increasingly detailed pre-specification prior to ontogenetic development. To what extent can the ontogenetic data be accounted for in terms of evolution selecting for less specific factors, such as increased neocortical plasticity and a greater range of learning mechanisms, to ensure adaptive outcomes rather than prior knowledge? Is it more useful to entertain the possibility that the highest level of evolution is to pre-specify simply a number of domain-relevant mechanisms which, after processing specific aspects of the environment, *become* increasingly domain-specific, that is, specialized, during ontogenesis? How might this change our perspective on developmental disorders?

Box 19.6   Models of developmental disorders of known genetic aetiology

The figure illustrates how the neuroconstructivist approach differs in its theoretical assumptions and resulting research strategies from both the nativist and empiricist accounts. Boxes and arrows are clearly not the most appropriate notation for a dynamic system, but the current representation hopefully captures some of the essential differences between neuroconstructivism and the other two theories. At the cognitive level, the neuroconstructivist approach stresses the difference between innate representations (invoked by most nativist linguists) and much lower-level innate computational and timing constraints from which representations progressively emerge as a function of development and of interaction with different types of environmental input. The multiple interactions between all levels, invoked by the neuroconstructivist approach, highlight why it is essential to start studies of developmental disorders in early infancy and then to trace the subsequent processes of development itself.

Theoretical assumptions	Nativist	Empiricist	Neuroconstructivist
Cause	genetic defect	genetic defect of limited interest; main focus on environmental causes	genetic defect; widespread an/or specific deficits depending on how early in prenatal development perturbation occurs;
Brain	specific deficit in prewired cortical circuit; plasticity solely as response to damage	general brain deficit expected; plasticity solely as a passive response to input	perturbation to normal patterns of pre- and postnatal brain development; plasticity as basic feature of normal and atypical cortical development
Cognitive	missing/damaged innate cognitive module	not a distinct level	modules develop by a process of gradual modularization; distinguish innate representations (rare at cortical level) from lower-level computational devices and differential developmental timing
Environment	environment static (acts as trigger only)	environment static (structures child's brain directly)	environment dynamic (changes as a function of infant's selection and processing of input)

Research strategies

Behavioral	domain-specific outcome	domain-general outcome	specific and general outcomes both important; the later the gene expression, the more specific the impairment expected
Seek cause	identify gene(s)	identify environmental factors	identify timing of gene expression and interactions with other genetic and environmental events
Choose domain of study	focus on single, impaired higher-level cognitive modules	focus on general processing efficiency and learning	identify lowest level of impairment and study its developmental effects on higher-level cognition re both proficiencies and impairments
Choose methodology	focus on cognitive tasks in impaired domain; search for selective impairments; brain imaging to highlight specific cortical areas involved; environmental input not studied	IQ and other such tasks; training for behavioral change; investigate direct effects of environment	devise tasks to differentiate behavior from cognitive processes; longitudinal brain imaging of both temporal and spatial changes; study changes in timing of environmental input
Choose targeted population	study behavior in endstate (middle childhood/adulthood); focus on phenotypes presenting specific or double dissociations	no specific age group targeted	study earliest possible markers of disorder in fetus and infancy; focus on differences and similarities across phenotypes

- What can we learn about subtle differences in the environmental input to atypically developing infants and children? In this respect, is it useful to replace the static notion of "environment" by that of the "child's progressive processing of environmental input"? To what extent does the infant/child contribute to its own subsequent brain specialization by selecting aspects of its environment to attend to at different times in development?
- How influential is subcortical specialization in the structuring of neocortex?
- Are developmental disorders really specific, or do they lie on a continuum, with seeming dissociations due to relatively small differences in developmental timing, gene dosage, neuronal formation, neuronal migration, neuronal density, biochemical efficiency affecting firing thresholds, variations in transmitter types, dendritic arborization, synaptogenesis, and pruning?
- Just as modularity theorists can show that specific disorders also predict more general impairments, so non-modularity theorists can show that dynamic systems predict dissociations that do not reduce to autonomous modules. Is the double-dissociation method necessarily the right tool for furthering our knowledge of developmental disorders?
- If we do discover a truly specific disorder of higher-level cognition with no other subtle impairments, how could this be explained without violating what is known about the probabilistic epigenetics of biological development? Can one region of neocortex develop abnormally with no effects on any other region?
- How do acquired developmental disorders differ from genetically based disorders?
- If we take development seriously, is atypical ontogenesis necessarily a window on the structure/functioning of the normal mind/brain, as seems to be taken for granted by many of those studying developmental disorders?

Acknowledgements

I should like to thank Mike Anderson, Susan Carey, Mark Johnson, and Steven Rose, as well as the anonymous reviewers, for comments on an earlier version of this paper.

References

1 Gottieb, G. (1992). *Individual Development and Evolution: The Genesis of Novel Behavior.* Oxford University Press.

2 Lightfoot, D.W. (1989). The child's trigger experience: degree-0 learnability. *Behav. Brain Sci., 12,* 321–375.

3 Gopnik, M. (1997). Language deficits and genetic factors. *Trends Cognit. Sci., 1,* 5–9.

4 Van der Lely, H. (1994). Canonical linking rules: forward versus reverse linking in normally developing and specifically language-impaired children. *Cognition, 51,* 29–72.

5 Pinker, S. (1994). *The Language Instinct.* Harmondsworth: Penguin.

6 Clahsen, H. (1989). The grammatical characterisation of developmental dysphasia. *Linguistics, 27,* 897–920.

7   Elman, J.L. et al. (1996). *Rethinking Innateness: A Connectionist Perspective on Development.* MIT Press.

8   Quartz, S.R., & Sejnowsky, T.J. (1997). A neural basis of cognitive development: a constructivist manifesto. *Behav. Brain Sci., 20,* 537–556.

9   Changeux, J.P., & Dehaene, S. (1989). Neuronal models of cognitive functions. *Cognition, 33,* 63–109.

10 Frith, U., & Happé, F. Why specific developmental disorders are not specific: on-line and developmental effects in autism and dyslexia. *Dev. Sci.* (in press).

11 Baron-Cohen, S. (1994). How to build a baby that can read minds: cognitive mechanisms in mindreading. *Cahiers de Psychol. Cognit., 13,* 513–552.

12 Tooby, J., & Cosmides, L. (1990). On the universality of human nature and the uniqueness of the individual: the role of genetics and adaptation. *J. Personal., 58,* 17–67.

13 Karmiloff-Smith, A. (1995). Annotation: the extraordinary cognitive journey from foetus through infancy. *J. Child Psychol. Child Psychiatry, 36,* 1293–1313.

14 Bishop, D.V.M. (1997). *Uncommon Understanding: Development and Disorders of Language Comprehension in Children.* Psychology Press.

15 Karmiloff-Smith, A. (1997). Crucial differences between developmental cognitive neuroscience and adult neuropsychology. *Dev. Neuropsychol., 13,* 513–524.

16 Liegeois, F., & de Schonen, S. (1997). Simultaneous attention in the two visual hemifields and interhemispheric integration: a developmental finding on 20–26 month-old infants. *Neuropsychologia, 35,* 381–385.

17 Mancini, J. et al. (1994). Face recognition in children with early right or left brain damage. *Dev. Med. Child Neurol., 36,* 156–166.

18 Frith, U. (1989). *Autism: Explaining the Enigma.* Blackwell Science.

19 Leslie, A.M. (1992). Pretence, autism and the theory-of-mind module. *Curr. Dir. Psychol. Sci., 1,* 18–21.

20 Frith, U. (Ed.) (1991). *Autism and Asperger Syndrome.* Cambridge University Press.

21 Frith, C., & Frith, U. (1996). A biological marker for dyslexia. *Nature, 382,* 19–20.

22 Skuse, D.H. et al. (1997). Evidence from Turner's syndrome of an imprinted X-linked locus affecting cognitive function. *Nature, 387,* 705–708.

23 Happé, F.G.E. (1996). Studying weak central coherence at low levels: children with autism do not succumb to visual illusions (a research note). *J. Child Psychol. Psychiatry, 37,* 873–877.

24 Gopnik, M. (1990). Feature-blind grammar and dysphasia. *Nature, 344,* 715.

25 Temple, C.M. (1997). Cognitive neuropsychology and its application to children. *J. Child Psychol. Psychiatry, 38,* 27–52.

26 Tallal, P. et al. (1996). Language comprehension in language-learning impaired children improved with acoustically modified speech. *Science, 271,* 81–84.

27 Fawcett, A.J., Nicolson, R.I., & Dean, P. (1996). Impaired performance of children with dyslexia on a range of cerebellar tasks. *Ann. Dyslexia, 46,* 259–283.

28 Pennington, B. (1997). Using genetics to dissect cognition. *Am. J. Hum. Genet., 60,* 13–16.

29 Gerhart, J., & Kirschner, M. (1997). *Cells, Embryos and Evolution.* Blackwell Science.

30 Johnson, M.H. (1997). *Developmental Cognitive Neuroscience.* Blackwell Science.

31 Dehaene-Lambertz, G., & Dehaene S. (1997). In defence of learning by selection: neurobiology and behavioral evidence revisited. *Behav. Brain Sci., 20,* 560–561.

32 Shankle, W.R. et al. (1998). Developmental patterns in the cytoarchitecture of the human cerebral cortex from birth to six years examined by correspondence analysis. *Proc. Natl. Acad. Sci. U.S.A., 95,* 4023–4038.

33 Neville, H.J. (1991). Neurobiology of cognitive and language processing: effects of early experience, in K.R. Gibson, & A.C., Petersen, (Eds.), *Brain Maturation and Cognitive Develop-*

ment: *Comparative and Cross-Cultural Perspectives*, pp. 355–380. New York: Aladine de Gruyter Press.

34 Morton, J., & Frith, U. (1995). Causal modelling: a structural approach to developmental psychopathology, in D. Cicchetti, & D.J. Cohen, (Eds.), *Manual of Developmental Psychopathology* (Vol. 1), pp. 357–390. John Wiley & Sons.

Index

Brent, M.R. 199
Broca, P. 154, 158
Brooks, P. 173, 175
Brown, Roger 135, 149, 234
bursts 137, 138, 323, 324
    second 135
Bybee, J. 204, 205, 207, 284

Canada 5
Carpenter, M. 119, 124
carrier frequency 15
Cartwright, T.A. 199
Casadio, P. 80, 101
case 267
    inflections 279
    markers 9, 182, 283–4
Caselli, M.C. 80, 95–101, 105, 171
Catalan 172
categories
    abstract 8, 170, 172, 173, 180
    contrastive 203
    grammatical, morphological realization of
        206
    grammatically specified notions 270
    linguistically relevant 278–80
    members not regarded as a homogenous
        set 203–4
    ontological 120, 121, 123
    pragmatic 282
    semantic 81, 282
    syntactic 173, 199, 273
    target 209
categorizations 204, 276, 307
    preposition 262
    psychological principles of 208
category-based abstraction 44, 45
causal role 229, 242
causality/causation 137, 230
Cazden, C.B. 299
CDI (MacArthur Communicative
    Development Inventory) 4, 50, 79, 138,
    140, 142, 149, 151, 154
    grammar scale 145
    Words and Gestures Scale 80, 81
    Words and Phrases Scale 80, 81
cells
    glial 309, 322
    proliferation 308
    specification 311
    stem 311
central nervous system 313

cerebellum 311
cerebral organization 55
certainty 263
Chafe, W. 263
Chafetz, J. 234, 243
"characteristic maturational course" 136
Chaucer, Geoffrey 8
checklists 101, 136, 138, 145
    baseline 85, 91
    ceiling 95
    grammatical complexity 139
    vocabulary 142, 146
chinchillas 16
Chinese 78, 79, 95
Chinese children 308
Choi, S. 78, 92, 95, 263, 272
Chomsky, Noam 8, 134, 137, 169, 176,
    183, 281, 304, 305
chronological age 148, 153
Chugani, H.T. 324
Church, K.W. 20
"citation form" 81
Clahsen, Harald 221
classifications 77, 82
clauses 188, 232, 233
    complement 252
    main-declarative-affirmative 234
    relative 142, 303
    subordinate complement 258
clicks 29
cline 282
clitics 274, 280
closed-class elements/items 273, 274,
    275–7, 280
closed-class words 95, 96, 135
    growth function for 100
    proportional development of 101
coding 50, 67, 68, 192, 232–3, 234, 237,
    240
    conservative strategy 236
cognition 147, 154, 182, 295
    assumptions about 273
    higher-level, more general constraints for
        343
    infant 272
    language and nonlinguistic 153
    verbs of 282
cognitive-behavioral phenotypes 340–2
cognitive processes 9, 268
    capacities 305
    development 4, 104, 272, 310